Englische Grammatik

Übungsbuch

für die Mittel- und Oberstufe

Englische Grammatik für die Mittel- und Oberstufe – Übungsbuch

Im Auftrag des Verlages erarbeitet von
Annie Cornford, Bamford; Dr. Paul Maloney, Hildesheim; Mervyn Whittaker, Bad Dürkheim

unter Mitarbeit der Verlagsredaktion
Irja Fröhling (verantwortliche Redakteurin), Elke Lehmann (Projektleitung)
sowie Christine House, Berlin

Beratende Mitwirkung
Marcel Sprunkel, Köln

Lizenzmanagement
Bettina Hamann

Illustrationen
Gregor Mecklenburg, Pinneberg

Gesamtgestaltung und technische Umsetzung
klein & halm, Berlin

Gestaltungskonzept
designcollective, Team für Mediengestaltung, Berlin

Umschlaggestaltung
Heike Börner, Berlin

Soweit in diesem Buch Personen fotografisch abgebildet sind und ihnen von der Redaktion fiktive Namen, Berufe, Dialoge und Ähnliches zugeordnet oder diese Personen in bestimmte Kontexte gesetzt werden, dienen diese Zuordnungen und Darstellungen ausschließlich der Veranschaulichung und dem besseren Verständnis des Buchinhaltes.

Das *Übungsbuch zur Englischen Grammatik* bezieht sich auf diese Grammatik.

ISBN 978-3-06-035284-5   ISBN 978-3-06-036134-2

www.cornelsen.de

Die in diesem Übungsbuch enthaltenen Mediencodes enthalten zusätzliche Unterrichtsmaterialien, die der Verlag in eigener Verantwortung zur Verfügung stellt.

1. Auflage, 2. Druck 2024

Alle Drucke dieser Auflage sind inhaltlich unverändert und können im Unterricht nebeneinander verwendet werden.

© 2024 Cornelsen Verlag GmbH, Mecklenburgische Str. 53, 14197 Berlin

Druck und Bindung: Livonia Print, Riga

ISBN 978-3-06-036127-4

PEFC zertifiziert
Dieses Produkt stammt aus nachhaltig bewirtschafteten Wäldern und kontrollierten Quellen.
www.pefc.de

PEFC/12-31-006

Inhalt

Inhalt

Inhalt

Wozu dient das *Übungsbuch zur Englischen Grammatik*?

Mithilfe der Übungen in diesem Buch kannst du deine Grammatikkenntnisse trainieren, selbst testen und bei Bedarf Fehler und Schwachstellen gezielt abbauen. So gewinnst du mehr Sicherheit bei der Anwendung der englischen Grammatik. Die Übungen helfen dir auch, wenn du ein Thema wiederholen und dich so auf Klassenarbeiten oder Klausuren vorbereiten möchtest.

Das Übungsbuch ergänzt die *Englische Grammatik für die Mittel- und Oberstufe* (978-3-06-035284-5). Du kannst es aber auch in Verbindung mit jeder anderen Grammatik verwenden.

Wie ist das Übungsbuch aufgebaut?

Das Übungsbuch folgt im Aufbau der Grammatik und enthält passende Übungen zu jedem der 25 Grammatikkapitel. Die letzten drei Kapitel der Grammatik sind zu einer *Mixed bag* zusammengefasst. Im Inhaltsverzeichnis ist jede einzelne Übung aufgelistet, sodass du gezielt ein Thema auswählen kannst.

Jedes Kapitel beginnt mit einer Übersichtstabelle, in der du mit einem Blick siehst, welche Übung welches Grammatikthema behandelt. Wenn dir die grammatischen Fachbegriffe nicht so vertraut sind, helfen dir die Beispielsätze zu verstehen, was geübt wird.

In der rechten Spalte findest du Verweise auf die *Englische Grammatik*. Dort kannst du die Erläuterungen zum jeweiligen Thema noch einmal nachlesen.

Task	Topic	Example	Englische Grammatik
1	Verb + *to*-infinitive	*We plan to stay at a hotel in Dover.*	10.3.2
2	Adjective + *to*-infinitive	*The problem was impossible to solve.*	10.3.4
3	Verb + object + *to*-infinitive	*Ms Blake reminded her students to finish their work on time.*	10.3.3
4	The *first/last/next/only* + *to*-infinitive	*Amelia Earhart was the first woman to fly solo across the Atlantic.*	10.3.5
5	*to*-infinitive or gerund after certain nouns (1)	*I hope we'll have a chance to visit our cousins. / Our chance of getting a cheap flight is very slight.*	10.3.6 11.6.3

Du kannst die Übungen in beliebiger Reihenfolge bearbeiten.

Die grün unterlegten Übungen am Kapitelende fassen mehrere Aspekte eines Themas zusammen oder behandeln weiterführende Themen. Sie sind anspruchsvoller und setzen mehr Wortschatz voraus und richten sich darum in erster Linie an die Oberstufe.

13	*to*-infinitive or gerund after certain nouns (2)	*Colin's decision to speak to the head teacher was not easy and the thought of telling him the truth filled him with fear.*	10.3.6 11.6.3
14	Improving your style with infinitives	*They told me that I should wait here. / They told me to wait here.*	10.3.3 10.3.7 10.3.8 10.3.9

Manchmal wird ein Thema in mehreren Kapiteln behandelt. In solchen Fällen findest du unter der Tabelle die Verweise zu weiteren Übungen in anderen Kapiteln.

10.3.2 Gerund or infinitive after certain verbs – see Chapter 11
10.3.3 Indirect commands and requests – see Chapter 15

Auf der letzten Seite jedes Kapitels gibt es einen *Quick Check* mit Testaufgaben zur Selbstkontrolle. Wenn du magst, kannst du den *Quick Check* auch durchführen, bevor du das Kapitel bearbeitest. Dann kannst du überprüfen, wie gut du das Thema schon beherrschst.

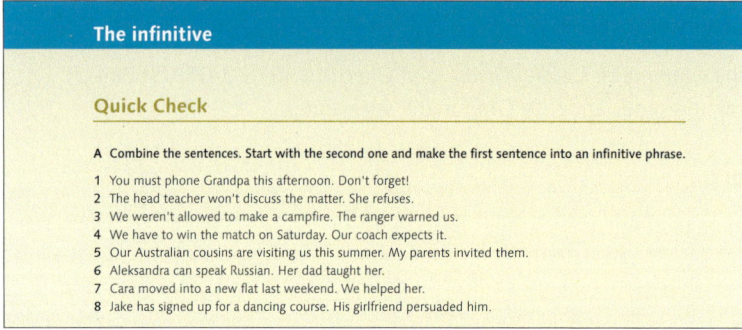

Was bedeuten die Hinweise in den Kapiteln?

→   Zu Beginn jeder Aufgabe findest du ein Lösungsbeispiel. Alle Beispiele sind durch den blauen Pfeil gekennzeichnet

✚   Die grün markierten Aufgaben am Kapitelende sind für die Oberstufe gedacht.

▶ 1.2.1   Bei jeder Aufgabe findest du einen Verweis auf den relevanten Abschnitt der *Englischen Grammatik*.

⊙   Dieses Symbol verweist auf ein Erklärvideo, das online verfügbar ist. Dafür gibst du auf www.cornelsen.de/webcodes den Code ein, den du bei der entsprechenden Aufgabe findest.

Erklärvideo online:

📄 ⊙ **cornelsen.de/webcodes**
✚ 🔊 **Code: cocoso**

Wo finde ich die Lösungen?

Die Lösungen für alle Übungen befinden sich im beigelegten Lösungsheft. Falls es verloren geht oder du lieber mit einem pdf arbeitest, kannst du es dir unter www.cornelsen.de/webcodes herunterladen. Gib dafür folgenden Code ein:

📄 ⊙ **cornelsen.de/webcodes**
✚ 🔊 **Code: pigapo**

Der Schrägstrich / zeigt an, dass es zu einer Übung mehrere korrekte Lösungen gibt. *The gallery is worth visiting / worth a visit* bedeutet: Die richtige Lösung lautet entweder *The gallery is worth visiting* oder *The gallery is worth a visit*. Eingeklammerte Wörter einer Lösung können weggelassen werden. *I told her (that) I was ill* bedeutet: Die richtige Lösung lautet entweder *I told her that I was ill* oder *I told her I was ill*.

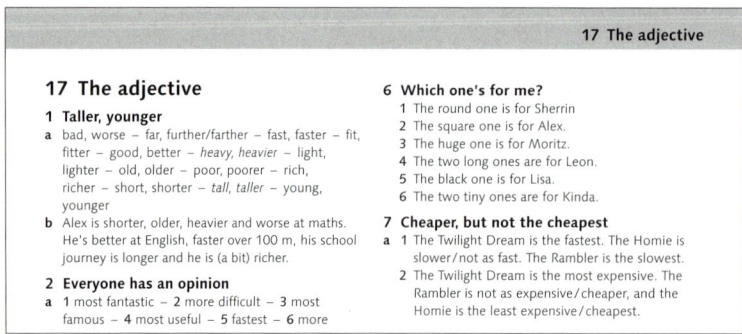

Viel Spaß und Erfolg beim Üben!

1 Sentence types and speech intentions

Task	Topic	Example	Englische Grammatik
1	Usual word order in statements	*Jeanette lives in Clifford Downs.*	1.2.1
2	Subject-verb inversion	*There's a dog in the garden.*	1.2.3
3	Negative statements	*Mirko didn't like the film.*	1.2.2
4	Yes/No questions	*Are you coming with us?*	1.3.1a
5	Questions with question words	*Why didn't anyone tell me?*	1.3.1b
6	Questions with prepositions	*What are you looking for?*	1.3.2d
7	Subject and object questions	*Who phoned you?*	1.3.3
8	Question words	*Which of the girls designed the poster?*	1.3.4
9	Answering yes/no questions	*Is it still raining? – No, it isn't. / I don't think so.*	1.3.5 1.3.6
10	Imperatives/Commands	*Don't wait – start today.*	1.4.1
11	Exclamations	*What a brilliant idea!*	1.5
12	Emphatic structures (1)	*I did do my homework, but I left it on my desk. It was curiosity that killed the cat.*	1.6
13	Emphatic structures (2)	*What worries me most is the cost of the project. Never before has it been possible to travel so cheaply.*	1.6

▶ Quick Check p. 17

1 Holiday plans   Usual word order in statements   ▶ 1.2.1

Erklärvideo online:
cornelsen.de/webcodes
Code: wozisi

These young people all have plans for their summer holidays. Put the words in the right order to find out what their plans are.

→ in Bathgate | to work as an au pair | Roxanne | going | from June to September | is
*Roxanne **is going to work** as an au pair in Bathgate from June to September.*

1 has | Elena | in Colchester | accepted | at the Oxfam shop | a temporary position
2 in Toulouse | is | in a trainee programme | Philip | taking part | at an aeronautics firm
3 this summer | in Ravenna | doing | a crash course in Italian | is | Dana
4 going | at his parents' hotel | Roger | is | in July and August | to help out | in Bristol
5 for a kitesurfing course | has | in Denmark | Oliver | next month | registered
6 has | the chance | to tour with a youth orchestra | Jackie | in August | been offered
7 volunteer work | is | for refugee children | at a summer camp | Mehmet | doing
8 her grandparents | Maleen | is | in July | visiting | in Breslau

2 A classroom   Subject-verb inversion   ▶ 1.2.3

a Describe the classroom in the picture below. What is there in the room? What isn't there? Write at least six sentences.

➜ *There aren't any students in the room.*

b NOW YOU What should there be in every classroom? Write down your ideas.

3 All wrong!   Negative statements   ▶ 1.2.2

Erklärvideo online:
▶ **Exercise 1**

All of the following sentences are wrong, so negate them. You can also correct them if you know the right answer!

➜ Christopher Columbus reached the New World in 1942.
*Christopher Columbus **didn't reach** the New World in 1942. (He reached it in 1492.)*

1 Neil Armstrong was the first man to set foot on Mars.
2 Koalas eat mainly bananas and coconuts.
3 Michael Jackson was shot by a gunman near Central Park.
4 The sun rises in the west.
5 Mobile phones have made communication more difficult.
6 Bill Gates made a lot of money by manufacturing windows.
7 The Golden Gate Bridge connects San Francisco and Los Angeles.
8 I will still be at school in 2045.

4 Information please!   *Yes/No* questions   ▶ 1.3.1a

Make new questions by replacing the underlined words in the sentences below with the words in brackets.

→ Lola reads <u>crime novels</u>. (fantasy novels?)
Does she read fantasy novels too?

1   Liam can speak <u>Gaelic</u>. (Welsh?)
2   Jana goes to <u>jazz concerts</u>. (rock concerts?)
3   My host brothers Jason and Eric play <u>baseball every weekend</u>. (football?)
4   <u>Jackie's brother</u> has an electric bike. (Jackie?)
5   Thomas Edison invented <u>the phonograph</u>. (telephone?)
6   The Goldsmiths <u>have bought a new car</u>. (sell the old one?)
7   While we were in London, we <u>went on a tour of the Globe Theatre</u>. (see a play?)
8   My friend Toby <u>has seen every James Bond film at least three times</u>. (read the novels?)
9   Our neighbours <u>go skiing every winter</u>. (go on holiday in summer?)
10 I'm going to see a <u>Broadway play</u> while I'm in New York. (a musical?)

5 The London Eye   Questions with question words   ▶ 1.3.1b

a   Lennard's class is planning a trip to London. They were given a list of questions on the London Eye. Below you can read the information they collected. Write the questions they had to answer.

→ ***How many*** *passenger capsules are there?*

> **The London Eye**
> ► 32 passenger capsules
> ► 135 metres tall (1)
> ► max. 25 passengers per capsule (2)
> ► opened to public 2000 (3)
> ► cost £70 million to build (4)
> ► 3.75 m visitors annually (5)
> ► open daily 10 am – 8:30 pm (6)

b   **NOW YOU** Choose some other sight in London that you would like to visit. Write five questions that you might ask before your visit.

6 Schoolyard gossip   Questions with prepositions   ▶ 1.3.2d

Write a question about each of the following statements.

→ Samantha is worried about something.
   What *is she worried **about**?*

1   Mateusz is angry at somebody.
2   Leyla and Fatma are laughing about something.
3   Harry is waiting for somebody.
4   Hanna is upset about something.
5   Roxanne and Delia are talking about somebody.
6   Karim is thanking Roberta for something.
7   Louise is staring at somebody.
8   Mr Baxter is looking for somebody.

1

7 A dramatic rehearsal   Subject and object questions   ▶ 1.3.3

The dress rehearsal of the annual play at Mansfield School was interrupted by a dramatic incident. Read what happened and then make questions for the answers below.

➔ I collapsed during the third act.

Danella

1 I caught Danny when she fainted.

Suzy

2 I brought her a bottle of water.

Jamal

3 I offered to phone for a doctor.

Sarah

4 I felt her pulse. It was OK.

Yannis

5 I texted Danny's brother Ron.

Yasemin

6 I picked up Danny with my mum's car.

Ron

7 I phoned the head teacher to postpone the premiere.

the drama teacher

➔ ...? – Danella
Who collapsed during the rehearsal? – Danella

1 ...? – Suzy.
2 ...? – A bottle of water.
3 ...? – Sarah.

4 ...? – Danny's pulse.
5 ...? – Yasemin.

6 ...? – His sister Danny.
7 ...? – The head teacher.

8 An interview with an exchange student   Question words   ▶ 1.3.4

Aiden Williams from Australia is an exchange student at Gymnasium Carolinum in Rostock. He is being interviewed for the school magazine by Karla Timmens. Choose the right words to complete the dialogue.

Karla Hi Aiden! Welcome to MeckPomm. You're a long way from home, aren't you? ➔ **What** | Which do you like best about German schools?

Aiden Hi Karla. Well, it's really OK here. Lucky for me, your English is a lot better than my German. And you have some great sports opportunities here.

Karla What | Which (1) is your favourite sport?

Aiden Surfing, most definitely. We've got a lot of great beaches for surfing in Australia.

Karla What | Which (2) of them is your favourite?

Aiden   Well, Bondi Beach is close to where I live. But the best places to surf are all on the west coast.
Karla   How is the water temperature | What is the water temperature like (3) down there right now?
Aiden   Well, it'd be around 20° centigrade, I guess. Warmer than here, anyway.
Karla   What for | What kind of (4) equipment do you use?
Aiden   Back home, I've got a really cool Barracuda shortboard I got second hand. And I wear a wetsuit, unless it's really hot.
Karla   Do you take part in competitions?
Aiden   Yeah – sometimes I even win.
Karla   What | Which (5) was the worst thing that ever happened to you in a competition?
Aiden   That was last year, when I had to compete against my best mate, Mike.
Karla   Who | Which (6) of you won?
Aiden   Neither of us – luckily. Say, aren't you going to write any of this stuff down?
Karla   I don't have to – I'm recording it on my phone.
Aiden   Clever! Y'know how | what (7) we call these things 'down under'?
Karla   No, tell me.
Aiden   Smartphones. Ha ha ha.

9 Q&A with Silvia   Answering *yes/no* questions   ▶ 1.3.5, 1.3.6

a At the bus stop, you meet your classmate Silvia. She always has lots of questions. Reply to them using a short answer.

➜ Do you have a bus pass? (yes) – *Yes, **I do**.*

1 Has the 7:42 bus arrived yet? (no)
2 Did you do the maths homework yesterday? (yes)
3 Did you understand the last task? (no)
4 Have you studied for the German test? (yes)
5 Will you give me the answers if I don't know them? (no)
6 Oh no, I've forgotten my lunch money! Can you lend me a couple of pounds? (yes)

b You and Silvia are on a class trip to a woodland campsite. Answer her questions using one of the verbs in the box.

think • suppose • hope • guess • be afraid

➜ Is Ms Jones still in a bad mood? – (Ich glaube ja.) – *I think so.*

1 Is it going to rain today? – (Hoffentlich nicht.)
2 Will we go on a hike again this afternoon? – (Ich fürchte ja.)
3 Do we have to collect wood for a bonfire this morning? – (Ich glaube nicht.)
4 Can we have a barbecue this evening? – (Ich hoffe ja.)
5 Will Ms Jones let us take the bus into town? – (Ich fürchte nicht.)
6 Is she going to make us clean the breakfast room again? – (Ich schätze ja.)

10 Walk, don't run Imperatives/Commands ▶ 1.4.1

a Use the imperative to say what these signs mean.

➜ ***Turn off*** your mobile.
   or: ***Do not use*** your mobile.

1  2  3  4

5  6  7  8

b Make the following imperatives sound more polite by rewriting them as questions.

➜ Step aside, please.
   Could I ask you to step aside, please?
   or: Would you mind stepping aside for a moment, please?

1 Open the door for me, please.
2 Don't smoke here.
3 Change this fifty euro note, please.
4 Please take a photo of me and my friend.

5 Please show me how to use this ticket machine.
6 Help me put my suitcase in the luggage rack, please.
7 Don't talk in the library. I'm trying to concentrate.
8 Wait here until I come back.

11 Secret thoughts Exclamations ▶ 1.5

a Laura and Jack have met at a café on their first date. 'Translate' the words from the thought bubbles into complete exclamations.

➜ Nice eyes!
   What nice eyes he has!

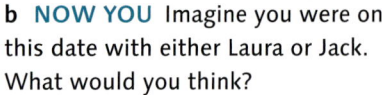

➜ Nice eyes!
1 Smart clothes!
2 Handsome!
3 A great sense of humour!

4 A beautiful smile!
5 Pretty face!
6 Intelligent!
7 I'm a lucky guy!

b **NOW YOU** Imagine you were on this date with either Laura or Jack. What would you think?

+ 12 Stressing your opinion Emphatic structures ▶ 1.6.1 – 1.6.4

Rewrite the sentences below to make them sound more emphatic. Use the technique shown in the examples. The underlined word or words show you which part of the sentence to emphasize.

→ It makes a difference where the food we buy comes from.
*It **does make** a difference where the food we buy comes from.*

1 Global warming leads to increased flooding and extreme weather conditions.
2 Every kilometre we drive in our cars contributes to air pollution.
3 Active volcanoes emit a huge amount of CO_2 into the atmosphere, but not nearly as much as China's industry.

→ Ella and Hassan designed the poster for the campaign, not Patty.
*It **was Ella and Hassan** who designed the poster for the campaign, not Patty.*

4 Daniel created our brilliant slogan.
5 The junior class gave us the most support.
6 We need publicity more than anything else.

→ The silly ending of the musical ruined it for me.
*What **ruined the musical for me was** the silly ending.*

7 I liked the music best.
8 The running gags got on my nerves.
9 The fantastic lead singer made the evening bearable for me.

→ It has seldom been as easy to travel as it is today.
*Seldom **has it been** so easy to travel as it is today.*

10 You hardly ever hear of people who dislike travelling.
11 Such large numbers of people have never before been on the move.
12 We have only recently begun to realize that mass mobility comes at a high price.

+ 13 A lesson in climate politics Emphatic structures ▶ 1.6.1

Rewrite the underlined passages below to make them sound more emphatic. Examples A–D can help you choose the right technique for each sentence.

A The story of the so-called 'ozone hole' shows that concerted action has a measurable effect.
*The story of the so-called 'ozone hole' shows that concerted action **does have** a measurable effect.*
B Scientists first observed in the Antarctic region that the ozone layer was getting thinner.
*It **was in the Antarctic region** that scientists first observed that the ozone layer was getting thinner.*
C The fact that a huge hole appeared in the ozone layer during the summer months really alarmed them.
*What **really alarmed them was** the fact that a huge hole appeared in the ozone layer during the summer months.*
D Scientists had never before observed such rapid changes in the earth's atmosphere.
*Never **before had scientists observed** such rapid changes in the earth's atmosphere.*

1

The earth's stratosphere contains a layer of ozone, a form of oxygen. This ozone layer (B) absorbs some of the sun's ultraviolet light before it can reach the surface of the earth. Ultraviolet light can cause skin cancer. Beginning in the early 1970s, scientists observed that the ozone layer was becoming thinner, especially over the Southern Hemisphere. Man-made chemicals called CFCs, used in spray cans and refrigerators, were held responsible. But experts began to warn only in the mid-1980s (D) that there could be up to 100,000 additional deaths from skin cancer every year if nothing was done to protect the ozone layer. In 1987, (B) the major industrial countries agreed to ban the production and use of CFCs. Since then, the ozone layer has recovered. This example shows (C) that action taken in time can be effective. Of course, the situation was much simpler than that of global warming. The only cause of the problem was the use of CFCs. The fact that only a handful of firms produced these chemicals made it much easier to reach an agreement (C). Furthermore, substitute chemicals that did not harm the atmosphere were already available. Moreover, ordinary people felt personally affected by the threat of skin cancer. By way of contrast, it is difficult to understand the connection between shopping trips in your SUV and flooding in Bangladesh. The link between cause and effect is simply too vague. And – let's be honest – reducing greenhouse gases means (A) changing every aspect of our lifestyle, not just throwing away the spray cans. But that is no excuse for doing nothing. We can only slow down global warming by drastically reducing our use of fossil fuels (D).

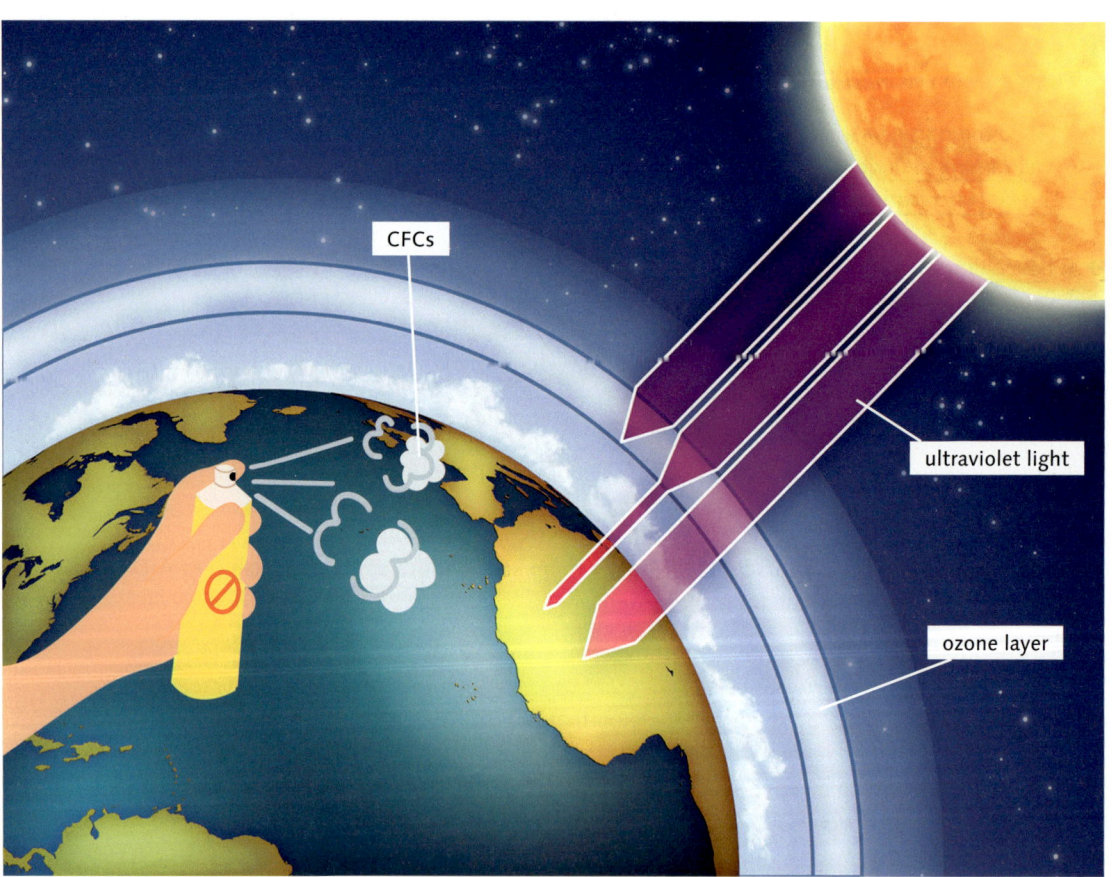

CFCs

ultraviolet light

ozone layer

Quick Check

A Put the words in the right order to make correct sentences.

1 Denise and Özlem | every Friday afternoon | tennis | play
2 will be | a meeting of the student council | There | next Monday
3 has | been | John | doing | not | on his tests | very well | recently
4 many times | We | this problem | have | discussed | already.

B Make the following sentences negative.

1 I will be at home this Christmas.
2 Marco did his homework yesterday.
3 Leonie and Jenna wanted to join the Photo Club.
4 Eating junk food is good for you.

C Write the question that the <u>underlined</u> part answers.

1 <u>Thomas and Jan</u> designed the poster.
2 The girls left the concert early <u>because it started to rain</u>.
3 The band will meet for a rehearsal <u>on Wednesday</u>.
4 Kieran does <u>weightlifting</u> at the local gym.
5 The class went to Salisbury <u>by bus</u>.
6 Tina has invited <u>sixteen</u> friends to her party.
7 Henrike met <u>Laszlo</u> at Kate's party.
8 Sarah gave the letter to <u>her brother</u>.

D Choose the correct solution.

1 Who | Which of the students is Jacqueline?
2 What | Which is your favourite flavour ice cream?
3 Do you know how | what this is called in French?
4 How is your brother feeling | What is your brother feeling like after his accident?
5 What | Which size do you take?
6 What colour has | is your parents' house?

E These incomplete sentences use different forms of emphasis. Complete them with the missing word or words.

1 'You forgot to lock the door.' – 'That's not true! I … lock the door when I left the house!'
2 'You don't like me.' – 'You know that's not true. I … like you.'
3 'You posted those embarrassing photos.' – 'That's not true! … Chris who posted them, not me!'
4 The Irish countryside is beautiful, but … I liked most was the hospitality of the Irish people.
5 The Hollywood blockbuster *Ben Hur* won eleven Academy Awards in 1959. Never before … one film … awarded so many Oscars.

2 The simple sentence and its elements

Task	Topic	Example	Englische Grammatik
1	Verbs with two objects	*I wrote a long letter to my uncle.* *I sent it to him yesterday.* *Did you give Joel the book?*	2.3.2
2	Verbs with *to* + indirect object	*We reported the break-in to the police.*	2.3.3
3	Phrasal verbs (1)	*Katie looked at me and smiled.*	2.3.4
4	Phrasal verbs (2)	*Please pick up those papers from the floor and throw them away.*	2.3.4
5	Prepositional verbs (1)	*My friend Mira comes from Tunisia.*	2.3.5
6	Prepositional verbs (2)	*Who was Leonie talking to?*	2.3.5
7	Adverbials	*Nowadays people often shop online.*	2.4.2
8	Subject complements	*The weather turned cold in September.*	2.2.1
9	Object complements	*The outlaws made Robin Hood their leader.*	2.2.2
10	Formal style	*Who do you look up to?* → *Who do you admire?*	2.3.4

▶ Quick Check p. 23

1 Who does what? – a game   Verbs with two objects   ▶ 2.3.2

a   Round 1: Combine the elements from the table to make sentences. Use the usual word order for direct and indirect objects.

➔ *Bankers lend* **their customers money**.

Who?	Does what?	To whom?
➔ ~~Bankers~~	~~lend money~~	~~their customers~~
1 Flight attendants	serve food and drink	passengers
2 Pharmacists	sell medicine	their customers
3 English teachers	teach English	their students
4 Tour guides	show interesting sights	tourists
5 Hotel receptionists	give the room keys	hotel guests
6 Lawyers	offer legal advice	their clients

b   Round 2: Now you need a different combination. Rewrite sentences 1–6 from part a, changing the order of the objects to emphasize the indirect object.

➔ *Bankers lend* **money to their customers**.

c Round 3: Answer the following questions using a personal pronoun.

➔ *What do bankers do with money? – They lend* **it to their customers**.

1 What do flight attendants do with food and drinks?
2 What do pharmacists do with medicine?
3 What do English teachers do with English?
4 What do tour guides do with interesting sights?
5 What do hotel receptionists do with the room keys?
6 What do lawyers do with legal advice?

2 **Please help me!** Verbs with *to* + indirect object ▸ 2.3.3

a Look at these snippets from the *Teens Today* advice page. Put the words in brackets in the correct order and complete the sentences. Add *to* if needed.

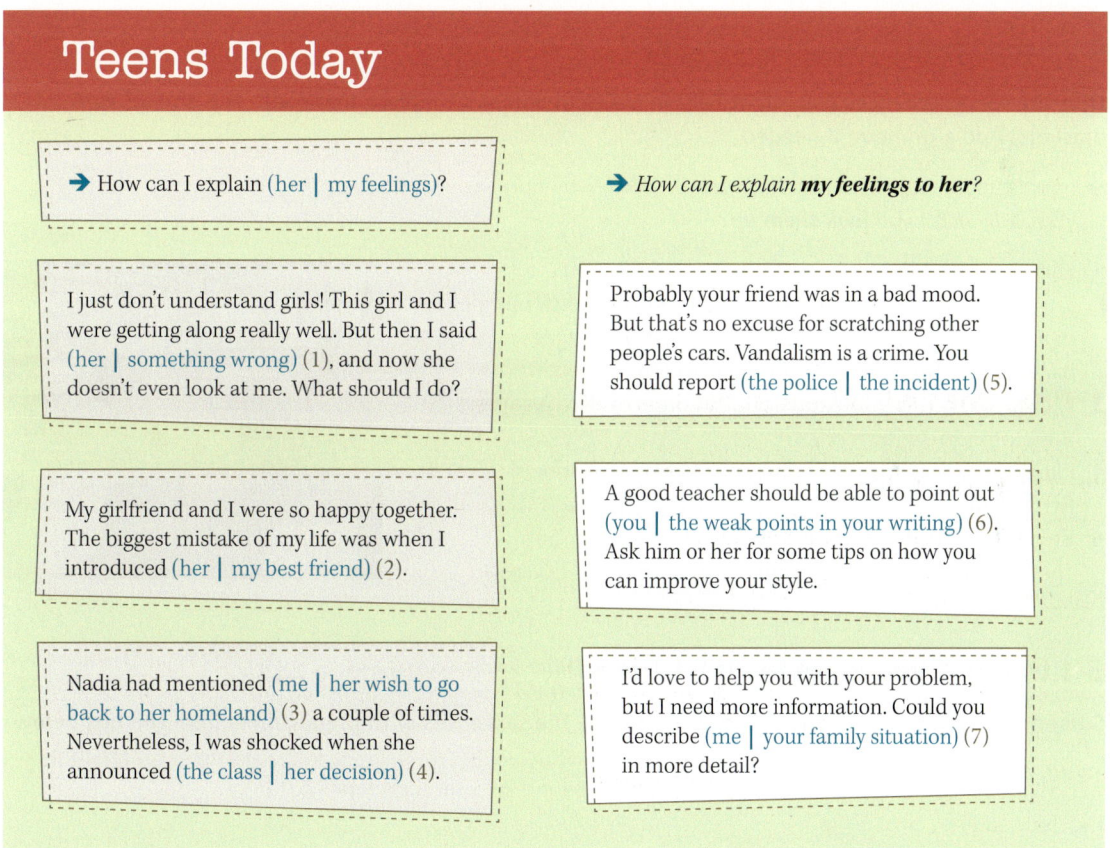

Teens Today

➔ How can I explain (her | my feelings)?

➔ *How can I explain* **my feelings to her**?

I just don't understand girls! This girl and I were getting along really well. But then I said (her | something wrong) (1), and now she doesn't even look at me. What should I do?

Probably your friend was in a bad mood. But that's no excuse for scratching other people's cars. Vandalism is a crime. You should report (the police | the incident) (5).

My girlfriend and I were so happy together. The biggest mistake of my life was when I introduced (her | my best friend) (2).

A good teacher should be able to point out (you | the weak points in your writing) (6). Ask him or her for some tips on how you can improve your style.

Nadia had mentioned (me | her wish to go back to her homeland) (3) a couple of times. Nevertheless, I was shocked when she announced (the class | her decision) (4).

I'd love to help you with your problem, but I need more information. Could you describe (me | your family situation) (7) in more detail?

b NOW YOU Choose a topic that interests you and write a brief letter to *Teens Today* asking for help. Use some of the verbs from a. If you are working with a partner, swap letters afterwards and write a reply to your partner's letter.

➔ *Dear XXX, I'm writing to you because I don't know what to do … Please help!*

2

3 A trip to Tunisia Phrasal verbs ▶ 2.3.4

Elena is telling her friends about a holiday trip to Tunisia with her cousin Alina. Complete the phrasal verbs by adding a word from the box.

> around • back • back • down • in • off • ~~off~~ •
> out • over • over • up

First, we spent over an hour on the runway waiting for our plane to take ➔ *off*. When we got off the plane in Monastir, I almost fell ... (1) from the heat. I was really nervous when a customs official went ...
5 (2) with my passport. I only began to relax when he came ... (3) and handed me my documents.
Then we took a taxi to our hotel and checked ... (4). After that, Alina said she was thirsty, so we looked ... (5) for a café. We found one near the hotel and sat ... (6). A young waiter came ... (7) to our table and 10 greeted us in Arabic. Alina got ... (8) her German-Arabic dictionary and wanted to look ... (9) the right phrase for 'We'd like something to drink'. Luckily, the waiter noticed the title of the book and asked us in perfect German what we would like. He told us 15 that he had lived in Duisburg before his family moved ... (10) to Tunisia.

4 In the library Phrasal verbs ▶ 2.3.4

Here are some sentences you might hear in a school library. Complete them with the phrasal verb in brackets. Add a pronoun if needed.

➔ I don't understand some of the words. – Well, why don't you ... (look up)?
*Well, why don't you **look them up**?*

1 This novel is so exciting, I just can't ... (put down).
2 I'm not a fan of horror stories. A while ago I ... (pick up) a copy of a Stephen King novel, but after the first few pages I ... (put back) on the shelf.
3 Excuse me, is this photocopier out of order? – No, just press the button to ... (turn on).
4 I keep forgetting my user number. – Maybe you should ... (write down).
5 If you enjoy reading, you should join the Reading Club. – The Reading Club? Sounds cool. I'll have to ... (check out).

5 I thought you were my best friend! Prepositional verbs ▶ 2.3.5

Sometimes even the best friends argue. Complete the sentences with prepositions from the box below.

> about • at (2x) • for (2x) • in • of • through • ~~to~~ • to

You aren't even listening ➔ *to* me.
I'm not asking ... (1) your help.
I wish you'd at least look ... (2) me when I talk ... (3) you.
You have no idea what I'm going ... (4).
Do you ever think ... (5) anyone but yourself?
I've always believed ... (6) our friendship.
I never dreamt that you would laugh ... (7) me behind my back.
If there's a problem, then let us talk ... (8) it.

6 Sorry, what did you say? Prepositional verbs ▶ 2.3.5

a Ellie is talking to her best friend Tahia on the phone while she is waiting for her train. It's noisy in the train station, so Tahia doesn't understand everything Ellie says. Write down her questions.

→ **Ellie**   I want to talk to you about   .
  Tahia   *Sorry, what do you want to talk about?*

1 I worry a lot about   .
2 I'm thinking of   .
3 I recently heard about   .
4 Last week I spoke to   .

5 He told me about   .
6 I asked him for   .
7 He promised to help me with   .

b NOW YOU Alone or with a partner, complete what Ellie said and write a mini story.

→ **Ellie** *I want to talk to you about your brother Malik.*

7 Tomorrow Utopia Adverbials ▶ 2.4.2

a Put the words in the right order.

→ will be | there | In 2050 | tourist flights | to the moon
  *In 2050 there **will be** tourist flights to the moon.*

1 peace | will be | There | in all countries of the world | by 2050
2 on public roads | will not find | You | anymore | human drivers
3 a cure for AIDS | will have discovered | in a few years | Researchers
4 by robots | all housework | In the near future | will be done |
5 to 100 years | will | live | People | often | or even older
6 will | people | Everywhere | access to clean water | have | in the world

b NOW YOU Add your own predictions for the future. Write three sentences including adverbials of time and place.

8 Christine's debut Subject complements ▶ 2.2.1

Complete the following text with words from the box below. Put the verbs in the correct form.

> be a great success • feel certain • feel sick • get nervous • look very friendly • seem strange •
> sound exciting • stay calm

Christine had always → **felt certain** that she was the best in her piano class. So she wasn't really surprised when her teacher offered her the chance to appear in a concert. The idea ... (1) at first, but as the
5 concert drew nearer, Christine began to ... (2). Her teacher told her to ... (3) and to concentrate on her playing. When the day of the concert finally arrived, Christine was so nervous that she almost ... (4).

It ... (5) to stand alone on stage with hundreds of eyes watching her. But then she noticed the people 10 in the first row: they all ... (6). Christine forgot how nervous she was and began to play. In the end, the concert ... (7). She got a huge round of applause from the audience and a bouquet of roses from her music teacher. 15

2

2

+ 9 America's first black president   Object complements   ▸ 2.2.2

a Complete the sentences below using the verb in brackets in the right tense. In some cases you need the passive form.

➜ Obama's election … him the first black president in US history. (make)
*Obama's election **made** him the first black president in US history.*

1 In 2008, Barack Obama … President of the United States. (elect)
2 At the time, black activists … Obama's victory the start of a new chapter in race relations. (consider)
3 Today, many people … the expectations placed on Obama unrealistic. (find)
4 Nevertheless, Obama … an outstanding figure in US political history. (consider)
5 For one thing, he … affordable health care a reality for millions of Americans. (make)
6 The Affordable Care Act of 2010 … 'ObamaCare' by the media in honour of its creator. (nickname)

b NOW YOU Make complete sentences expressing your own thoughts and feelings on the issues below. Use phrases from the box on the right.

• weapons exports
• discrimination
• violent protests
• animal experiments
• GM foods
• hunger

> find sth. difficult to understand • make sb. angry • consider sth. a scandal • think sth. should be made (il)legal

+ 10 A difficult time in life   Formal style   ▸ 2.3.4

Make the style of the following text more formal by replacing phrasal verbs with verbs that belong to the written language. Find a suitable verb from the box and use it to replace the underlined words. (There are two more words than you need.)

➜ *Quarrels **erupt** over seemingly trivial issues.*

> contradict • deny • despair • discuss • ~~erupt~~ • experience • explore • permit • recall • subside • tolerate

Adolescence is a difficult time in the lives of children and their parents. Quarrels break out over seemingly trivial issues. Parents refuse to see why they should put up with (1) their son's or daughter's
5 eccentric, unpredictable behaviour. Formerly docile teens suddenly start talking back to (2) their elders at every turn. Attempts at talking about (3) differences of opinion typically end in shouting matches. All too often, parents just give up (4) and wait for
10 the storm to blow over (5). They might be more understanding if they were to think back to (6) their own adolescence. Many of the conflicts their children are going through (7) are similar to the problems they had as teenagers.

Adolescence is mainly a behavioural trial period: 15
teens are trying out (8) new behaviours as they search for their own identity. If parents kept this in mind, they might regard their children's sudden changes of mood more calmly.

Quick Check

A Find and correct the mistakes. There is one in each sentence.

1 My brother plays in his free time computer games.
2 Could you explain me again how to solve these tasks?
3 I had never seen Florian's video before, so I was really impressed when he showed me it.
4 Selima's courage made her to a leader of the protest movement.
5 If you're not using these dictionaries, please put them on the shelves back.
6 At what are you guys laughing?
7 That's a really nice dress – why don't you try on it?
8 Ms Wilson looked angrily when she entered the classroom.
9 By 2030 will students get most of their education online.
10 James Joyce is considered as one of the greatest writers of his century.

B Complete the sentences below by adding the word(s) in brackets. You may also have to add *to* or *for*.

1 Mr Flanagan showed a film about life on the Aran Islands. (his class)
2 Hakan met Karim at a café in the city centre. (yesterday afternoon)
3 I mentioned that I was leaving for the States at the weekend. (her)
4 Ms Gomez made dinner before she left the house. (her children)
5 'That's a lovely necklace you're wearing.' – 'Thanks. My aunt bought it.' (me)
6 I buy fresh fish at the supermarket. (never)
7 The parcel service delivered the books on Friday. (the shop)
8 Filiz was elected at the first meeting of the year. (chairperson)

C Complete the replies using a suitable phrasal verb from the box.

> leave out • put back • send back • take off • tidy up • turn off

1 That music is driving me crazy. – Then you can ….
2 These shoes are very uncomfortable. – Why don't you …?
3 My room is such a mess. – Well, you could ….
4 I bought these jeans online, but they don't fit. – Why don't you …?
5 I can't do task 8. – Then you can just ….
6 Shall I leave the pen here? – No, please … on my desk.

D Write questions based on the words in brackets.

1 I've just bought a birthday present. – (Für wen gekauft?)
2 I did have the key to the store room, but I don't have it anymore. – (Wem gegeben?)
3 It isn't a secret anymore – I've heard it from a couple of people. – (Von wem gehört?)
4 I have to wait here a few more minutes. – (Worauf warten?)
5 Sophie phoned to thank me yesterday. – (Wofür danken?)
6 I got so angry yesterday. – (Worüber geärgert?)

2

3 Full verbs

Task	Topic	Example	Englische Grammatik
1	The s-form and the *ing*-form (1)	*talks, says, takes, runs* *talking, saying, taking, running*	3.2.2 3.2.3
2	The s-form and the *ing*-form (2)	*The cat usually sits by the window but she's sitting on my desk now.*	3.2.2 3.2.3
3	The *ed*-form	*Jed played really well.*	3.2.4
4	Irregular verbs	*He was so good that he won a prize.*	3.2.4
5	Tense and time	*She's just going to the shops now.* *She's going to the shops tomorrow.*	3.3
6	Simple and progressive forms (1)	*Marc enjoys DIY. He was working on his house, when he fell off the ladder.*	3.4
7	State verbs	*Ah, now I understand!*	3.5.2
8	Verbs of perception	*How do you feel today?*	3.5.4
9	Verbs with several meanings	*Wait, I'm thinking … Yes, I think you're right!*	3.5.3
10	Simple and progressive forms (2)	*They moved here ages ago. By next year, they will have been living here for 20 years.*	3.4

▸ Quick Check p. 30

3.1.2 *Be, have, do* – see chapter 4, 3.1.3 Modal auxiliary verbs – see chapter 5

1 Spelling matters   The s form and the *ing*-form ▸ 3.2.2, 3.2.3

a Use the clues to complete the puzzle with the s-form of the verbs.

She is a student who always ➔ ***completes*** her projects on time.

1 Our baby girl only … when she's hungry or tired.
2 My brother always … his homework at the last minute.
3 My neighbour often … to my house for coffee.
4 Jack is so lazy. He never … at home.
5 My uncle is a pilot. He … all around the world.
6 My grandma's neighbour is so helpful. He always … her heavy shopping bag.
7 My grandpa … TV every evening.
8 The school bus always … from this stop.
9 Tom … his clothes online.

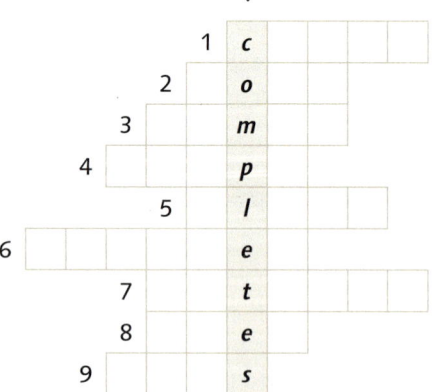

b Fill in the *ing*-form of these verbs.

come – ➔ ***coming***	control – … (1)	die – … (2)	hope – … (3)
offer – … (4)	plan – … (5)	play – … (6)	sit – … (7)
smoke – … (8)	stop – … (9)	swim – … (10)	work – … (11)

2 Pinocchio often lies   The s-form and the *ing*-form   ▶ 3.2.2, 3.2.3

Sam is reading a classic children's story from the 1880s called Pinocchio.
Read the text and choose the correct spellings.

Sam ➜ is studieing | **is *studying*** languages at university, so at the moment he is trieing | is trying (1) to read Pinocchio in the original Italian. The idea that a liar's nose growes | grows (2) longer comes from this story. It begins | beginns (3) in Tuscany. An Italian carpenter is planning | is planing (4) to make a piece of wood into a leg for his table when, suddenly, the wood cries out | crys out (5). The carpenter is so afraid that he gives | givs (6) the wood to his neighbour Geppetto, who makes it into a boy named Pinocchio. Geppetto teachs | teaches (7) the boy to walk and he soon runs | runns (8) away. As Pinocchio's behaviour gets | getts (9) worse and worse, his nose starts | startes (10) to grow. The book is great fun, even for a modern reader. Sam has | haves (11) problems understanding every word of the text, but that doesn't matter because he knows | knowes (12) the story from the Disney film.

3 Pronunciation matters   The *ed*-form   ▶ 3.2.4

How are the simple past *ed*-endings of regular verbs pronounced? Complete the table with the past tense forms of the words from the box.

[-d]	[-t]	[-ɪd]
➜ enjoyed	➜ asked	➜ ended

ask • end • enjoy • hate • help • laugh • live • need • paint • pick • play • seem • shop • try • wait • want • wash • wish

4 He came, he saw, he overcame his fears   Irregular verbs   ▶ 3.2.4

a Complete the missing simple past and past participle forms of these irregular verbs. You can find all the forms you need in the grid.

be – ➜ **was** / were – been
become – became – … (1)
begin – … (2) – begun
choose – chose – … (3)
eat – … (4) – eaten
go – went – … (5)
grow – … (6) – grown
hide – hid – … (7)
hit – … (8) – hit
make – made – … (9)
see – … (10) – seen
shoot – … (11) – shot
speak – … (12) – spoken
win – … (13) – won
write – wrote – … (14)

R	B	M	Y	C	A	M	E	L	L	I
I	K	B	P	H	P	I	S	S	U	G
N	B	E	C	O	M	E	M	H	R	R
H	A	X	P	S	X	Z	G	O	N	E
I	E	A	T	E	Y	V	J	T	O	W
T	P	N	L	N	A	S	*W*	B	B	Q
R	G	H	L	N	F	M	*A*	D	E	N
S	A	W	D	C	L	G	*S*	V	G	N
P	S	Y	D	W	M	H	A	D	A	B
O	T	S	W	R	I	T	T	E	N	R
K	A	L	O	N	N	A	W	D	A	A
E	O	N	N	D	H	I	D	D	E	N

b Complete the text about a sports star using the simple past of the verbs given.

When tennis legend Andy Murray ➜ **won** (win) his second Olympic gold medal in 2016, he ... (make) (1) history. It all ... (begin) (2) in Dunblane, a small Scottish town where Murray ... (grow up) (3). He ...
5 (go) (4) to the local primary school which ... (hit) (5) the headlines in 1996, when a gunman ... (shoot) (6) sixteen children and a teacher in a terrible massacre. The young Andy Murray ... (hide) (7) in a classroom, but he ... (see) (8) it all. He never ... (speak) (9) much
10 about this in later interviews, but he ... (write) (10) about it in his autobiography *Hitting back*. Perhaps this terrible experience helped him overcome his fears on the court. In 2001, he ... (be) (11) one of just

a few kids to win a top event for junior players twice. And in 2016, he ... (become) (12) the world number 15 one.

5 She's known him since kindergarten   Tense and time   ▶ 3.3

a Read the dialogue between Bev and Anja, focussing on the verbs in bold. Decide what tense they are in and what time they refer to.

Anja	Hi, Bev! What **are** you **doing** tonight?
	➜ tense: *present* time: *future*
Bev	Sorry Anja, I can't talk now, I**'m** just **going** out.
Anja	To Elmer's? I heard he **is having** a party tonight.
Bev	Oh, I didn't realize you **knew** him.
Anja	Yeah, I**'ve known** Elmer for years.
Bev	When **did** you last **see** him?
Anja	I **haven't seen** him for ages.
Bev	Well, if you **met** him in the street, ...
	... you **wouldn't recognize** him.
Anja	Really? Anyway, **are** you busy tomorrow?
Bev	Yes, I**'m working** all day, I'm afraid.
Anja	If you **had** five minutes now, ...
Bev	Listen, I**'ll ring** you back in a minute, OK?

b Now translate these parts of the girls' conversation into German. Watch out for the tenses!

➜ What are you doing tonight?
Was machst du heute Abend?

1 I'm just going out.
2 I've known Elmer for years.
3 When did you last see him?

4 If you met him in the street, you wouldn't recognize him.
5 Are you busy tomorrow?
6 If you had five minutes now, ...

3

6 Who usually cooks? Who's cooking now? Simple and progressive forms ▶ 3.4

a Choose the correct tense.

Helen I can smell something nice!
Who ➜ cooks | **'s cooking**?

Rose My son, Harry. He often cooks | is often cooking (1) for us at the weekend. He's a vegetarian; he doesn't eat | isn't eating (2) meat.

Helen What does he prepare | is he preparing (3) tonight?

Rose A type of Hungarian goulash.

Helen What happens | is happening (4) if you make | are making (5) goulash with no meat?

Rose It actually tastes | is tasting (6) quite nice. A little red wine in the sauce makes | is making (7) all the difference. Watch out, Harry! The sauce boils over | is boiling over (8).

Helen Does he often make | Is he often making (9) such a mess in the kitchen?

Rose Yes, I'm afraid he does | is (10)! He needs | is needing (11) an assistant chef. And guess who usually clears up | is usually clearing up (12) after him?

b NOW YOU Write five sentences about who usually cooks in your family and what they like making.

7 What do you know? State verbs ▶ 3.5.2

Complete the three dialogues with the simple present or present progressive of the verbs in brackets.

Kemal and Lisa ➜ **are discussing** (discuss) smartphones.

Kemal I ➜ **need** (need) a new phone. It … (not matter) (1) what it costs.

Lisa What … … (you, mean) (2)? You … (own) (3) the latest model already.

Kemal You … (not understand) (4). They … (bring out) (5) the S10Plus next week.

Lisa I … (believe) (6) it's very expensive. In fact, I know it … (cost) (7) over £300.

Mr and Mrs Singh are shopping at the market.

Mr Singh Look, they … (sell) (8) fish at half price here today.

Mrs Singh But it … (smell) (9) funny. I … (not buy) (10) that.

Mr Singh Hmm, it … (seem) (11) OK to me. You know how much I … (love) (12) fish. In fact, I … (prefer) (13) it to meat.

Mrs Singh All right. I hope you … (enjoy) (14) it!

Austin is talking to a colleague, Sofia.

Austin I believe your son Ben … (work) (15) in the same bar as my daughter.

Sofia Really? That … (sound) (16) unlikely. He … (study) (17) hard for exams at the moment.

Austin Susie … (talk about) (18) him quite a lot. At least, I … (think) (19) it's your Ben.

Sofia Huh? Well, he never … (tell) (20) me anything.

8 I could smell smoke   Verbs of perception   ▸ 3.5.4

a Amanda had a scary experience. Read her account and choose the correct verb.

It was a dark and cloudy night, and the air ➔ **tasted** | seemed of electricity, as it sometimes does before a storm. I saw | heard (1) a
5 rumble of thunder and, as I sat, waiting for the lights to change, I looked | saw (2) an owl silently flying past.

By the time I got to the Snake Pass, I saw | felt (3)
10 large raindrops on the windscreen and soon it was raining hard. I was driving slowly when suddenly I realized | noticed (4) a figure standing at the side of the road. A young girl, all alone. I stopped to offer her a lift. She listened | seemed (5) distracted and
15 hardly spoke, except to tell me her address. I felt | sounded (6) she wasn't happy, but I was soon glad to be home and dry myself and I heard | thought (7) no more about her.

The next morning, my car saw | seemed (8) oddly differ-   20
ent to me and I really didn't understand why. It tasted | smelled (9) of smoke, but I'm not a smoker. Then I found the strange girl's wet scarf   25
under the passenger seat, so on my way to work, I stopped outside her house. It sounded | seemed (10) to be empty, but a neighbour looked | saw (11) me and came out to talk. 'Does a young girl live here?' I began. 'Not anymore,' came   30
the answer. 'They all moved away after the accident.' I felt | heard (12) a shiver running down my back. 'Oh?' – 'Yes, she was killed on the Snake Pass. Must be a year ago now.' 'How awful,' I replied. 'Was … was she a smoker?' – 'Yes, she was. Why do you   35
ask?'

b NOW YOU Describe a time when something scary happened to you or someone you know. Use at least five different verbs of perception.

✚ 9 It's the thought that counts   Verbs with several meanings   ▸ 3.5.3

Jake's friends Lena, Caro and Amelie are planning a birthday party for him. Complete the sentences using the simple present or the present progressive.

Lena

Five days before the party, Lena is talking to Caro.

➔ **count**
I'**m not counting** (not) how much this party will cost.
It's the element of surprise that really **counts**.
I'**m counting** on you and Amelie to help!

think
We … (1) of having a surprise party for Jake in our garden.
And we are going to have fireworks! What … you … (2) of that idea?
Everyone else we've spoken to … (3) it's a great plan!

Caro

Three days before the party, Caro is talking to Amelie.

depend
The success of the party … (4) on the weather.
Lena … (5) on me to order the party tent. I'm not sure how big it should be. I guess it … (6) on how many people we plan to invite.

measure
We're hiring the dance floor online. I need to know what the tent … (7).
I believe dance floors normally … (8) 15 square metres.
Lena … (9) the space we have in the garden now, to make sure it will fit.

The day before the party, Amelie is talking to Lena.

expect

I … (10) you'd like me to come over and discuss things.

I'm afraid I can't leave yet, I … (11) Jake's present to be delivered.

It's late. I … (12) the postman's been delayed.

mean

I … (13) to make his birthday cake for days, but I haven't had time.

So that … (14) I'll have to buy one instead.

But if I order it online, it … (15) waiting for the postman again!

It's Jake's birthday! Finally!

hold

Wow, what a crowd! How many people … a tent of this size usually … (16)?

I'm glad my friends … (not) (17) a surprise party every year! I don't know half of these people.

And whose dog is that? Oh dear, is that a firework the dog … (18) in its mouth?

✚ 10 What's been happening? Simple and progressive forms ▶ 3.4

A UN delegate has recently met Amena, a teenager from Syria. Read his report and complete Amena's story, choosing the correct form of the verbs.

Teenagers from many different backgrounds ➔ **have** | are having much in common. Amena is a normal sixteen-year-old, interested in the usual things: music, her friends, her mobile phone.
5 However, like millions of other young people around the world, Amena is a refugee. Now, she is living | has been living (1) in England. Before that she lived | has lived (2) in a camp in France after escaping from Aleppo, where she had been doing |
10 has been doing (3) very well as a promising pupil in a good school.
She and her family had been living | have been living (4) in a tent for three years before they finally sought | were seeking (5) asylum in the UK. They
15 had crossed | were crossing (6) the Syrian border into Turkey illegally. For some of the journey, she and her siblings hid | have been hiding (7) under a car seat. It was both dangerous and frightening. They didn't manage | weren't managing (8) to take
20 anything with them when the bombs have been falling | fell (9) and have been destroying | destroyed (10) their home.

In the camp in France, everything changed | was changing (11) for Amena. She didn't go | hasn't gone (12) to school anymore; the camp children didn't have | weren't having (13) any books. How did she feel | was she feeling (14)?

'Life in the camp was hard – boring and depressing. I'm much happier now. By the end of this year, I will live | will have been living (15) in Leicester for six months. I will have learned | will have been learning (16) enough English to take the school leaving exams. I have decided | have been deciding (17) to study nursing in college. When I am | will be (18) qualified, hopefully the war in my country will be over. I am | am being (19) happy in England, but I need | am needing (20) to go back to Syria and help rebuild lives there.'

Quick Check

A Which word is the odd one out in each line and why?

1 offering – running – getting – sitting
2 played – carried – stayed – enjoyed
3 gone – forgotten – written – showed
4 was – were – been – done
5 smoking – jumping – opening – shouting
6 jumped – talked – stopped – listened
7 stay – stayed – stood – staying
8 fall – fell – felt – fallen

B Find and correct the mistakes. There's one in each sentence.

1 Paul prefered the old version, but I liked the new one better.
2 Graham leaved an hour ago, I'm afraid you've missed him.
3 Are you sure you should be openning that parcel?
4 Do you know what happend to Sami last night?
5 Tieing your shoelaces is hard with only one hand.
6 You lyed to me. Please tell me the truth in the future.
7 Are you comming? We can't wait all day.
8 I red a really good book while I was on holiday.

C Choose the correct verb form.

1 That's a smart bike. Who does it belong | is it belonging to?
2 Incredible! I'm sorry but I don't believe | am not believing you!
3 She wants | is wanting a new job.
4 Tom saw a ghost on the stairs? I think he imagines | is imagining things!
5 You can't do it? What on earth are you meaning | do you mean?
6 Please don't rush him. He thinks | is thinking of the answer.
7 We enjoy | are enjoying our summer holidays at home this year – no airport stress!
8 I don't suppose | am not supposing you could babysit for us tonight?

D Translate the sentences into English. Be careful with the tenses!

1 Ich lebe in Berlin.
   Ich lebe seit zehn Jahren hier.
   Vorher habe ich in Frankfurt gelebt.

2 Morgen spielen Tim und ich Tennis.
   Mittwochs spielen wir immer Tennis.
   Wir spielen seit 2016 zusammen.

3 Wir essen gerade zu Abend.
   Gewöhnlich essen wir um acht Uhr.
   Meine Mutter isst kein Fleisch – sie ist Vegetarierin.

4 The verbs *be*, *have* and *do*

Task	Topic	Example	Englische Grammatik
1	*Be, have, do* as full or auxiliary verbs (1)	*Are you OK or do you feel ill? – I'm having a rest and doing nothing.*	4.1
2	The auxiliary verb *be*	*She is looking for a new job.*	4.2.2
3	The full verb *be* with *there is / there are*	*There are several different options.*	4.2.3
4	The full verb *have (got)*	*He has (got) a nasty cold.*	4.3.3
5	The full verb *have* as activity verb	*He's having a party next Saturday.*	4.3.4
6	The auxiliary verb *have*	*They haven't answered my email yet.*	4.3.2
7	The full verb *do*	*He was doing his homework when I rang.*	4.4.3
8	The auxiliary verb *do*	*Didn't you get the message she left?*	4.4.2
9	*Be, have, do* as full or auxiliary verbs (2)	*Being a stunt driver will be tricky if he doesn't have a driver's licence.*	4.1
10	*Be, have, do* as full or auxiliary verbs (3)	*I'm curious to know how long you have been doing this job.*	4.1

▸ Quick Check p. 40

1 Are you tired? *Be, have, do* as full or auxiliary verbs ▸ 4.1

a Read the sentences and decide if the underlined word is a full verb ⬚F or if it is an auxiliary verb ⬚A.

➔ Tim is ⬚F always tired, but is ⬚A he doing ⬚F anything about it?

1 Bernie often has ⬚ a sore throat, but he says that he has ⬚ stopped smoking.
2 I am ⬚ so sorry that you aren't ⬚ feeling any better yet.
3 You're ⬚ looking worried. Do ⬚ you need any help with your homework?
4 Marie said she hadn't ⬚ slept well because she had ⬚ had ⬚ a bad dream.
5 Did ⬚ Pete hurt his leg while he was ⬚ doing ⬚ his last ski jump?
6 Yolanda said she wasn't ⬚ coming out with us because she had ⬚ been ⬚ ill.

b Complete the text about teenage sleeping patterns with the correct form of the verbs *be*, *have* or *do*.

A study has shown that if you ➔ **don't have** (not have) enough sleep, the chances of ... (have) (1) an accident, an injury or an illness are much higher. Everyone knows that sleep ... (do) (2) you a lot of good. Enough sleep ... (be) (3) very important for good health and can help you deal with the stress of ... (be) (4) a teenager. As an adolescent, your sleep patterns change to later times, which means you ... (have) (5) late nights and then oversleep. Most teenagers ... (not have) (6) enough sleep or they ... (have) (7) irregular sleep patterns. To sleep better, ... (not do) (8) anything exciting before bedtime, such as late-night texting or chatting online. It is better ... (do) (9) some gentle yoga exercises or ... (have) (10) a nice warm bath before you turn out the lights.

c NOW YOU What do you do before you go to bed and how much sleep do you normally have?

31

2 Is Venice sinking? The auxiliary verb *be* ▶ 4.2.2

Complete this text about Venice using the verbs in brackets in the correct tense. Sometimes you need the passive.

Venice ➔ *is made up* (make up) of 118 islands which
... (connect) (1) by bridges. The palaces, churches and
other buildings stand on wooden masts or poles. In
the past, these supported only fishermen's houses,
5 but today this method of building ... (use) (2) to
support the whole city.
One of the reasons that tourists find the city so
charming is that there are no cars or roads. This
might explain why Venice ... (know) (3) best for its
10 canals and gondolas. It ... (estimate) (4) that there
are about 350 of these long boats transporting people
around the city. According to a local tradition, if a
couple ... (kiss) (5) when their boat is going under
the Bridge of Sighs at sunset, they will stay in love
15 forever!

Venice is such a beautiful and romantic city. So why
has its population dropped from 120,000 to 60,000
in the last 50 years?
Many scientists worry
that the city is in dan-
ger. They have warned
that the Mediterranean
... (rise) (6) and that by
the year 2100, it could be
over 1.5 metres higher.
Many people believe this
... (happen) (7) because
of climate change. Not

only that, but Venice has been sinking on its wood-
en poles a little more every year. These two dangers 30
together mean that this historic city ... (cover) (8) in
water by the beginning of the next century.

3 There's a lot to see The full verb *be* with *there is / there are* ▶ 4.2.3

a Youth hostels are popular with hikers and climbers. Read this text about
a youth hostel in Wales and complete the sentences with *there* + a form of
the verb *be*.

Do you enjoy hiking, climbing or cycling? Why not
get away from the city and visit our youth hostel? ➔
There is no Wi-fi and no mobile phone signal either,
so you get a complete break from the internet and
5 social media.
The word 'youth' suggests that youth hostels are for
young people only, but we have family rooms too.
The beds are all comfortable, and ... (1) a kitchen for
visitors who like to cook for themselves. If you
10 prefer, ... (2) tasty meals on offer in our restaurant.
Now ... (3) building plans to extend the dining areas,
so by next summer ... (4) seating for many more of
our guests.
... (5) a famous castle, which you shouldn't miss,
15 only eighteen kilometres away. ... (6) other attractions
even closer, like a mountain railway, just a ten-
minute drive from the hostel.

What did the guests say?

'When we were there, ... (7) some visitors who
freaked out without Wi-fi, but I loved it!'
Marion, Germany
'I was told that ... (8) a massive car park but
when we arrived, ... (9) no spaces left – so get
there early!' *Jamie, UK*
'It was raining all weekend so ... (10) not a lot
to see. Plus ... (11) so many groups of visitors
from overseas that the restaurant was packed at
mealtimes.' *Francine, France*
'... (12) really such a thing as comfortable beds
in youth hostels? I don't think so! My bunk bed
was uncomfortable and too narrow. Never
again.' *Nico, the Netherlands*

b NOW YOU Write four sentences about a place where you stayed during your last holiday: a hostel,
a guest house, a friend's house. Use *There was / wasn't* and *There were / weren't*.

4 He doesn't have any brothers or sisters The full verb *have (got)* ▸ 4.3.3

a Not all families are the same. Complete the text about a teenager in China with the correct form of *have* from the box.

> didn't have • doesn't have • don't have • had (2x) • has (2x) • have • ~~have~~ • having • won't have

My name's Cheng Wang, and I live in Beijing with my parents, who ➔ **have** a successful printing business. In the 1970s, our country ... (1) a single-child policy which meant that people ... (2) more than
5 one child. So I ... (3) any aunts, uncles or cousins.

Although China's policy has now changed, my parents don't want any more kids so I ... (4) any brothers or sisters in the future. Many people think that the advantages of ... (5) only one child are great-er than the disadvantages. I sometimes worry about the 'Little Emperor Syndrome'. This is when a 10
child who ... (6) any brothers or sisters gets too much attention from parents and grandparents. It's true that I go to a great school – it ... (7) the best exam results in the city. I also ... (8) private English lessons, private piano lessons, and so on. Of course, 15
life for an only child ... (9) its negative sides too. There is a lot of pressure on kids like me to do well at school and in all the other activities I am lucky enough to do. My days are very busy. And some-times I think I would be happier if I ... (10) a brother 20
or sister to share things with.

b Make questions about Cheng and answer them using the full verb *have*.

➔ his parents | a shipping business
Do his parents **have** a shipping business? – No, they **don't**. They **have** a printing business.

1 China | single-home policy | 1970s
2 Cheng's grandparents | more than one child
3 Cheng | any brothers or sisters | in the future

4 Cheng | private guitar lessons
5 his life | only | good sides
6 kids like Cheng | a lot of free time

c NOW YOU Write five sentences about your own family. Use phrases from the box to start your sentences.

> I have • I don't have • My family doesn't have • We had • I didn't have •
> I won't have • My mum/dad has • If I had

5 Having a good time? The full verb *have* as activity verb ▶ 4.3.4

a There are many expressions with *have* to talk about actions. Use the pictures and the prompts to make questions and answers about John and Clare's camping holiday.

➜ ***Does** Clare usually* **have** *a bath at the campsite? – No, she doesn't. She usually* **has** *a shower.*

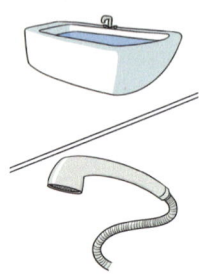

➜ Clare | usually | a bath | at the campsite? | a shower

1 they | normally | a cooked lunch? | just a sandwich

2 John | a good bike ride | yesterday? | a long walk

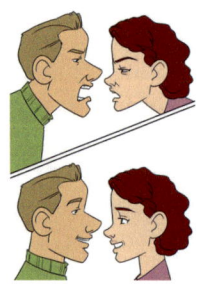

3 Clare | a glass of cola | later? | a glass of juice

4 they | an argument | at the moment? | a friendly conversation

5 they | usually | a coffee | in the evening? | a cup of tea

b Lottie and George aren't having a very good holiday. Complete George's message home, using his notes and a form of the verb *have*.

From:	George
Re:	Hi everyone!

Hi everyone
I'm sitting in a bar on a beautiful Greek island but I feel like ➜ **I'm having a bad dream**! As you know, Lottie and I … (1) here on Kos. We both wanted … (2) from studying and exams. Unfortunately, so far we … (3) – and I mean really, really bad. On the second night, I … (4) after eating some awful seafood. When I was better, we went to a sports centre to … (5). That was fine until after our game when I … (6) with the guy who wanted 50 euros for the rackets! Then, last night Lottie … (7) while we … (8) on some rented mountain bikes. She fell off and broke her arm. As I am writing this, she … (9) on her arm in hospital. I'm not looking forward to the flight home. Who knows – perhaps I … (10) first!
I'll keep you posted. ☺ George

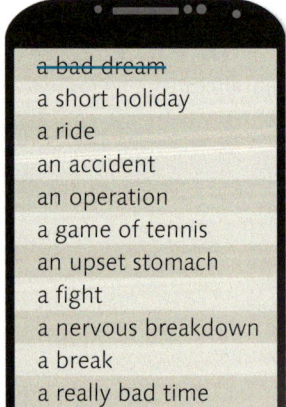

~~a bad dream~~
a short holiday
a ride
an accident
an operation
a game of tennis
an upset stomach
a fight
a nervous breakdown
a break
a really bad time

c NOW YOU Write an email about a holiday you had recently – did you have a good time?

6 I haven't seen you for ages   The auxiliary verb *have*   ▶ 4.3.2

Martha and Lulu have met up for a coffee. Choose the correct tense to complete their conversation.

Martha Hey, Lulu! Good to see you!

Lulu You too, Martha! We ➔ ***haven't seen*** | haven't been seeing | haven't seen each other for ages. You're looking good.

Martha So are you. Have you had | Are you having | Will you have had (1) your hair cut? It looks different.

Lulu Thanks! And yeah, there has been | have been | having been (2) some big changes in my life.

Martha Well it have been | hasn't been | has been (3) ages since we had a chat.

Lulu I know. So, where do we begin? Had you ordered | Have you ordered | Hadn't you ordered (4) the coffees yet?

Martha Yes, I had | haven't | have (5) actually – two cappuccinos, is that OK?

Lulu Yes, that's great, thanks. I won't have stopped | hadn't stopped | haven't stopped (6) drinking coffee yet!

Martha So what has happened | hadn't happened | hasn't happened (7) since we last met? What's new?

Lulu I'd be surprised if you have been hearing | having heard | hadn't heard (8) about me and Jake.

Martha Yeah, I saw from your status that you hadn't split up | had been splitting up | had split up (9). Sorry about that.

Lulu It's OK now. By tomorrow, I have been | had been | will have been (10) single for seven weeks but hey, who's counting?

Martha Hmm, so tell me all about the break-up.

7 Do it yourself   The full verb *do*   ▶ 4.4.3

a When to use *do* and when to use *make*? Decide for each item.

➔ ***do*** *a job*   ➔ ***make*** *breakfast*

> ~~breakfast~~ • a cake • a cup of tea • ~~a job~~ • a mess • a mistake • a test • lunch • the beds • the dishes • the housework • the ironing • the shopping • very well • your hair • your homework

b How much does the average teenager do to help around the house? Here are some teenagers' comments. Complete the sentences with the correct form of *do* or *make* and an expression from **a**.

Most of my friends would rather ➔ ***do their homework*** than help around the house.

1 Not many young people …, but most of their clothes don't need it anyway.
2 My brother always … when he's cooking and he never cleans up. There are dirty plates and pans everywhere!
3 When mum …, Clara sometimes goes to the supermarket with her.
4 My friend's a great baker – she … for me on my birthday last year.
5 Has anybody … yet? It's nearly two o'clock and I'm hungry!
6 Oh no, the dishwasher is broken! That means we have to … ourselves.
7 Pete would … if you asked him: the English way, with milk in it.
8 I hate … but the cleaning, the ironing, the dishes, it all has to be done!

c **NOW YOU** What jobs do you do around the house? What jobs don't you do? Write four sentences, two with the verb *do* and two with *make*.

8 Don't believe everything you read   The auxiliary verb *do*   ▶ 4.4.2

a Friends on social media – they are not always who you think they are. Read this advice and complete it, using the correct form of the verb *do* and the words in brackets.

Chatting online is fun, but ➔ ***do you know*** (know) who you're actually talking to?

Many people meet new partners on online dating sites.

Most people who use dating sites are honest and give true information about themselves and their motives for joining. However, there are others who … (not always tell) (1) the truth. So you need to know how to keep your identity safe, when you meet people online.

What are the basic dos and don'ts of online dating?
- … (not share) (2) private information when you first meet someone on online dating sites. This way you avoid identity theft.
- … (think) (3) carefully about when and how you meet someone in person.
- … (not rush) (4). Take your time to get to know someone. Learn as much as you can about a person before contacting him or her outside of the dating site. … the site … (offer) (5) you added security? If so, use it – it's there to protect you.
- Also take care when you talk about yourself. You … (not need) (6) to tell your whole life story the first time you chat – and you shouldn't. There's enough time to share detailed information as your relationship grows.
- Check to see if the person you're chatting to is on other social networking sites. It's a good idea to use an image search to check the profile photos – … his or her picture … (match) (7) what they've told you about themselves?
- … (not send) (8) your new online friend any money. Always keep your bank account information private. If a person you have just met online tells you a sad story and asks for money, end all contact immediately and report the person to the dating site.
- And finally, … (not forget) (9) that you can stop talking to a person who makes you feel uncomfortable or worried. Again, report anything that … (not seem) (10) right to the dating site.

b Complete Pat's story, using the words from the box.

> ~~don't stop~~ • didn't look • don't feel • doesn't matter • don't do • didn't think • didn't do

Pat's story

A first date with someone new is exciting, but my advice is, ➔ ***don't stop*** playing safe. I had read all the tips about checking someone's profile photo be-fore I joined a dating site, but I … (1) they were im-
5 portant and so I … (2) that first. It was quite a shock when I met up with my online 'friend'. He … (3) like his photo. He was really old – nearly as old as my dad. Yuk! So … (4) what I did. Check someone out really carefully and if you meet, meet in a public place and stay there. If you … (5) comfortable, just   10 leave. It … (6) how well you got on when chatting online or on the phone. If you're not happy when you meet face-to-face, say goodbye and leave.

c **NOW YOU** You're advising your younger brother or sister about the risks of meeting someone on social media. Write six sentences starting with *Don't* …

+ 9 Being a lifeguard   *Be, have, do* as full or auxiliary verbs   ▶ 4.1

Jake Ellis works at a swimming pool in Buxton, a spa town in the north of England. We interviewed him for our website's career page.

a Read the interview and complete the questions the interviewer asks.

Interviewer	We have with us this morning Jake Ellis, who works at a swimming pool in Buxton. Welcome Jake.
	➜ could | tell us | what | do?
	Could you tell us what you do?
Jake	I teach swimming, I'm a lifeguard and a Duty Officer.
Interviewer	what | mean | be | a Duty Officer? (1)
Jake	It means that you're in charge of the building, opening up, locking up, making sure everything's running smoothly through the day, that all the staff are doing what they're supposed to be doing, that sort of thing.
Interviewer	how long | you | do | this job? (2)
Jake	For about five years, off and on. I've been travelling and have done all sorts of things in between.
Interviewer	I see. how | you | train for it? (3)
Jake	I trained at college. You have to do a life-saving award, which is the National Pool Lifeguard Award. For the lifeguard training, it's about twenty hours, so you do it over so many weeks. Then you have to do it again every two years. Plus, I've been doing staff training at regular intervals.
Interviewer	On pool duty, you're basically just sitting on the side and watching, aren't you?
Jake	Doesn't sound very interesting, does it?
Interviewer	I'm sure it gets boring sometimes. your mind | wander? (4)
Jake	Yeah, when it's quiet. There's lots of time for thinking, but when it's busy, you focus on what's going on in the water.
Interviewer	you | often | have to | stop kids messing about? (5)
Jake	Oh yes. But I don't have a problem with being strict. I'm quite good at getting people to do what I want them to do.
Interviewer	how | you | do that? (6)
Jake	I put on my dominant face. You just have to tell them and they don't tend to argue if you've told them straight. I don't think I look like a pushover, even though I'm not much older than some of them.
Interviewer	you | get used to | doing shifts | yet? (7)
Jake	Yes, I have really. I do the same shifts every week, which is OK. You know what you're doing from week to week, so you can plan what to do. I work Saturdays, but I don't very often do Sundays. Most people think being a lifeguard is easy, but you're actually in charge of people's lives, which you don't think about all the time.
Interviewer	what | you | like least | about your work? (8)
Jake	I suppose the lifeguarding part of it, because it can be boring.
Interviewer	what qualities | a lifeguard | need | be good at the job? (9)
Jake	Patience. To be good at this job, you need to be patient. And to be able to be diplomatic with people. If you're talking to a parent with a child and asking them not to do a certain thing, the parents always know best. You have to be polite, but firm.
Interviewer	what | you | do | in your leisure time? (10)
Jake	I don't seem to have a lot of leisure time. Football sometimes, going out with my mates.
Interviewer	and what you | think | you | do | in ten years' time? (11)

4

Jake	Hopefully, I'll have completed all my staff training by the end of this year, so I hope to be teaching more than I am now. I'm not so keen on the lifeguarding. More and more older people are coming to us, wanting to learn to swim, and that's quite a challenge.
Interviewer	people | become | more health conscious | in recent years? (12)
Jake	Oh yes. People are definitely more aware of what they should be doing to keep fit.
Interviewer	why | be | swimming | such a good way | keep fit? (13)
Jake	Because it's easy to do. You're watched all the time, so it's not dangerous. And it's good for your whole body, you have a very good aerobic workout, it's good for your breathing, good for your lungs.
Interviewer	I | hate | the chlorine | in swimming pools, | you? (14)
Jake	Yes, I do, but there's nothing we can do about that. If it wasn't chlorinated, it'd be dirty. Actually, Buxton pool doesn't have as much chlorine as some pools. Because of the minerals in our spa water, it doesn't have to be chlorinated as much. It's nice water.
Interviewer	Talking to you has *almost* made me feel like having a swim! Jake, thank you very much indeed for talking to us today.

b Read the interview again and find five examples of *do, be* and *have* as full verbs, and five examples of each as auxiliary verbs.

✛ 10 So you want to be a spy? *Be, have, do* as full or auxiliary verbs ▸ 4.1

a Secret service agent Tasha Swift (not her real name) writes about being a spy. Read her article and choose the correct form of the verbs.

Part of a recent strategy by UK intelligence agencies – MI5, MI6 and GCHQ – ➜ *has been* \| have been to try to make intelligence work more appealing to women. A female colleague of mine said she had
5 spent lots of time people-watching from a café table, so she should be good at surveillance. My former boss joked that she thought middle-aged women made great spies, because they were used to be \| being (1) invisible!
10 It isn't really a laughing matter, though. Historically, it's been a man's world. In the early twentieth century, when the intelligence agencies were started \| have started (2), spies were recruited from the army. Later, the recruits came from the top universities,
15 especially Cambridge, where the brightest students were thought to be – and of course in those days, they were mainly men. Fortunately for women, things have changed \| are changed (3) since then. But – male or female – what qualities do you need \|
20 are you needing (4) to make it as a spy? It's a really tough recruitment process. I remember my first interview, which was three hours long, when I was asked about every aspect of my life since I have been \| was (5) a teenager. Then there was a
25 weekend course where I was in competition with other candidates. The course involved analysing data and role-playing. This was followed by more intensive interviews, some of them with a psychiatrist. I think I was successful because I managed to stay calm, even when provoked. 30

If you see yourself as a James or even a Jane Bond, you're not likely to be accepted into the intelligence agencies. Unlike 007's adventures, it won't all be fast car chases, gun fights and exotic locations. Mostly, there are \| there is (6) less glamorous as- 35 pects to the work. The key qualities you will need are firmness, toughness and the ability to keep your mouth shut. You are forbidden to tell anyone what you make \| do (7) for a living. One of the most difficult aspects of my work as a spy was that I wasn't 40 even allowed to tell my partner the true nature of my job. In other words, you have to lie to your nearest and dearest. On the other hand, if you tell a lie in any of your interviews, you won't be accepted. There must be nothing in your past that could make you a 45 target for blackmail.

So if you think the life of a spy might be for you, don't even mention that you're applying, and whatever you do, don't put \| do put (8) it on social media!

b Owen read this article quickly on a crowded train, but he misunderstood some of it. Correct his statements.

→ MI5 and MI6 are US intelligence agencies.
  No, they aren't. They are UK intelligence agencies.

1 The writer of the article said she'd be good at surveillance.
2 Her former boss was serious when she said women were invisible.
3 Spies were originally recruited from top universities.
4 Nothing has changed since the early 20th century.
5 The writer's first interview lasted two days.
6 She was selected because a psychiatrist provoked her.
7 According to the article, you have to be like Agent 007 to become a spy.
8 Intelligence agents are allowed to share secrets with their closest relatives.
9 In the recruitment process, it doesn't matter what you have done in your past.
10 If you're going to apply for a job as a spy, you should share it on social media!

4

Quick Check

A Complete the sentences with the correct form of the verb *be*.

1 Your call … important to us and … answered as soon as possible.
2 … a teacher can … a wonderful job, but at times it … very frustrating.
3 … (not) impatient with him! He … (not) feeling at all well today.
4 You … (not) in class yesterday, … you?
5 I … (not) going swimming tomorrow, because I have a cold.
6 If she … (not) so lazy, she … top of her class.
7 Why … (not) you coming? – I …, but later.
8 I … (not) looking forward to … away from home for so long.

B Complete the sentences with words from the box.

> don't have • had • had had • hasn't had • have •
> have you had • used to have • were having

1 I … a big family, but I … many relatives in my town.
2 We … a picnic when she … an accident.
3 The twins … a secret language when they were small, but they've forgotten it now.
4 They felt much better after they … something to eat.
5 … that scooter for long?
6 Sheila … an answer to her question yet.

C *Do* or *make*?

1 Have you done | made your homework already?
2 What a great cake! Who did | made it?
3 The neighbours were doing | making too much noise.
4 Could you do | make your own bed, please?
5 Tony's been doing | making fine in his new class.
6 I can't do | make maths, but I'm OK at foreign languages.

D Find and correct the mistakes. There's one in each sentence.

1 It gives three different desserts on the menu.
2 My friends didn't be very nice to me yesterday.
3 Did the girls their own hair?
4 Your brother have a lot of friends!
5 Be not so silly, spiders can't hurt you.
6 He did a few elementary mistakes in his test.
7 What does Paul do? – He's looking for his keys.
8 Do you much sport?

5 Modal verbs

Task	Topic	Example	Englische Grammatik
1	Ability: *can, could*	*Jo can speak Spanish really well.*	5.3.1
2	Ability: *be able to*	*Don't worry – you'll be able to repair your bike if you try.*	5.3.1
3	Permission and prohibition: *can, could, may, must not, be allowed to* (1)	*You mustn't leave your car here.*	5.3.2
4	Permission and prohibition: *can, could, may, must not, be allowed to* (2)	*My friends and I were allowed to have a party.*	5.3.2
5	Necessity, compulsion: *must, have (got) to, needn't* (1)	*We mustn't forget Gran's birthday. – You needn't worry. I've set an alarm on my phone.*	5.3.3
6	Necessity, compulsion: *must, have (got) to, needn't* (2)	*You must go to London – it's a great city.*	5.3.3a
7	Necessity, compulsion: *must, have (got) to, needn't* (3)	*We'll have to paint the living room ourselves.*	5.3.3
8	Obligation and advice: *should, ought to, be supposed to*	*You oughtn't to worry too much. It's going to be fine.*	5.3.4
9	Request, demand, suggestion: *can, could, will, would*	*Could you help me with my homework, please?*	5.3.5
10	Probability, possibility	*Paul might come later, if he has time.*	5.3.9
11	Mixed exercise (1)	*The children were allowed to stay in their parents' hotel room for free.*	5.3
12	German 'sollen': Offers, invitations, suggestions	*Shall we start or had we better wait?*	5.3.7
13	Grades of obligation	*Rena really ought to contact her supervisor. Fred called. You're to be at the meeting place in twenty minutes.*	5.3.3 5.3.4
14	Modals in the perfect infinitive	*Ben is a nice guy, but he really shouldn't have got me those flowers.*	5.3
15	Offers, invitations, suggestions	*Shall we go now? It's late.*	5.3.6 5.3.7
16	Mixed exercise (2)	*Would you say that again? What do we have to do?*	5.3

▶ Quick Check p. 51

▶ Erklärvideo zu Modalverben ▶ **Exercise 1**

▶ 1 Can you or can't you?   Ability: *can, could*   ▶ 5.3.1

Erklärvideo online:
📄▶ cornelsen.de/webcodes
＋🔊 Code: cocoso

a Look at the pictures. What can or can't you do? Fill in the missing forms.

You ➔ **can** swim here, but you ➔ **can't** have a shower.

1 You … meet your friends here, but you … do what you want.

2 You … play a CD on this, but you … download music.

3 You … travel very fast, but you … eat, sleep and party.

4 You … stay here for some time, but you … leave when you want to.

5 You … have a meal here, but you … have an ice cream.

6 You … watch a football match here, but you … watch a film.

7 You … get to faraway places quickly, but you … move around much inside.

8 You … listen to music with this, but you … put it in your pocket.

b NOW YOU What could or couldn't you do when you started primary school? Write three sentences with some of the ideas from the box or your own ideas.

➔ *I* **could** *write my name, but I* **couldn't** *read a whole book.*

> read a whole book • ride a bike • ski • read a few words • count money • go to school on my own • use a mobile phone • skate • swim • tie my shoe laces • write my name

2 Making your dreams come true Ability: *be able to* ▶ 5.3.1

Erklärvideo online:
▶ Exercise 1

a Read Anton's report on his family and fill in the right form of *be able to* from the box.

> are able to (2x) • aren't able to • had never been able to • 'll be able to (2x) • be able to •
> was able to • wasn't able to • weren't able to • won't be able to

Do you sometimes want to do something, but give up because you think it's impossible?

My gran is afraid of flying, so my grandparents → *had never been able to* take a holiday abroad. But
5 then the Channel Tunnel was built, and now they ... (1) travel to France without any problems. My dad ... (2) buy his first car until he was 30, but then he won the lottery and ... (3) get his dream car. Everyone in my family seems to have a dream. Now my brother's
10 saving up and soon he ... (4) fulfil his biggest wish – to cross the USA on Route 66. My own dream is hitching a ride on a cargo ship; that way, I ... (5) travel to South America for free.

It's similar with education: my mother and her sis-
ters ... (6) have a career, because my grandfather 15 thought higher education wasn't necessary for girls. Still, that didn't stop my mum from getting a degree from the Open University later! Today, we think everyone should ... (7) study, and my sister and I both are students at top colleges. We ... (8) pay for it 20 thanks to the money we get from the government. If something seems impossible to you, you should ask yourself if you really ... (9) do it, or if you don't really want to. Me, I believe in getting things done; don't leave things too late or you ... (10) do them! 25

b This is an excerpt from Kayla's report. Look at the underlined forms of *be able to* and rewrite the sentences with *could/couldn't* if possible.

My sister's biggest dream was being able to (1) swim. She used to be scared of water and wasn't able to (2) swim until she was a teenager. Once, she fell in a lake. Luckily, a young man jumped in and was able to (3) rescue her. We weren't able to (4) take 5 her anywhere near water for years after that. But finally, last year, she was able to (5) pass her swimming test.

3 You mustn't leave your bike here Permission, prohibition ▶ 5.3.2

Erklärvideo online:
▶ Exercise 1

Look at these signs from an English secondary school and explain what you mustn't do and what you are allowed to do when you see these signs. The expressions in the box will help you.

> drink the water from this tap • eat here •
> go into this room • fill up your water bottles •
> play ball games • ride your bikes • take a book
> to read • use your mobiles

→ You **mustn't** drink the water from this tap.
→ You**'re allowed to** play ball games here.

▶ **4 Rules, rules, rules** Permission, prohibition ▶ 5.3.2

Erklärvideo online:
▶ **Exercise 1**

a Class 9YE spent a few days at a youth hostel in the Lake District. There was a sign with rules at the reception. Later, they talk about the trip.

→ *We **were allowed to** use the playing fields whenever we liked, but we **weren't allowed to** play noisy games after 8 pm.*

→ DO use the playing fields whenever you like
          DON'T play noisy games after 8 pm – it annoys our neighbours
1 DO help yourself to drinks from the fridge
   2 DON'T leave glass bottles lying around
3 DON'T make fires anywhere in the grounds
   4 but DO use our barbecue area
5 DO take any sports equipment you need from the cupboard
   6 DON'T climb on the table-tennis tables   Thank you.

---

b In a few years, you might be a youth group leader at a holiday camp. What will the kids in your group be allowed to do and not allowed to do? You can use the ideas in the box.

→ *The kids **will be allowed to** play rough games. They **won't be allowed to** go swimming in deep water.*

> play rough games • go swimming in deep water • wander off on their own • have a barbecue •
> use their mobiles when they're hiking • sleep outside their tents • collect mushrooms for lunch •
> stay up as late as they like • play computer games • watch videos

▶ **5 A new school** Necessity, compulsion ▶ 5.3.3

Erklärvideo online:
▶ **Exercise 1**

Sara is starting out at a new school and a helpful student gives her a few tips. Complete the text with *must, mustn't* or *needn't*.

You → *needn't* eat in the school canteen, but then you → *mustn't* forget to bring a packed lunch. You … (1) join a club, but it's a good way of meeting new people. We usually do one foreign language here; if you do Spanish, you … (2) do French. We get a lot of homework, but you can check up on your assignments online, so you … (3) write everything down. You can share my books in the classes we have together – you … (4) bring all of them to school each lesson. Oh, and Ms Masters is really strict. You … (5) pay attention in her lessons, and you … (6) talk to me, or we'll both be in trouble. And remember this: you … (7) ever be rude to the school secretaries – if they don't like you, they can make your life really difficult. And of course you … (8) forget the date of the Senior School Dance – everybody goes and it's great fun!

6 London for beginners Necessity, compulsion ▶5.3.3a

Erklärvideo online:
▶ Exercise 1

a Dave is giving Luan some tips on what to do on his first trip to London. Complete his sentences with *must* or *have to / don't have to*.

Well, you really ➔ **must** go down to the River Thames. It's easy to find, you just ... (1) walk downhill from the hotel. Oh, and when you cross the road, you ... (2) be very careful to look to the right for
5 traffic. Now, you ... (3) take your camera with you so you can take pictures of the spectacular city skyline from the bridge across the river.
You should also take a walk along the South Bank – just turn left at the end of the bridge. You can see
10 so much from here and you ... (4) spend any money. There's another amazing place that you ... (5) visit: the Tate Modern. It's an art gallery with lots of fun exhibitions inside. Look across the Thames from

there and you'll see St. Paul's Cathedral – you ... (6) take a selfie with the cathedral in the background. 15 Go along the path a bit further and you'll see The Globe, Shakespeare's theatre, but I wouldn't go in, because you ... (7) pay to get in. Another sight coming up as you go on is Tower Bridge, but if you want a photo of the 20 bridge opening, you ... (8) wait for a ship to come along.

b **NOW YOU** A good friend from England is visiting your town. Write down tips would you give him or her. Use *must, have to* and *don't have to*.

➔ *You* **must** *visit the shopping mall. You* **don't have to** *spend any money – you can just go window shopping. You* **have to** *watch out for pickpockets though.*

7 Do it yourself Necessity, compulsion ▶5.3.3

Erklärvideo online:
▶ Exercise 1

The year 10 students at Parkland School asked the head teacher if they could have their own room for the breaks. Use the correct form of *have to* to complete their discussion. Sometimes you need the negative, and sometimes more than one answer is possible.

Mia	OK, guys. Listen to this. I've just had an email from the headteacher. She says 'If we give you a room, you ➔ **'ll have to** decorate it yourselves.' Will that be a problem?
Leon	No, not at all. We can manage. I don't think we ... (1) paint the walls because the caretaker painted all the rooms in the summer holidays.
Marek	But we ... (2) ask him to put up some curtains, otherwise the younger kids will be able to look in.
Paula	Good point. But we ... (3) decide on what colour we want before we can buy the curtains.
Mia	Yeah, sure. What about some sofas?
Leon	We ... (4) buy any because my uncle has two sofas that he wants to throw out.
Mia	But how can we get them here? My sister ... (5) pay for a trailer last month when she moved. It was really expensive.
Marek	Don't worry. My dad's got a van. I only ... (6) ask him – it won't be a problem as long as he ... (7) transport the sofas during working hours.
Paula	OK – you two will sort out the sofas, right? Now, what about lighting? It would be much better if we ... (8) buy lights because they aren't cheap.
Leon	We can wait until the winter. We ... (9) buy them now.
Mia	I agree. But in the next holidays we ... (10) find ways to make some extra money.

⊙ 8 Don't worry   Obligation, advice   ▶5.3.4

Erklärvideo online:
▶ Exercise 1

a Sara's new school is OK, but she still has some problems and needs some advice. Make three sentences with *should / shouldn't* and three with *ought to / oughtn't to*.

→ She remembers an unkind word a boy said to her on her first day. (she | not worry too much about what people say)
*She **shouldn't** worry / **oughtn't to** worry too much about what people say.*

1 She's behind the rest of the class in French. (her parents | arrange extra lessons)
2 In breaks, she finds herself all alone in a corner. (she | join a group of students when they go outside in the break)
3 She would love to be asked to join the class's online group. (she | not wait to be asked)
4 She feels the maths teacher is being unfair to her. (she | talk to the teacher and tell her about it)
5 Last week, she missed a day at school and hasn't got the notes from the lessons. (she | ask a classmate to lend her the notes)
6 Teachers complain that she won't join in. (she | not be afraid of making mistakes)

b Come up with your own suggestions to solve two more of Sara's problems.

– Sara would love to join the badminton club after school, but she doesn't know if she's good enough.
– It's her birthday next week and she'd like to bring some treats for the class, but she's unsure what to bring.
– Joining the ski trip would be an ideal way to find friends, but who's going to pay?

c As a senior student, you're a class buddy. Explain the school rules to Sara using *(not) supposed to*.

→ *You**'re supposed to** be quiet in the corridors during lessons.*

Be quiet in the corridors during lessons.
Please stand in the queue for lunch. (1)
No talking during registration. (2)
Try to join at least one after-school club or activity. (3)
Do homework at home, not at school. (4)
No eating or drinking during lessons. (5)
Don't come to school in flip-flops. (6)

⊙ 9 Could you help me?   Request, demand, suggestion   ▶5.3.5

Erklärvideo online:
▶ Exercise 1

Philipp is staying in a host family in Britain and there are some things he needs to ask his host parents. Write polite questions for him, using the words in brackets.

→ He'd like to borrow a hairdryer. (could)
***Could** I borrow a hairdryer, please?*

1 He wants to know if they would wake him at 7.30. (will)
2 He'd like to use the microwave. (can)
3 He wants to know if they could collect him from the station at 10 pm. (could, possibly)
4 He'd like to open the window. (can)
5 He wants to know if he could stay out a bit later. (couldn't)
6 He wants them to prepare a packed lunch for him tomorrow. (could)

10 Where is everyone? Probability, possibility ▸5.3.9

Erklärvideo online:
▸ Exercise 1

The Literature Club has an important meeting today, but several students are missing. The others are talking about where they might be. Choose the correct modal verbs to complete the dialogue.

Ethan   Where's Patrick? He ➔ can | *might* be at home because art was cancelled.

Emily   Anna does art too, but she said she would | might (1) definitely come.

Mehmet   I saw Deniz and Mirko at lunchtime. They have a game later, so they can | must (2) still be at school.

Ethan   But with Deniz, you never know. He may | would (3) be on his way here, but he might | must (4) be asleep at home!

Emily   True. And Paul's not here either. But you must | might (5) find him at his girlfriend's house.

Robin   I'll text him. And Tabita must | can (6) be in the library if she isn't here – she's always there.

Ethan   Right, and I know that Kilic is babysitting this afternoon, so you will | would (7) find her at her neighbour's. Perhaps next time we could | may (8) send everyone a message to remind them of the date and time.

11 A weekend in Berlin Mixed exercise ▸5.3

Erklärvideo online:
▸ Exercise 1

Aunt Rixa has agreed to let Anton and his friends use her Berlin flat over a long weekend. She's very kind and there are only a few rules. Fill the gaps in each blog entry with the modals given in the boxes.

February 12th – Wednesday

My aunt rang earlier today. She says I ➔ *can* stay at her flat from Friday to Monday morning. And the good news is I ... (1) take three friends with me. As soon as we arrive, we ... (2) collect the key at her neighbour's flat. Aunt Rixa promised that everything will be ready for us: we ... (3) to make the beds or anything. We just ... (4) switch on the heating, and then we ... (5) do what we want.

> don't have to •
> have to • can •
> have to • may • can

February 16th – Sunday

The flat is great and Aunt Rixa is the best! We'd bought some food, but when we arrived, we ... (6) even fit everything into the fridge, because it was full of delicious food! We ... (7) keep our drinks out on the balcony! We've had such a great time here, and now it's almost over. Aunt Rixa said we ... (8) clean up, but we thought we ... (9). If we're helpful, she ... (10) invite us to stay again in summer!

> ought to • didn't
> have to • might •
> had to • couldn't

February 18th – Tuesday

Berlin was awesome! If you ever make the trip, you ... (11) visit the Reichstag Gallery! From up there, you ... (12) enjoy a 360° view over the city. And you ... (13) miss the Berlin Wall Museum either. Good news: you ... (14) pay a penny to visit either of these places.

> mustn't • needn't •
> must • can

5

+ 12 To eat or not to eat?   German 'sollen'   ▸5.3.7

Carl's class is going to see a movie. He and his friends are almost ready to go, but some of them are hungry. Translate their sentences taking care to use the right form for German 'sollen/sollten': *shall / should / ought to / had better / be supposed to / be to*. More than one answer is sometimes possible.

Carl	→ *Shall* I order some pizzas?
Lisa	We … (1) wait for the others.
Deniz	Well, they … (2) hurry up a bit!
Amela	Let's get the pizzas from that new place – Pizza Paradise. They … (3) be the best in town.
Carl	But then we'll have to walk there. They really … (4) have a delivery service!
Deniz	Remember we … (5) be at the cinema by eight!
Amela	Eight? Then we … (6) leave in five minutes. Those who are hungry … (7) just grab an apple or a banana.
Lisa	OK – the others … (8) be along any moment now.

+ 13 Work experience   Grades of obligation   ▸5.3.3, 5.3.4

a Annabelle is going on a work placement. The school placements coordinator gives her group some instructions before they start. For each sentence, say which of the underlined words is the stricter instruction.

→ Everybody listen up, please. As you know, your placement starts in ten days. You <u>should</u> already have contacted your firm and introduced yourself. If you haven't, you <u>must</u> do it today.
must *is stricter*

1 Right. On day one you <u>are to</u> arrive punctually and present yourself to your supervisor. In fact, you <u>ought to</u> leave home at least ten minutes earlier than usual in case anything happens on the way.
2 <u>You're not supposed to</u> dress too casually, especially on your first day And from then on, you <u>are never to</u> leave the grounds of the firm during working hours without informing your supervisor first.
3 You are getting a great opportunity for work experience and <u>should</u> make good use of it. But if you are ever worried about anything, you <u>must</u> phone me at school straight away, remember that.
4 For instance, if you find yourself photocopying and making coffee all day, you <u>needn't</u> do those jobs; <u>you're supposed to</u> be learning about careers and the workplace there.
5 You <u>have to</u> hand in your written report one week after your return to school, so you <u>shouldn't</u> leave it too late to start.
6 At the end of your time, you <u>ought to</u> have learned a lot about the workplace – and you <u>might</u> want to present your experience to the rest of the class.

b Now test your knowledge of modals by suggesting possible alternatives to the ones used in the sentences.

→ *Everybody listen up, please. As you know, your placement starts in ten days. You **ought to** already have contacted your firm and introduced yourself. If you haven't, you **have to** do it today.*

+ 14 It could have been worse Modals with perfect infinitive ▸ 5.3

Keiran has been to the hospital to visit his friend Louise, who had a nasty accident with her bike.
Now he is telling their friends all about it. Finish his sentences with a modal and the perfect infinitive.

Poor Louise, she looked really sad and lonely. She ➜ ***ought to have told*** (ought to | tell) me earlier that she was in hospital. Well, anyway, we talked about the accident. Apparently, the lorry driver hadn't seen

5 her coming along on her bike. He really ... (should | look) (1) more carefully. But he just turned right while she went straight ahead. Louise ... (could | be killed) (2)! Next thing that happens is, he just drives on without stopping; I'm sure he ... (must | notice)

10 (3) what had happened!
And now there's Louise lying there saying she blames herself! It's his fault, I told her – he ... (can | use) (4) his wing mirror, couldn't he? But she feels she ... (might | slow down) (5) a bit too. It

15 makes me so angry! There have already been so many accidents that ... (should | be avoided) (6). You see these 'ghost bicycles' at crossroads all around the city painted white.

... (could not | they | think) (7) of something to stop these accidents long ago? Nowadays you can fit sen- 20 sors to the side of lorries and they sound if a bike comes too close. That ... (would | save) (8) dozens of cyclists that are injured or dead now.

5

◎ + 15 Shall we go now?

Erklärvideo online:
▸ **Exercise 1**

Offers, invitations, suggestions – *can, could, shall, would* ▸ 5.3.6, 5.3.7

You've been chosen to welcome an international group of students on the first day of their visit to your school. Use the prompts to make polite suggestions, offers or invitations.

➜ would | like | to follow me | the meeting room
Would you like to follow me to the meeting room, please?

1 would | help yourselves to | tea and biscuits | from the buffet
2 shall | we all | introduce ourselves | to begin with
3 could | all | mark | home country | with a flag | on this map
4 may | I present | a short film about our school
5 would | wait here | while I fetch the head teacher | speak to you
6 will | join us | when we go to the town hall | meet the Mayor

⊳ ✚ **16 Would you say that again?** Mixed exercise ▶5.3

Erklärvideo online:
▶ Exercise 1

It's often possible to express an idea in different ways. Rewrite the second sentence with another verb so it means the same as the first.

➔ Perhaps he'll come later. – He ... later.
  *He **might come** later.*

1 Don't wait for me. – You ... for me.
2 I was told to return by midnight. – I ... by midnight.
3 She never learned to swim as a child. – She ... as a child.
4 It isn't necessary to come with me. – You ... with me.
5 It's a pity I didn't ask her before now. – I ... her before now.
6 He has been instructed to do 25 hours of social service. – He ... 25 hours of social service.
7 People say Ice Dreams is the coolest place in town. – Ice Dreams ... the coolest place in town.
8 They didn't let me use the sauna. – I ... the sauna.
9 I think he is obliged to share the prize money with me. – He ... share the prize money with me.
10 I'm advising you to get vaccinated against malaria. – You ... against malaria.
11 It's likely that he has arrived in Hong Kong now. – He ... in Hong Kong now.
12 Crossing the police line is prohibited. – You ... the police line.
13 We won't have the opportunity to see you on our visit. – We ... you on our visit.
14 I'm quite certain this is the place I hid the money. – This ... the place I hid the money.
15 Is it not possible for you to make the deadline? – ... the deadline?

5

Quick Check

A Rewrite the sentences using the new time word or phrase and changing the tense of the modal verb accordingly. Sometimes different modal forms are possible.

1 Sorry, I can't help you today. (tomorrow)
2 She must go to the dentist next week. (yesterday)
3 Students mustn't take knives to school. (when I was on exchange in the US)
4 Mum has to collect me from football practice. (last Tuesday)
5 They needn't do any homework. (last week)
6 They were allowed to go home early yesterday. (today)

B Spot the mistake in each sentence and correct it. Sometimes two solutions are possible.

1 Yesterday I could talk to my tutor.
2 You mustn't go swimming with us, but you are very welcome to join us.
3 Can you Italian?
4 You needn't to do it if you don't want to.
5 The sign says you aren't able to drink the water from the tap.
6 Aren't you supposed put bottles and cans into your suitcase?
7 Tim don't have to work this weekend.
8 Our new flat is much nicer than the old one. We should move years ago.

C Translate the missing words into English.

1 Du darfst hier nicht Fahrrad fahren.
  You … cycle here.
2 Meldung vom Chef: Ihr sollt sofort zurückkehren.
  Message from the boss: you … return immediately.
3 Wir mussten das Auto reparieren, ehe wir nach Hause fahren konnten.
  We … repair the car before we … drive home.
4 Du brauchst keine Angst haben.
  You … be afraid.
5 Soll ich dir einen Tee kochen?
  … I make you a cup of tea?
6 Wir sollten lieber loslaufen, sonst verpassen wir die anderen.
  We … make a start or we'll miss the others.
7 Du wirst sehen, Jessica wird nicht mitkommen dürfen.
  You'll see, Jessica … to come with us.
8 Das Taxi könnte etwas später ankommen.
  The taxi … arrive a little later.

D Choose the better modal phrase to fit the context.

1 I ought to | must phone her, but I don't feel like it.
2 You won't be allowed to | can't use Mum's car, I bet you.
3 We aren't supposed to | mustn't disappoint Grandma again.
4 Had you to | Did you have to give the secret away?
5 We had better not | haven't got to make a noise.
6 Would | Might you lend me your notes, please?
7 The boss oughtn't to have | mustn't have called Emily lazy.
8 I could | was able to talk to Jule yesterday and she agrees with our plan.

5

6 Present tenses

Task	Topic	Example	Englische Grammatik
1	Simple present: third person singular	*Felix works hard, he never finishes before 7 pm.*	6.1.2
2	Simple present with repeated or regular actions/events	*My parents leave the house at seven every day.*	6.1.3a
3	Simple present: questions and negatives	*Does your sister play the guitar? Yes, but she doesn't practise much.*	6.1.1
4	Simple present with adverbs of frequency	*Janek sometimes speaks Polish at home.*	6.1.3a
5	Simple present for universal truths	*Ice melts in the sun.*	6.1.3a
6	Present progressive for temporary actions	*Lara's working as a waitress this summer.*	6.2.2b
7	Present progressive for actions/events in progress	*Take an umbrella, it's raining.*	6.2.2a
▶ 8	Simple present or present progressive? (1)	*Ben usually goes by bus but he's walking today.*	6.3
▶ 9	Simple present or present progressive? (2)	*We're going to the cinema. The film starts at 8.*	6.3
10	Simple present with certain verbs	*He needs more help.*	6.1.3e
▶ 11	Simple present or present progressive? (3)	*I hope you're doing something nice today.*	6.3
12	Present progressive to talk about developments	*It's becoming harder and harder to get a job.*	6.2.2
13	Simple present to talk about books, films, etc.	*The film stars Eddie Redmayne as physicist Stephen Hawking.*	6.1.3c

▶ Quick Check p. 59

1 'He, she, it …' Simple present: third person singular ▶ 6.1.2

Complete the table with the third person singular of the verbs in the box.

> ~~come~~ • ~~cry~~ • ~~do~~ • enjoy • feel • fly • go • hear • hurry • know • leave • like • miss • need • own • say •
> sleep • speak • study • take • teach • think • try • watch • wake up • wear • work • worry

-s	-es	-ies
→ comes	→ does	→ cries

2 The day starts early   Simple present with repeated or regular actions/events   ▶ 6.1.3a

Nora's family has a daily routine. Complete the text with the correct form of the verb in brackets.

Nora ➔ *lives* (live) with her parents near Manchester. Her parents ➔ *work* (work) in the city. They ... (leave) (1) for work at seven every day, so weekday mornings are always the same. Her dad ... (wake up) (2) first

5   and ... (go) (3) to the kitchen to make tea. Before her mum ... (have) (4) a shower, she ... (try) (5) to wake Nora by banging on her door. Nora never ... (hear) (6) her alarm so she definitely ... (need) (7) that wake-up call. Students at her school ... (wear) (8) a

10 uniform, so at least she ... (know) (9) what to wear. Nora ... (worry) (10) a bit about missing her bus because it sometimes ... (come) (11) early, so there's no time for breakfast. However, life ... (feel) (12)

much more relaxed at the weekend. Her parents ... (sleep) (13) late, and Nora ... (enjoy) (14) a big plate   15 of waffles and ... (watch) (15) breakfast TV in her pyjamas.

3 About Joe   Simple present: questions and negatives   ▶ 6.1.1

Joe has a new job in Edinburgh. Complete the questions and answers using the simple present.

➔ Joe | travel to Edinburgh by train – No | he | fly | because | not like trains
  ***Does* Joe *travel* to Edinburgh by train? – No, he *flies*, because he *doesn't like* trains.**

1 the new job | interest him – Well | it | offer a lot of opportunities | but | not pay very well
2 Joe | miss his hometown – Of course, he | miss his girlfriend | but | skype with her most evenings
3 Joe and his girlfriend | meet every weekend – No, they | not see each other more than twice a month
4 Joe | have many hobbies – He | not have much free time | but | try to go jogging after work
5 his girlfriend | do a lot of sport – Yes, she | do more sport than Joe | because | not work such long hours
6 they | want to move to Edinburgh – No, they | like the city, but | not want to live there

4 What do they usually do?   Simple present with adverbs of frequency   ▶ 6.1.3a

a How often does Janek do these things? Put the adverbs in the correct place in the sentences.

✗	(✓)	✓	✓✓	✓✓✓
never	sometimes	usually	often	always

➔ Janek goes for a run. (✓)
  *Janek **sometimes** goes for a run.*

1 He plays tennis in the winter. ✗
2 He doesn't cycle to school. ✓✓
3 He is late for class. (✓)
4 He and his mates discuss sport. ✓✓
5 He doesn't eat healthy food. ✓✓✓
6 He goes to the gym. ✓✓✓

6

b Complete these sentences about Janek's friends. Use information from the grid.

	run	play tennis	cycle	be late	discuss sport	eat healthy food	go to the gym
Mike	(✓)	✓✓✓	✗	✓✓✓	✓✓	(✓)	✗
Basia	(✓)	✓✓✓	(✓)	✗	✓✓	✗	✓

➔ Mike and Basia go for a run with Janek.
*Mike and Basia **sometimes** go for a run with Janek.*

1 Mike and Basia … tennis together on Fridays.
2 Basia … to school, but Mike … – he's too lazy!
3 Mike and Basia are very different. Mike … late, but Basia … late for school.
4 They … sport – especially when they meet at the park after school.
5 Mike … healthy food, but Basia doesn't.
6 Mike … to the gym. Basia … at the weekend.

c **NOW YOU** Write five sentences about what you do and how often you do it.

5 Great minds think alike   Simple present for universal truths   ▶ 6.1.3a

a Match the sentence parts to form common expressions.

➔ *Money doesn't grow on trees.*

1 You get
2 All you need
3 All good things come
4 Still waters run
5 Practice makes
6 ~~Money doesn't grow~~
7 What goes around
8 Everyone makes
9 Couples that play together,

a perfect.
b mistakes
c ~~on trees.~~
d stay together.
e is love.
f in threes.
g deep.
h comes around.
i what you pay for.

b **NOW YOU** How would you translate these expressions? Do you think they have any truth in them?

6 I'm working this summer   Present progressive for temporary actions   ▶ 6.2.2b

School's out for summer and lots of students are doing holiday jobs. Use the present progressive to say what they're all doing.

➔ Cara | help | local playgroup | until the end of July
*Cara**'s helping** at the local playgroup until the end of July.*

1 Jules | pick strawberries | Hall Farm | for four weeks
2 Petra | help out | corner shop | until September
3 Toni | sell ice creams | park | for a month
4 Helena | work as a lifeguard | swimming pool | for a while
5 Bertie and his brother | stack shelves | supermarket | for six weeks
6 Tasha | look after dogs | local kennels | until she goes on holiday

7 I'm still waiting   Present progressive with actions/events in progress   ▶ 6.2.2a

Moira's late for a date. She's phoning her boyfriend to explain why.
Complete the call with the verbs from the box in the present progressive.

> come • do • happen • join • joke • look for • not have • not stop •
> ~~queue~~ • run • sit • trainspot • wait

Greg Where are you? I've bought the tickets and there's a huge queue already.
Loads of people ➜ **are queuing** up to get into the gig. … you … (1)?

Moira Of course I'm coming. I wouldn't miss this concert for anything. But
unfortunately, I … (2) on a bench on the platform at the moment.

Greg What … you … (3) there?

Moira I … (4), it's my new hobby.

Greg What!? You can't be serious!

Moira No, of course I'm not serious. I … only … (5). Where's your sense of humour, Greg? I … (6) for
the train, that's all. It's not my fault that all the trains … (7) late today. Oh, I think I can hear it.
Yes, it's coming now.

Greg Great. Well, it's only two stops, right? You should be here in ten minutes. I … (8) the queue now,
so hurry up. I might not be able to save you a good place at the front.

Moira Oh no, the train … (9)!

Greg What? Not stopping? Why on earth not? So what … (10) now?

Moira No idea. Everyone … (11) someone to ask. And they … (12) much luck. Sorry Greg, you'll have
to go in alone. Greg? Are you still there?

6

▶ 8 Usually … but not today   Simple present or present progressive?   ▶ 6.3

Erklärvideo online:
cornelsen.de/webcodes
Code: mokonu

Miriam's fed up. She's broken her leg, so she can't do the things she usually
does. Use the notes under the pictures to make sentences.

➜ *She usually **does** gymnastics, but she**'s watching** it on TV today.*

➜ do gymnastics | watch it on TV

relax in her bedroom | lie on the sofa

have lessons at school | study alone

play in a band | listen to iTunes

meet friends in town | chat online

help in the garden | watch her dad

▶ 9 A survey Simple present or present progressive? ▶ 6.3

Erklärvideo online:
▶ **Exercise 8**

Mark from Lifestyle Consumer Group is at the supermarket.
Choose the correct words to complete the interview.

Mark Excuse me. I **➜ 'm doing** | do | does | don't do a survey about shopping habits. Can you spare a minute or two?

Woman Sure, that's fine. I not do | not doing | 'm not doing | don't do (1) anything right now.

Mark Great. So, do you shop | you shop | are you shopping | you are shopping (2) here regularly?

Woman Yes. Normally, I don't buy | buy | buying | 'm buying (3) the basics here – you know, things like flour, sugar, toilet paper.

Mark And you're happy with the things you buy?

Woman It's OK. On the whole, you get | 're getting | gets | don't get (4) good value for money at this supermarket.

Mark So where go you | do you go | you are going | are you going (5) for your fresh food generally – fruit and vegetables and so on?

Woman We buys | don't buy | buying | 're buying (6) more and more fruit and veg from the market these days.

Mark And why's that?

Woman The food isn't packaged so it 's staying | stay | doesn't stay | stays (7) fresher for longer.

Mark OK thanks. Just one last question. Are you finding | You find | Do you find | You are finding (8) the staff at the supermarket helpful and friendly?

Woman I 'm hoping | hope | don't hope | doesn't hope (9) so – I'm the manager!

Mark The manager? Oh dear, then I think | don't think | doesn't think | 'm not thinking (10) I'll be able to use your responses, sorry.

6

10 What a mess! Simple present with certain verbs ▶ 6.1.3e

Katrina's room is a mess and she needs to tidy it up. Complete the text with the correct form of a verb from the box.

> feel • know • love • need • not agree • not need •
> not want • own • promise • suggest • ~~want~~

Katrina's mum **➜ wants** her to get rid of all her stuff. She ... (1) that her daughter is not really an untidy girl. Although she is a teenager now, Katrina still ... (2) some of her favourite toys and ... (3) to throw them out. Her mother says that
5 Katrina first ... (4) to sort out all the books and comics which are lying all over her bedroom floor. Mrs Jones sensibly ... (5) that the best ones should go to a charity shop, along with the old video games that Katrina ... (6) any more. In short, Mrs Jones ... (7) that it really is time for Katrina to grow up and get
10 rid of everything from her childhood, including her soft toys. Poor Katrina ... (8) to do her best, but she ... (9) with her mother when it comes to Big Teddy, the most precious thing she ... (10).

11 Choose and explain Simple present or present progressive? ▶ 6.3

Erklärvideo online:
▶ **Exercise 8**

a Choose the correct form of the verb to complete the email.

From: Colm

Re: greetings from France

Hi Nigel

Hannah and I ➜ camp | **are camping** in France at the moment. I sit | 'm sitting (1) outside the campsite loos – it's the only place where you always get | 're always getting (2) a decent signal. We stay | 're staying (3) on this site for the whole summer and, despite the lack of good Wi-fi, we have | 're having (4) a brilliant time. Hannah begins | 's beginning (5) to relax, partly because the weather improves | 's improving (6) – and everybody knows | 's knowing (7) how she loves | 's loving (8) the sun! And also, because she doesn't worry | isn't worrying (9) about exams at the moment.

So how do we usually spend our mornings? We always get up | 're always getting up (10) really early and jump | are jumping (11) into the lake. At least that's what Hannah does | 's doing (12) – you know me, I'm not a big swimmer. But I plan | 'm planning (13) to get fitter, so I often run | 'm often running (14) round the lake while she swims | 's swimming (15).

In the afternoons, we generally explore | 're generally exploring (16) the countryside on our bikes and by evening, all we want | 're wanting (17) to do is cook some food and sleep! What do you do | are you doing (18) for the rest of the holidays? Something exciting, I hope | 'm hoping (19).

Better go now – Hannah waits | 's waiting (20) for me!

See you, Colm

b Then explain your choices: A (repeated regular event), B (state verb), C (events in progress), D (temporary actions) or E (developments).

➜ *Hannah and I* **are camping** *in France at the moment.* C

12 The world is getting hotter Present progressive to talk about developments ▶ 6.2.2

Complete the text with the verbs from the box in the present progressive.

affect • become • cause • die • freeze • get • ~~happen~~ • increase • melt • multiply • not do • not get • occur • spread • suffer from • take

Climate change is nothing new, but it matters because ➜ it's *happening* faster now than ever before. ... we ... (1) sufficient action to prevent climate change? Average global temperatures ... (2).
5 Last year was the warmest year on record, making it the third consecutive year with record-setting surface temperatures. The ice in the Arctic regions ... (3) more in the summer and ... (4) less in the winter. This situation ... (5) the habitats of mammals
10 such as the walrus, the polar bear and the Artic fox.

Warmer winters mean germs and bacteria ... (6). According to a study published in the journal Nature Climate Change, mosquitoes and other pests ... (7) northwards from hot tropical countries. The study showed a clear relationship between rising tem- 15 peratures and the increased range of crop pests. Meanwhile, more people ... (8) from heat-related illnesses, especially older people over 65.

As we understand more and more about climate change, it … (9) clear that
20 mature forests are extremely important. We now know that deforestation …
(10) as many greenhouse gas emissions as all the cars and trucks on the
planet. Preserving our ancient forests has to be a priority.
It is estimated that more than 800 million people … (11) climate change impacts
such as droughts and extreme weather. While some parts of the world
25 … (12) enough water, others … (13) too much. Serious floods …
(14) every 10 to 20 years instead of every 100 years. Yet, even
now, some people refuse to admit that we have a
problem, whilst campaigners for a greener world
insist that we … (15) enough.

+ **13 Reader's review**   Simple present to talk about books, films, etc.   ▶ 6.1.3c

Paula Hawkins' best-selling psychological thriller, *The Girl on the Train*, tells the story of three young women.

a The paragraphs in this review have become mixed up. First put the verbs in brackets in the correct form.

A The plot … (thicken) because at the same time,
she … (become) fascinated by another young
couple who … (live) a few doors away and her
discontent with her own lonely life … (increase).

B Rachel … (find) it difficult not to stare into Tom
and Anna's house and … (envy) their happiness.
Sometimes, she even … (visit) her old home and
… (frighten) Anna with her crazy accusations.

C Are you reading anything at the moment?
Because if not, I can thoroughly recommend this
book. Rachel, the main narrator, is the girl on
the train. She ➜ **takes** (take) the same commuter
train to work every day, despite being unemployed and an alcoholic.

D Her ex-husband Tom now … (live) there with his
new wife Anna and their baby girl. Rachel … (get)
maddened by jealousy and regret, especially as
one of the causes for her divorce was her inability
to have a child with Tom.

E At some point earlier in the story, she's lost her
job, but she … (continue) to take the same
journey, pretending to her flat mate that she still
… (have) a job. Every day her train … (stop) at a
signal opposite her former home, in a cosy
suburban street.

F The plot gets complicated with the disappearance
and murder of this perfect but unfaithful wife.
How is Rachel involved? You won't be able to
put this book down until you find out …

G Then one day, from her seat in the train, Rachel
… (witness) something shocking: she … (see)
the perfect wife in her garden, embracing
another man. Soon after, the woman disappears.

H She … (fantasize), often in a drunken state,
about the perfect life this unknown couple …
(enjoy) together: he is handsome, she is beautiful,
they are in love.

I However, because Rachel's drinking is out of
control, she is an unreliable witness and often …
(not remember) what has happened. As she
frequently … (retain) no memory of events the
night before, the police … (not believe) her story
and indeed … (warn) her to stop stalking her ex.

b Now put the paragraphs in the correct order.

1	2	3	4	5	6	7	8	9
C								F

c NOW YOU Write a review of a book or film you've recently enjoyed. Use the simple present tense.

Quick Check

A Put the adverbs in the correct place. There is sometimes more than one possibility.

1 We help each other when we work as a team. (usually)
2 She's excellent at time management. (always)
3 Do you regret taking on too many projects? (sometimes)
4 They don't spend enough time checking their answers. (always)
5 The dog sleeps at my feet under my desk. (normally)
6 Paula goes to the dentist if she can avoid it. (never)
7 My car starts first time on cold mornings. (hardly ever)
8 We're the last to arrive at parties. (rarely)
9 He doesn't get so anxious about meeting new people. (usually)
10 They argue about who's going to do the washing-up. (frequently)

B Choose the correct verb form.

1 Kim babysits | is babysitting for her neighbours this week.
2 The three of us come | are coming from the same village.
3 Do you think | Are you thinking we can open the windows?
4 Sometimes I forget | am forgetting to wear my bike helmet.
5 Two wrongs don't make | aren't making a right.
6 You'll need to put on a warm coat – it snows | 's snowing.
7 It becomes | 's becoming even easier to keep in touch these days.
8 We don't often print | aren't often printing documents any more.
9 The price of electricity goes up | is going up and up these days.
10 How much does it cost | is it costing to fly to Brazil?

C Find and correct the mistakes. There's one in each sentence.

1 The best Sherlock Holmes film is starring Benedict Cumberbatch.
2 My sister always crys during films with sad endings.
3 It's a shame that she doesn't plays the violin any more.
4 I'm thinking it's high time you got yourself a job.
5 Our guests aren't strict vegetarians, but they don't eat usually meat.
6 Belinda works as an assistant in a care home this summer.
7 We're runing short of time, so please hurry up.
8 Do he know how to get here by public transport?
9 I'm not believing that it's all their own work.
10 He's an amazing chef but he makes not good desserts.

D Make these sentences negative.

1 Jules has a new car.
2 I see the point in going outside in this weather.
3 She remembers her accident. She knows exactly what happened.
4 Please leave your trainers out in the corridor.
5 We're planning to visit you today.
6 Jennie's new jeans go well with her top.

6

7 Past and perfect tenses

Task	Topic	Example	Englische Grammatik
1	Present perfect (simple form) – Forms	I'm not at home - I've gone away.	7.1.1
2	Present perfect (simple form) – Use (1)	Have you ever tried frogs' legs?	7.1.2a
3	Present perfect (simple form) – Use (2)	Nothing much has changed in my life.	7.1.2b
4	Present perfect progressive – Forms	Suzie and Kim have been talking on the phone for hours.	7.2.1
5	Present perfect progressive – Forms and use	They have been working out all morning.	7.2
6	The use of since and for	since four o'clock – for five hours	7.6
7	Present perfect simple and progressive contrasted	I've read four chapters of this book. I've been reading it since breakfast time.	7.3
8	Simple past – Forms and use	It all happened a long time ago.	7.4
9	Present perfect and simple past contrasted	We've moved to Berlin – we moved here last week.	7.5
10	Past progressive – Forms and use	At 10:30 pm I was walking home.	7.7
11	Simple past and past progressive contrasted	We weren't driving fast when the accident happened.	7.8
12	Past perfect simple – Forms and use	She had acted in six films before she was twelve.	7.9
13	Past perfect and simple past contrasted	The film had already started when we got to the cinema.	7.10
14	Past perfect progressive	Everyone knew that he had been lying.	7.11
15	Used to	Things used to be different, when I was a child.	7.12.1
16	Mixed past forms (1)	Katie played football when she was a child, but she hasn't played for years now.	7
17	Present perfect simple and simple past contrasted	My application still hasn't arrived. I posted it last week.	7.5
18	Mixed past forms (2)	I was waiting at the crossing when the man walked by.	7
19	Mixed past forms (3)	Max has gone to Paris, he lived there as a child.	7
20	Mixed past forms (4)	Home had changed when I returned.	7

▶ Quick Check p. 71

1 A checklist Present perfect (simple form) – Forms ▶ 7.1.1

a Write down the past participle forms of the verbs in the box in two lists: regular and irregular forms.

buy • do • drive • feed • finish • forget • give • hide • lock • pack • take • tell • text • wrap • write	regular	irregular
	➔ *finished*	➔ *bought*

b Before you go off to your grandma's for the weekend, you look at your family's checklist to see what everyone has/hasn't done. Make sentences using some of the verbs from part a.

➔ *I***'ve packed** *my rucksack.*
➔ *I* **haven't finished** *my presentation for chemistry.*

My jobs:
- ~~pack rucksack~~ ✓
- ~~finish presentation for chemistry~~
- lock cupboard ✓
- hide diary

Jobs for my sister and me:
- feed the cat ✓
- wrap Grandma's present
- text Dad ✓

Mum's jobs:
- buy train tickets ✓
- give key to neighbour
- tell Grandma when we're arriving ✓

2 Have you ever tried frogs' legs? Present perfect (simple form) – Use ▶ 7.1.2a

a Here are some signal words for tenses. Which three are NOT used with the present perfect?

yesterday • never • before • not … yet • last week • today • three days ago • ever

b This is a questionnaire from a magazine. First, translate the questions into English.

➔ Bist du jemals mit Delphinen geschwommen?
*** Have you ever swum*** *with dolphins?*

1 Bist du schon einmal in England gewesen? …
2 Bist du schon mal im Krankenhaus gewesen? …
3 Hast du jemals dein Handy zerbrochen? …
4 Bist du schon mal erster Klasse geflogen? …
5 Hast du schon einmal deine Schlüssel verloren? …
6 Hast du jemals einen Preis gewonnen? …

7 Bist du in deinem Leben schon mal auf einem Pferd geritten? …
8 Hast du schon einmal in einem Fünf-Sterne-Hotel übernachtet? …
9 Hast du schon mal einen schlimmen Autounfall gesehen? …
10 Hast du schon mal für zehn Leute Abendessen gekocht? …

c NOW YOU Ask a partner and make notes. Answer the questions for your partner too. Then, report on your own and your partner's answers.

➔ *Yes, **I have** | No, **I haven't**.*
➔ *I **have swum** with dolphins but my partner **hasn't**. **We have** both **been** …*

3 Nothing much has changed in my life   Present perfect (simple form) – Use   ▶ 7.1.2b

a   Gilbert, the Giant Tortoise, is one of the oldest animals in the zoo. Today, he looks back over his long life. Complete the text with the help of the words in brackets.

→ I ... (live) here for ages.
   I've lived here for ages.

1   Every morning since 1990 I ... (wake up) in this cage.
2   I ... (eat) about 15,000 lettuces in the last 40 years.
3   I ... (always, want) to go on holiday to Africa.
4   My human helpers ... (always, be) kind to me.
5   I ... (never, have to) go to the vet.
6   But I ... (have) any adventures either.
7   And I ... (often, ask) myself if I will live to 100.

b   Imagine you're doing an interview with Gilbert's zookeeper. Write three questions using the present perfect.

→ How long **has** Gilbert **lived** here?

4 Consequences   Present perfect progressive – Forms   ▶ 7.2.1

Match the actions on the left to the consequences or responses on the right.

→ *Your grandma has been calling all day. – I'll phone her back now.*

1   ~~Your grandma has been calling all day.~~
2   It's been raining ever since I came out of school.
3   He's been asking me for my number since I walked in through the door.
4   I've been having problems with my computer for weeks now.
5   Those kids next door have been partying all night.
6   I've been dyeing my hair blond for years now.
7   My mate has been paying for his phone for years.
8   She's been reading that book for months now.
9   That guy in the corner has been staring at you since we came in.

a   Oh no, that's my ex!
b   Yeah, I didn't get much sleep either.
c   ~~I'll phone her back now.~~
d   He shouldn't have signed the contract.
e   You should get a new one.
f   I know, I'm really wet too.
g   Just tell him no – you don't want him to call you!
h   I bet everyone thinks it's the natural colour.
i   It can't be very exciting.

7

5 What have they been doing? Present perfect progressive – Forms and use ▶ 7.2

Look at these pictures and make sentences to explain what the people have been doing.

➔ *They**'ve been cooking.***

6 I've been playing for 11 years. The use of *since* and *for* ▶ 7.6

a *Since* or *for*? Choose the right word for each of these time phrases.

➔ **since** midnight

> ... ~~midnight~~ • ... a week • ... last month • ... ages •
> ... I left you • ... centuries • ... many days •
> ... we last talked • ... Christmas • ... a long time

b Make sentences with the present perfect progressive and use *since* or *for*:

➔ I started learning the piano when I was five. Now I'm sixteen. (for)
   I've been playing *the piano for eleven years.*

1 They started band practice at ten – it's two in the morning now and they're still playing! (for)
2 I wrote the first entries of my blog in January. (since)
3 She took her first riding lessons six months ago. (for)
4 My brother wants this really cool bike and he started saving up last Christmas. (since)
5 They started working on our hockey pitch at the beginning of March and now it's the end of September! (for)
6 I started having dancing classes last year. (since)
7 The class took up learning Spanish in Year 9 and they're at the end of Year 11 now. (for)
8 The marathon began at eight and here we are still running four hours later. (since)

7 Keep trying   Present perfect simple and progressive contrasted   ▸ 7.3

Complete these sentences with the correct forms of the verbs (present perfect simple or present perfect progressive).

➔ My friend … (apply) for a placement since September; she … (apply) to six companies so far
*My friend **has been applying** for a placement since September; she **has applied** to six companies so far.*

1 My dad … (help) me to repair my motorbike since my accident. Now he … (help) me to fix the engine, so it should be ready for the trip tomorrow.
2 I … (see) the same doctor for months now. I … (just, see) a different one and now I feel fine.
3 We … (learn) English for six years now, and our teacher says we … (learn) roughly 5000 words so far.
4 I … (write) invitations for my party all evening. I … (write) 15 so far.
5 Our team … (try) to make it into the second league all season, but our coach … (not try) everything yet.
6 Me and my best mate … (save) up for a trip to Rome since Easter, but we … (not save) enough to book the flight.

8 A history quiz   Simple past – Forms and use   ▸ 7.4

To do this history quiz, first complete the questions with the verbs in the simple past form (be careful, you sometimes need the passive). Then choose the right answer.

Who ➔ **won** (win) the World Cup in Wembley in 1966?
a The German team   b ➔ ***The English team***

1 When … the Berlin Wall … (fall)?
  a 1961   b 1991   c 1989
2 The New York terrorist attacks … (be carried out) on September 11th of which year?
  a 1971   b 1994   c 2001
3 How many years … the First World War … (last)?
  a four   b seven   c five
4 Who … (write) *Romeo and Juliet*?
  a Goethe   b Shakespeare   c Brecht
5 The famous song *Yesterday* … first … (be sung) by which pop group?
  a Abba   b The Rolling Stones   c The Beatles
6 Which political leader … (not win) the Nobel Peace Prize?
  a Barack Obama   b Mahatma Gandhi   c Willy Brandt
7 On which country … the first atomic bomb … (be dropped)?
  a Japan   b North Korea   c Greenland
8 The first *Star Wars* movie … (be made) in which year?
  a 2001   b 1977   c 1986

7

▶ 9 About Jo   Present perfect and simple past contrasted   ▶ 7.5

Erklärvideo online:
📄 ⊙ cornelsen.de/webcodes
➕ ◁) Code: seboja

a There are signal words for simple past and for present perfect in the box. Put them in the correct list. [Note: In this exercise, you should follow the rules for British English.]

> ~~already~~ • ~~two days ago~~ • in 2014 • just • when? • at the weekend • never • yesterday • ever • not … yet • so far • since • last night • on Tuesday • at 8:30 • always • ago

signal words for simple past	signal words for present perfect
➔ *two days ago*	➔ *already*

b Choose the correct tense in the following sentences about Jo's family life.

➔ I have been born | was born in Wuppertal 15 years ago.
  I **was born** in Wuppertal 15 years ago.

1 My parents have got married | got married the year after I was born.
2 When I was small, we have moved house | moved house three times.
3 But now we have lived | lived at the same place for years.
4 They haven't had | didn't have another child since I was born, but I'm still hoping for a sister.
5 My dad used to work in an office, but he has retrained | retrained as a social care worker last year.
6 Mum has always worked | always worked in an IT firm.
7 My grandma has come | came to live in our town after my grandad has died | died.
8 I have a cousin too, but I haven't seen | didn't see him yet because my uncle and aunt live in Mexico. I really want to go there one day.

c NOW YOU Write five sentences on what has or hasn't happened in the life of your family. Use time markers like *ago, when I was six, not … yet, often, always, last* and choose your tenses carefully.

10 Everyone has an alibi   Past progressive – Forms and use   ▶ 7.7

a Oh no! The Crown Jewels have been stolen! The police have been talking to several people, but everyone has an alibi. Say what they were all doing. Who do you think stole the Crown Jewels?

Bill Fingers	I ➔ **was having** (have) a drink at the pub.
Bad Bess	Evil Edna and me … (enjoy) (1) a boat trip down the Thames.
Joe Bloggs' wife	He wasn't in London. He … (stay) (2) in Brighton at the time – here's his Brighton hotel bill!
Agile Ali	It can't have been me – I … (lie) (3) in bed in hospital.
The Kelly Gang	We … (not work) (4) that day – it was our day off.
The first Kramer Twin	No, not me, I … (visit) (5) my twin brother in prison that morning.
The second Kramer Twin	Me? No, ask my prison guard – I … (make) (6) mailbags in the prison workshop all morning – non stop!

b NOW YOU Imagine you needed an alibi for a crime. Can you remember what you were doing at this time yesterday, in your last English lesson, and last Saturday night? Write three sentences.

▶ 11 The moon was shining

Simple past and past progressive contrasted   ▶ 7.8

Erklärvideo online:
cornelsen.de/webcodes
Code: wusadi

Stories often begin by telling you what was happening when something changed the situation. Complete these sentences with verbs in the past progressive or the simple past.

Beginnings	What happened then
1 The moon ➜ **was shining** (shine) and the cicadas … (sing) in the trees. It was a fairy-tale evening. The sad notes of her flute … (sound out) through the cooling summer air.	A beautiful youth ➜ **stepped** (step) out of the bushes. He … (catch) her eye and she … (freeze).
2 Crash! The ship … (smash) its way through the mountains of waves, the passengers … (be thrown) this way and that.	Suddenly they … (hear) a terrific crack! and … (feel) the ship hit something very large and very hard.
3 Absolute silence. No one … (move) in the classroom. Everyone … (shake) with fear. What … (go on)?	The Demon Teacher … (break) the silence. 'Good morning,' he … (whisper), 'and welcome to my lessons.'
4 The Zargs … (come) closer by the minute. The Xenii … (be pushed back) by the ultimate force of the Gamma gun. They … (not even fight) any more.	Suddenly, the Xenii … (be stopped). They … (stand) stuck to the ground. A blinding white fog … (cover) them.

12 Extraordinary talents   Past perfect – Forms and use   ▶ 7.9

a Some young people had already been very successful before they were out of their teens. Complete these sentences using the past perfect form of the verbs in the box.

become · be chosen for · be signed for · design · speak · use · win · write

➜ Jeffrey Xiang … the world's U20 Chess Champion by the time he was fifteen.
Jeffrey Xiang **had become** *the world's U20 Chess Champion by the time he was fifteen.*

1 When she was 17, Helena Coggan … already … two books.
2 Eleanor Green … the England gymnastics team before she was fourteen.
3 At just 15, Ben Pasternak … already … a gaming app, *Impossible Rush*, that was downloaded 1.3 million times.
4 Before he turned 13, Shuham Banerje … Lego bricks to create a braille printer for blind people. The Intel company bought the idea.
5 Before his 14th birthday, Karamoko Dembele … for Celtic Football Club's U20s.
6 At 17, Malala Yousafzai … already … the Nobel Peace Prize.
7 By the time she was 14, Harley Bird … the voice of Peppa Pig in the films for over seven years.

b **NOW YOU** Small achievements count too. What had you done by the time you were a) five b) ten c) fifteen? Write three sentences.

➜ *I* **had learned** *to swim by the time I was five.*

7

13 Not my lucky day Past perfect and simple past contrasted ▶ 7.10

Erklärvideo online:

cornelsen.de/webcodes
Code: buheza

There are days when everything goes wrong. Complete these sentences using the simple past or the past perfect of the verbs given.

→ I … (wake) up in the morning with my phone on the stone floor next to my bed.
  I **woke** up in the morning with my phone on the stone floor next to my bed.
→ The screen … (be broken) in the fall.
  The screen **had been broken** in the fall.

1 On the way to school, I … (meet) a friend who … (see) a special offer for my favourite phone in the paper.
2 Luckily, I … (save up) just enough money by working in the holidays, because even as a special offer, it still … (not be) cheap.
3 After school, I … (cannot) find the advert; the paper with the ad … (be thrown out) that morning.
4 When I … finally … (find out) where to go, I … (take) the bus to the store.
5 But it just … (not seem) to be my lucky day – all the phones on offer … (sell out).
6 There's a happy ending though. On the bus home, a friend … (tell) me where she … (get) a new screen for her broken phone for just €35.

14 The boy who cried wolf Past perfect progressive ▶ 7.11

a There's a famous story about a shepherd boy who got so bored with his job that he went around town screaming 'A wolf is attacking the sheep!' All the townspeople had been busy before he came but dropped their work to help him. Who had been doing what when the boy raised the false alarm? Choose from the verbs in the box.

> dig up • feed • play • put up • repair • sell • ~~serve~~

→ A waiter … tea.
  A waiter **had been serving** tea.

1 Two builders … a wall.
2 A mechanic … a cart.
3 A shop assistant … groceries.
4 A farmer and his wife … their cows.
5 Three workers … the road.
6 A little girl … in the street.

b Here's the rest of the story. Complete the text using the simple past or the past perfect progressive of the verbs given.

When the townspeople → **arrived** (arrive) in the fields, they … (realize) (1) that the shepherd boy … (lie) (2) to them. So they … (go) (3) back to town. But, all this while, the wolf … (hide) (4) in the bushes. He
5 … (know) (5) that the townspeople wouldn't come to help the liar a second time. At last, this was the chance which the wolf … (wait) (6) for. He … (jump out) (7), … (attack) (8) the sheep and … (enjoy) (9) a delicious dinner.

15 Things used to be different   Used to   ▶ 7.12.1

a   Things used to be different when your grandparents were young. Write sentences with *used to* in order to say what life was like then.

➜ Drivers wear seat belts now.
*They **didn't use to** wear them.*

1 People don't smoke in restaurants nowadays.
2 Not many students go to single-sex schools now.
3 There aren't many corner shops around today.
4 You don't have to wear swimming caps in pools.
5 You are allowed to vote at 18.

6 Women don't have to ask their husbands when they take a job.
7 We have smartphones and the internet.
8 Most male teachers don't wear ties to school.

b   **NOW YOU**   Look back on your own past. What things did or didn't you use to do, or like, or believe when you were younger? Write four or five sentences.

16 Sports and me   Mixed past forms   ▶ 7

The new sports teacher wants to hear about the experiences the students in her class had with sports. Complete the text using the past tense that fits best for the context. Look out for signal words.

Teacher   So, let me ask you: What sports ➜ **have you done** (you, do) so far?
Robin   Well, I … (play) (1) volleyball a lot when I was younger, but then one day I … (break) (2) a finger, so I … (have to stop) (3).
Elena   Mira and I … (go riding) (4) for about five years now. It's fantastic – we … (go) (5) trekking in the last holidays.
Finn   My parents … (take) (6) me to tae kwon do when I was younger; but now I like judo better.
Luca   I … (never, do) (7) any sports outside school.
Ms G   What about the others? … (you, ever, ask) (8) to do other sports in your PE lessons?
Tarık   Yeah, I remember once, when Oliver and I … (play) (9) football in the break, our last PE teacher … (see) (10) us and … (promise) (11) to coach us.
Leyla   In year 7, we … (play) (12) basketball tournaments against the other classes; why … (that, be stopped) (13) now?
Mika   Alex and I … (ask) (14) our music teacher to give us dancing lessons all year. But he … (say) (15) no. And his reason? He … (never, do) (16) dancing at school. But we … (talk) (17) to our friends at another school yesterday, and they … (practise) (18) a hip-hop number nearly every week this term.

+ 17 A job interview   Present perfect simple and simple past contrasted   ▶ 7.5

These sentences are from a job interview. Translate them and choose the tenses carefully.

➜ Warum haben Sie sich um diesen Job beworben?
*Why **did** you **apply** for this job?*

1 Wie lange leben Sie schon in Bayern?
2 Wir sind vor acht Jahren hergezogen.
3 Ich wohne schon seit fünf Jahren in München.
4 Seit meinem 10. Geburtstag spiele ich Tennis.
5 Ich habe letztes Jahr mein Abitur bestanden.

6 Sie schreiben für die Zeitung. Wann haben Sie damit angefangen?
7 Ich habe noch nicht entschieden, welches Fach ich studieren will.
8 Haben Sie schon einmal länger als drei Monate im Ausland gelebt?

+ 18 The story of a rescue Mixed past forms ▶ 7

This is the story of a car driver who rescued an old man with Alzheimer's, who was trying to cross the railway tracks. Put the verbs in the right form, choosing carefully between simple past, past progressive and past perfect.

I ➔ **was waiting** (wait) outside the school where I ➔ **was collecting** (collect) my ten-year-old when I ➔ **noticed** (notice) an old gentleman opposite. He ... (walk) (1) along with some difficulty. When my son
5 ... (get in) (2) the car, I ... (drive) (3) on down the road towards where it crosses the train tracks. The white lights were flashing to show that a train ... (approach) (4) the crossing. When I ... (stop) (5) the car, I saw the old man again – and he ... (head) (6) straight
10 onto the crossing.

'This can't be right,' I thought to myself. Out of the corner of my eye, I ... (see) (7) that now the red lights ... (flash) (8) to show that the gates ... (come) (9) down. Meanwhile, the old gentleman ... (already, reach) (10) the tracks. 15

I jumped out of the car, ... (run) (11) under the closing gates and ... (look) (12) to my right. Only a couple of hundred metres away, the train ... (speed) (13) towards us. I sprinted forward, ... (take) (14) the old man by the hand and ... (say) (15), 'Sir, we need 20 to move'. He obviously ... (not know) (16) what ... (happen) (17).

I took his arm and he ... (start) (18) to walk – step by slow step – while the train driver ... (whistle) (19) at us to clear the tracks. Seconds later, the train ... 25 (pass) (20) close behind us. We ... (only just, make) (21) it across.

I couldn't believe what ... (just, happen) (22). But, when I got back to my car, my son ... (wait) for me (23). 'Great move, Dad, and I've got you on film!' He 30 ... (wave) (24) his mobile at me. He ... (record) (25) everything from start to finish.

+ 19 Tricky tenses Mixed past forms ▶ 7

a A change in tense often means a change in meaning. Read the sentences and answer the questions.

➔ I lay awake all night. (Is it still night when he is speaking? – **No.**)

1 When she arrived at the party, everybody was having fun. (Did they have fun before she came?)
2 Max has been to Paris, and Gina has gone to Paris. (Who is there now?)
3 Eggy Rock has made more than twelve albums. (Is Eggy still alive and singing when the speaker says this?)
4 When the teacher came into the room, the students were sitting on their desks. (Were they on their desks when she came in?)
5 I've had a toothache all afternoon. (Does he still have a toothache now?)
6 She had her hair cut this morning. (Is it still morning now?)
7 How long did Peer stay in the interview room? (Is he still there?)
8 The Minister hadn't eaten before the parade. (Has the parade started yet?)
9 Ayesha has done really well in her first year in Germany. (Is she in her second year now?)

7

b Now try to translate these sentences, watching out for the correct tenses.

→ Im ersten Semester hatte ich gute Ergebnisse, aber in diesem Semester hatte ich bisher nicht so viel Erfolg.
I had good results in my first term, but this term, I haven't had much success so far.

1 Als ich hereinkam, saßen alle da und redeten, aber als die Königin eintrat, standen sie alle auf.
2 Mein Freund ist gerade nach New York gegangen, aber ich bin noch nie da gewesen.
3 Wie lange ist dein Auto schon in der Werkstatt? Du hast es letzte Woche hingebracht, oder?
4 Kelly hat schon den ganzen Morgen Kopfweh. Gestern ging es ihr auch nicht gut.
5 Wie viele Alben hat John Lennon aufgenommen, und wie viele hat Adele bisher aufgenommen?
6 Jo hat sich letzte Woche endlich die Haare schneiden lassen. Sie hat sie sich noch nie so kurz schneiden lassen.

✛ 20 Rachel's year abroad   Mixed past forms   ▸ 7

a It's exciting when you go away on a year abroad, but what is it like when you come back? That is what this article is about. Read it through, then choose carefully which tenses to use in the gaps.

The year abroad → **was** (be) something that Rachel → **had been looking forward to** (look forward to) for ages. When she finally … (fly) (1) out to New Zealand, she adored all the challenges that she … (be confronted) (2) with. She … (make) (3) new friends, … (do) (4) her best to learn the language – and simply … (not have) (5) the time to become homesick. But coming back … (be) (6) a big disappointment, she says. 'It felt like I … (take) (7) a step backwards.'

Over in New Zealand, she … (meet) (8) different people with different outlooks, … (have) (9) new experiences and … (stand up) (10) for herself. Now back in Britain, she … (live) (11) with her parents again and … (try) (12) to acclimatize to her old surroundings. Rachel … (change) (13), but people at home had too. In the year she … (live) (14) in Auckland, some old friendships … (be lost) (15), while other friends … (get) (16) closer. Now she … (wonder) (17) why people thought she'd be the same person she … (always, be) (18), and how she could readjust to the life she … (have) (19) before.

Even though it … (be) (20) hard to get used to being back home again, she wouldn't want to … (miss) (21) the year off. 'I … (become) (22) more self-confident and more tolerant,' she says. 'And I … (decide) (23) to include some of the things I … (learn) (24) abroad into my new life at home.'

b **NOW YOU** Think back to an event in your life that made a big change, maybe moving house or changing schools. Write a report like the one above and and talk about what happened while, before and after the event. Try to make use of tenses like the past perfect or the present perfect progressive too, to help express the order of the events in the past.

Quick Check

A Fill the gaps with *since*, *for*, *ago* or *yet*.

1 I haven't watched this programme … I was in primary school.
2 That shop closed down years ….
3 I've only been learning Spanish … one year.
4 I haven't been to the United States … 2001.
5 My sister hasn't taken her driving test …, and she's nineteen now.
6 Tamira waited … one and a half years before she was accepted on the course.
7 Have you sold your bike …?
8 I need a new school bag, I got this one ages ….

B Translate the German parts of these sentences (present perfect or simple past).

1 (Wir wohnen) in this part of town for eight years.
2 Sam looks a bit green in the face – that's the third ice cream (das sie heute gegessen hat).
3 (Ich habe ihn nicht gesehen) yesterday.
4 (Diese Armbanduhr habe ich) since my fourteenth birthday.
5 I've only just arrived. When (hat die Party begonnen)?
6 (Wir haben noch nicht gelesen) a play by Shakespeare.
7 (Wie lange kennst du) your dance partner?
8 He took the flight (am Tag als die Ferien angefangen haben).

C Choose the best form for the verbs

1 I used to go | have gone to the cinema a lot when we lived in town.
2 When it collided with the bike, the lorry turned | was turning off right.
3 I wanted to know if she had taken | took my bag.
4 Mr Heller wasn't collecting | hasn't collected my work yet.
5 The team has been preparing | was prepared for the match all season.
6 The poor horse was tired out and didn't want | hadn't wanted to take the last jump.
7 You could see that the teacher had been expecting | has been expecting a different answer.
8 Thanks to three placements this year, I gained | have gained a lot of experience in hotel work.

D Correct the marked mistakes.

1 We learn French for four and a half years now.
2 I lost my contact lens while I put it in after PE.
3 I prepare my presentation all day.
4 As kids, we didn't used to have meals in school.
5 Why haven't you told me that we had maths homework yesterday?
6 I follow his blog ever since he left for Canada.
7 We got to the cinema late and the film has already started.
8 My partner hasn't given the source of the text in his report, so he lost 2 points.
9 My family bought our house here for ten years.
10 One of my best friends moved away and I wasn't hearing from him until yesterday.

7

8 Expressing future time

Task	Topic	Example	Englische Grammatik
1	*Will*-future for spontaneous decisions/predictions	*Wait, I'll open that door for you.*	8.1.2
2	*Will*-future for predictions	*You won't find a repair shop open on Sunday.*	8.1.2a
3	*Going to*-future for plans or intentions	*She's going to be a technician.*	8.2.2a
4	*Going to*-future – present signs or indications, *Will*-future for predictions	*Look at the worksheets on the table – there's going to be a test!* *I'm sure it will be difficult.*	8.2.2b 8.1.2
5	*Will-* and *going to*-future contrasted	*Ben will be 17 tomorrow, and we're going to give him a big surprise.*	8.1 8.2
6	Present progressive for arrangements	*Are you coming to the meeting tonight?*	8.3
7	Future progressive	*I'll be visiting Grandad in hospital this afternoon.*	8.5
8	Simple present with future meaning (timetable future)	*My train leaves in five minutes.*	8.4
9	Mixed future forms (1)	*The match starts at 7 pm. Are you coming too?*	8
10	Future perfect	*She won't have finished her essay yet.*	8.6
11	Other ways of expressing future time	*I'm about to phone for some pizzas – does anybody else want one?*	8.7
12	Mixed future forms (2)	*The airport opens next year. They'll have built the new terminal by then.*	8

▶ Quick Check p. 78

1 Wait, I'll help you! *Will*-future for spontaneous decisions/predictions ▶ 8.1.2

Jenna's birthday party is just about to start, and there are lots of things going on. Match the sentences to form mini dialogues.

➜ *The phone's ringing! – I'll get it!*

1 ~~The phone's ringing!~~	a Don't worry – I'll dance with her.
2 Remember, Pia's our surprise guest.	b ~~I'll get it.~~
3 I hope Emma doesn't flirt with me again.	c I'll go and let them in.
4 Oh no, I forgot to put onions on the pizza!	d That means there'll be karaoke. Great!
5 Tarik is going to sing later.	e It's OK, I'll clean it up.
6 What if the neighbours complain about the noise?	f I won't tell anyone she's coming.
7 Oh dear, I've broken a glass!	g Nobody will notice.
8 Oh, there's someone at the door already!	h They won't. I saw them go out.

2 An exchange trip · *Will*-future for predictions · ▸ 8.1.2a

a Finn is going on an exchange to Canada. He's wondering what it will be like. Complete his sentences with *will* or *won't* and the words in brackets.

➔ I (hope | I | not be) the only guest in the family.
*I hope **won't be** the only guest in the family.*

1 I (not suppose | I | talk) much at the beginning.
2 I (not expect | I | get) enough to eat, but I can always buy some snacks.
3 I (hope | I | have) a room of my own.
4 I (think | there | be) a school bus.
5 I (probably | meet) other German students.
6 I (be sure | I | be able to) do a lot of sports there.
7 I (guess | the teachers | be) stricter there.
8 I (definitely | not have) much free time.
9 I (not expect | I | skype) with my parents every day – but maybe every weekend.
10 I (wonder | if | I | get) homesick.

b Do you agree with Finn's predictions? Or do you think some things will be different than he imagines? Write three sentences with *I think* or *I don't think*.

➔ *I don't think he'll meet other German students.*

3 Plans for the future · *Going to*-future for plans or intentions · ▸ 8.2.2a

a School will soon be over and the students are making plans for the future. Read the information and guess who is going to do what. Use the ideas in the box.

> go on a work and travel tour • do a hotel management training course •
> spend the summer in Auckland • ~~study medicine~~ • cycle across the Alps •
> apply for a job at the local supermarket • become an au pair somewhere •
> do nothing for a couple of months • look for a placement at a film production company

➔ Nele has always wanted to be a doctor.
*She**'s going to study** medicine.*

1 Anna and Ayse want to travel, but their savings are only enough for the flight out.
2 Leon loves working with children.
3 Jonas needs a break. He needs some time off.
4 Finn, Yuri and Emma are happiest when they're on their bikes.
5 Nasrin needs money and doesn't want to leave home yet.
6 Karim hopes to train for a job that will allow him to work in exciting places around the world.
7 Hanna and Darius are lucky. They have family in New Zealand.
8 Lily dreams of a career in the media.

b **NOW YOU** What are you going to do when you finish school? And what are your friends' plans? Write three or four sentences.

8

4 What's going to happen?

Going to-future – present signs or indications, *will*-future for predictions ▸ 8.2.2b, 8.1.2

a Look at the pictures and write down what is going to happen next. The expressions in the box will help you.

> do a test • land in • light • lose •
> miss • ~~pull~~ • score • steal • win

➔ *The children **are going to pull** the string.*

  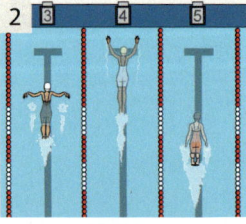      

b What do you think will happen AFTER the events you have described? Remember to use the *will*-future for predictions.

➔ *The man **will** probably **be** angry.*

▶ 5 A shopping trip *Will-* and *going to*-future contrasted ▸ 8.1, 8.2

Erklärvideo online:
cornelsen.de/webcodes
Code: rezace

Hanna, Reka and Leon are going to town to do some shopping. Finish the sentences, using either the *going to-* or the *will*-future.

Reka Let's go by bus, that ➔ ***'ll be*** (be) faster.
Leon All right. I prefer biking, but it looks like it … (rain) (1). What are everyone's plans?
Hanna Oh, I've decided, I … (buy) (2) that camera I wanted.
Reka Really? I'm sure it … (be) (3) cheaper on the internet.
Hanna I know, but I need it for the photography competition this week. I… (be) (4) a famous photo-grapher one day!
Leon Yeah, right. … (we, check out) (5) that ice cream parlour again?
Reka Sorry, I have no money this month. My sister … (be) (6) 18 in May, and my brothers and I … (buy) (7) her a new phone.
Leon Don't worry, I … (pay) (8) – you paid for the ice creams last week!
Hanna Well, then I … (have) (9) the biggest ice cream on the menu! Just kidding! OK, are we ready? We've got three minutes – there … (not be) (10) another bus for an hour if we miss this one.

6 Are you coming with us? Present progressive for arrangements ▸ 8.3

It's Saturday, and the Brown family are discussing their plans for the week with their daughter Kelly and their Italian exchange student Pietro. Make sentences with the present progressive.

→ **Mrs Brown**   I | visit | Grandma | on Monday
  I'm visiting Grandma on Monday.

1 I | make pizza | for you | at the weekend

7 Charlie and I | meet | on Thursday after school

2 I | skype with my parents | after dinner

6 Steve come over | for dinner | next Friday

3 I | have coffee with Jo | on Tuesday afternoon

5 My friend Suzie | help me revise maths | tonight

4 anybody | take me for my walk | today?

7 Summertime Future progressive ▸ 8.5

Everyone at school is looking forward to their summer holidays. What will they be doing this time next week? Complete their sentences using the future progressive.

Paul   Next week → *I'll be lying* (lie) on the beach.
Sirin And I … (sightsee) (1) in Paris. I can't wait.
Paul   What about you, Kim? What … (you, do) (2) this time next week?
Kim   Me? I … (sit) (3) in a plane on my way to Peru.
Emily Peru? Wow! Ben and I … (rock climb) (4) in the Alps.
Mia   You guys are so lucky! I … (work) (5) at the supermarket while you're all having fun.
Paul   Oh no! Poor you.
Mia   Well, it's only for two weeks. And then in August, Mum and I … (cycle) (6) along the Loire.
Emily Aw, that sounds nice. See? It isn't all bad.

8 We leave at 8.51 Simple present with future meaning ▸ 8.4

Rajiv has been asked to organize a class trip to Brighton to see a play. Complete his presentation of the itinerary with the verbs in the correct tense. Be careful – not all the verbs are in the simple present form.

Theatre Trip to Brighton
Tuesday, 11th March
Meet at station 8.30 am
Train out: 8.51 – 9.22
Show: 10.00 – 11.45
Train back: 1.33 – 2.10 pm

OK, so we → *go* (go) on our theatre trip next Tuesday. We … (meet) (1) at 8.30 am at the train station. The train … (leave) (2) here at 8.51 and … (arrive) (3) at 9.22. Then we … (not have) (4) much time to get to the theatre because the show … (start) (5) at ten. The play … (finish) (6) at 11.45, and the train home … (not leave) (7) until 1.33 pm, which means that we … (have) (8) some time. So, Ms Reid, would you like to have a hamburger with us on the way to the station? Of course, we … (pay) (9). Aren't we nice? We … (return) (10) home at 2.10, and so, sadly, we … (miss) (11) afternoon lessons that day. Er, I mean, … (we, get) (12) those lessons off, Ms Reid?

8

9 Next year ...   Mixed future forms   ▶ 8

It's New Year's Eve, and people are chatting.
Pick the better form of the verb.

Patsy   I think ➔ it snows soon | ***it's going to
snow soon***.

Len   We're going to the mountains | We'll go
to the mountains (1) tomorrow.
Are you coming | Do you come (2)?

Patsy   Yeah, of course. Say, do you like *Dinner for One*? Wait, I switch on | I'll switch on (3) the TV for you.

Joel   Hey, Alex! Where are you going to live | will you be living (4) this time next year?

Alex   No idea! But I do know I'm not going to light | I don't light (5) any fireworks later. I hate fireworks!

Bev   If I try to phone my family later after midnight, I'm sure I won't get through | I'm not going to
get through (6).

Ethan   Any New Year's resolutions? What are you going to change | What are you changing (7) next year?

Olivia   I bet I'm not going to keep | I bet I won't keep (8) my New Year's resolutions.

Ethan   If we won't fill | we don't fill (9) our glasses now, we'll be | we're (10) late for the New Year!

➕ 10 Maths problems   Future perfect   ▶ 8.6

a Here are four mathematical problems. Read them
carefully and calculate the result. Write down the answer
in a full sentence using the future perfect.

➔ Sidra came to Germany in January 2016. She'll be 18 in
July 2028. How long will she have been in Germany on
her birthday?
*She**'ll have been** here for twelve and a half years.*

1   Mirko is saving up for the racing bike of his dreams. It costs €1500. He's got €850, but his after-school
job only pays €65 a month. When will he have saved enough?

2   It's 9.00 am. Little Red Riding Hood is walking through the forest to visit Grandma. It's four miles to go
and she walks at two miles an hour. The wolf is heading the same way and will arrive at noon. Will he
have already arrived when she reaches Grandma's?

3   In 2010, the world was using oil at the rate of about 40 million tonnes every ten years; experts calculated
then that there were about 200 million tonnes in the ground. So, at this rate, by what year will our oil
reserves have run out, roughly?

4   The world's fastest tortoise takes about 4 seconds to walk a metre. Say his keeper puts him in the
middle of a large lawn in their park, 100m from the edge, and takes a short break, returning 7 minutes
later. Will the tortoise have left the lawn when he returns?

b   NOW YOU Make up a maths task like the ones above, and give it to your partner. The question
should be: What will or won't have happened at a certain time in the future?

+ 11 The optimist   Other ways of expressing future time   ▸ 8.7

a Ben is sure that his family are 'on a roll' this year; he's really optimistic for everybody. Read what he says and then rewrite each sentence using the phrase given.

➔ Mum will get a promotion at work very soon now. (about to)
*Mum is **about to get** a promotion at work.*

1 My grandad will probably retire this year. (would like to)
2 Our family will be moving to a bigger house before summer. (be certain to)
3 Maybe my sister will marry in September. (hope to)
4 Our cat is going to have kittens any day now. (be about to)
5 If nothing bad happens, I'll pass my school leaving exam at the end of term. (expect to)
6 The girl I fancy will definitely fall madly in love with me. ☺ (be sure to)
7 But my football team probably won't stay in the league at the end of the season. ☹ (be unlikely to)

b NOW YOU What about you? What is about to or sure to or unlikely to happen next in your life? Write four or five sentences using phrases like the ones in a to express the future.

+ 12 Challenges ahead – but progress too   Mixed future forms   ▸ 8

Challenges are in store for us in the future – but so are a lot of bright ideas to deal with them. Complete the sentences with the best form to express the future.

What ➔ **will the future bring** (future, bring)? We hear a lot about the challenges that … (face) (1) us in the years to come. But when the challenges do arrive, people … (not just sit) (2) on their hands. Here are just a few of the helpful inventions that … (become) (3) available to us over the next few years.

Before the end of the decade, robotics … (advance) (4) tremendously. The robots … (not just do) (5) all the boring factory work that we don't want to do. They … (also, read) (6) human emotions, providing help and even care for people who need it.

There is a lot of evidence that people will live much longer in the future. Groups like *Jugend forscht* are already working on prototypes of gadgets that … (make) (7) life easier for older people. One such project is a cup fixed to a gyroscope; in a care home of the future this … (stabilize) (8) it in the hand of a Parkinson's patient – the drink … (not spill) (9) out.

Here are just two examples of progress in medicine: Year by year, doctors … (be able to) (10) transplant more organs more easily. Or how about this: Supposing you got a tattoo done as a teenager. Maybe you … (not want) (11) it anymore when you … (grow up) (12). Scientists are optimistic that, in a few years' time, they … (be able to) (13) provide a solution to remove it much less painfully than today.

In a couple of decades, we … (all live) (14) in a super-mobile world. By then, self-driving cars and trucks … (be perfected) (15), ensuring that the number of serious accidents on our highways … (drop) (16). Furthermore, drones … (be developed) (17) that … (be able to) (18) deliver emergency supplies to people that today are too remote to reach.

And with the help of all those robots, we … (be likely to) (19) be enjoying a four-day working week in the not-too-distant future. So, what … (you, do) (20) on your three-day weekends?

8

Quick Check

A Complete the sentences using either the present progressive or the *will*-future.

1 We're off to the burger bar for lunch; … (you, come) with us?
2 Believe me, you … (not be able to) use that ticket on this train!
3 You want to drop off a parcel at your friend's? I … (drive) you there, OK?
4 I talked to Geoff this morning; we … (meet) down at the club tonight.
5 You need to have a talk with the boss; I'm sure he … (help) you out.
6 We … (go) to that cool new café tomorrow. Would you like to come?
7 I can't stand Ally and her gang. So I … (not go) to Jack's party.
8 The pizzeria is closed and they … (not open again) until Monday.

B Decide which form fits the context best.

1 Oh hello Steve, I was about to | certain to call you!
2 I've had enough of delayed flights; next year, I take | 'm going to take the train.
3 When I come in tonight, my parents will wait | will be waiting for me.
4 I'll be there at nine o'clock. Or will you have left | will you leave by then?
5 As soon as he will have | has his results, he will call us.
6 He's failed the exam twice and he told me he will not | 's not going to try again.
7 Don't hurry your breakfast; stores in Britain mostly don't | aren't going to open before ten.
8 Have you heard? We 're spending | 'll spend tonight on the beach.

C Find and correct the mistakes in each sentence.

1 Stay there. I help you!
2 From the look of the clouds, it snows soon.
3 If you don't hear from us, we are going to be out.
4 My friend will become a vet. At least, that's what he says.
5 Don't go so fast – you crash into that lorry!
6 My parents spend Easter in Majorca this year.
7 We call you when we get home.
8 We spend next Christmas in Thailand.

D Use the most fitting tense to finish these sentences.

1 I can't meet you in the afternoon, … (weil ich meine Hausaufgaben noch nicht gemacht haben werde)
2 If this computer crashes one more time, … (schreie ich)
3 Maybe we should try to book the evening flight; … (er startet um 19.00 Uhr)
4 I can't do this maths homework. – I … (helfe dir) later.
5 How many tickets for that show … (wirst du bestellen?)
6 Grandma won't be free tomorrow afternoon, because … (sie passt auf ihre Enkelkinder auf)

9 The passive

Task	Topic	Example	Englische Grammatik
1	Active and passive	*We did it together. The work has been done.*	9.1
2	Tenses: Simple present	*are done*	9.2.1
3	Tenses: Simple past	*were done*	9.2.1
4	Tenses: Present perfect	*have been done*	9.2.1
5	Tenses: Past perfect	*had been done*	9.2.1
6	Future tenses	*will be done / are going to be done*	9.2.1
7	Modal verbs + passive infinitive	*Can anything be done?*	9.2.2
8	The use of the passive	*Do you know when John Lennon was shot?*	9.3
9	Passive sentences with *by*	The History Boys *was written by* Alan Bennett.	9.4
10	Prepositions in passive sentences	*Crime statistics are being looked at carefully.*	9.5.1b
11	Passive verbs with one object	*She thought she was being followed.*	9.5.1
12	Passive verbs with two objects	*The first prize was awarded to her sister.*	9.5.2
13	The passive participle	*I've never seen a ship being launched.*	9.6.3
14	The passive infinitive and gerund	*She hopes to be chosen for the new modelling show on TV. She loves being filmed.*	9.6.1 9.6.2
15	Verbs of speaking and thinking (1)	*It is thought that the President will attend the meeting.*	9.5.3
16	Verbs of speaking and thinking (2)	*Several children are reported to have been injured in the explosion.*	9.5.3

▶ Quick Check p. 89

1 How your time is spent Active and passive ▶ 9.1

Here are some interesting statistics from a new survey on how young teenagers spend their free time.

a Read the sentences and write ⟦A⟧ if the underlined word is an active verb or ⟦P⟧ if it is a passive verb.

→ Many teenagers in the UK don't spend **A** much time outside. Their time is spent **P** inside.

1 Both girls and boys like ⟦ ⟧ playing computer games.
2 Chatting on social media is preferred ⟦ ⟧ by girls.
3 Less TV is watched ⟦ ⟧ today than it was ten years ago.
4 Fitness has become ⟦ ⟧ a typical teenage problem.
5 Many teenagers are driven ⟦ ⟧ to school by their parents.
6 New sports centres have been opened ⟦ ⟧ in the bigger towns and cities.
7 A lot more after-school activities are offered ⟦ ⟧ than 20 years ago.
8 Not many teenagers get ⟦ ⟧ weekend or holiday jobs.

b NOW YOU What do you do in your free time? How much of that time is spent outside? Write three sentences about yourself and your friends with active verbs and three sentences with passive verbs.

⊙ 2 How often is it done? Tenses: Simple present ▶9.2.1

Erklärvideo online:
🗋⊙ **cornelsen.de/webcodes**
╋◁) **Code: mogazo**

Leila has a weekend job in a 4-star hotel. We asked her about the tasks she has to do every day. Use the words given to make questions and answers as in the example.

→ tables | polish
*How often **are** the tables **polished**? – **They are polished** every day.*

1 beds	make	3 baths and toilets	clean	5 towels	change
2 bins	empty	4 television	check	6 mini-bar	refill

b There are some tasks that aren't done every day. Make questions and negative sentences.

→ walls | not paint
***Are** the walls **painted** every day? – No, **they aren't painted** every day.*

1 windows	clean	3 grass in the garden	cut	5 restaurant menu	update
2 mirrors	polish	4 fire alarm	test	6 dining room	redecorate

c NOW YOU What cleaning jobs are done in your house every day? What isn't done daily?

⊙ 3 A quick quiz Tenses: Simple past ▶9.2.1

Erklärvideo online:
▶ **Exercise 2**

Form the quiz questions in the simple past passive. Choose an answer from the box.

> Alexander Fleming • Athens • ~~Charles Lindbergh~~ • Lena • London • 1990 • 2006 •
> Sergey Brin and Larry Page • Snow White and the Seven Dwarfs

→ who | first solo non-stop flight across Atlantic | complete by
*Who **was** the first solo non-stop flight across the Atlantic **completed by**? **It was completed** by Charles Lindbergh.*

1 when | the World Cup | play in Germany
2 where | the world's first underground railway | build
3 where | first modern Olympics | hold
4 who | the Eurovision Song Contest | win by in 2012
5 what | first animated Disney movie | call
6 when | Germany | officially reunite
7 who | first antibiotic | discover by
8 who | Google | invent by

Alexander Fleming in his lab

9

▶ 4 Town hit by earthquake   Tenses: Present perfect   ▶ 9.2.1

Erklärvideo online:
▶ Exercise 2

a A news editor has been asked to write headlines for these incidents. First complete the sentences with a verb from the box. Then change the sentences into headlines as in the example.

> arrest • destroy • find • open • ~~photograph~~ • rescue • win

→ Someone has … a young princess on a French ski slope.
*Someone has **photographed** a young princess on a French ski slope.*
YOUNG PRINCESS PHOTOGRAPHED ON FRENCH SKI SLOPE

1 Someone has … a missing walker from a Swiss mountain. MISSING WALKER …
2 Kids have … ten little dogs in a rubbish bin in Corby. …
3 A gold medallist has … a new swimming pool. …
4 The police have … the bank robbers. …
5 A German film has … an Oscar. …
6 A hurricane has … thousands of homes. …

b Isla is reading out the headlines from her news updates app. Read the headlines and write what Isla says to her friend, using the passive and the present perfect tense.

→ TOWN IN ITALY HIT BY EARTHQUAKE
*A town in Italy **has been hit** by an earthquake.*

1 TWO GIRLS INJURED BY CROCODILE
2 NEW GERMAN CHANCELLOR ELECTED
3 HOLIDAY COTTAGES BURNT DOWN IN CORNWALL
4 CHIEF OF POLICE ARRESTED FOR SHOPLIFTING
5 NEW SHOPPING CENTRE OPENED IN MANCHESTER
6 TOP MODEL VOTED WORST DRESSED CELEBRITY

▶ 5 The window had been broken   Tenses: Past perfect   ▶ 9.2.1

Erklärvideo online:
▶ Exercise 2

a There's been a break-in in your street. Complete the police officer's report, using the passive and the past perfect tense.

SOCO report

When I arrived at 6 Holly Lane, the burglar → **had already gone** (already go) and the owners, two sisters Edna Barlow (83) and Betty Barlow (79), were very upset. Their dog, who must have heard the burglars and run out into the garden, … (shoot) (1).

5 Fortunately the dog … (not kill) (2), only injured, and it … (already take) (3) to the vet by a kind neighbour. The kitchen window … (break) (4), so that is how the burglar entered. The bedrooms … (search) (5), and there were clothes, books and personal items all over the floor. All the cupboards … (empty) (6). Some of the women's jewellery … (steal) (7), including a valuable diamond ring. Luckily, the cash box, which was hidden in
10 a safe behind a picture on the wall, … (not find) (8). Having checked for fingerprints, I realized that the burglar must have worn gloves. However, on further examination, it became clear that the bathroom … (use) (9) because the toilet seat was up. Fingerprints … (leave) (10) on the seat. I am optimistic that these prints will give us enough information to catch the burglar.

9

b The chief of police has read the SOCO report and wants more information. Complete the memo he writes to the officer using the passive and the past perfect tense.

→ police | call | too late to catch the burglar?
Had the police **been called** too late to catch the burglar?

1 the burglar | see | by anyone before he entered the house?
2 he | attack | by the dog before he shot it?
3 the burglar | inform | by someone that there was jewellery in the house?
4 anyone | see | watching the house in the days before the break-in?
5 this house | break into | before?
6 the same fingerprints | find | in other break-ins in this area?

▶ 6 **What will be done when?** Future tenses ▶ 9.2.1

Erklärvideo online:
▶ **Exercise 2**

Your student committee is arranging the end of year school party, and the school principal is worried about the things that still have to be done. Complete the dialogue, using the passive and the future tense.

Principal I have some more questions about your school party. Where → **will** this party **be held** (hold)?
You A room … (reserve) (1) at the Holiday Inn on Broad Street.
Principal That's a very chic hotel for a school party. What sort of dress code … (expect) (2)?
You Oh, don't worry about that, sir! Only the most glamorous dresses … (wear) (3)!
Principal Well, I only hope the boys know how to dress smartly too. When … (the final reservation, make) (4)?
You That … (do) (5) on Friday, as soon as we have the exact numbers.
Principal I hope there won't be any alcohol there.
You Don't worry, sir. Everyone … (offer) (6) water and juice only.
Principal Well, that's good, because parents always want to know. And how will you all get home?
You Several taxis … (order) (7) for the night of July 11th. And the band … (book) (8) for that night too.
Principal On July 11th? What about your school exams? They … (not finish) (9)!
You Yes, they will! All the exams … (complete) (10) by the 10th – I've checked.

Principal Ah, I see. All right, but the results … (not announce) (11) by then.
You Exactly, sir. So we can all have a good time without having to worry about our results!
Principal And … (the teachers, invite) (12)?
You The teachers, sir?

7 It must be done   Modal verbs + passive infinitive   ▶ 9.2.2

Erklärvideo online:
▶ Exercise 2

There's a new fitness centre in town, but there are a lot of dos and don'ts. Complete the rules using modal auxiliary verbs and the passive infinitive.

➔ An adult must accompany any children under the age of 18.
*Any children under the age of 18 **must be accompanied** by an adult.*

1 You can use all the equipment in the gym – at your own risk. All the equipment …
2 You must show ID cards at reception. ID cards …
3 You may not bring in any food or drink (except water). No food …
4 Customers should pick up towels, water bottles and put litter in the litter bin. Towels …
5 In the interests of hygiene, you must clean each piece of equipment for the next user. Each piece …
6 You should bring only clothing suitable for working out. Only clothing …
7 Customers must not wear boots, street shoes or sandals. No boots, …
8 You may not take photographs in the gym or the changing rooms. No photographs …

8 Where were your jeans made?   The use of the passive   ▶ 9.3

Erklärvideo online:
cornelsen.de/webcodes
Code: gawiyo

a Jeans have an interesting history. Here is an article about everyone's 'must-have' item of clothing. Complete it with the correct passive form of the verbs given.

Who doesn't have a favourite pair of blue jeans? You can wear the same pair of jeans for years, if you treat them right – and then one day they ➔ *can be cut up* | must be cut up for summer shorts!

5 What has been known | is known (1) about the origin of jeans? Here are a few facts. They are made | are making (2) of denim. The word 'denim' originally came from the name of a strong material which were called | was called (3) 'serge de Nîmes',
10 after the French town of Nîmes.

The indigo dye that they use to colour denim is an organic dye with a characteristic blue colour. It hasn't been used | has been used (4) in India for centuries, and that is actually where it gets its name
15 from.

Perhaps the most famous name in jeans is Levi. Levi Strauss left his native Germany in 1851 to open a store in New York, where denim was sold | had been sold (5). Two years later, during the Gold Rush,
20 he moved to San Francisco, where another store will be opened | was opened (6). Levi was soon making strong denim work trousers for the gold miners. The rest is history.

Some believe that whole ecosystems will be
25 destroyed | have been destroyed (7) by our hunger for jeans since Levi's time. Today, you can buy cheaper jeans, which must be produced | are produced (8) in India or China, but is this the right or ethical thing to do? The process uses lots of water, often in places where there is not enough of it. 30
There are sometimes health problems for factory workers too.

The good news is that, when it comes to eco-friendly jeans, Levi's are again in the lead. Their effect on the environment have been reduced | has been 35 reduced (9) in recent years by using less water in the factories. In addition, a 'Worker Well-being' programme should be introduced | has been introduced (10) in many Levi factories. The aim of this programme is to improve the lives of the men, 40 women and children who make the jeans.

9

b Correct the statements using information from the text.

➜ Denim has been used in India for centuries.
*Denim **hasn't been used** in India for centuries. Indigo dye **has been used**.*

1 Gold was sold in Levi's first New York store.
2 His San Francisco store was opened in 1851.
3 Cheap jeans are destroyed in India and China.

4 A lot of oil is used in the making of jeans.
5 The lives of the factory workers will be saved by the "Worker Well-being" programme.

c **NOW YOU** When you buy jeans, what's important to you? Do you know where your jeans were made?

9 Who stole the *Mona Lisa*? Passive sentences with *by* ▶ 9.4

Read the sentences about famous art thefts. Make passive sentences using the active sentences given. Use the word *by* only when necessary.

➜ Leonardo da Vinci painted the *Mona Lisa*.
*The Mona Lisa **was painted by** Leonardo da Vinci.*

1 An Italian called Vincenzo Perugia stole the *Mona Lisa* from the Louvre in Paris.
2 Someone took Edvard Munch's famous painting *The Scream* from a Norwegian museum in 2004.
3 Detectives found Munch's stolen painting in 2006, but the thieves had treated it badly.
4 Someone stole Vincent van Gogh's *Poppy Flowers* from a museum in Cairo in 1978.
5 Ten years later, police discovered van Gogh's stolen painting in Kuwait, but art thieves broke into the museum again in 2010.
6 The police arrested two men, but no one has seen the painting since.
7 An art thief in Paris stole Picasso's *Le pigeon aux petits pois* but threw it into a rubbish bin when he got scared.
8 The Parisian rubbish collectors emptied the bin. They took the rubbish away and probably destroyed the painting.

10 Vandals or victims? Prepositions in passive sentences ▶ 9.5.1b

Nico is a social worker reporting on vandalism and violence in schools. He has found that many of the teenagers have not been well cared for at home. Change the active sentences from his report into passive sentences to make it more formal.

➜ Today, people often talk about problem teens on TV and on social media.
*Today, problem teens **are** often **talked about** on TV and on social media.*

1 Some kids had broken into schools.
2 Someone will have to pay for the repairs.
3 The police say that someone should talk to the vandals.
4 We know that someone is always laughing at the bullied kids.
5 In troubled homes, someone was always shouting at kids.
6 Social workers suggest that parents haven't brought these kids up properly.
7 Unqualified babysitters had looked after some of the children from a very young age.
8 We should consider special family situation in these cases.

11 The stuff that dreams are made of   Passive verbs with one object   ▶ 9.5.1

Dreaming is the subject of serious scientific study, but the interest in it is not new. Use the underlined words to change the active sentences into passive sentences.

→ Dreams have always fascinated <u>people</u>.
   *People **have always been fascinated** by dreams.*

Is it possible to interpret dreams? Is there a hidden message behind them? Since the days of Sigmund Freud, people have written <u>many books</u> (1) about that topic. But we still don't know what our dreams mean or why we dream at all. Dreams are often illogical, but people accept <u>them</u> (2) as normal. And no matter if a dream is clear or confusing, we forget <u>most of our dreams</u> (3).
Are there really hidden meanings in your dreams? Someone asked <u>three teenagers</u> (4) this question:
Myra: Hidden meanings? I'm not sure. My dreams are certainly weird. I often dream that people laugh at <u>me</u> (5) because of my clothes. This could mean I'm worried about how I look, but I don't think I care that much about what I wear.
Jonas: I think there might be. I get very nervous the night before an exam. I often dream that I'm running a marathon and someone has taken <u>my shoes</u> (6) just before the start. I interpret that as a hidden message.

Dana: Definitely. I used to have the same dream again and again. A monster with a long tail followed <u>me</u> (7) everywhere – I had no idea what that was about, but it wasn't very nice. Then I realized it was about a problem I had with a girl in my friendship group. In the end, we talked about it, and when we had solved <u>our problem</u> (8), the dreams stopped.

12 Were you given a form to fill in?   Passive verbs with two objects   ▶ 9.5.2

Susie and her friend Bella are doing some work experience in two different schools.

a Susie had to write a report about her experience. Rewrite the parts which are underlined without changing the meaning.

→ First <u>they gave me</u> a long form to fill in.
   *First **I was given** a long form to fill in.*

Then <u>the receptionist gave me</u> (1) a card with my name on it. <u>They showed me</u> (2) around the school. After that, <u>a teacher took me</u> (3) to the teachers' room. <u>They offered me</u> (4) a cup of coffee. <u>They haven't introduced me</u> (5) to any of the children yet. <u>Nobody asked me</u> (6) if I had any brothers or sisters. <u>A young teacher invited me</u> (7) to watch a lesson. <u>They're going to tell me</u> (8) more tomorrow.

b Bella's day was very different. Use the sentences from part a and the words in brackets to form Susie's questions and Bella's answers.

→ a long form | just a form to sign
   ***Were you given** a long form to fill in, Bella? – No, I **wasn't given** a long form. I **was** just **given** a form to sign.*

1 a card with your name on it | an ID badge
2 around the school | around one classroom
3 to the teachers' room | to the canteen
4 a cup of coffee | a light lunch
5 to any of the children | to all the dinner ladies
6 if I had any brothers or sisters | a lot of questions about my parents
7 to watch a lesson | to teach a lesson
8 tomorrow | next week

9

+ 13 Super talented? The passive participle ▶9.6.3

Sara had often dreamed of seeing a live talent show.

a Make one longer sentence using the pairs of sentences, starting with the words given and using the passive participle.

➔ Sara's town was chosen for a live performance of her favourite talent show. She decided to ask about tickets. Sara's town …

*Sara's town **having been chosen** for a live performance of her favourite talent show, Sara decided to ask about tickets.*

1 She was told how much the tickets cost. She changed her mind. Having been …
2 She was sent an advert for free tickets to the talent show. She applied for some. Having been …
3 The TV sponsor awarded her two tickets. She invited a friend. Two tickets …
4 She invited her friend. She waited for his answer. Her friend …
5 She received his answer. She arranged where to meet him. His answer …
6 Arrangements to meet outside the TV studio were made. They stood in a long queue. Arrangements …

b Match the sentence parts to complete Sara's description of her evening in the TV studio.

➔ *Have you ever watched a talent show **being made**?*

1	~~Have you ever watched~~	a	when the contestants were chosen.
2	We couldn't see the stage very well,	b	being told when they should laugh.
3	I hadn't watched the earlier show	c	the judges being introduced.
4	We were too late to hear	d	we were among the last to get in.
5	There was a long delay in semi-darkness	e	~~a talent show being made?~~
6	Having been shown to our seats,	f	having been given terrible seats.
7	Having been told to queue outside,	g	while the lights were being repaired.
8	Some audience members weren't happy	h	we finally saw our first performer.

+ 14 Bees need to be protected The passive infinitive and gerund ▶9.6.1, 9.6.2

a A Scottish beekeeper is interviewed for a radio programme about endangered species. Read the interview and choose the correct passive forms to complete the sentences.

Interviewer Why are bees so important to us?

Beekeeper Bees pollinate many hundreds of different plants. It ➔ ***should be understood*** | should understand | must understand that those plants would simply not be able to reproduce without them.

Interviewer How do farming methods affect bees?

Beekeeper Well, the modern farming systems depend on the work of bees, which must not be ignored | isn't being ignored | must have been ignored (1). Bees play a large role in agriculture. Farmers' bee colonies are moved around to different agricultural areas, and it is in this way that their crops are pollinated.

9

Interviewer	And these crops are important for human food, aren't they?
Beekeeper	Of course. And it needs remembering | must be remembering | is worth remembering (2) that many foods enjoyed by humans would disappear if the plants were not pollinated by bees.
Interviewer	Do you mean fruit?
Beekeeper	Not just fruit. Plants that are grown for cattle feed also has to be pollinated | mustn't be pollinated | have to be pollinated (3), and of course it is from cows that people get most of their dairy products. Moreover, the by-product of bee pollination is of course honey.
Interviewer	But we know that bees are endangered. Can you tell us why they should have been protected | must be protected | will be protected (4)?
Beekeeper	If a condition known as 'Colony Collapse Disorder' affects a bee hive, every single worker bee dies or vanishes. If this happens, the queen bee is left with only young bees that have not yet fully grown. Many hives will have been affected | must have been affected | needed to be affected (5) in 2014, when almost 40% of bee hives died in that year alone.
Interviewer	Yes, I remember reading a report about that survey. But do we know the reasons for this disorder?
Beekeeper	Farming methods that are used today are thought to be one of the main reasons. Bees need moving | are worth moving | dislike being moved (6) from farm to farm: it upsets them. Many of the bees' natural feeding areas have been lost, and chemical pesticides are harmful to bees too.
Interviewer	And, I suppose, climate change has had its impact on bees?
Beekeeper	Yes, climate change is definitely also a factor, but perhaps the biggest danger to bees is disease. The disease that is to be feared | doesn't need to be feared | shouldn't be feared (7) most is the varroa mite (Varroa destructor). As its Latin name suggests, this tiny parasite is very destructive.
Interviewer	Now, I understand that you live and work on one of two Hebridean islands which have become famous in the world of bees. Tell us about that.
Beekeeper	Yes, that's right, the islands of Colonsay and Oronsay are the first being given | to be given | not being given (8) sanctuary status for native Black bees.
Interviewer	Where exactly are these islands?
Beekeeper	They are off the west coast of Scotland. They were chosen as a nature reserve because the bee colonies there are genetically pure and had avoided to be attacked | being attacked | attacking (9) by the varroa parasite.
Interviewer	And I believe you were instrumental in protecting those colonies by law?
Beekeeper	I was indeed. I campaigned for a law worth passing | to be passing | to be passed (10) which made it illegal to bring any other bees onto the islands. The law was successfully passed in January 2013.
Interviewer	Well, good luck and thank you very much for joining us today.

b Why are bees so important? Summarize the basic facts from the interview, using the passive.

+ 15 It is thought that … Verbs of speaking and thinking ▶ 9.5.3

Much has been written about the stone circle at Stonehenge. There have been many theories about why it is there.

a Complete the text with the verbs in brackets.

The mystery of who built Stonehenge, and why it was built, continues to fascinate. The stone circle at Stonehenge ➜ **is thought to have been** (think | have | be) erected in early Neolithic times, possibly as a pagan celebration of the sun. It … (prove | be) (1) designed with mathematical precision, as the entrance of the circle matches perfectly the direction of the midsummer sunrise and the midwinter sunset.

This group of enormous standing stones … (believe | be) (2) the world's most famous prehistoric monument. It … (know | have | be) (3) built in several periods. Two types of stone were used at Stonehenge. The larger stones are called 'sarsens'. The tallest stands nine metres high and weighs 25 tons. The sarsens … (think | have | be) (4) carried 32 kilometres to the site.

The smaller 'bluestones' weigh much less, but they were brought from Wales, a distance of 225 kilometres. The first sarsen … (believe | have | be) (5) put there about 5,000 years ago. Nobody knows how such heavy stones … (can | have | be) (6) transported so far with the primitive tools they had then.

Many small hills over graves from the early Bronze Age have been found nearby. These … (say | be) (7) 'burial mounds' or 'tumuli'. Stonehenge … (seem | have | be) (8) visited often in the Roman period from AD 43, because many Roman objects have been discovered there. Today, along with a smaller and less famous stone circle at Avebury, Stonehenge forms the heart of a World Heritage Site.

b There are other passive verbs in the text. Find five of them.

➜ The mystery of who built Stonehenge, and why **it was built**, continues to fascinate.

+ 16 They're known to be rich Verbs of speaking and thinking ▶ 9.5.3

Owners of super yachts are feeling sorry for themselves. Make passive sentences with the words given.

➜ Antibes | think | be the biggest yacht port in Europe.
 *Antibes **is thought to be** the biggest yacht port in Europe.*

1 Billionaires' Quay | know | be home to the world's super yachts
2 The Cote d'Azur | say | be the playground of the rich and famous
3 It | think | that yacht owners here are among the wealthiest people in the world
4 This year Antibes | expect | be much quieter than usual
5 Taxes on fuel | know | rise from 15 % to 55 %
6 It | think | that this rise will cost the boat owners up to 20,000 euros a week
7 It | expect | that such an increase will upset many super yacht owners
8 Some billionaires | report | complain to the French president

Quick Check

A Complete the sentences using the correct passive forms.

1 Chatsworth House … (use) as a location in the 2005 film of *Pride and Prejudice*.
2 The Spanish language … (understand) in many parts of the world.
3 This printer … (repair) twice but it still doesn't work.
4 All the tickets … (sell out) soon, so hurry and book yours.
5 When we arrived, the official speeches … (already make).
6 … the articles for our school paper … (write) yet?

B Complete the sentences using modal auxiliaries and the passive.

1 Solutions to most the world's problems … (could | find) if politicians listened to each other.
2 Doors and windows … (should | shut) every evening before you leave the building.
3 Library books … (must | return) by the correct date.
4 No phones or tablets … (may | take) into the exam room.
5 All our projects … (should | finish) by yesterday but some are not ready.
6 Loud music and shouting … (cannot | tolerate) after midnight tonight.

C Rewrite the sentences with the passive form of the verbs, using the word *by* when necessary.

1 These days people do a lot of their food shopping on Sundays.
2 She told us to help ourselves to tea or coffee.
3 Someone has taken my coat by accident. This is not mine!
4 J.R.R. Tolkien wrote *Lord of the Rings*.
5 In 2016 they started the Tour de France in Yorkshire.
6 The bank manager asked Tom for all his contact details.

D Find and correct the mistakes.

1 It is believe that the French cave paintings at Lascaux are the oldest in the world.
2 The cyclist's accident was caused through ice on the road.
3 Jeans must not been worn to school.
4 Everyone knows who the Harry Potter books were written from.
5 It was a shocking event that will be talked for many years about.
6 Our house is thought to have built in the early 1900s.

E Complete the sentences using the correct passive forms.

1 On our last visit, we … (show) the quickest way to get to the museum.
2 Since his accident, my grandpa … (advise) not to drive without his glasses.
3 It … (recommend) that Hannes wore smart clothes for his interview.
4 When the meeting was over, we … (tell) to run or we'd miss the last bus.
5 I … (advise) to use an electric toothbrush when I was ten.
6 The Princess Royal … (expect) to attend the horse show tomorrow.

9

10 The infinitive

Task	Topic	Example	Englische Grammatik
1	Verb + *to*-infinitive	We *plan to stay* at a hotel in Dover.	10.3.2
2	Adjective + *to*-infinitive	The problem was *impossible to solve*.	10.3.4
3	Verb + object + *to*-infinitive	Ms Blake *reminded her students to finish* their work on time.	10.3.3
4	The *first/last/next/only* + *to*-infinitive	Amelia Earhart was *the first woman to fly solo* across the Atlantic.	10.3.5
5	*To*-infinitive or gerund after certain nouns (1)	I hope we'll have *a chance to visit* our cousins. / Our *chance of getting* a cheap flight is very slight.	10.3.6 11.6.3
6	*For* + noun/pronoun + *to*-infinitive	Why is that so hard *for you to accept*?	10.3.7
7	Question word + *to*-infinitive	Viktor doesn't know *what to do* with his free time.	10.3.8
8	Phrases + infinitive	You'*d better talk* to your parents first.	10.4.2
9	Verbs of perception + object + infinitive	I *saw them beat* Bayern München 1:0.	10.4.4
10	*Let/Make* + object + infinitive	Carolyn *let me use* her mobile. But she *made me pay* for the call to New York.	10.4.3
11	Infinitives with and without *to*	We *must wait* here. / We *have to wait* here.	10.3 10.4
12	Negative infinitives	I *didn't tell* you to open the window. I told you *not to open* the window.	10.2.5
13	*To*-infinitive or gerund after certain nouns (2)	Colin's *decision to speak* to the head teacher was not easy and the *thought of telling* him the truth filled him with fear.	10.3.6 11.6.3
14	Improving your style with infinitives	They told me *that I should wait* here. / They told me *to wait* here.	10.3.3 10.3.7 10.3.8 10.3.9
15	Passive, perfect and progressive forms of the infinitive	The software *needed to be updated*. You were *supposed to have finished* your work by Friday. / Your work was *supposed to have been finished* by Friday. Terry *may be working* in the garden.	10.2.2 10.2.3 10.2.4

10.3.2 Gerund or infinitive after certain verbs – see Chapter 11
10.3.3 Indirect commands and requests – see Chapter 15

▶ Quick Check p. 98

1 A gap year in Canada   Verb + *to*-infinitive   ▸ 10.3.2

a Stephanie is thinking about doing a gap year after finishing school. Translate the verbs in brackets using a verb from the box in the correct form.

➜ Stephanie … (wollen) go abroad after graduation.
*Stephanie **wants to** go abroad after graduation.*

1 She … (vorhaben) go to Canada for a year.
2 She … (hoffen) find a family that will take her on as an au pair.
3 If that doesn't work out, she'll … (versuchen) find a part-time job.
4 Her English teacher has … (anbieten) help her with the application.
5 She … (müssen) earn enough money to get by on her own.
6 She … (erwarten) become really good at English during her year in Canada.
7 If she … (es schaffen) find a job in Quebec, she can practise her French too.
8 She has … (beschließen) do translation work when she comes back to Europe.

decide
expect
hope
manage
need
offer
plan
try
~~want~~

b NOW YOU Perhaps you are thinking about doing a gap year. Write three sentences about your hopes and expectations for that year.

1 I would like …   2 I hope …   3 I expect …

2 After the test   Adjective + *to*-infinitive   ▸ 10.3.4

a The students in class 9E have just finished writing an English test. Complete the sentences below using an adjective from the box and a *to*-infinitive.

afraid • difficult • ~~easy~~ • important • impossible • pointless • sure

➜ **Selima**   'I had no trouble answering the questions.'
*Selima thinks the questions were **easy to answer**.*

Jared   'I couldn't always understand the speaker. He had a funny accent.'
Jared says the speaker was … (1)
Tom   'I know I'm going to get a good mark.'
Tom thinks he is … (2)
Lisa   'I simply couldn't do the last two tasks. Not a chance.'
Lisa is unhappy because the last two tasks were … (3)
Larry   'I don't want to see my test score. I'm too scared.'
Larry is … (4)
Carl   'Worrying about your score won't do you any good.'
Carl believes that it is … (5)
Teacher   'You must learn from your mistakes – that's what counts.'
The teacher tells the class that it is … (6)

b NOW YOU Imagine your best friend has failed a test and is afraid to tell their parents. What could you say? Use some of the expressions from part a.

10

3 Before the class trip   Verb + object + to-infinitive   ▶ 10.3.3

Herr Haberkorn is giving his English class some last-minute instructions before they leave for their class trip to London. Use the verb in brackets and a *to*-infinitive to express his statements indirectly.

➜ 'Be at the airport by 6 am.' (tell)
   *He **told them to be** at the airport by 6 am.*

1 'Bring your ID cards with you.' (remind)
2 'Exchange your money at a local bank.' (advise)
3 'In your free time, you can explore London in groups of three or more.' (allow)
4 'Don't go anywhere on your own.' (warn)
5 'Use your English.' (encourage)
6 'Please thank your parents for their support.' (ask)

4 Susan's Halloween party   The first/last/next/only + to-infinitive   ▶ 10.3.5

Susan gave a Halloween party for five of her friends. The table below gives you some information about them. Make complete sentences about Susan's guests using *the first / the last / the only* and an infinitive phrase.

	Mehmet	Felicia	Jackie	Ron	Peter
arrived at	09:10 pm	08:45 pm	09:20 pm	10:05 pm	10:05 pm
left at	11:05 pm	00:15 am	01:20 am	00:45 am	00:45 am
came by	bike	bus	bike	car	car
costume	vampire	witch	ghost	zombie	zombie

➜ Felicia | guest | arrive.
   *Felicia was **the first guest to arrive**.*

1 Ron and Peter | guests | arrive
2 Jackie | guest | leave
3 Mehmet | guest | leave
4 Felicia | guest | come by bus
5 Ron and Peter | guests | come by car
6 Jackie | guest | wear a ghost costume
7 Mehmet | guest | wear a vampire costume

5 That's the way to do it   To-infinitive or gerund after certain nouns   ▶ 10.3.6, 11.6.3

a Sort the nouns below into three groups: nouns that can be used with an infinitive (the ability to think), nouns that can be used with of + gerund (the advantage of having a big family) and nouns that can be used with an infinitive or a gerund (the chance to win / the chance of winning).

> ability • advantage • attempt • chance • courage • danger • decision • dislike • dream • hope • idea • need • opportunity • plan • possibility • reason • right • risk • strength • time • thought • way • will • willingness • wish

ability   chance   advantage

b Make complete sentences by attaching the second part of the sentence to the first using either *to* + infinitive or *of* + gerund. Sometimes both solutions are possible.

→ Leonie had the courage | face the difficulties in her life.
*Leonie had the courage **to face** the difficulties in her life.*

1 We want to give you the opportunity | show us your talent.
2 Is there any possibility | book an earlier flight?
3 Everyone has the right | form their own opinions.
4 The class made a final attempt | persuade the teacher to put off the test.
5 As a vet, Carmen is now living her dream | work with animals.
6 We'll continue the search as long as there is still hope | find survivors.
7 I was surprised at Ted's willingness | support our campaign.

6 A problem for you to solve   *For + noun/pronoun + to-infinitive*   ▸ 10.3.7

Complete the following sentences using *for* + noun/pronoun + *to*-infinitive.

→ Look at the time! We have to leave.
*It's time **for us to leave**.*

1 We can't start over again. It's too late.
  It's too late …
2 Don't try to carry that box. It's too heavy.
  That box is …
3 I've made a list of your most common mistakes. I want you to correct them.
  Here's a list of mistakes …

4 Your history teacher gave me a worksheet. You should do it in class.
  She gave me a worksheet …
5 The students had difficulty with Shakespeare's English. They didn't always understand it.
  Shakespeare's English was …
6 OK, I made a mistake. But you needn't get so angry about it.
  That's no reason …

7 Miriam's questions   *Question word + to-infinitive*   ▸ 10.3.8

Miriam has just come to London to study and she still has lots of questions. Write about her questions using a phrase from the box and a question word with a *to*-infinitive.

> Miriam would like to know …
> She isn't sure …
> She doesn't know …
> She wants to find out …

→ What should I do if I feel ill?
*Miriam doesn't know **what to do** if she feels ill.*

1 Who can I talk to if I have a problem?

2 What should I do if I lose my room key?

3 Where can I get an adapter for my laptop?

4 How can I meet other new students?

5 Which travel pass for public transport should I buy?

6 How can I find a cheap second-hand bike?

10

8 Giving (and taking) advice   Phrases + infinitive   ▶ 10.4.2

a Giving advice can be tricky, and it's best to be diplomatic about it. Rewrite the sentences using one of the phrases from the box and an infinitive.

> ➜ I think you should tell him the truth.
> **You'd better tell** him the truth.

> You'd better (not) … • Why not …? •
> I'd rather (not) … • I'd sooner (not) …

1 Why don't you phone him?
2 I'd prefer to put it in writing.
3 You could write him a letter.
4 I'd prefer to text him.
5 You really shouldn't have that conversation on the phone.
6 I don't want to see him ever again.

b Using one of the phrases from part a, complete the reply to each of the following statements.

> ➜ Terry has invited me to his party, but I've got a driving test the next morning.
> **You'd better** go to bed early.

1 You should go jogging every morning before school. It's the best way to keep fit!
   – … sleep a little longer.
2 I hate these glasses. They make me look like a nerd.
   – … try wearing contact lenses.
3 Let's go clubbing tonight.
   – … spend a quiet evening at home.
4 Every morning, I wake up with a really bad headache.
   – … see a doctor about that.
5 I know a really good Japanese restaurant in Mayfair. They've got fantastic sushi.
   – … go for a pizza. I don't like sushi.

9 A day in the life   Verbs of perception + object + infinitive   ▶ 10.4.4

Private detective Clive Gumshoe has been hired by actress Yvonne Sellafield, who believes that her husband Rick is having an affair. Below is the report he gives Ms Sellafield. Complete the sentences with a verb from the box (sometimes more than one answer is correct).

> watch • see • hear • listen to • notice

At 1:53 pm, I ➜ *watched* an attractive young woman get out of a taxi and enter the Victoria Hotel in Baker Street. Five minutes later, I … (1) Rick S. come around the corner and go into the hotel.
5 I followed him into the lobby. He went directly to the hotel bar, where the young woman was waiting for him. I … (2) them greet each other with a kiss and then sit down together at a table. I sat down at a nearby table where I could watch them easily. I … (3)
10 Rick S. tell the woman that he could only stay for an hour. Then I … (4) him take a small box out of his jacket pocket and hand it to her. When she opened it, I … (5) a big smile appear on her face. I … (6) them finish their drinks in a hurry and get up to leave. Rick S. handed the waitress a bank note, then 15 I … (7) them cross the lobby and disappear in a lift. At 3:14, I … (8) Rick S. come out of the lift and go to the reception desk. Standing just behind him, I … (9) him make a reservation for the following Friday. Then he left the hotel – alone. 20

10 Lucky Steve   *Let/Make + object + infinitive*   ▸ 10.4.3

Steve Donahue from Liverpool has found a great job as an au pair for the Rogers family in Melbourne. Complete the sentences with a form of *let* or *make*.

➔ The Rogers … him use their swimming pool whenever he likes.
*The Rogers **let** him use their swimming pool whenever he likes.*

1 Mrs Rogers … him use her car.
2 They don't … him do hard work.
3 They … him have a week off every two months.
4 They … him skype his friends back home in Britain.

5 Sometimes the Rogers' children … him play games with them.
6 He always … them win.
7 It … him laugh to see their happy faces.

11 Help wanted!   Infinitives with and without *to*   ▸ 10.3, 10.4

A German girl posted this message on an online forum for au pairs. Read her text and the comments, then decide whether or not *to* must be used in each of the gaps.

> Helpless: I've been an au pair for an American family for two months now. They've got five kids and live out in the country, in Ohio. I have my own room, and the family is really nice, but the only way to go anywhere here is by car, and I don't have one. And because I am always in and around the house, I spend all my time playing with the kids, helping them with their homework, doing housework, gardening … you name it. It's like I'm on the job 24 hours a day. I don't know if I should complain to my host parents – they don't have much money. They own two cars, but the parents need them all the time (together they have three jobs). Still, this isn't what being an au pair is supposed to be like, is it?

Comments:

Crazy Horse   You'd better ➔ look for a new job fast!

Starlet   That sounds pretty unfair. You ought … (1) talk to your host parents and ask them … (2) let you … (3) borrow a car at least once a week.

Buzzy   There's no reason for you … (4) put up with working conditions like that. It might be a good idea … (5) contact your home organization and complain.

Lawyer girl   What you describe sounds like modern slavery. You needn't … (6) work more than ten hours a day or 45 hours a week, and you must … (7) have a chance … (8) have free time. You also have the right to a free weekend once a month. Why not … (9) talk with your host parents about the problem? Or would you rather … (10) go on living like a slave?

10

12 How (not) to take a test   Negative infinitives   ▶ 10.2.5

Mr Williams' students don't always pay attention to what he tells them before a test. Use the information in the table below to say what he told them and what he didn't tell them to do.

→ He told them **not to use** red ink.

→ He **didn't tell them to use** red ink.

What Mr Williams said:

1 Don't copy from your neighbour.
2 Don't write more than one answer to each question.
3 Don't forget to write your name at the top of the page.

What Mr Williams didn't say:

4 Copy from your neighbour.
5 Write more than one answer to each question.
6 Forget to write your name at the top of the page.

+ 13 Time to clean up   *To-infinitive or gerund after certain nouns*   ▶ 10.3.6, 11.6.3

Niels P. went scuba diving on Ibiza and discovered something that changed his life and may help to save our planet.
Complete the sentences below using a *to*-infinitive or *of* + gerund and the words in brackets.

→ Niels got the idea … (start a campaign) when he went to Ibiza a few years ago.
*Niels got **the idea of starting a campaign** when he went to Ibiza a few years ago.*

1 He wanted to go scuba diving. But his dream … (explore an underwater paradise) came to an abrupt end when he found himself surrounded by plastic trash.
2 That was when he felt the need … (do something about this problem).
3 He made the decision … (collect photos) of beaches ruined by plastic pollution.
4 He saw the chance … (reach large numbers of people) via the internet.
5 When he returned home, he started a website called DrasticPlastic.net to give people the possibility … (post photos showing the effects of plastic pollution).
6 Niels is also grateful to research institutes for their willingness … (let him use their photos of plastic found in dead marine animals).
7 To date, more than 40,000 people have taken the time … (post photos from all over the world).
8 Niels thinks this is a good way … (call attention to a worldwide problem).

✚ 14 The fairy bell   Improving your style with infinitives   ▸ 10.3.3, 10.3.7, 10.3.8, 10.3.9

Improve the style of the following text by using an infinitive phrase instead of the parts in brackets.

One evening, some farmers are sitting in a pub in a small Irish town and playing a card game. When one of the farmers reaches into his pocket ➜ **to get some money** (because he needs some money), he
5 discovers that his money is gone, and a quarrel breaks out.

A stranger, who until then has been sitting quietly in the corner, comes over and says that he knows how ... (1) (he can
10 settle the argument). He reaches into his pocket and takes out a small silver bell. He tells the men at the table that this is a magic bell given to his great grandfather by a
15 fairy. The stranger puts the bell on the table and asks the owner ... (2) (if he could fetch the old iron pot) from the fireplace and put it over the bell. Then he ... (3) (says that he should turn off the lights). When it is completely dark, the stranger ... (4) (says
20 to the farmers that they should come) to the table one by one and put their hands on the pot. When the thief touches the pot, the bell will ring. The stranger waits ... (5)
25 (until everyone has taken his turn). But the bell doesn't ring. Then the stranger ... (6) (says that the owner should turn the lights on) again. He ... (7) (tells the farmers that they should show him their hands). All but one of them
30 have black hands. The only man ... (8) (who has white hands) is the thief, because he was ... (9) (afraid and wouldn't touch the pot).

✚ 15 Shakespeare's theatre   Passive, perfect and progressive forms of the infinitive   ▸ 10.2.2 – 10.2.4

Rewrite the sentences below using an infinitive construction instead of the underlined words.

➜ The first permanent theatre that was built in London was called simply 'the Theatre'.
The first permanent theatre **to be built** *in London was called simply 'the Theatre'.*

1 Since actors weren't allowed to perform plays in London, the first theatres were built across the Thames in Southwark.
Since plays couldn't ... in London, the first theatres were built across the Thames in Southwark.

2 It is believed that in the late 1580s a young man named William Shakespeare was working as an actor and writer in London.
A young man named William Shakespeare is believed ... as an actor and writer in London in the late 1580s.

3 Nowadays, people tend to connect Shakespeare's name with the Globe Theatre.
Nowadays, Shakespeare's name tends ... with the Globe Theatre.

4 But it seems that Shakespeare was already a well-known figure in London when the Globe was built in 1599.
But Shakespeare seems ... a well-known figure in London when the Globe was built in 1599.

5 Experts think that the wood used to build the Globe was taken from the Theatre.
The Globe is thought ... with wood taken from the Theatre.

6 It appears that Shakespeare ended his acting career in 1610, three years before the Globe was destroyed by fire.
Shakespeare appears ... his acting career in 1610, three years before the Globe was destroyed by fire.

10

Quick Check

A Combine the sentences. Start with the second one and make the first sentence into an infinitive phrase.

1 You must phone Grandpa this afternoon. Don't forget!
2 The head teacher won't discuss the matter. She refuses.
3 We weren't allowed to make a campfire. The ranger warned us.
4 We have to win the match on Saturday. Our coach expects it.
5 Our Australian cousins are visiting us this summer. My parents invited them.
6 Aleksandra can speak Russian. Her dad taught her.
7 Cara moved into a new flat last weekend. We helped her.
8 Jake has signed up for a dancing course. His girlfriend persuaded him.

B Make complete sentences using an infinitive.

1 I | sorry | hear about your accident
2 Leroy | glad | be back home in Atlanta
3 You | old enough | make your own decisions
4 My parents think | I | too young | stay out all night
5 The last two tasks | too difficult | Vitali | solve
6 It wasn't easy | me | say goodbye | my friends
7 Farah's parents think | important | her | get good marks
8 Will | be possible | us | make a day trip to Greenwich

C Rewrite the following sentences using an infinitive phrase instead of the underlined words.

1 My mum asked me if I would look after my little brother.
2 Our teacher reminded us that we had to bring our ID cards on Monday.
3 How could you forget that you should close the windows before leaving the house?
4 I still haven't worked out how I can change my settings on this site.
5 Rakhida promised that she would help us with the posters for the concert.
6 The band members agreed that they would meet an hour earlier for the sound check.
7 The angry hotel guest demanded that he should be allowed to speak to the manager.
8 We decided that we would take the train instead of driving.
9 Hillary Clinton was the first woman who ran for president.
10 Larissa hopes that she will win a prize in the competition.

D Each of the sentences below contains one mistake. Find and correct it.

1 I can't afford going away this summer.
2 If you don't mind, I'd rather to wait for the bus.
3 My parents don't want that I study medicine.
4 The teacher made the students to leave their mobiles outside the room.
5 We're driving to the coast this weekend. Would you like coming with us?
6 You ought have told me earlier about your problem.
7 I expect that you will help me with the project.
8 This song always lets me feel sad.

10

11 The gerund

Task	Topic	Example	Englische Grammatik
1	The gerund as subject	*Shopping is fun.*	11.4
2	The gerund as object	*Sue enjoys painting.*	11.5.1
3	Gerund or infinitive after certain verbs	*I like to cook/cooking.*	11.5.1 11.5.2
4	Gerund or infinitive: same verb, different meaning	*Oh no! I forgot to pack my mobile!* *I'll never forget seeing Paris by night.*	11.5.3
5	Adjective + preposition + gerund	*Jackie is really good at doing card tricks.*	11.6.1
6	The gerund after prepositions	*Frank left the shop without paying.*	11.6
7	Noun + preposition + gerund	*What are the disadvantages of living in the country?*	11.6.2
8	Fixed phrases with the gerund	*There's no point waiting any longer.*	11.7
9	Verb + preposition + gerund	*Don't worry about catching the train.*	11.6.3a
10	Verb + object + preposition + gerund	*Thank you for helping us with the project.*	11.6.3b
11	The passive form of the gerund	*Samantha enjoys being photographed.*	11.2.2

▶ Quick Check p. 104

1 Talking about hobbies   The gerund as subject   ▶ 11.4

Form gerunds from the words on the left and use them to complete the sentences on the right.

➔ *Collecting stamps is a bit old-fashioned.*

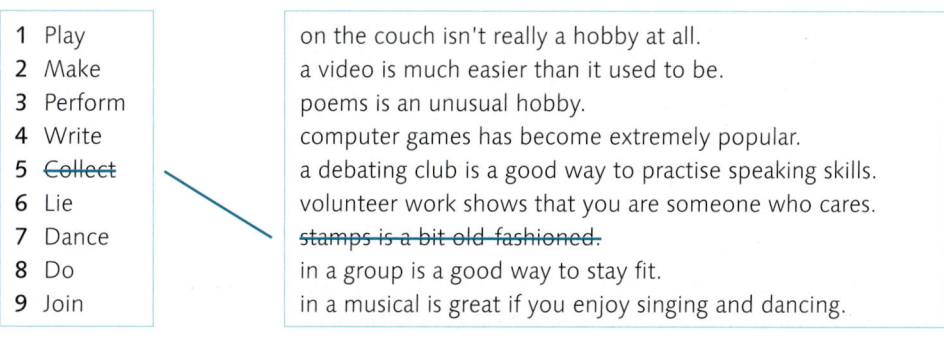

1 Play	on the couch isn't really a hobby at all.
2 Make	a video is much easier than it used to be.
3 Perform	poems is an unusual hobby.
4 Write	computer games has become extremely popular.
5 ~~Collect~~	a debating club is a good way to practise speaking skills.
6 Lie	volunteer work shows that you are someone who cares.
7 Dance	~~stamps is a bit old-fashioned.~~
8 Do	in a group is a good way to stay fit.
9 Join	in a musical is great if you enjoy singing and dancing.

The gerund

▶ 2 A dream career? The gerund as object ▶ 11.5.1

Luis is a brilliant football player. He has been offered a place at an exclusive sports academy in southern Germany. Complete the sentences below using the underlined verbs and a gerund phrase.

Erklärvideo online:
📄▶ cornelsen.de/webcodes
➕🔊 Code: boqemu

→ You could <u>apply</u> to a sports academy.

→ His coach suggested …
*His coach suggested **applying** to a sports academy.*

1 I may <u>accept</u> the offer.
2 It'd be great to <u>have</u> the chance to concentrate on my sports skills.
3 It'd be OK if I had to <u>practise</u> a lot every day.
4 But I won't be able to <u>see</u> my friends every day – that will be hard.
5 And I'll have to keep fit, so I can't <u>go</u> to any more all-night parties!
6 I sometimes <u>wonder</u> if it really is the right decision.
7 I still <u>feel</u> unsure about leaving home.
8 But then I think, hey man, you could <u>play</u> in a major-league team some day.

1 Luis is considering …	4 But he would miss …	7 He admits …
2 Luis says he would enjoy …	5 And he would have to give up …	8 But then he imagines …
3 He says he wouldn't mind …	6 Luis can't help …	

▶ 3 What belongs where?

Gerund or infinitive after certain verbs ▶ 11.5.1, 11.5.2

Erklärvideo online:
▶ Exercise 3

a Sort the verbs below into three groups: verbs that can be used with a gerund, verbs that can be used with an infinitive and verbs that can be used with a gerund **or** an infinitive.

> ~~risk~~ • ~~agree~~ • ~~like~~ • practise • hope • start • finish • dislike • keep • decide • seem • mention • offer • hate • continue • plan • expect • promise • want • prefer • begin

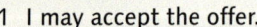

risk   like   agree

b NOW YOU Choose three verbs from the box on the left and three ideas from the box on the right, and write sentences about you and/or your friends (using a gerund or an infinitive).

→ *My friend Leon **hates doing** homework.*
  *Or: My friend Leon **hates to do** homework.*

love • like • enjoy • want • hate • prefer • expect • plan • hope	do homework • babysit for the neighbours • read novels • do sport • have a family • live abroad • earn a lot of money • be rich and famous

11

4 A bank robbery

Gerund or infinitive: same verb, different meaning ▶ 11.5.3

Erklärvideo online:
▶ **Exercise 2**

There was a bank robbery yesterday in the High Street. Timothy is telling the police what he saw.
Choose the correct form of the verbs.

I was just getting on the bus when I realized that I had forgotten ➜ buying | **to buy** a litre of milk at the supermarket. That meant walking | to walk (1) back to the supermarket and then waiting | to wait (2)
5 twenty minutes for the next bus. On the way I saw my mate Roger, who had just come out of the newsagent's, and we stopped talking | to talk (3). I remember noticing | to notice (4) a man in a black leather jacket standing in front of the bank on the opposite side of the street. I meant saying | to say 10
(5) goodbye to Roger, but at that moment a second man came running out of the bank with a metal suitcase in his hand. The two men ran over to a blue Ford Mustang and jumped in. I tried getting | to get
(6) a look at their faces, but I couldn't see them 15
clearly. And now for the good news: I did remember writing down | to write down (7) the car's registration number – here it is!

5 Talking about feelings Adjective + preposition + gerund ▶ 11.6.1

Combine the sentences below using a gerund phrase and a preposition. You must add a preposition.

➜ Suzie is going to L.A. for a year. She's really excited.
  *Suzie is really **excited about going** to L.A. for a year.*
➜ She doesn't know many people there. She's a bit worried.
  *She's a bit **worried about not knowing** many people there.*

1 We didn't make it to the final. We were very disappointed.
2 Jared won first prize for his short story. He's proud.
3 Catriona's not coming to my party. She's really sad.
4 Marco suggested going to the cinema. I wasn't interested.
5 I know I hurt your feelings. I'm really sorry.
6 Sandra is taking her driving test tomorrow. She's very nervous.
7 Tarik left his mobile in the café. He's really angry.
8 In the end, we didn't have to rewrite our essays. We were glad.

6 Liz and Jeremy The gerund after prepositions ▶ 11.6

Rewrite the sentences about Liz and her brother Jeremy using the preposition in brackets and a gerund phrase.

➜ Liz may be the smallest girl in her class, but she knows how to get her own way. (in spite of)
  ***In spite of being** the smallest girl in her class, Liz knows how to get her own way.*

1 Jeremy earns extra pocket money. He does garden work for the neighbours. (by)
2 Liz meets her friends in the afternoon. But first she finishes her homework. (before)
3 Jeremy sometimes leaves the house even though he hasn't done his homework. (without)
4 Jeremy wants to do a gap year when he has finished school. (after)
5 Liz wants to study drama. She doesn't want to do a gap year. (instead of)
6 Liz and Jeremy get on well, even though they are very different. (in spite of)

11

7 Travel-India.com   Noun + preposition + gerund   ▶ 11.6.2

Travelling to India

- ◉ How to meet interesting people
- ◉ How to find the best hostels
- ◉ Why you shouldn't travel alone
- ◉ What to eat …

What questions might the girl in the photo have? Complete the questions below using a gerund phrase.

→ What is the best way | meet interesting people?
*What is the best **way of meeting** interesting people?*

1 What's the best way | find a good hostel?
2 What is the main reason | not travel alone?
3 What about the risk | eat the wrong food?
4 How great is the danger | get robbed?

5 What are the advantages and disadvantages | travel by train?
6 Is there any chance | see the 'real' India?
7 What about the possibilities | find help in an emergency?

8 A difficult task   Fixed phrases with the gerund   ▶ 11.7

Tarik and Filip are having problems in their maths lesson. Rewrite the underlined sentence parts using the words in brackets.

→ **Tarik**   These maths exercises are awful.
  Filip   I know. <u>I hate doing exercises like this</u>. (It's no fun | do)
  ***It's no fun doing** exercises like this.*

Tarik   Can you help me with this task?
Filip   Sorry, <u>I'm already into the next task</u>. (I'm busy | do) (1)
Tarik   Should I ask Dan for help?
Filip   <u>It doesn't make much sense to ask him</u>. (There's no point | ask) (2)
Tairik   Do you understand task 5b?
Filp   Are you kidding? <u>I had trouble with 5a</u>. (I had a hard time | understand) (3)
Tarik   <u>I don't know why I should just sit here</u> if I can't solve the tasks. (It's no use | sit) (4)
Filip   <u>Why don't you ask Mr King for a couple of tips?</u> (How about | ask) (5)
Tarik   <u>It's a waste of time</u>. He never helps! (It's not worth | ask) (6)

9 Josh's dream   Verb + preposition + gerund   ▶ 11.6.3a

Combine the sentence parts with a preposition from the box to write about Josh's dream.

→ Josh often talks | become a famous musician.
*Josh often **talks about becoming** a famous musician.*

1 Josh dreams | make it big in the music scene.
2 He sometimes thinks | leave school and tour with his band.
3 His parents think he should concentrate | get better marks at school.
4 Josh seldom worries | fail his exams.
5 He's sure he will succeed | pass all his courses.
6 He's looking forward | finish school and spend more time on his music.

> about • in • of • on • to

✛ 10 The hotel theft   Verb + object + preposition + gerund   ▶ 11.6.3b

Inspector Carnaby was sent to the Royal Seaside Hotel to investigate a mysterious theft.
Rewrite sentences 1–7 using a gerund phrase and the verb in brackets. You must add a preposition.

→ Carnaby told the guests not to leave the hotel before they had been questioned. (stop)
*Carnaby **stopped the guests from leaving** the hotel before they had been questioned.*

1 He told the staff not to withhold information – it would have serious consequences. (warn)
2 The barman gave him a useful tip, for which he was grateful. (thank)
3 The hotel manager was angry with the chambermaid because she had left the door of one of the rooms open. (criticize)
4 The chambermaid said the bellboy hadn't locked the door. (blame)
5 Carnaby believed that the chambermaid was not telling the complete truth. (suspect)
6 In the end, Carnaby said the chambermaid had stolen the jewellery. (accuse)
7 The manager was pleased that Carnaby had solved the crime so quickly. (congratulate)

✛ 11 What teens hate most   The passive form of the gerund   ▶ 11.2.2

a Here is a 'most hated' list from a teen magazine. Rewrite each of the items using a gerund in the passive form and a verb from the box on the right.

→ When grownups call them 'spoiled'
*They hate **being called** 'spoiled' (by grownups).*

1 When teachers treat them unfairly
2 When adults talk down to them
3 When people stare at them
4 When their parents don't take them seriously
5 When authority figures push them around
6 When people expect them to conform
7 When older people give them advice
8 When their parents constantly tell them what to do

> • They're fed up with …
> • They hate …
> • They complain about …
> • They object to …
> • They can't stand …
> • They dislike …

b **NOW YOU** What do you really dislike?

Quick Check

A **Choose the correct verb form. Sometimes both are correct.**

1 Tarek suggested going | to go to a café for something to eat.
2 The students continued writing | to write, even though the bell had rung.
3 We hope being | to be able to meet with our cousins while we are in the USA.
4 Julia is a mystery to me – I think she actually enjoys doing | to do history.
5 Would you like watching | to watch a DVD this evening?
6 I'm really sorry – I meant phoning | to phone you, but somehow I forgot.
7 Has Aleksandra finished painting | to paint the poster yet?
8 To improve your technique, practise playing | to play for at least 15 minutes every day.
9 Viktor has tried to stop smoking | to smoke at least five times.
10 I know you dislike walking | to walk, so I've already phoned for a taxi.

B **Correct the marked mistakes. Add prepositions where necessary.**

1 I'm really looking forward to see my family again.
2 Philip's idea to leave school and join the navy shocked his parents.
3 We had trouble to install this program. — I still don't understand why.
4 Is there any possibility to see a musical while we're in London?
5 A mobile is useful to make phone calls while you're on the go.
6 How long did it take Fiona to get used to live in Malaysia?
7 Mandy finally succeeded to persuade her parents to let her go to the rock festival.
8 David didn't want to try skiing because he was afraid to break his arm or leg.

C **Translate the words in brackets using a gerund.**

1 Please close all windows (bevor Sie das Gebäude verlassen).
2 I can't believe Sharon would just move away (ohne Auf Wiedersehen zu sagen).
3 You can improve your English (indem du jeden Tag fünf neue Wörter lernst).
4 I can remember (dich zum ersten Mal zu treffen).
5 Are any of you interested (das Museum zu besuchen)?
6 The sun is shining – let's walk (anstatt den Bus zu nehmen).

D **Rewrite the following sentences, replacing the underlined words with a gerund construction. Add prepositions where necessary.**

1 Priscilla is so publicity-hungry – I think she actually enjoys it when paparazzi chase her.
2 The head teacher congratulated the students who had won the prize.
3 I would like to thank you because you have been so patient with me.
4 Daniel dislikes it when his parents treat him like a child.
5 Paul apologized because he was late.
6 Nobody likes the feeling that others are laughing at them.

11

12 Participles

Task	Topic	Example	Englische Grammatik
1	Participles used like adjectives	*A helping hand would be nice.* *I can't do the dishes with a broken arm.*	12.4.1a
2	Adjectives ending in -ing and -ed	*The film sounds interesting. Are you interested in watching it?*	12.5
3	Using a participle instead of a relative clause	*Most of the people waiting in the queue were middle-aged or older.*	12.4.2
4	Verbs + present participle	*Do you want to go swimming with us?*	12.6.1
5	Verbs + object + present participle	*I saw Tarik and Lia sitting in a café.*	12.6.2
6	Mixed exercise	*Mira was frightened. She heard someone coming closer.*	12.4 12.5 12.6
7	Participle clauses of time (1)	*While working for Oxfam, Jill learned a lot about being poor.*	12.7.1
8	*Have* + object + past participle	*When did you last have your teeth checked?*	12.6.3a
9	Two-part participle attributes	*This is a well-written essay.*	12.4.1b
10	Infinitive or participle after verb of perception	*I saw him break into the shop. /* *I saw him breaking into the shop.*	12.6.2
11	Expressions with participles	*Judging by her reaction, Suzanne wasn't pleased with the results.*	12.4.2 12.6.2a 12.8c
12	Participle clauses of time (2)	*Having saved his work, Karim shut down his laptop.*	12.7.1
13	Participle clauses of reason, circumstance and result	*Wanting to help, I volunteered to do the cooking. Feeling bored and angry, Jason walked up and down the street.*	12.7.2 12.7.4
14	Using participle clauses (mixed exercise)	*Having received low marks in maths and French, Frank enrolled in summer school.*	12.4.2 12.7

▶ Quick Check p. 112

1 What's what? Participles used like adjectives ▶ 12.4.1a

a Translate the participles into German.

→ confusing – **verwirrend**

damaged – ... (1)   depressing – ... (2)   frightened – ... (3)   frustrating – ... (4)
relaxing – ... (5)   shocked – ... (6)   surprising – ... (7)   worried – ... (8)

b Choose a verb from the box and complete the caption for each of the pictures below using a participle – present or past.

> break • bury • fall • ~~fly~~ • fry • help • sleep • talk

➜ a ***flying*** saucer

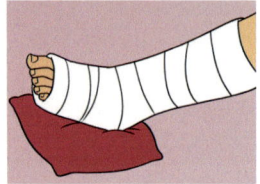

1 a … leg

2 a … tree

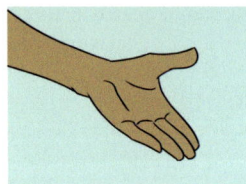

3 a … hand

4 a … bird

5 a … treasure

6 a … cat

7 a … egg

2 A fascinating city   Adjectives ending in *-ing* and *-ed* ▸ 12.5

Erklärvideo online:
cornelsen.de/webcodes
Code: sowobi

a Kim went on a trip with her parents. Complete the sentences by choosing the right adjective for for each gap.

Kim was really ➜ exciting | ***excited*** when her parents said they wanted to spend a week in New York. She had always been interesting | interested (1) in New York and was thrilling | thrilled (2) at the idea
5 of seeing the city. On their first day, they walked around downtown Manhattan, which Kim found rather confusing | confused (3). The next day, they visited Central Park. Kim was surprising | surprised (4) at how large it was. On the third day, it rained a lot, so her parents took her to three museums, 10 which Kim found quite boring | bored (5). The next day was sunny, so they went to the observatory of One World Trade Center to enjoy the amazing | amazed (6) view of New York. In the afternoon, they visited the 9/11 Memorial Museum – a really 15 moving | moved (7) experience. By the end of the week, they were all very tiring | tired (8), but they agreed that there was no place quite like New York.

b **NOW YOU** Describe a trip you went on with friends or your family. Write about what you saw and how you felt. Use adjectives with participle endings.

12

3 Who's who? Using a participle instead of a relative clause ▶ 12.4.2

a Carl wants his friend Tomas to join the school newspaper staff. He shows him a photo from their last meeting. Rewrite his sentences using a participle phrase instead of the relative clause.

→ The guy who is wearing a white T-shirt is Jamal.
*The guy **wearing a white T-shirt** is Jamal.*

1 Mirella is the girl who is talking to Jamal.
2 Claire is the girl who is using the notebook.
3 The girl who is sitting next to Claire is Kathy.
4 Thanh is the guy who is sitting on Claire's left.
5 The girl who is holding a coffee cup is Shana.
6 And the guy who is taking the photo is me, of course!

b Here are some topics for articles that were discussed at the meeting. Make headlines by using a participle phrase instead of the relative clause.

→ Why schools that were built before 1970 aren't safe
*Why schools **built before 1970** aren't safe*

1 Cars that are steered by computers – no longer science fiction
2 The food that they serve in our cafeteria is awful
3 Photos that you post online never really go away
4 Stuff that you buy on the internet isn't always cheaper
5 Some films that were made for TV are better than Hollywood
6 Why children that are born into poor families stay poor

4 My dog Toby Verbs + present participle ▶ 12.6.1

Toby is a very well-trained dog. Rewrite the underlined parts of the following sentences. Use a present participle.

→ Every afternoon before I come home, he <u>sits and waits</u> for me in the hall.
*Every afternoon before I come home, he **sits waiting** for me in the hall.*

1 When I open the door, he doesn't <u>come and run</u> up to me, because he knows I don't like it.
2 Instead, he <u>remains on his bed and sits there</u> until I call him.
3 Then I get his lead and we <u>go and walk</u> in the park.
4 Once I made the mistake of letting him run free. At first, he just <u>stood there and looked</u> at me with a confused expression on his face.
5 Then he <u>went and ran</u> after a cat.
6 In the end, I had to <u>go and look for</u> him. It seems even the best-trained dog isn't perfect!

12

5 Hanging out   Verbs + object + present participle   ▶ 12.6.2

a Steve is writing an email to his best friend Zach. Complete the sentences below using a verb from the box.

> chat • hang out • look • sit • smile • talk • tell • touch

Yesterday I saw you and Jack ➔ **hanging out** with some other kids. I had gone to the city centre with my mum. I left her ... (1) at the shoes in a shop window and told her I'd be back in a minute. I wanted
5 to check out the fanzines at the newsstand, but then I found you guys ... (2) by the fountain. I noticed you ... (3) to that new kid in our class. I heard you ... (4) him about our club. I noticed a girl with a red cap ... (5) on the ground. I saw her ... (6) at the new kid. I was just going to come over and say hi when I felt someone ... (7) my arm. I turned around ...

b NOW YOU Write an ending to the story.

6 Down by the lake   Mixed exercise   ▶ 12.4 – 12.6

Read Jake's story and complete the sentences by filling in the missing participles. Use the verbs in brackets.

Jake couldn't believe it. Laura had dumped him – just like that. First she had kept him ➔ **waiting** (wait) for over an hour at their usual meeting place by the lake. Then she had told him they couldn't be
5 together any longer. No explanation, nothing. Jake couldn't believe that the girl ... (say) (1) those words to him was really his girlfriend Laura. And then she had turned her back on him and left him ... (stand) (2) there. Feeling ... (confuse) (3) and helpless, Jake
10 watched her ... (walk off) (4) down the shore. Finally, he broke out of his trance and followed her at a distance. He stopped when he saw Laura ... (sit) (5) on the stairs of the boathouse. He could hear her ... (talk) (6) to someone on her mobile. Jake stayed ... (hide) (7) in the shadows. A few minutes later,
15 someone came ... (climb) (8) down the steep path to the boathouse. It was his classmate Eric. Laura jumped up and ran over to him. Jake felt the blood ... (rush) (9) to his face as he watched the couple ... (hug) (10) on the beach. He turned away and ran off
20 into the darkness.

7 What happened when?   Participle clauses of time   ▶ 12.7.1

Match the sentence parts that belong together. Then make a participle clause of time out of the first part of the sentence.

➔ **While picking apples**, Roger fell off the ladder and broke his leg.
➔ **Seeing his girlfriend with another boy**, Rick ran over and shouted at her.

1 While she was visiting her aunt in Teheran	a Roger fell off the ladder and broke his leg.
2 When she saw a man with a gun	b Rani took it inside and gave it some milk.
3 While he was picking apples	c Karel found a handbag full of money.
4 When she found a cat at her door	d Sarina learned to speak a little Persian.
5 While he was training for the competition	e the kids all ran to the window.
6 When he saw his girlfriend with another boy	f Sam injured his leg.
7 While he was walking to school	g Mrs Higgins phoned 999.
8 When they heard a loud crash	h Rick ran over and shouted at her.

12

8 Changes   *Have + object + past participle*   ▶ 12.6.3a

Nothing ever stays the same. Complete the following dialogues using the words in brackets.

→ Hey, have you got a new mobile? – No, it's my old one. I … (it | repair).
  *I **had it repaired**.*

1 Julie looks so blonde. Before the holidays she was more brunette. – I bet she … (her hair | dye).
2 Didn't there use to be a youth club in Haverford? – Yeah, but the building was in really bad shape.
  The city council … (it | tear down) a couple of years ago.
3 Your room looks so tidy. What happened? – My parents … (it | paint) last month, so I had to clean it out.
4 That bridge I drove across on the way here looks brand new. – Yes, the town … (a new one | build)
  last year.
5 Hey, that wasn't my speech that the boss read at the meeting! – Sorry, I meant to tell you.
  He wasn't happy with it, so he contacted a professional speech writer and … (parts of it | rewrite).
6 I thought your parents had a silver car. – Yeah, they did, but after the accident they … (it | repaint)
  a different colour.

9 A well-written story   *Two-part participle attributes*   ▶ 12.4.1b

**Complete the sentences below with words from the table. Use the verbs in the participle form
(past or present).**

→ Living in China for a year was a really … experience.
  *Living in China for a year was a really **eye-opening** experience.*

well	repeat
~~eye~~	fit
freshly	organize
tight	construct
time	~~open~~
much	prepare
carefully	save

1 … jeans are in this year.
2 Saunders' Deli is famous for their … sandwiches.
3 A good detective novel needs a … plot.
4 In some ways, the computer is a … device.
5 What we need is a … campaign to keep our city clean.
6 'Everything has its price' is a … saying.

✚ 10 At the department store   Infinitive or present participle after verbs of perception   ▶ 12.6.2

**The department store in High Street has a new store detective, and he really takes his job seriously.
Choose the right form of the verb. Sometimes both forms can be used.**

The store detective observed a boy in a hoodie
→ look | **looking** at the DVDs. He watched the boy
take | taking (1) one of the DVDs and put | putting
(2) it in his pocket. The detective ran after him as he
5 walked out of the store, and caught him by the arm.
The boy struggled to free himself. 'Forget it,' he
hissed. 'Or do you want everyone to see you make |
making (3) a fool of yourself?'
Later that day, he noticed a girl carry | carrying (4)
10 three pairs of jeans over her arm. He saw her go |
going (5) into a fitting room and close | closing (6)

the curtain. From where he was standing, he could
hear her talk | talking (7) to someone on her phone.
A few minutes later, he saw the curtain open |
opening (8) again. The girl came out of the fitting
room wearing brand-new jeans. She went over to a
mirror. The detective looked into the fitting room.
He could see the other two pairs hang | hanging (9)
on a peg. Turning back to the mirror, he noticed the
girl grin | grinning (10) at him. 'Everything OK,
Sherlock?' she asked.

12

+ 11 Don't keep me waiting   Expressions with participles   ▶ 12.4.2, 12.6.2a, 12.8c

a Choose the correct translation from the two possibilities.

→ jemanden warten lassen
   a → *keep someone waiting*   **b** let someone wait

1 jemanden beim Mogeln erwischen
   a catch someone by cheating   **b** catch someone cheating

2 ein Roman, der auf Tatsachen basiert
   a a novel basing on fact   **b** a novel based on fact

3 genau genommen
   a strictly speaking   **b** strictly spoken

4 ein Computerprogramm zum Laufen bringen
   a get a program running   **b** bring a program to run

5 alles in allem
   a considering all things   **b** all things considered

6 Menschen, die sich um die Umwelt sorgen
   a people concerning the environment   **b** people concerned about the environment

7 ein Film, der aus mehreren Episoden besteht
   a a film consisting of several episodes   **b** a film consisted of several episodes

8 im Hinblick auf den Energiesektor
   a with regarding the energy sector   **b** regarding the energy sector

b NOW YOU Choose four expressions from part a and use each in a sentence of your own.

+ 12 It's a small world   Participle clauses of time   ▶ 12.7.1

Complete these sentences about Ben's cycling holiday last month.
Decide whether or not you want to use a conjunction *(when/while)*.

→ get off | the train in York | meet | former classmate of mine
   ***Getting off the train in York**, I met a former classmate of mine.*

1 have tea | in a sidewalk café | see | my ex-girlfriend walk by
2 go into a bookshop | to buy a map | be surprised | to find a former classmate of mine at the cash desk
3 cycle | through the Yorkshire Dales | have to stop | to repair my bike
4 look into my toolkit | discover | that a tool was missing – the one I needed.
5 sit next to my bike | and | wonder what to do | hear a car stop | just behind me
   Luckily for me, the driver was a bike mechanic.
6 have repaired my bike | he | drive off | and | I | continue my tour
7 have finally reached Cowgill | feel very hungry | so | go into the first café I found
8 look up | to give the waitress my order | see | that it was my cousin Jeanne

b NOW YOU Imagine three strange coincidences that might happen to you. Write a sentence about each of them. Use a participle clause of time in each.

✚ 13 The Golden Gate Bridge Participle clauses of reason, circumstance and result ▶ 12.7.2, 12.7.4

Rewrite the sentences below. Replace the underlined words with a participle clause. You may have to make small changes to the punctuation.

➔ As it has appeared in numerous films, the Golden Gate Bridge is one of the most famous bridges in the world.
***Having appeared in** numerous films, the Golden Gate Bridge is one of the most famous bridges in the world.*

1 Because it is surrounded by water on three sides, for many years the city of San Francisco was cut off from the rest of the Bay area.
2 As they were looking for an alternative to ferry traffic, the Board of Supervisors asked the city engineer to examine the possibility of building a bridge across the Golden Gate Strait.
3 The Department of War was against the project; they feared that any kind of bridge would hinder navigation in the Bay.
4 As they were determined to get their bridge, the Supervisors hired engineer Joseph Strauss to oversee the project.
5 Because he had already designed and built several large bridges, Strauss was confident that he could make the project succeed.
6 Strauss insisted on high safety standards; he spent $130,000 on a huge safety net.
7 The bridge was painted bright orange; this makes it easier to see in the fog.
8 The Golden Gate Bridge is used by over 120,000 people daily and is one of America's most famous landmarks.

✚ 14 Does the Web really connect us? Using participle clauses (mixed exercise) ▶ 12.4.2, 12.7

Rewrite the underlined parts of the text using a suitable participle. You may have to make small changes to the punctuation.

➔ A society works only if it has something that holds it together.
*A society works only if it has something **holding it together.***

Social scientists talk about bonding and bridging as the two main forms of social connection. Bonding means the connection between people who belong to the same group (1); bridging refers to creating
5 ties between members of different groups.
When the internet was still young, many thought it would become the ultimate bridging tool, that it would unite people around the world in one global village (2). Now we know that the opposite is true. People use the internet very selectively, they read
10 only opinions (3) that support their views and form communities (4) with others of a similar background and political perspective. Instead of making people broader-minded, the internet tends to strengthen the views we already have and makes us
15 less tolerant (5) towards those who disagree.

Of course, the internet has also brought benefits, for example for members of social minorities, such as gay, lesbian and transgender individuals, who are now able to link up with others who face similar 20
challenges (6). Another group that has benefitted from the bonding talent of the internet consists of people who suffer from rare diseases (7). Whereas in the past it was almost impossible for these individuals to find advice and support, today there 25
are dozens of online self-help groups that make it possible (8) for people who will never meet in person to swap information on therapies and medication.

12

Quick Check

A Choose the correct participle to complete the sentences.

1 Ken was thrilling | thrilled to see so many stars in person.
2 Lynn was disappointing | disappointed when she didn't get the leading role in the play.
3 What was the most interesting | interested experience you had in China?
4 When did you have your house repainting | repainted?
5 Chelsea got annoying | annoyed when her boyfriend texted her to say he would be late.
6 Some of the students complained that the exam instructions were very confusing | confused.
7 I thought the story was really funny, but Karen didn't look amusing | amused.
8 Didn't I see you at the newsstand looking | looked at the sports magazines?

B Rewrite the sentences using a participle phrase instead of the <u>underlined</u> relative clause.

1 People <u>who live in glass houses</u> shouldn't throw stones.
2 The money <u>that was found in the bag</u> had been stolen the day before.
3 Four of the people <u>who were killed in the crash</u> were tourists from Australia.
4 Passengers <u>who are flying on to New York</u> are asked to go to Gate 7.
5 The buildings that <u>had been damaged by the earthquake</u> had to be torn down.
6 The girl <u>who is sitting next to Philip</u> is my sister.

C Complete the sentences by making a two-part participle from the words in brackets.

1 My parents only want to travel to … countries. (countries where people speak English)
2 How can anyone be so stupid as to sit down on a … chair? (one that has been freshly painted)
3 Roger's dad is a typical … salesman. (one who talks fast)
4 No veggie burger for me! I'm a real … Texan. (one who eats meat)
5 It's nice to read a … novel for a change. (one that is well written)
6 My grandfather was a … coal miner. (one who works hard)

**D In each of the following sentences there is one mistake. Find and correct it.
You may have to change more than one word.**

1 The paintings stealing from the museum were never found.
2 Leon's brother went to Mali as part of a mission keeping peace.
3 Photos having been edited on a computer sometimes look unnatural.
4 Nina was really exciting when she heard about the concert.
5 My laptop keeps crashing. – Why don't you let it repair?
6 All of the here mentioned issues will be dealt with in the next chapter.
7 There are a lot of fast-moved action scenes in his latest film.
8 Kensington has many in the 18th century built houses.
9 I saw a wolf cycling through Brandenburg.
10 Generally spoken, IT specialists have well-paid jobs.

12

13 Main clauses and subordinate clauses

Task	Topic	Example	Englische Grammatik
1	Main clauses vs subordinate clauses	*It's going to rain today. / ... because it's going to rain today.*	13.1
2	Compound sentences	*You can wait, or you can leave without me.*	13.1.1
3	Complex sentences	*After he had made a rough sketch, Linus added some details.*	13.1.2
4	Subordinating conjunctions	*You can use my laptop as long as I don't need it.*	13.2
5	*That*-clauses	*I wish that you had told me.*	13.3 / 13.4
6	Adverbial clauses	*Phone me as soon as you arrive.*	13.2
7	Adverbial phrases vs adverbial clauses	*Joel waited patiently during the rehearsal / while the band was rehearsing.*	13.2

13.5 Relative clauses – see chapter 16

▶ Quick Check p. 117

1 Teens and phones   Main clauses vs subordinate clauses   ▶ 13.1

a The following clauses are from an article on teens and smartphones. Decide if they are main clauses MC or subordinate clauses SC. Capital letters and punctuation have been left out.

→ how they use their smartphones **SC**

1 many teens hardly ever use their smartphones for telephoning ☐
2 as a recent study of communication habits discovered ☐
3 because they prefer texting to talking ☐
4 a few didn't know that smartphones can be used for making phone calls ☐
5 most of them only use their phones for going online ☐
6 that it's faster to type a text message than to talk to someone ☐
7 and you needn't waste time making small talk ☐
8 but they don't know how to really communicate ☐

b Use your own ideas to complete the subordinate clauses from part a.

→ **We asked teenagers** how they use their smartphones.

13

2 No excuses! Compound sentences ▶ 13.1.1

a The music teacher Mr Nelson is unhappy about the discipline of the school band.
Complete the sentences below with *and*, *but*, *or* or *so*.

The list of rehearsal dates has been on the notice board for weeks, ➔ **but** only a few students came to the rehearsal on Friday. You all know that we have a concert next month, … (1) we still need a lot of practice. I asked you to contact me if you can't come, … (2) nobody did. You all have my phone number and my email address, … (3) that can't be the problem. You can always reach me by mobile, … (4) you can text me if you prefer. Some of you can't even play your part correctly, … (5) you don't practise at home. We have a lot of work to do today, … (6) let's get started!

b Ted, one of the drums players in the band, wrote Mr Nelson an email explaining why he couldn't come to the rehearsal. Complete his sentences using ideas of your own.

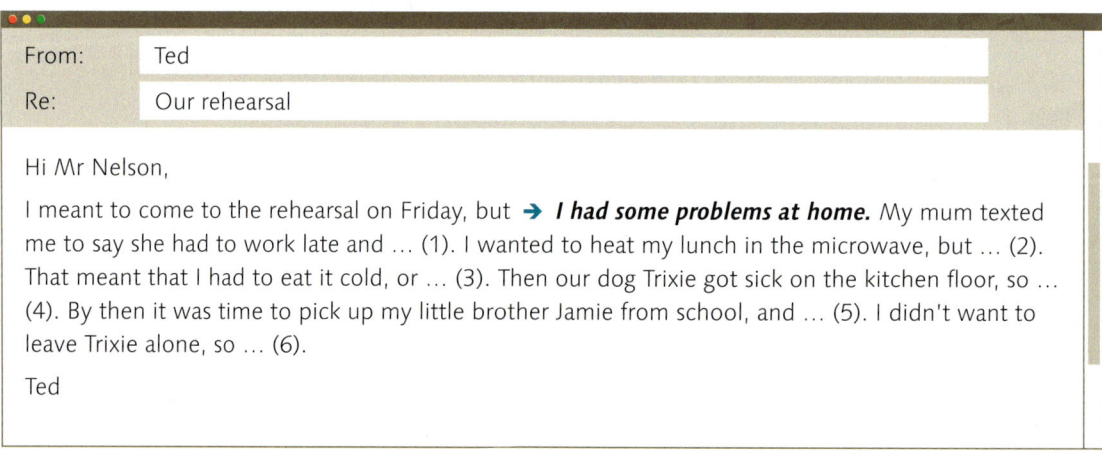

From:	Ted
Re:	Our rehearsal

Hi Mr Nelson,

I meant to come to the rehearsal on Friday, but ➔ *I had some problems at home.* My mum texted me to say she had to work late and … (1). I wanted to heat my lunch in the microwave, but … (2). That meant that I had to eat it cold, or … (3). Then our dog Trixie got sick on the kitchen floor, so … (4). By then it was time to pick up my little brother Jamie from school, and … (5). I didn't want to leave Trixie alone, so … (6).

Ted

3 Sport and you Complex sentences ▶ 13.1.2

a Combine the sentence pairs using a conjunction from the box.

> as long as • because • before • even though • ~~if~~ • unless • when • while

➔ You've never done sport before. | It's a good idea to join a sport club
   If you've never done sport before, it's a good idea to join a sport club.

1 Some people are allergic to sport. | They think it's really hard work.
2 You do sport every day. | It gets much easier.
3 Sport can even help you to think clearly. I often get my best ideas. | I'm jogging.
4 Sport is good for your health. | You stay within your limits.
5 You may feel tired at first. | You'll feel more energy with every workout.
6 You can choose any sport you like. | You have a health problem.
7 Go to your doctor for a checkup. | You begin doing a really tough sport.

b NOW YOU Write five sentences about a sport or hobby you do regularly. Use a conjunction from the list above in each of your sentences.

4 Emily's first trip to Germany   Subordinating conjunctions   ▶ 13.2

Read about Emily's first trip to Germany. Choose the right conjunction.

Emily had been looking for a summer job as an au pair in Germany, so she was very happy ➔ as | **when** she got a job with the Becker family in Recklinghausen. On the day of her flight, she was a bit
5 nervous, because | while (1) she had never flown alone before. Her parents drove her to the airport in Manchester and said goodbye. Emily checked in her suitcase and waited in the departure lounge unless | until (2) it was time to board. As soon as |
10 As long as (3) she saw her boarding time on the screen, she jumped up and went quickly to her gate. An hour later, her plane landed at Heathrow, when | where (4) she caught her connecting flight to Düsseldorf. At the airport in Düsseldorf, Emily
15 went to the baggage claim to get her suitcase.

While | Because (5) she was waiting for her suitcase, Emily texted her parents to say she had arrived. There were so many suitcases, but Emily couldn't see hers. She was very unhappy while | as
20 (6) she left the baggage claim without her suitcase. The Becker family were waiting for her and were very surprised that she only had a small rucksack. After | By the time (7) she had explained to her host parents about her missing suitcase, they went with
25 her to the British Airways desk and filled in a form. The woman there was very friendly and she promised that they would send Emily's suitcase to her new home in Recklinghausen whenever | as soon as (8) it arrived.

5 Caught in the act   *That*-clauses   ▶ 13.3 – 13.4

Match the sentence halves that belong together to read about a disappointing experience one boy had at school.

➔ *When I arrived at school that morning, my classmate Ralph told me that my mate Kevin had been caught cheating on his chemistry exam.*

1 ~~When I arrived at school that morning, my classmate Ralph told me~~	a that he would do anything so stupid.
2 The teacher discovered	b that Kevin hadn't listened to my advice.
3 Kevin's a smart guy—I couldn't believe	c ~~that my mate Kevin had been caught cheating on his chemistry exam.~~
4 I was really disappointed	d that he would pass the exam.
5 I had spent a whole afternoon explaining the terms to him until I was sure	e that Kevin wasn't the honest, hard-working guy I thought he was.
6 I had to accept the fact	f that Kevin was using his mobile to look up answers on the internet.

+ 6 Lilly and Lucy   Adverbial clauses   ▶ 13.2

a Match the underlined adverbial clauses in the sentences below with the clause types in the box.

A clause of time	E conditional clause
B clause of place	F clause of comparison
C clause of reason	G clause of purpose
D clause of contrast	H clause of result

➜ <u>Wherever Lilly and Lucy appear together</u>, they attract attention.
   B (clause of place)

1 <u>As the girls are the same size</u>, they love swapping clothes.
2 In spite of being twins, they aren't nearly as similar <u>as most people expect</u>.

3 <u>While Lilly loves riding and dancing</u>, Lucy prefers reading and listening to music.
4 But she likes to watch <u>while Lilly is dancing with her club</u>.

5 Lilly is generous. She lets Lucy borrow her things and keep them <u>as long as she wants</u>.
6 Lucy lets Lilly borrow her gear too, <u>as long as she doesn't need it herself</u>.

7 They have been together day and night <u>since they were born</u>.
8 They don't talk much to each other, <u>since they already know what the other one wants to say</u>.

9 Lilly and Lucy look almost identical, <u>so that their teachers sometimes mix them up</u>.
10 The girls plan to study at the same university <u>so that they can share a flat</u>.

b Now write three sentences using different adverbial clauses. Swap them with a partner – can they identify the clauses you have written?

+ 7 Elizabethan London   Adverbial phrases vs adverbial clauses   ▶ 13.2

The underlined parts of the sentences below are adverbial phrases. Rewrite them as adverbial clauses that have the same meaning. Choose a conjunction from the box.

> ~~after~~ • although • as • before • if • when • while

➜ <u>After the death of Henry VIII in 1558</u>, his daughter Elizabeth was crowned Queen of England.
   ***After Henry VIII died in 1558**, his daughter Elizabeth was crowned Queen of England.*

1 <u>During the reign of Elizabeth I</u>, London became a centre of culture and commerce.
2 <u>Because of the frequent plagues</u>, most people avoided towns and cities.
3 <u>In case of fire</u>, little could be done to stop the flames from spreading.
4 <u>Before the creation of the Metropolitan Police in 1829</u>, crime was part of everyday life in London.
5 <u>In spite of the dangers of city life</u>, London attracted thousands of people from all over England.
6 <u>By the end of the Elizabethan Age in 1603</u>, London had grown to a bustling city of over 200,000.

Quick Check

A Use the conjunctions in the box to complete the sentences.

because • but • or • since • so • unless • whenever • yet

1 The open-air concert was cancelled … there had been a storm warning.
2 Feel free to use my bike … you need it.
3 I've known Catriona … we went to primary school together.
4 Cal promised to buy bread on the way home, … then he forgot.
5 You needn't do the 'extra' task … you finish the test early.
6 We can go to the cinema this evening, … would you prefer to go clubbing?
7 Rob says he's my friend, … he never has time for me.
8 The last train had already left, … I phoned for a taxi.

B Choose the right conjunction to complete the sentences.

1 We must stop global warming now, or | so it will be too late.
2 Just raise your hand when | if you have trouble with any of the tasks.
3 Most of the students had already finished the exam as | when the bell rang.
4 Ahmad asked for a room of his own because | so that he could concentrate on his studies.
5 Take an umbrella with you if | unless you enjoy getting wet.
6 Joshua wanted to be on time, so | yet he got up ten minutes earlier.
7 Every time | As soon as I go to the city centre, I see Kaitlyn with her new boyfriend.
8 While | By the time he was waiting for his brother, Karim got a message from Nasrin.

C Match the underlined conjunction in each sentence to the conjunction from the box that has the same meaning. (There is one more conjunction than you need.)

although • as • as long as • as soon as • every time • whereas • wherever

1 Larry couldn't finish his presentation on time because his computer wouldn't start.
2 Whenever I see a rainbow, I think of my last holiday in Connemara.
3 Everywhere I go, I see people staring at their smartphones.
4 Lucia loves hip hop, while her sister Maria only likes techno.
5 Even if the weather was bad, we had a great weekend with our friends in Prague.
6 With this ticket, you can use public transport as often as you want if you stay in Zone I.

D Find and correct the mistakes. There's one in each sentence.

1 As the doorbell rang, Philip got up and went to see who it was.
2 Wait here until I will come back.
3 Everytime I hear this song, I remember our first date.
4 I've bought you a T-shirt. When you don't like the colour, I can exchange it.
5 During Samantha was waiting for the bus, she saw her boyfriend with another girl.
6 Julio told me, that he was flying home for the holidays.
7 Kevin entered the classroom looking as he had just climbed out of bed.
8 Ms Pritchard stepped back that she could get the whole class in the photo.

14 Conditional sentences

Task	Topic	Example	Englische Grammatik
1	*When or if?*	*I'll phone you when I get home. If it's after 10 pm, I'll phone you tomorrow.*	14.1
2	Conditional sentence 0	*If you stand here, the software automatically scans your face.*	14.3
3	Conditional sentence I	*If you don't start soon, you'll never finish on time.*	14.4.1
4	Conditional sentence I: Other tenses in the if-clause and the main clause	*If you've lost your ID, fill in this form and you can get a new one.*	14.4.2
5	Conditional sentence II (1)	*If you won a million euros, what would you do with it?*	14.5.1
6	Conditional sentence II (2)	*Sorry, I'm busy this weekend. If I had more time, I'd help you.*	14.5.1
7	Mixed exercise: Comparison of conditional sentences I and II	*If Victor's leg is OK, he will run in the race on Saturday.* *If Victor's leg was OK, he would run in the race on Saturday.*	14.5.2
8	Conditional sentence III	*If it hadn't rained so hard yesterday, we would have walked to the underground station.*	14.6.1
9	Mixed exercise: Comparison of conditional sentences II and III	*If Tim had more money, he would buy a new mobile.* *If Tim had had more money, he would have bought a new mobile.*	14.6.2
10	*Would or had?*	*If you'd paid attention, you'd know what I'm talking about.*	14.6.1
11	Understanding conditional sentences	*If Lars had known how cold the water was, he wouldn't have jumped in.* *Did Lars jump into the water?*	14.5 14.6 14.7
12	Mixed conditional sentences	*If you had started earlier, you would be ready now.*	14.7
13	Conditional sentences with other conjunctions	*I'm in favour of the project provided we get the funding we need.*	14.1
14	Speculating	*If Juliet had awakened a few minutes earlier, Romeo would have realized that she wasn't dead.*	14.6.1 14.7

▶ Quick Check p. 126

▶ Erklärvideo zu Conditional sentences ▶ **Exercise 3**

1 Travelling to Celle   *When or if?*   ▶ 14.1

Leonie's pen friend Ellie is coming to visit her in Celle. Leonie sends her an email explaining how to reach Celle from Hanover Airport. Choose *if* or *when* to fill each gap.

From:	Ellie
Re:	Your visit

Hi Ellie!

I'm sorry I can't meet you at the airport in Hanover. But don't worry – it's easy to get to Celle by train. Here are a few tips:

➔ **When** you've collected your luggage, go to Terminal C, where you can get on the S-Bahn. … (1) your train ticket doesn't allow you to use the S-Bahn, buy a ticket to Celle at the ticket machine before you board. … (2) the train stops at Langenhagen Mitte, get off and go to Platform 1. There you can board the Metronom to Celle. It's a double-decker train, so … (3) the lower level is full, you can usually find a seat on the upper level. The trains only run once an hour, so … (4) you miss your connection you'll have to wait a while. … (5) you arrive in Celle, call me on my mobile. … (6) the traffic isn't too bad, Dad and I can meet you at the station in about twenty minutes.

See you soon!
Leonie

2 If A, then B   Conditional sentence 0   ▶ 14.3

Match the sentence parts from the table to form conditional sentences.

➔ **If** *the temperature falls below 0°C, water freezes.*

1 ~~the temperature falls below 0° C~~	a the young plants die
2 the battery is weak	b skating isn't allowed
3 you right-click the icon	c ~~water freezes~~
4 you choose the 'portrait' option	d the yellow light starts to blink
5 the ice is less than 15 cm thick	e some birds don't fly south
6 there isn't enough rain	f the camera focusses on the face
7 the winter is mild	g the context menu opens

3 Before the exam Conditional sentence I ► 14.4.1

Erklärvideo online:
 cornelsen.de/webcodes
 Code: sigifi

a Read the text about Jannik. Then complete the sentences below the text by putting the verb in brackets in the right form.

Jannik has his final exam in chemistry tomorrow. The battery of his smartphone needs to be recharged so that it can wake him on time. He wants to wake up early, so that he will have time to catch the early bus to school, because the later bus is always full. Full buses make him nervous. He wants to do well on the exam, because he needs a good mark in chemistry to pass.

➔ If he … (not recharge) the battery, the alarm … (not ring).
 *If he **doesn't recharge** the battery, the alarm **won't ring**.*

1 If the alarm … (not ring), he … (not wake up) early.
2 If he … (not wake up) early, he … (miss) the early bus.
3 If he … (miss) the early bus, he … (have to) take the later bus.
4 If he … (take) the later bus, he … (feel) nervous when he arrives at school.
5 If he … (feel) nervous, he … (not get) a good mark.
6 If he … (not get) a good mark, he … (not pass).

b NOW YOU Think of four things you will do tomorrow. Make sentences that say what will happen if you do (or don't do) them.

➔ *If I clean my room, my mum will be happy.*

4 Good advice Conditional sentence I ► 14.4.2

Erklärvideo online:
► Exercise 3

a Match the sentence halves that belong together. Add commas where necessary.

➔ **If** you **aren't** part of the solution, you **are** part of the problem.

1 ~~If you aren't part of the solution~~	a	you may fail.
2 If you want to hear good advice	b	you'll never love what you do.
3 Don't walk	c	~~you are part of the problem~~.
4 If you don't do what you love	d	if you can fly.
5 You'll never win	e	if you're not willing to lose.
6 If you try	f	listen to your heart.
7 If you don't try	g	you've already failed.

b NOW YOU Choose one of the above sentences. Explain what you think it means and why you chose it.

14

Erklärvideo online:
▶ **Exercise 3**

⊙ **5 Studying abroad** Conditional sentence II ▶ 14.5.1

Linda wants to study in the US after finishing school. She is talking to her parents about it. Put the verb in brackets in the right form.

→ If I … (go) to the US for a year, my English … (get) a lot better.
 *If I **went** to the US for a year, my English **would get** a lot better.*

Linda:
1 If I … (be accepted) by a US college, I … (get) a room in a students' hostel.
2 I … (never feel) lonely if I … (live) in a students' hostel.
3 It … (not be) so expensive if I … (get) a scholarship.
4 If I … (need) more money, I … (look for) a part-time job.

Linda's parents:
5 If you … (study) in the US, we … (not be able to) visit you often.
6 There … (be) no one to look after you if you … (be) ill.
7 You … (feel) lonely if you … (leave) all your friends behind.
8 If we … (not have) three other children, we … (think) about letting you study abroad.

14

Erklärvideo online:
▶ **Exercise 3**

⊙ **6 Boring holidays** Conditional sentence II ▶ 14.5.1

a It is the school holidays, but Jack's not having a good time. Make sentences about his situation using conditional type II.

→ *If my dad **had** a job, we could **go** on holiday.*

→ My dad doesn't have a job, so we can't go on holiday.

1 We don't have a car, so I can't go to the disco in Bradford.

2 My girlfriend is in Spain with her family, so there's no one to hang out with.

3 There are no parties, so I won't get any invitations.

4 My PC doesn't work, so I can't play computer games.

5 I don't have enough money, so I can't get it repaired.

6 There are no shops in our village, so I can't get a part-time job.

b Give Jack some advice on how he can spend his holidays. You can use ideas from the box below.

→ *If I were you, I would do small jobs for the neighbours.*

do small jobs for neighbours • look for volunteer work • take bike trips in the countryside •
interview people in the village • write a mystery story

▶ **7 Maybe**   Comparison of conditional sentences I and II   ▶ 14.5.2

Erklärvideo online:
▶ **Exercise 3**

Look at the pictures and complete the sentences with the correct form of the verb.

➔ *If it … raining, we **can go** on a bike tour this afternoon.*

➔ *If it **stopped** raining, we … on a bike tour this afternoon.*

➔ *If it **stops** raining, we can go on a bike tour this afternoon.*
  *If it stopped raining, we **could go** on a bike tour this afternoon.*

If I **buy** a lottery ticket, maybe I … (1) the jackpot.

If I … (2) a lottery ticket, I probably **wouldn't win** anything.

If I **enter** the race, I … (3) first.

If I … (4) the race, I'd **come in** last.

If I **get** an 'A' on the exam, my parents … (5) happy.

If I … (6) an 'A' on the exam, my mum **would be** shocked.

8 Things could have been different Conditional sentence III ▶ 14.6.1

Erklärvideo online: ▶ Exercise 3

Each of the sentences below presents a fact and its consequence. Write sentences expressing what could, would or might have happened under different circumstances.

➔ Jamie didn't study for his final exams, so he didn't pass.
*If Jamie **had studied** for his exams, he **might have passed**.*

1 Shirin didn't go to the audition, so she didn't get a part in the musical.
2 Frank overslept, so he arrived late for his job interview.
3 Pauline forgot her umbrella, so she got really wet on the way to school.
4 Carlo spent all his money on a new mobile, so he couldn't go to the concert.
5 The Bakers' car broke down, so they couldn't go on holiday.
6 Our dog Spike barked when he heard a stranger at the window. The man ran off.

14

9 Chances Comparison of conditional sentences II and III ▶ 14.6.2

Erklärvideo online: ▶ Exercise 3

Larissa and her grandma are looking at photographs on Larissa's laptop. Larissa is thinking about her future, her grandma about her past. Complete their sentences.

➔ *If I **went** to law school, I **could become** a lawyer.*

➔ *If I **hadn't married** your grandfather, I **could have become** a dancer.*

Larissa's thoughts	Her grandma's thoughts
➔ go to law school – become a lawyer	➔ not marry your grandfather – go to dancing school
1 study creative writing – write a bestselling novel	5 go to dancing school – develop my talent
2 become an astronaut – fly to Mars	6 become a dancer – travel around the world
3 have a brilliant idea – found a startup	7 travel around the world – meet interesting people
4 do research – win a Nobel Prize	8 meet interesting people – not marry your grandfather

10 If you'd worked harder ... *Would or had?* ▶ 14.6.1

Jared's German teacher wants to help him to get better marks.
Write out the underlined words.

→ If you did your homework regularly, <u>you'd</u> get better marks. – *you would*

1 You would have got a better mark this term if <u>you'd</u> studied for the vocabulary tests.
2 If you had a larger vocabulary, <u>you'd</u> find it easier to express yourself.
3 If <u>you'd</u> practised more for the last test, you might have passed.
4 You wouldn't have these problems now if <u>you'd</u> worked steadily from the start.
5 Perhaps <u>you'd</u> find it easier to learn if you practised with a friend.
6 <u>You'd</u> learn a lot of German if you did a summer language course in Germany.

11 What really happened? *Understanding conditional sentences* ▶ 14.5–14.7

Yes or no? Answer the questions under each sentence.

If Sarah had learned German, she could have read her grandmother's old letters.
→ Did Sarah learn German? **No, she didn't.**
→ Could Sarah read her grandmother's letters? **No, she couldn't.**

Victor wouldn't have got lost in Moscow if he had been able to read street signs in Cyrillic.
1 Did Victor get lost in Moscow?   2 Can he read Cyrillic?

Leila would come to the party if she didn't have to babysit for her older sister.
3 Is Leila coming to the party?   4 Does she have to babysit for her older sister?

If he hadn't injured his leg, Leon might have become a professional football player.
5 Is Leon a professional football player?   6 Did he injure his leg?

If Kaitlyn had learned Chinese instead of Spanish, she could have got a job at the State Department.
7 Does Kaitlyn work at the State Department?   8 Can she speak Chinese?

If Terry hadn't dropped out of medical school, he could be a doctor now.
9 Did Terry drop out of medical school?   10 Is he a doctor?

⊙ 12 Uncle Horace *Mixed conditional sentences* ▶ 14.7

Erklärvideo online:
▶ Exercise 3

Uncle Horace is always telling his nieces and nephews what a great man he is.
Complete the sentences with the correct form of the verbs in brackets.

→ I went to school with Bill Gates. If I ... (want) to, I ... (get) a job at Microsoft.
*If I **had wanted** to, I **could have got** a job at Microsoft.*

1 If I ... (invest) in Microsoft back then, I ... (be) a multimillionaire today.
2 I'm a financial genius. If I ... (have) more money, I ... (start) my own consulting firm.
3 I was a great runner when I was young. If I ... (not break) my leg in 1972, I ... (run) in the Olympics.
4 I was the star of the Debating Club. If I ... (go) into politics when I was younger, I ... (be) President today.
5 I ... (become) a Hollywood star if I ... (concentrate) on my acting talent while I was in college.
6 If I ... (not always be) so busy, I ... (write) my autobiography.
7 If you kids ... (take) my advice, you ... (become) just as successful as I am.

✚ 13 Flatsitting Conditional sentences with other conjunctions ▸ 14.1

Mike is flatsitting for his friend Liam, and Liam wants to make sure he knows exactly what to do.
Choose the correct word or words.

You're welcome to use my flat while I'm away ➔ **on condition that** | in case you clean it before you leave.
You can use my Wi-fi as long as | unless (1) you don't do anything illegal.
Feel free to eat whatever is in the fridge providing | supposing (2) you replace it before I come back.
Don't use the cappuccino machine on condition that | unless (3) you know how to clean it properly.
Text me on my mobile in case | supposing (4) anything unexpected happens.
You're welcome to have a party unless | as long as (5) the guests don't wreck the flat.
We've got air conditioning, but you won't need it in case | unless (6) the weather turns unusually hot.

✚ 14 What if ...? Speculating ▸ 14.6.1, 14.7

a Read the text below, then draw suitable conclusions from the facts using conditional sentences.

Cars and the city

The rise of the automobile in the first two decades of the twentieth century had an enormous impact on the city, especially in the US. The broad pedestrian promenades and the narrow alleyways of 19th-century New York or Baltimore were replaced by wider streets and car parks to accommodate the increasing number of automobiles. Highways were built into the heart of the city to guarantee the mobility of motorists, while no money was invested in public transportation.

With increasing mobility, middle-class white families left the crowded urban centres for the suburbs with their endless streets of one-family houses with double garages. They took both spending power and political influence with them, leaving behind the poor and disadvantaged. Crime and decay became part of everyday life.

As inner cities became less attractive, the exodus to the suburbs accelerated. Huge shopping malls, connected only by highways, sprung up like mushrooms outside the city centres. The rush-hour ritual – crawling to work in the city in the morning, crawling back home to the suburbs in the evening – became part of everyday life for millions of Americans.

What if the automobile had never been invented? What consequences would that have had for urban culture in the US?

➔ *The original street pattern of the city centres **would have been preserved**. Wide roads and car parks **wouldn't have been built** …*

b **NOW YOU** Write two or three sentences about each of those topics.

1 What if East and West Germany hadn't been reunited in 1990?
2 What if human beings could live forever?
3 What if your parents had moved to the USA when you were little?

Quick Check

A Choose the right conjunction (*when* or *if*) for each gap.

1 You can call me on my mobile … you need any help.
2 … everyone has a ticket, we can get the next train.
3 … autumn comes, the leaves turn brown and fall to the ground.
4 You can earn a lot of money on an oil rig … you don't mind the loneliness.
5 … anyone calls this afternoon, tell them I'm in a meeting.
6 … the update is finished, restart the computer.
7 Please call me … you get home.
8 I'll return your book … I see you again.

B Choose the correct form of the verb to complete the sentences.

1 If you don't hurry up, we miss | will miss our train.
2 The problem will only get worse if we don't do | didn't do anything about it.
3 Water starts | is starting to boil if it is heated to 100° C.
4 I take | will take the photos for our article if it's OK with you.
5 If you don't have | won't have any butter, you can use margarine instead.
6 Don't sign up for the test if you aren't | weren't ready to take it.
7 If Carina doesn't want | didn't want to write the article, I can do it.
8 If the sea level continues to rise, many coastal cities are | will be under water.

B Complete the sentences with the correct form of the verb in brackets.

1 I'd be glad to help you if I … (not have) so much to do this weekend.
2 Lena could get a part in the musical if she really … (want) to.
3 I wouldn't have bought such an expensive smartphone if it … (not be) on sale
4 If you had asked me, I … (lend) you my tablet.
5 If I … (be) you, I'd talk to my teacher first.
6 If we had phoned Marc in time, he … (drive) us to the party.
7 We … (not have to) wait in the queue if we bought our tickets online.
8 If the wind hadn't been so strong, our team … (have) a better chance of winning the regatta.

D Each of the following sentences contains one mistake. Find and correct it.

1 If Karol would have worked harder, he would have got better marks.
2 When you can't do the tasks alone, ask Francine for help.
3 If Tarik hadn't to help his parents, he could come to the party.
4 If our train had arrived on time, we hadn't missed the beginning of the concert.
5 I'm expecting a visitor – send her into my office if she arrives.
6 If I would be a filmmaker, I would make a film about the food industry.
7 If I hadn't failed my maths exam, I were at university now.
8 We'll be late for the show if we won't catch the next bus.
9 Let me know if there would be anything I can do for you.
10 If Piotr didn't break his leg, he could have played for our team.

14

15 Indirect speech (Reported speech)

Task	Topic	Example	Englische Grammatik
1	Features of direct and indirect speech	Bill: 'I can't come to your party.' Bill says he can't come to my party.	15.1 15.2
2	Reporting with say and tell	He said he wasn't coming. He told me he was sick.	15.1
3	Changes in tenses: present to past	Darius: 'I'm going to Berlin.' He said he was going to Berlin.	15.4.2
4	Changes in tenses: past / present perfect to past perfect	Max: 'I met a clown yesterday!' He said he had met a clown the day before.	15.4.2
5	Changes in tenses: modals	Zoe: 'I'll help you if I can.' Zoe told me she would help me if she could.	15.4.2
6	Indirect questions (1)	Ida: 'Do you have my address?' Ida asked me if I had her address.	15.5
7	Indirect questions (2)	Dan: 'What is the matter, Paul?' Dan asked Paul what the matter was.	15.5
8	Indirect commands and requests	Dad: 'Jo, close the door and don't leave the lights on.' Dad told Jo to close the door and not to leave the lights on.	15.6a 15.6b
9	Indirect suggestions	Gina: 'Let's eat here.' Gina suggested that they should eat there.	15.6c
10	Changes in tenses: mixed exercise (1)	Nigel: 'I'll be home by nine.' Nigel promised to be home by nine.	15.4
11	Changes in phrases of time and place	Kylie: 'I'm busy working here all this week.' She said she was busy working there all that week.	15.3
12	Indirect advice and warning	Saul: 'Don't text when you are driving.' Saul advised me not to text when I was driving.	15.6b
13	Changes in tenses: mixed exercise (2)	Ella: 'I'm sure winters are getting colder. Why is that?' Ella said she was sure winters are getting colder and wondered why that was.	15.4
14	Various reporting verbs	He advised working harder and recommended that I should spend less time partying.	15.6

▶ Quick Check p. 137

▶ Erklärvideo zur Veränderung von Zeitformen in der indirekten Rede ▶ Exercise 3

▶ **1 What's that, dear?** Features of direct and indirect speech ▶ 15.1, 15.2

Erklärvideo online:
cornelsen.de/webcodes
Code: karuwa

Amelie has taken her new boyfriend Giles to visit her grandmother, who doesn't hear very well. Amelie has to repeat most of what Giles says. Complete her sentences in indirect speech.

15

Giles	Hello, I'm Giles. I'm pleased to meet you.
Granny	What's that, dear?
Amelie	He says ➔ **he's** pleased to meet you.
Giles	Amelie and I came in my new car.
Amelie	He says … (1) new car.
Giles	I've never been to this village before.
Amelie	He says … (2) to this village before.
Giles	Have you been living in this house for long?
Amelie	He wants to know if … (3) in this house for long.
Giles	My parents had a holiday home not far from here once.
Amelie	He says …. (4) a holiday home not far from here once.
Giles	My mum and dad don't live together anymore.
Amelie	He says … (5) together anymore.

Giles	Amelie and I will be getting married soon.
Amelie	He says that … (6) married soon.
Giles	I hope you can come to the wedding.
Amelie	He says … (7) to the wedding.
Giles	Amelie will definitely send you an invitation.
Amelie	He says that … (8) you an invitation.

> What did he say?

2 A wet weekend Reporting with *say* and *tell* ▶ 15.1

Lukasz was invited to a friend's cottage for the weekend, but he never arrived. Use the correct form of *say* or *tell* to complete the email in which he explains what happened.

From:	Lukasz
Re:	Stupid weather!

Hi Kevin

Your voicemail has just ➔ **told** me you are busy at the moment – I hope you're not mad at me. I left early, because the weatherman … (1) that a storm was coming. You … (2) me that the cottage was hard to find, but I have a navigation app on my phone, so I … (3) to myself that it wouldn't be a problem. I should have known that if the app … (4) you not to take the motorway, you usually end up on some tiny roads. At one point, it … (5) me to go right, but I should have gone left. Suddenly I came across a sign that … (6) the road ahead was flooded. Stupidly, I didn't turn round, and the car stopped. I called a garage but they … (7) me it would take hours to reach me because of all the rain. When the mechanic finally came, he … (8) he could take me home, but not to your place. So, here I am, back home again. I'm really sorry to miss the fun. Hope you're having a good time.

Cheers, Lukasz

3 The perfect family? Changes in tenses: present to past ▶ 15.4.2

Erklärvideo online:
📄▶ cornelsen.de/webcodes
➕🔊 Code: xajutu

We showed four friends a picture of a family eating together and asked them what meals were like in their homes. Answer the questions with *He/She said …*

Yuri I think the perfect family sits down to eat together, but we hardly ever do! We order pizzas on Wednesday after football training, and Friday is fish and chips night. We're all perfectly healthy, so I'm not complaining.

Mandy That looks like a weekend breakfast. On weekdays, we don't have time for breakfast in our house. My mum leaves the house first and has a coffee at work.

Jed We don't have breakfast together but my parents want us to have our evening meal together. My dad's a better cook than my mum, so he makes dinner for us every night.

Lillian We all have breakfast at different times, and we all get home at different times too, so it's hard to eat together. We have Sunday lunch with my grandparents.

15

➡ What did Yuri say about the perfect family?
*He said he **thought** the perfect family **sat down** to eat together, but **they** hardly ever **did**.*

1 What did Yuri say about Wednesdays and Fridays?
2 What did Lillian say about eating together?
3 What did Mandy say about her mum?
4 What did Jed say about his parents?

5 What did Yuri say about his family's health?
6 What did Lillian say about Sunday lunch?
7 What did Mandy say about breakfast?
8 What did Jed say about his dad?

4 Alibi Changes in tenses: past / present perfect to past perfect ▶ 15.4.2

Erklärvideo online:
▶ Exercise 3

The police are investigating a crime, and they think Susie and Finn were involved. They have both given statements, but many of the facts don't match up. Read the statements and complete the sentences below in indirect speech.

<u>Susie's statement:</u> Finn and I don't usually go out on a weekday, but on the night of January 5th, we met at six o'clock and had a quick snack in a sandwich bar on East Street. Finn wanted to see an old Spanish film at the Showroom Cinema, so we took a bus there and bought tickets at the box office for the 8:30 film. We had time for a quick drink at the bar and Finn left just before the start of the film to go to the toilet. I hated the film but Finn loved it.

<u>Finn's statement:</u> Susie and I often have a date on Wednesdays. We met at 5:30 on the night in question and we ate at the new curry place on East Street. Susie has always been interested in Spanish films, so we booked tickets online for the eight o'clock show of *Pan's Labyrinth*. We missed the bus so we walked to the Showroom and got there just in time for the film. We didn't have a drink and I didn't even have time to go to the toilet. We both really enjoyed the film.

➡ Susie said she and Finn … out on a weekday, but Finn said … a date on Wednesdays.
*Susie said she and Finn **didn't usually go** out on a weekday, but Finn said **they often had** a date on Wednesdays.*

1 Finn said … at half past five, but Susie …
2 Susie said … on East Street, but Finn …
3 Finn said … Spanish films, but Susie …
4 Susie said … tickets at the box office, but Finn …

5 Finn said … to the Showroom Cinema, but Susie …
6 Susie said … a drink, but Finn …
7 Finn said … the toilet, but Susie …
8 Susie said … the film, but Finn …

Indirect speech (Reported speech)

▶ 5 So little time Changes in tenses: modals ▶ 15.4.2

Erklärvideo online:
▶ Exercise 3

There are so many interesting places to visit that it's hard to decide where to go. We asked some young people where they would choose to spend a gap year.

→ I can't decide which South American country to visit.
I would love to hike to Machu Picchu. (1)
I really should learn Spanish before I go. (2)

I'll probably tour Eastern Europe by train. (3)
I won't go to Warsaw because I've been there before. (4)

I may stay with my aunt and uncle in Sydney. (5)
I can't go to Australia without visiting Uluru. (6)

I may not go far because I'd like to see more of the British Isles. (7)
I'll definitely visit the Shetland Islands. (8)

→ Joel said he …
*Joel said he **couldn't decide** which South American country to visit.*

1 Joel also said …   4 He added that …   7 Patsy thought …
2 He admitted that …   5 Ollie told us …   8 She decided that …
3 Len said …   6 He explained that …

▶ 6 Questions, questions Indirect questions ▶ 15.5

Erklärvideo online:
▶ Exercise 3

Elleray High School is doing a project entitled 'Misunderstandings'. All the kids have been asked to contribute their experiences. Read the text Phyllie wrote, then complete the questions she was actually asked.

> **WANTED**
> experienced, energetic young person to look after my Little One.
> Two hours morning and evening.
> Call Mrs Brady on ~~███████~~

Last month I had the funniest job interview ever. I was looking for some babysitting work to help pay for my summer holiday. I saw this ad online, so I rang the woman. She asked me all sorts of questions, starting with quite normal ones, like my name and age. She asked me how long I'd lived in the village, and if I'd left school. Then she asked me what courses I had studied. She asked if I had a clean driving licence and if I could stay calm in an emergency. Fair enough, I suppose. But then she asked me how far I walked every day and how many pets I had! And she wanted to know what kind of dogs I preferred. I suddenly realized there'd been a misunderstanding. She didn't want a babysitter at all – she wanted a dog sitter! I didn't get the job by the way…

→ 'What's … ?'
'What's **your name and how old are you**?'

1 '… in the village?'   3 '… courses …?'   5 '… in an emergency?'   7 '… pets …?'
2 '… school?'   4 '… driving licence?' 6 '… every day?'   8 '… dogs …?'

Erklärvideo online:
► Exercise 3

7 They wanted to know   Indirect questions   ► 15.5

Hari's neighbours have just started renting their apartment out to visitors. The visitors asked Hari a lot of questions, so he decided to send his neighbours an email. Rewrite their questions in indirect speech.

→ Is there Wi-fi in the apartment?

1 What's the password for the internet connection?

2 How can I get onto the balcony?

3 Where do you keep the key?

4 Can we use the garden?

5 Why was the freezer switched off?

6 How do we use the microwave?

7 Should we write a review on the internet?

8 Can we get some of our money back?

15

| From: | Hari |
| Re: | The apartment |

Your visitors wanted to know → **if there was Wi-fi in the apartment**. They also wondered … (1), because of course they needed that to log on. Someone asked … (2) because the weather was so hot. They decided to have breakfast out there. One of them tried to open the door to the balcony but found it was locked, so she asked … (3). The kids wanted to play football, but of course the apartment is very small so they asked … (4). The parents wanted ice for their drinks, but there wasn't any. Actually, they were wondering … (5). At dinner time, they needed to know … (6). They really weren't very happy and were wondering … (7). They clearly thought the apartment was over-priced and before they left, they asked … (8).

8 Party planners   Indirect commands and requests   ► 15.6

Bea is a German au pair, and she's organizing a children's party with the help of two English friends, Jacky and Pam. She's telling Jacky what she wants them to do. Find and correct Bea's mistakes.

→ You and Pam promised that you help me with the party, right?
*You and Pam **promised to help me** with the party, right?*

1 I've asked the children that they invite some other five-year-olds.
2 Pam promised that she isn't here later than four.
3 Pam warned us to start too late, since tired kids are unhappy kids.
4 She advised me that I don't let the other kids' parents stay all evening.

5 Pam offered me to help with the food.
6 I've told to Pam that she should make a cake.
7 I've suggested to have dinner at six o'clock.
8 Pam told me don't forget to prepare some games for the kids.

15

9 Be kind to yourself   Indirect suggestions   ▶ 15.6c

a Laura's aunt Teresa broadcasts a popular life hack video online. Laura is interviewing her for a project in her health class about stressed teens. First underline all Teresa's advice.

Laura   Why do I always feel tired? Is it normal for a teenager?

Teresa It's nothing to do with age. If I were you, ➜ **_I'd get more sleep_**. I know that's easier said than done, but don't drink too much tea or coffee. Caffeine's not good for you, especially not late at night. You should try some natural health products for stress or panic attacks.

Laura   I've tried those. They don't seem to work for me.

Teresa Are you eating properly? Try eating less sugar. Have a healthy diet of fresh fruit and vegetables.

Laura   I don't think I eat badly. Maybe I snack too much, but no more than most teenagers.

Teresa How about taking more exercise, like a regular walk in the park or a swim? And if I were you, I'd spend less time in front of the computer screen.

Laura   But I have so much work! I can't stop using the computer! I'm often late handing in projects.

Teresa OK, so you should manage your time better. We can talk about that together, if you like. Why don't you say 'no' or 'I need more time'? You're not superwoman and you can't do everything.

Laura   No, I guess not.

Teresa I could show you some relaxation techniques like breathing or simple yoga exercises.

Laura   I might try that. Thanks, Teresa, you're a star.

b Complete the report Laura wrote for her project. Use indirect speech.

I interviewed my aunt, Teresa, who had some really good tips for me. I told her that I often feel tired. She ➜ **_suggested getting more sleep_** (suggest | get more sleep). She ... (warn | drink tea or coffee) (1). She ... (advise | try natural health products) (2). She ... (ask | eat properly) (3). Teresa ... (suggest | eat less sugar) (4). She ... (recommend | have a healthy diet) (5). She ... (suggest | take more exercise) (6) and ... (advise | 5 spend less time | computer) (7). She ...(propose | talk about managing my time better) (8). She ... (advise | say no) (9). Teresa also ... (offer | show relaxation techniques) (10). I think this is excellent advice for stressed teenagers.

c NOW YOU Have you ever watched a really interesting life hack video online? What did the vlogger advise, suggest or propose? Write three sentences.

▶ 10 My hero   Changes in tenses: mixed exercise   ▶ 15.4

Erklärvideo online:
▶ Exercise 3

a This is from a radio phone-in programme, in which callers were asked about the most important person in their life. Complete the texts below with the correct forms of the verbs.

Elena

'The most important person in my life is definitely my mother – she's my hero. She has always been a great support to me. I suppose some people will say that that's completely normal and they may be right. But I honestly think my mum is special. It doesn't matter what she's going through, she always manages to 5 laugh. She's taught me to be positive at difficult times, and I will always be glad she did.'

The first caller, Elena, said the most important person in her life ➜ **_was_** definitely her mother, who ... always ... (1) a great support to her. She said she supposed some people ... (2) that that ... (3) normal and she agreed that they ... (4) right. But she honestly ... (5) that her mum ... (6) special. She said it ... (7) what she ... (8) through, she always ... (9) to laugh. She said her mum ... (10) her to be positive and that she ... always ... (11) 10 glad she had.

Deniz

'Several people have played a big part in my life, in addition to my parents. I feel that the most important person in my teenage years was my football coach, Jimmy. I've been thinking about him a lot recently. I can remember training sessions when I felt so frustrated and ready to give up. At those times, Jimmy made me
15 try just a little bit harder.'

The next caller, Deniz, said that several people … (12) a big part in his life, in addition to his parents. He said he … (13) that the most important person in his teenage years … (14) his football coach. He said he … (15) a lot about him recently. He went on to say he … (16) remember training sessions when he … (17) ready to give up. He said his coach … (18) him try a little bit harder.

b NOW YOU Ask a friend or one of your parents about an important person in their life. Then write four sentences about what they said.

➔ *… told me that … was an important person in his/her life. He/she explained …*

11 Change of plan   Changes in phrases of time and place   ▶ 15.3

Kylie wants to meet up with some old school friends. First she rang Julia, then Mikey. And now she's telling Zoe about their conversations.

Julia	'I tried to contact you last week.'
Julia	'I'm going to the doctor's tomorrow.' (1)
Julia	'I'm not feeling very well at the moment. I may have caught a cold.' (2)
Kylie	'You should really try to rest all this week.' (3)

Mikey	'I'm too busy today.' (4)
Mikey	'I tried to call you several times last week.' (5)
Kylie	'I had some terrible news yesterday.' (6)
Kylie	'Our favourite café closed down two days ago.' (7)
Mikey	'Oh no! But that's OK because we can all meet here at my place.' (8)

And now she's telling Zoe about their conversations.

First I called Julia. Julia said ➔ **she had tried** to contact me ➔ **the week before**.

1 She said …
2 Then she said …
3 So I said …
4 Mikey said …

5 Mikey said …
6 I said …
7 Then I told him …
8 Mikey said …

✚ 12 Stay safe Indirect advice and warning ▶ 15.6b

There's a lot to think about before you travel.
Choose the correct words to complete these travel tips.

You are ➔ **advised to** | warned to | advised that start preparing for
your trip, especially long trips, four to six weeks before you go.

It recommends | recommends that | is recommended that (1) you read the latest health and safety advice
for the country you're travelling to.
Find out if you need any special medication for travelling and make sure your immunizations are up to
date. If diseases such as malaria are a risk, you are normally suggested | told | warned (2) to start taking
the tablets before travelling.
The Department of Health advises you preparing | you to prepare | you prepare (3) a travel kit, including
sun cream, painkillers and antiseptic.
Whether you're off on a six-month trek to the Andes or a family holiday in Italy, you are asked | advised |
recommended (4) that someone back at home should know where you are going. Your travel plans should
be known in case of accidents, especially if you are doing dangerous activities like skiing or mountain
climbing.
Most airlines advise to | advise | advise you to (5) get up from your seat and walk around whenever you
can on long-haul flights. Drink regularly, but avoid alcohol, and wear loose, comfortable clothes.
Finally, when you get where you're going, you are warned not to eat | are recommended to not eat | are
advised that you eat (6) street food or drink tap water in some places.

⏵ ✚ 13 Wish you weren't here Changes in tenses: mixed exercise ▶ 15.4

Erklärvideo online:
▶ Exercise 3

Journalists use both direct and indirect speech to make their articles interesting. Rewrite the numbered
sentences in direct speech if they are indirect, or in indirect speech if they are direct.

➔ Local people warn that giant cruise ships and the rise of internet vacation platforms would make mass
tourism a problem in many holiday destinations.
*'Giant cruise ships and internet vacation platforms will make mass tourism a problem in many holiday
destinations,' warn local people.*

A leading travel agent reported that a number of
anti-tourist protests had taken place (1) in some of
Europe's most popular holiday destinations. Some
of the biggest problems have been in Spain, which
5 has around 75 million visitors a year. In the beautiful city of Barcelona, the rise of internet vacation
platforms has resulted in local families not being
able to afford to live in the city. Spanish activists
vandalized a tourist bus, painting it with the words
10 'Tourism is killing neighbourhoods' (2). A spokesperson told this paper that today's model of tourism
displaced families and harmed the environment (3).
Even various tour operators admitted that Spain
was rather full. A written statement from them con-
15 firmed that they had had an all-time high in tourist
numbers to Spain that year (4).

Other demonstrations have taken place in southern
Europe. Venice, which has more than 20 million
tourists a year, is more at risk than most cities.
Enormous cruise ships are of particular concern. A 20
Venetian restaurateur told us that these huge ships
had become symbols of the impact of mass tourism
(5). 'Each ship may bring 3000 visitors, who all
arrive at the same time. Our old city cannot take so
many people.' (6) He went on to say that this would 25
harm the foundations of the city, which were
already very fragile (7).
This, according to a member of the UN, is 'a very
serious problem that needs to be discussed in a very
serious way' (8).
30

+ 14 Guerrilla gardening   Various reporting verbs   ▸ 15.6

People in cities all over the world are planting in places where nothing is growing. James has been to a conference to learn more from gardening enthusiasts. Rewrite the text in indirect speech as freely as you think suitable. Leave out unnecessary details and change words to make the situation clear. Remember to use various reporting verbs, such as *explain*, *argue*, *advise* or *agree*.

James	Here at Sheffield University, they are having a conference called 'From Grey to Green: Adventures in Radical Urban Gardening'. I'm talking to the speakers, who are themselves all radical gardeners, about guerrilla gardening. My first question is to a fashion designer from Los Angeles – hello, can I ask you please, what is guerrilla gardening exactly? Can you explain the basic concept?
Man	Sure. Guerrilla gardening is when the people who live in cities make their city greener in secret. We do this by planting flowers at night, growing a garden, seed bombing in public places, that kind of thing.
James	Seed bombing? That sounds aggressive.
Man	But it isn't aggressive at all. It just means, when I find an empty piece of land, or even just the space between the road and the sidewalk, I throw down handfuls of seeds in 'earth bombs'. These will grow into plants and flowers and make that space more beautiful. Most cities are short of green places, but I think improving what we call 'dead land' can be done in any sad little space. You should just look around you and you'll see that places in car parks, up walls, even rooftops can all be transformed.
James	What kind of people are guerrilla gardeners? I mean, are you all activists?
Man	I don't agree with that term, actually! All sorts of people are interested in improving life in the city. I'm in the fashion business, but I am also passionate about access to healthy food for everyone. You know, in LA, you can't get a fresh apple or banana without getting into your car and driving to a store.
James	And what is your reaction to that?
Man	There was an ugly patch of grass outside my house, which people were dropping litter on. So I dug up the grass and planted sunflowers and banana trees. You can do that in the Californian sunshine! Now, my aim for the future is to plant edible gardens in schools, parks, empty plots and shelters for the homeless. Why should we have dusty patches of grass when we could be growing food?
James	So, basically, this is what guerrilla gardening is all about, but it is illegal. Every vacant piece of land belongs to someone, after all. So it's like graffiti or vandalism. Let's ask another of the speakers – excuse me, I have a question about this kind of activity. Do you agree that it is against the law?
Woman	Yes, it is technically illegal, but we have three simple rules. One is: Make sure the land or area is vacant. Two is: Make the space better than how you found it. And, most importantly, rule number three is: If you don't ask for permission, don't let anyone catch you doing it!
James	I understand that you design gadgets for secretive gardening activities. Your drawings look like something out of a James Bond movie – can you tell us about them?
Woman	OK, so what can you do if you need to dig a hole without being noticed? Let me show you. This gadget comes in a chic little handbag. You make the hole, collect the extra earth in your bag and hurry away.
James	Very clever!
Woman	Thank you – I like it! I'm pretty proud of this one too.
James	And what is it? It looks like a camera.

Speaker Yes, it does, doesn't it? In fact, it can shoot out flower seeds into any bit of wasteland. I can assure you that next summer, flower meadows will shine like jewels in places all over Sheffield, in public places and on housing estates. Children will be able to enjoy the flowers, watch butterflies – we're bringing nature into our grey urban spaces.

James And is that the main objective of guerrilla gardening?

Woman Some urban gardeners say the planting must be edible. Others say it only has to be beautiful. But we have to be careful. We sometimes come up against authorities who don't like what we're doing and we have to fight them. Someone at this weekend's conference planted a garden on a piece of dead land. Wiltshire County Council noticed it and said 'It's against our health and safety regulations, it must be destroyed.' The woman fought back and won, so the garden remains. That is a lesson to us all.

15

Guerrilla gardening:

an article by James Robertson

I asked a fashion designer from Los Angeles ➔ *what guerrilla gardening was exactly*. He said that guerrilla gardening was when the people who ➔ *lived* in cities ➔ *made* their city greener in secret. He explained ➔ *that they did this* by planting flowers at night, growing a garden and seed bombing. He argued that seed bombing ...

Quick Check

A Report what was said in indirect speech.

1	**Bella**	'I really don't like hot milk.'	Bella said …
2	**Neil**	'Do you want to come with me, Paula?'	Neil asked …
3	**Jude**	'Answer the phone for me!'	Jude told me …
4	**Karim**	'I think it may snow here.'	Karim thought …
5	**Lilly**	'Can you help me with my homework?'	Lilly asked Bill …
6	**Laura**	'What time is the last bus?'	Laura wanted to know …
7	**Ina**	'Bye, Josh. I'll call you tomorrow.'	Ina told Josh …
8	**Ryan**	'You're right, this lemon cake is delicious.'	Ryan agreed …
9	**Owen**	'Do you think I'll need a coat?'	Owen wondered …
10	**Faye**	'I saw this film when it first came out.'	Faye told us …

15

B Fill in the missing forms.

Pete and Jill were discussing their winter holiday plans. Jill said she … (not want) (1) to do what they … (always, do) (2) in the past. Pete asked her what she … (mean) (3). She replied that she … (not enjoy) (4) last year's skiing holiday. She added that skiing holidays … (be) (5) always very expensive. Pete was surprised and said that he'd thought they … (have) (6) a brilliant time. He asked her where she … (prefer) (7) to go the following year and she suggested … (go) (8) to the Caribbean. He warned her that a trip like that … (cost) (9) as much or more than skiing. At that point she wanted to know why he … (ask) (10) her in the first place.

C Write what was said in direct speech.

1	Bella said that she preferred vegetarian food.	**Bella** …
2	Neil told us that he was going to the beach.	**Neil** …
3	Jude wondered if the call had been for him.	**Jude** …
4	Karim asked if he could borrow a warm sweater.	**Karim** …
5	Bill offered to meet me at the station the next day.	**Bill** …
6	Laura wanted to know if it had been raining.	**Laura** …
7	Ina said she knew how much the tickets cost.	**Ina** …
8	Ryan told Jane to help herself to a drink.	**Ryan** …
9	Owen warned me not to touch the hot plates.	**Owen** …
10	Faye asked me if I was going by myself.	**Faye** …

D Find and correct the mistakes.

1 My maths teacher told us don't forget our homework.
2 My aunt said to us to take our shoes off at the door.
3 Phillip wants to know when does the show end.
4 Belinda told to me that she was feeling unwell.
5 Can you say me the time, please?
6 The interviewer asked me what was I studying.
7 My mother wants that I help her with the shopping.
8 The teacher asked if I do usually go to chess club.

16 Relative clauses

	Task	Topic	Example	Englische Grammatik
▶	1	The relative pronouns *who*, *which* and *that*	*Tamara is the girl who is talking to Lennart.*	16.2.2
▶	2	The relative pronoun as object (contact clauses)	*Here are the photos (that) I took at the premiere.*	16.2.3
▶	3	Relative clauses with prepositions	*That's the film (that) I told you about.*	16.2.4
	4	The relative determiner *whose*	*Is Samed the guy whose parents come from Uzbekistan?*	16.2.5
	5	*Whose* or *who's*?	*See that guy who's standing next to Noah? He's the one whose sister won a prize.*	16.2.5
	6	Non-defining relative clauses	*Barack Obama, who was elected President in 2008, had a Kenyan father.*	16.3.1 16.3.2
	7	*Which* relating to a clause	*We had to walk five miles in the pouring rain, which wasn't exactly fun.*	16.3.3
	8	Mixed exercise (1)	*Bill Gates started a firm. He named it Microsoft. → Bill Gates started a firm which he named Microsoft.*	16
	9	Defining and non-defining relative clauses in contrast	*The man who broke into the shop was arrested. Connor P., who broke into Smithfield's on 9 June, was arrested two days later.*	16.1b
	10	Mixed exercise (2)	*Stephen King has two sons. They are both writers. → Stephen King has two sons, both of whom are writers.*	16
	11	Formal and informal style	*To whom are you referring? / Who are you talking about?*	16.2.4 16.3.2

▶ Quick Check p. 145

▶ 1 The bag snatcher The relative pronouns *who*, *which* and *that* ▶ 16.2.2

Erklärvideo online:
cornelsen.de/webcodes
Code: sogiza

Read the text below, then complete the captions. Use a relative clause with *who*, *which* or *that*.

It was a nice Saturday afternoon. In the park, three kids were playing with their dog. Two men were playing chess. A girl was checking her mails. A woman was sitting on a bench.

5 The woman got up and walked away, but she forgot her handbag. A young man passed by on his bike. He noticed that she had forgotten her bag and called to her. But a small plane was flying over the park, so she couldn't hear him. At that moment, a man wearing a blue cap grabbed the bag and ran off. 10 The cyclist tried to catch him, but the man ran into the bushes. While he was running away, he lost his cap.

These are the kids ➔ *who were playing with their dog.*

1 These are the men …

2 This is the girl …

3 This is the woman …

4 This is the handbag …

5 This is the young man …

6 This is the plane …

7 This is the man …

8 This is the cap …

16

2 Which one? The relative pronoun as object (contact clause) ▶ 16.2.3

Erklärvideo online:
▶ Exercise 1

Answer the questions using a relative clause without a relative pronoun (contact clause).

➔ – Hey, look! There's that girl!
– What girl?
– The girl **I met at Jackie's party** (I met her at Jackie's party).

1 – I need my book back.
– Which book?
– The book … (I lent it to you last week).

2 – I'm doing a presentation on Water.org.
– Water.org? What's that?
– It's a nonprofit organization … (Matt Damon founded it in 2009).

3 – I feel a bit sick. It must be that hamburger.
– What hamburger?
– The one … (I ate it before I came here).

4 – I've given my old bike to a refugee.
– Your old bike?
– Yes, it's the bike … (I bought it second hand a couple of years ago).

5 – The film was okay, but I liked the other one better.
– Which one?
– The film … (We watched it last weekend).

6 – I got an 'A' for my painting.
– What painting was that?
– The one … (I painted it for the competition).

3 That boy I told you about · Relative clauses with prepositions ▸ 16.2.4

Erklärvideo online:
▸ Exercise 1

Read the sentences below, then answer the questions. Use a relative clause.

→ Who is Carlotta?
*Carlotta is **the girl Maria is talking to**.*

→ Maria is talking to Carlotta.

1 Ken is waiting for Lucas.

2 Harry is running after Spots.

3 Camilla is shouting at Roger.

4 José is flirting with Lucy.

5 Tarek is laughing at Laszlo.

1 Who is Lucas?
2 Who is Spots?

3 Who is Roger?
4 Who is Lucy?

5 Who is Laszlo?

4 Parents and their jobs · The relative determiner *whose* ▸ 16.2.5

Steve and Cindy are doing a project on careers and have collected the names of students whose parents have interesting or unusual jobs. Now they're comparing notes. Complete the dialogue with the help of their notes.

Cindy's notes	Steve's notes
Annabel Cranston – mother: ballet dancer *Irina Gorchukov – father: diplomat* *Brian Lovell – mother: author of fantasy novels* *Louise Dano – parents: opera singers*	*Tim Corey – father: police detective* *Caleb Manson – father: bodyguard* *Mara Lippincott – father: stuntman*

Cindy Who's Tim Corey? Isn't he the guy
→ ***whose*** father is a police detective?
Steve Right. And what about Annabel Cranston?
Cindy She's the one … (1).
Steve Who is this Irina Gorchukov?
Cindy Irina? She's the girl … (2).
Steve What about Brian Lovell?

Cindy Don't you remember? Brian's the guy … (3). But why is Caleb Manson on the list?
Steve He's the one … (4). What about Louise Dano?
Cindy She's the girl … (5). And then there's Mara Lippincott – why is she on the list?
Steve She's the one … (6).
Cindy Wow, what a collection!

5 Cleaning up   Whose or who's?   ▶ 16.2.5

The PE teacher Mr O'Hara is going through the sports gear that has been left in the locker room. Pete and Karim are helping him. Complete the dialogue using *whose* or *who's*.

O'Hara Here's a pretty nice sweatshirt. Any idea ➜ **whose** it could be?

Karim I think it belongs to Yuri.

O'Hara Yuri? … (1) that?

Pete Yuri Savatzky from Year 10. His brother Pavel is on the rugby team.

O'Hara Pavel Savatzky? You mean the guy … (2) top player this season?

Karim Right, that's him. Hey, look at these trainers! Ugh – they look terrible. No wonder somebody left them here.

O'Hara … (3) are they? Any idea?

Pete They could be Kevin's. Let me have a look. – Yeah, they're Kevin's all right.

Karim Isn't Kevin the guy … (4) family owns the Clifford Hotel?

Pete Yeah. Anyone … (5) rich enough to own a hotel should have enough money for better trainers for their son.

O'Hara I agree with you there. I always feel sorry for kids … (6) parents don't seem very interested in them.

6 The birth of a vampire   Non-defining relative clauses   ▶ 16.3.1, 16.3.2

a Below there is a short text about Bram Stoker, the author of the novel *Dracula*. Seven relative clauses are missing; you find them on the right. Match the sentences and the clauses, then copy the complete sentences, adding commas where needed.

➜ *Bram Stoker,* **who became famous as the author of Dracula**, *was born in Dublin in 1847.*

1 ~~Bram Stoker … was born in Dublin in 1847.~~
2 He was still a student at Trinity College when he became the theatre critic for the Dublin Evening Mail …
3 Through his work as a theatre critic he became friends with Henry Irving …
4 Stoker later became the manager of the Lyceum Theatre in London …
5 Stoker had begun writing fiction early in life and he wrote many novels, but his biggest success was *Dracula* …
6 Before he began writing, Stoker spent many years studying the folklore of Transsylvania …
7 Stoker's charismatic vampire Count Dracula … has inspired authors, playwrights and filmmakers from F. W. Murnau to Stephenie Meyer.

a which belonged to Irving
b who was one of the best-known actors of his time
c which at that time was the leading Irish newspaper
d ~~who became famous as the author of Dracula~~
e whose bite makes vampires of his victims
f which was published in 1897
g which he never visited in person

b NOW YOU Collect information on a famous person and write a short biography. Use relative clauses wherever possible.

7 Sports Day at Hatherford   *Which* relating to a clause   ▶ 16.3.3

Sports day at Hatherford School is always an exciting event. Combine the sentences below by making the second sentence a relative clause that refers to the first sentence.

→ Larry Neff won the 100-metre sprint. That amazed everyone.
  Larry Neff won the 100-metre sprint, which amazed everyone.

1 During the 400-metre race Brian Kennedy fell and hurt his leg. That meant that he had to spend the rest of the day on the bench.
2 The volleyball team of Form 10BH won all their matches. That made them very proud.
3 Bertie Lewis won the 5000-metre run. That didn't exactly come as a surprise.
4 At lunch break, some of the teachers showed their sports talent. That gave everyone something to laugh at.
5 Linda Moretti broke the school record for girls' long jump. That made her friends cheer wildly.
6 Kelly Mulligan cleared 170 cm on the high jump. No one had ever done that before.

8 From starlet to superstar   Mixed exercise   ▶ 16

Combine the sentences below by making the second sentence a relative clause of the first. Add commas if necessary.

→ Ariana Grande was born in Boca Raton, Florida in 1993. Her real name is Ariana Grande-Butera.
  Ariana Grande, **whose real name is Ariana Grande-Butera***, was born in Boca Raton, Florida in 1993.*

1 From 2010 to 2013, Grande played a character in the popular TV series *Victorious*. That brought her national attention.
2 In 2013, she released her first studio album. It was called *Yours Truly*.
3 Her second album, *My Everything*, was a huge success. It made Grande famous.
4 In 2017, Grande went on a world concert tour. Her third album, *Dangerous Woman*, was released in 2016.
5 At the end of her concert in Manchester Arena, a bomb exploded, killing 23 people. They were leaving the concert hall.
6 Grande organized a benefit concert for the victims. It took place in Manchester on June 4.

16

✚ 9 The water crisis   Defining or non-defining relative clauses in contrast   ▸ 16.1b

The following text on the global water crisis contains a number of relative clauses. Read the text and decide for each numbered gap whether a comma is needed.

➔ Everybody knows the kind of water [?] that falls from the sky.
 Everybody knows the kind of water that falls from the sky.

But in many parts of the world, there isn't enough rainfall to satisfy the needs of farmers and urban populations. Instead, these people rely on groundwater [?] (1) which is the water found in so-called
5 aquifers far below the surface. For years now, farmers in many regions of the world have been pumping groundwater [?] (2) which they use to irrigate their crops [?] (3) up to the surface. About two-thirds of the groundwater [?] (4) that is consumed yearly
10 [?] (5) goes into irrigation. The rest is needed for drinking water for the world's cities [?] (6) which have rapidly expanded in recent decades. Scientists warn that we are using up water reserves at a rate [?] (7) that will have drastic effects in the future.
15 Pumping the water out of the ground leaves millions of tiny air pockets in underlying rock layers [?] (8) which may then collapse under pressure. The Chinese capital Beijing [?] (9) which depends heavily on the huge North China Plain aquifer
20 [?] (10) is actually sinking at a rate of ten centimetres a year in some places.

16

✚ 10 Crowdfunding   Mixed exercise   ▸ 16

Connect the sentences below by making the sentence in brackets a relative clause of the other sentence. Add commas where needed.

The word crowdfunding may be new, but crowdfunding itself isn't. One of the most famous examples is the Statue of Liberty ➔ **which was intended as a gift from the French people to the American**
5 **people** (it was intended as a gift from the French people to the American people).

The American Committee of the Statue of Liberty ... (it was responsible for raising money to build the pedestal) (1) had great difficulty finding enough
10 supporters. Joseph Pulitzer used his newspaper *The New York World* to start a fundraising campaign ... (with it he solved the problem) (2). He received money from more than 160,000 people ... (most of them donated less than a dollar) (3).

15 Modern crowdfunding began with the rise of the internet ... (it makes it easier to reach a large number of people in a short time) (4). Rock musicians ... (they needed money for a tour or a new album) (5) were among the first to discover the possibility of
20 raising money by getting many people to donate relatively small sums. Often there are special prizes for those ... (they donate larger amounts) (6), for example an autographed CD or a backstage invitation. Since then, crowdfunding has become a billion-
25 dollar business ... (it is often used by start-ups to raise capital for new projects) (7). Websites such as Kickstarter and Indiegogo connect people ... (they have new ideas) (8) with others ... (they are willing to support them) (9). To date, more than 10 million
30 people worldwide have donated to online campaigns ... (this shows that crowdfunding in one form or another is here to stay) (10).

+ 11 First impressions Formal and informal style ▸ 16.2.4, 16.3.2

a The sentences below contain forms that are too formal for the context. Improve the style by using less formal expressions (*when, where, why*, contact clauses) in place of the underlined relative pronouns.

➔ I'll never forget the day <u>on which</u> I first came to Germany.
*I'll never forget **the day (when) I first came** to Germany.*

1 A friend of mine had given me the phone number of the youth hostel in Mannheim, <u>at which</u> I planned to stay.
2 The train <u>on which</u> I was travelling had a breakdown, so I arrived two hours late.
3 I phoned the youth hostel, but the man <u>to whom</u> I talked told me they were full up.
4 I left the station and looked around for streets <u>in which</u> there might be a cheap hotel.
5 But all the hotels <u>to which</u> I went had no free rooms.
6 The reason <u>for which</u> all hotels were booked out was the trade fair in Mannheim.
7 Not knowing what else to do, I went to a nearby park and looked for a quiet bench, <u>on which</u> I spent my first night in Germany.
8 But the person <u>with whom</u> I shared my first German breakfast has turned out to be a really good friend.

b Sanjit has applied for an interesting position at an IT company. Read those snippets from the emails he exchanged with them and replace the underlined parts of the sentences with more formal structures.

➔ The person <u>I spoke to</u> yesterday asked me to contact you regarding my application.
*The person **to whom I spoke** yesterday asked me to contact you regarding my application.*

1 The position <u>you have applied for</u> has also been advertised internally.
2 The assessment centre <u>which suitable applicants will be invited to</u> will take place on 13 March.
3 The contract must be signed and returned within two weeks from the date <u>when it was received</u>.
4 As soon as the contract is signed, we will have a meeting <u>where we will discuss</u> the next steps.
5 The project is similar to others <u>I've worked on</u> before.
6 Would it be possible for me to receive a list of the other people <u>I'll be working with</u> on this project?

Quick Check

A Complete the sentences with *who, that, which* or *whose*.

1 The girl … was hurt in the car accident is in my biology class.
2 What's the name of that boy … went to school with Lisa?
3 We need a list of all the students … profiles have been hacked.
4 The Tower of London, … was built in the 11th century, is one of London's most famous landmarks.
5 A newcomer won the Oscar for Best Actor, … surprised a lot of people.
6 What's the name of that couple … used to live next door to us?
7 George W. Bush is one of two presidents … fathers were also presidents.
8 A heavy snowstorm hit the city at rush hour, … led to chaotic traffic jams.
9 The Burj Khalifa in Dubai, … was completed in 2008, is presently the tallest building in the world.
10 Carla kept jumping up and running to the window, … made everyone nervous.
11 The gentleman … portrait is hanging on the wall is my great-grandfather.
12 J. R. R. Tolkien, … wrote *The Lord of the Rings*, was a language professor at Oxford.

16

B Look at the sentences below and decide whether the <u>relative pronoun</u> can be left out.

1 What's the name of the man <u>who</u> invented the telephone?
2 Miranda is the girl <u>who</u> I introduced you to at Carlo's party.
3 I didn't like that film <u>that</u> we watched in English last week.
4 Bill Gates was the first person <u>who</u> realized that software was big business.
5 This is the book <u>that</u> I was telling you about yesterday.
6 The food <u>that</u> is served in the cafeteria is usually quite good.
7 The woman <u>who</u> I met at the airport told me she was from Chicago.
8 The house <u>that</u> we stayed at was built in the 18th century.
9 The hills <u>which</u> you can see in the distance are part of the Harz Mountains.
10 Mateusz is the guy <u>whose</u> mother is an opera singer.
11 Philip knows somebody <u>who</u> works for a software firm.
12 All the people <u>that</u> I spoke to shared my opinion.

C There is one mistake in each of the following sentences. Find and correct it.

1 Sri Lanka, that is in the Indian Ocean, used to be called Ceylon.
2 Jeanette remembered to bring her pocket calculator to the maths lesson, what surprised everyone.
3 Passengers who are travelling on to the US, should go to Gate 10.
4 Only students who's marks are B- or higher can take part in the programme.
5 Hey – isn't this the flash drive for that you were looking?
6 Don't believe everything what Melissa tells you.
7 Winning that prize was the best thing could have happened to you.
8 My girlfriend Sandra, whose family comes from Poland speaks four languages.
9 We need the names of all the customers to who this letter was sent.
10 Kathleen? That's the girl whose sitting next to Robert.

17 The adjective

Task	Topic	Example	Englische Grammatik
1	Comparison with -er/-est	*fast, faster, fastest*	17.2.2 17.2.4
2	Comparison with *more/most*	*the most successful team this season*	17.2.3
3	Sentences with comparisons (1)	*Shhh! We need to be as quiet as a mouse.*	17.2.5
4	Sentences with comparisons (2)	*Tennis is better than squash, but not as good as badminton.*	17.2.5
5	Adjectives with two forms of comparisons	*The latest results are on the last page.*	17.2.4
6	*One/Ones* after adjectives	*I'd like the red one, please.*	17.1.3
7	More comparisons	*Adjectives make your writing more effective.*	17.2
8	Adjectives used to refer to abstractions	*The best thing about school is meeting your friends.*	17.3
9	Adjectives used to refer to people	*Help the homeless.*	17.3

▶ Quick Check p. 151

⊙ Erklärvideo zu Steigerung und Vergleich von Adjektiven ▶ Exercise 1

⊙ **1 Taller, younger** Comparison with -er/-est ▶ 17.2.2, 17.2.4

Erklärvideo online:
📄⊙ **cornelsen.de/webcodes**
➕◁) **Code: vekaco**

a Make a table and fill in the comparative forms of the adjectives in the box.

bad · far · fast · fit · good · ~~heavy~~ · light · old · poor · rich · short · ~~tall~~ · young

Positive form	Comparative form
tall	*taller*
heavy	*heavier*
…	…

b Look at the information about Max and Alex in the table. Compare Alex to Max; use adjectives from the table in **a**.

→ *Alex is shorter, and he's …*

	Height	Age	Weight	Mark in maths	Mark in English	Time over 100 m	School journey	Pocket money
Max	162 cm	15 years, 1 month	58.9 kg	2	4	13.5 seconds	3.8 km	€20/month
Alex	159 cm	15 years, 8 months	59.6 kg	3	1	12.2 seconds	7.7 km	€6/week

2 Everyone has an opinion Comparison with *more/most* ▶ 17.2.3

Erklärvideo online:
▶ Exercise 1

a Here's what people think about different issues. Read the sentences carefully and put in the comparative or superlative form of the adjective with or without *more* or *most*.

➜ I got the Alpha tablet because the other one was … (expensive).
I got the Alpha tablet because the other one was **more expensive**.

1 That gold medallist is the … (fantastic) athlete I've ever seen.
2 I'm no good at maths so, for me, sudokus are … (difficult) than crosswords.
3 That actor from TV is the … (famous) person I've ever taken a selfie with.
4 This photo app is the … (useful) app I have. It's great!
5 This place is great – it's got the … (fast) internet connection ever!
6 I don't like science fiction – the more I read, the … (bored) I get.
7 My hometown is the … (beautiful) place in the world for me!
8 Cycling is sometimes … (slow) than skating.

b NOW YOU Write five sentences about your own opinions, using comparatives and superlatives.

3 English – it's as easy as pie Sentences with comparisons ▶ 17.2.5

Erklärvideo online:
▶ Exercise 1

17

a Find the right words to go with these traditional English expressions.

➜ as poor as
a church mouse

as pretty as …

as hungry as …

as quick as …

as busy as …

as tough as …

as dry as …

as hot as …

b Herr Schmidt is very proud of how well he speaks English. Tonight, he has taken an English friend to his favourite restaurant. Fill in the comparisons he uses.

Let's eat, please! I'm ➜ *as hungry as a wolf*. And I need a drink, too. My mouth feels … (1). I'm warning you: Don't order the curry in this restaurant. It's … (2). The waiters are fast here, you'll see. The food will be here … (3). The steaks here are very good. Last week I went to a different place and the steak was … (4). Oh, it's nice to relax a bit, after a day like this – I've been … (5). The bill? Oh, I can't pay, I'm … (6).

▶ **4 Comparisons quiz**   Sentences with comparisons   ▶ 17.2.5

Erklärvideo online:
▶ **Exercise 1**

a **Do you know the right answer? Compare the two things with the help of the adjective.**

➔ a pint | a litre | much
*A litre is **more than** a pint.*

1 London | Berlin | big
2 Mars | Saturn | far
3 Mont Blanc | Zugspitze | high
4 a diamond | a ruby | expensive

5 an elephant | a lion | fast
6 Shakespeare | Rowling | difficult to read
7 cricket | football | popular

b **Try making the same comparisons now using *less* or *not as … as*.**

➔ *A pint is **less than** / **not as much as** a litre.*

c **NOW YOU** **Make three quiz questions for your partner like the ones above – and try to answer his or hers.**

▶ **5 Teacher talk**   Adjectives with two forms of comparisons   ▶ 17.2.4

Erklärvideo online:
▶ **Exercise 1**

Mrs Allen always makes sure every student knows exactly what to do. Complete the sentences with the right form of the adjective.

➔ You failed your test, but I'm giving you one last | latest chance.
*You failed your test, but I'm giving you one **last** chance.*

1 There's going to be a fire drill later today. Remember: we all go to the nearest | next exit together.
2 OK, you don't need any further | farther instructions, you can start with the test.
3 The last | latest student who used this computer left her or his phone there.
4 The next | nearest time we have English, I'll have your marks ready.
5 Make sure you've checked up on the last | latest information for your chosen country before you give your presentation in class.

6 Which one's for me?   *One/Ones* after adjectives   ▶ 17.1.3

Your class has prepared the Secret Santa ('Wichteln') gifts that you can see in the box. You have the list, and it's your job to describe the gifts so the right person gets them. The adjectives in the box will help you.

➔ Mona – ***The striped ones are for Mona.***

1 … Sherrin
2 … Alex
3 … Moritz
4 … Leon
5 … Lisa
6 … Kinda

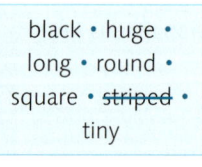

black • huge •
long • round •
square • ~~striped~~ •
tiny

▶ 7 Cheaper, but not the cheapest   More comparisons   ▶ 17.2

Erklärvideo online:
▶ Exercise 1

	Top Speed	Fuel consumption	Length	Price
Rambler	125 km/h	7.5 l/100km	6.99 m	€ 49,000
Twilight Dream	145 km/h	8.3 l/100km	7.7 m	€ 64,500
Homie	133 km/h	6.6 l/100km	4.95 m	€ 39,999

a Your grandparents are buying a caravan. You have done some research for them and have found the statistics in the table. Tell them how the three models compare.

→ How environmentally friendly are they?
Well, the Homie is the most environmentally friendly. The Rambler is less environmentally friendly; and the Twilight Dream is the least environmentally friendly.

1 How fast are they?
2 How expensive are they?
3 How long are they?

b NOW YOU Would your grandparents really like a caravanning holiday? If not, explain why. And if so, which vehicle would be the right one for your grandparents? Say why.

✛ 8 The best thing about school   Adjectives used to refer to abstractions   ▶ 17.3

a Tarik has almost finished school. Here's what he thinks about it. Translate the German parts of the sentences. Remember to add *thing* or *part* to the adjective in the English translation if necessary.

→ (Das Beste an der Schule) is the breaks.
*The **best thing** about school is the breaks.*

1 (Das Schwierigste an Sprachen) is getting the grammar right.
2 (Das Nette am Sportunterricht) is that we get to move around rather than sitting around.
3 In maths, you just need to think logically – (das ist das Großartige daran).
4 Our geography teacher always manages to focus (aufs Interessanteste) of a topic.
5 (Das Wichtigste) that I have learned is how to find out what really interests me.
6 (Das Komische) is that I love history now, and it was always a subject I hated.
7 When I finish school I want to, well, take some time out (um mal Gutes zu tun).
8 I don't have anything planned. I suppose I'm just looking forward to facing (das Unerwartete).

b NOW YOU Write three or four sentences about your experience of school, using phrases like *the challenging part, the most rewarding thing, ...*

17

+ 9 The rich and the poor Adjectives used to refer to people ▸ 17.3

a 'Give me your tired, your poor …' – these words at the foot of the Statue of Liberty in New York Harbour were written to welcome the ships carrying immigrants arriving in America, and fleeing their hard lives in Europe. How would you translate them?

b The tired and the poor are an everyday sight on our streets too. Read this report on homeless people. Decide whether the adjective can stand alone or whether it needs a prop word like *person/people, man/men, woman/women.*

In the centre of most big cities, you can see many homeless ➔ *people* living on the streets.

The reasons why they are there are varied. They might belong to the unemployed … (1) or the poor … (2) in the city and have no place to stay. Quite a few are newly-arrived … (3) from other countries.

Homelessness hits many social groups. The elderly … (4) are affected as well as the young … (5). Even the rich … (6) cannot be sure that they, too, won't end up walking the streets with their possessions stuffed in carrier bags. After a divorce or an illness, formerly wealthy … (7) can easily see themselves losing their grip on their lives.

If they are lucky, such people will be provided with food and clean clothes by a number of concerned … (8) who spend their free time looking after them. These voluntary helpers, working alongside municipal social workers, will try to feed the hungry … (9) and see to it that the sick … (10) get medical attention.

Once someone is 'down and out', it is difficult for them to get back to leading a steady life. So, what can be done to support the lonely … (11)? Providing warm soup and, more importantly, lending an open ear to the concerns of the needy … (12) who queue up at the help centres at nightfall is one way of reaching out to them. And projects like those that allow a small number of homeless … (13) to sell magazines to passers-by can be an opportunity for a new start.

If you're interested in helping long term, why don't you donate to one of the many charities which support the most vulnerable … (14) in society? Who knows – you might change a life!

Quick Check

A Fill the gaps with the correct form of the adjectives (positive, comparative or superlative).

1 …   –   smaller   –   …
2 nice   –   …   –   …
3 …   –   …   –   tidiest
4 easy   –   …   –   …
5 …   –   worse   –   …
6 difficult   –   …   –   …
7 …   –   more boring   –   …
8 important   –   …   –   …

B Find and correct the mistakes in these comparisons.

1 The new model of the phone is expensiver than the one before.
2 I don't think geography is so interesting as history.
3 Tea or coffee? – I think tea is best.
4 My test results were higher as last year's.
5 There's going to be a thunderstorm; I've just checked the last forecast.
6 I chose this school because it was the next to my home.
7 Only the fit people should attempt the Iron Man challenge.
8 Chili bananas are the unpopularest item on the menu.
9 The book is much more better than the film.
10 The test was more easy than I was expecting.

C Translate the German words in these sentences.

1 I'd like one of those T-shirts; do you have (ein grünes), please?
2 (Das Spannende beim Reisen) is that you never know what's coming next.
3 He never forgot (die Armen), even when he became rich and famous himself.
4 If you want to make chips from potatoes, it's best to choose (die großen).
5 There's (nichts Schlimmeres als) mosquitoes on the beach.
6 Cycling is (die umweltfreundlichste) way to travel.
7 On the barbecue, a sausage doesn't need (so lang wie) a steak.
8 Just take a look in the mirror – you're (bildhübsch)!
9 The (einzige) thing which I couldn't live without is my phone!
10 (Je älter) my grandma gets, (desto vergesslicher) she becomes.

D Fill the gaps with suitable adjectives in the correct form.

1 The test was more difficult than the last one? – Really? I thought it was … .
2 The green T-shirt looks smaller than the blue one. – No, it doesn't. It looks … .
3 Fruit is cheaper at the market than at the supermarket. – Not where I live – there it is … .
4 My school report was better than last year. – Lucky you! Mine was … .
5 This film is so boring. – You're right. The book was much … .
6 I'd buy the red suitcase because it is lighter. – But I prefer the blue one even if it is … .

17

18 The adverb

Task	Topic	Example	Englische Grammatik
1	Adverbs derived from adjectives	*nervously, happily*	18.2.1
2	Adjectives and adverbs in contrast (1)	*The new teacher laughed nervously.*	18.1
3	Adverbs with the form of adjectives	*hard, fast*	18.2.1 18.2.2
4	Adverbs with two forms	*hard, hardly*	18.2.3
5	The use of adverbs	*It's really important.*	18.1
6	Adjectives after certain verbs	*Sarah looks angry.*	18.1
7	Basic positions (1)	*I can see you at five tomorrow.*	18.3.1b
8	Basic positions (2)	*See you at school tomorrow.*	18.3.1.c
9	Comparison of adverbs (1)	*well, better, best; strongly, more strongly*	18.4
10	Comparison of adverbs (2)	*laughs louder than / as loudly as*	18.4
11	English verbs instead of German adverbs	*Ranjit happened to be passing.*	18.5
12	Adjectives and adverbs in contrast (2)	*The widely known story of Frankenstein is …*	18
13	Adverbs to enhance your style	*Surprisingly, Grandma was snoring loudly when little Red Riding Hood arrived.*	18

▸ Quick Check p. 159

1 I can usually do this easily   Adverbs derived from adjectives   ▸ 18.2.1

a Find ten adjectives in this word snake.

b Make a list with the adjectives on the left and the adverbs on the right.

➔ *slow – slowly*

c Choose the correct adjective or adverb to complete the text.

My best friend Jada is ➜ terrible | **terribly** shy. She cries easy | easily (1), when people are loud or aggressive.

5 Last week our teacher, Mr Mills, got angry | angrily (2) and shouted at her. He said Jada hadn't prepared her presentation very good | well (3). She started crying. Mr Mills said a little criticism was normal | normally (4), and she should calm down.

But I disagree. He's not a good | well (5) teacher, and he's the one who needs to calm down! I true | 10 truly (6) hate Mr Mills! Poor Jada.

2 We loved Katzi dearly   Adjectives and adverbs in contrast   ▶ 18.1

Erklärvideo online:
cornelsen.de/webcodes
Code: qogaqe

a Change the adjective to an adverb where necessary.

We got our new cat Katzi after we had read an advert in the ➜ *local* newspaper. The (kind)
5 (1) people were giving her away for nothing, so we called them (quick) (2). We chose her (easy) (3) from among the
10 four brothers and sisters. Poor Katzi was very sick in the car on the way home. But she soon became a (happy) (4) member of the family. She (usual) (5) stayed out at night, but (normal) (6) returned the following morning. After

about three years, Katzi 15 had four (beautiful) (7) kittens and (quiet) (8) carried them off to a (safe) (9) place. She was a (good) (10) mum and 20 looked after them very (careful) (11).

When we (final) (12) moved to the city, we had to give her away to some (close) (13) friends. We 25 were very (sad) (14) when it was time to say good-bye, but we knew our friends would look after Katzi (good) (15).

b Find the word(s) that each adjective or adverb refers to.

➜ the local *newspaper*

3 Jakob's knee problems   Adverbs with the form of adjectives   ▶ 18.2.1, 18.2.2

a Adjective (red), adverb (blue) or both? Put the words from the box in the right section of the diagram.

> ~~polite~~ • ~~loudly~~ • ~~well~~ • quick • daily • friendly • fantastically • early • badly •
> fast • exactly • far • cheerful • shyly • helpful

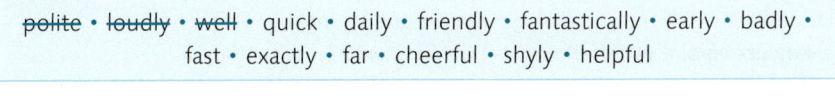

polite   well   loudly

b Jakob hurt his knee while playing football, but he still has to go to work. Complete the sentences with an adverb.

→ I'm early this morning!
*Jakob got to work **early** this morning.*

My daily routine is a lot more complicated now.	Jakob needs to take the bus twice … (1)
Fortunately, the bus was really quick today.	His bus got through the traffic … (2)
My home isn't far, just the other side of town.	He doesn't live … (3) away.
I usually walk, but with my injured knee, I'm not so fast.	He can't walk very … (4) at the moment.
The bus driver was very friendly.	Jakob said the bus driver smiled at him … (5)
I like it when people are polite.	He likes it when people behave … (6)
I always try to be cheerful when I chat to others.	Jakob always chats to people … (7)
I must go. Hopefully I'll be well again soon.	He doesn't feel … (8) now, but hopefully he soon will.

c Look at the diagram in a and at sentence 8 above. When can 'well' be an adjective?

4 It's hardly a problem   Adverbs with two forms   ▶ 18.2.3

Complete the sentence pairs with the correct form of the adverbs – one with *-ly* and one without.

→ It's not … to find the answer. It's … a problem.
*It's not **hard** to find the answer. It's **hardly** a problem.*

close • fair • free • ~~hard~~ • late • most • near

1 You can get into the Marine Park … . Then you can wander around … inside.
2 It was … aggressive the way you spoke to Jeff. If you ask me, it wasn't … what you did.
3 Look how … Tim and Maya are dancing. And look how … Maya's boyfriend is watching them.
4 I haven't been to gym practice … . That's why I forgot where it was and turned up …
5 My dad … cooks the meals in our house. His kebabs are what I like … of all.
6 The twins live really … the school. They can … fall out of bed and into the classroom.

18

⊙ 5 What is really important to you? The use of adverbs ▸ 18.1

Erklärvideo online:
▸ Exercise 2

a Look at the picture and choose the right adverb to describe Nele's attitude to things.

→ Schoolwork is extremely | not particularly important.
*Schoolwork is **not particularly** important.*

1 Talking to my friends is terribly | not really important to me.
2 Pretty clothes and make-up are definitely | hardly essential for my happiness.
3 Electronic equipment is absolutely | hardly essential for my lifestyle.
4 The environment is something I am totally | not especially committed to.
5 Sport is something incredibly | not really important to me, too.
6 I believe travelling is an absolutely | not really a vital part of growing up.

b **NOW YOU** What is important and not so important for you? Write your answers.

6 I feel fine Adjectives after certain verbs ▸ 18.1

a Read the following sentences, then use the words in the box to respond to the news. There are two more adjectives than you need.

> bored • cool • fit • fresh • ~~relaxed~~ • scary • stuffy • suspicious • unfair

→ Finn's just come back from his summer holiday. – Yes, he looks …
*Yes, he looks **relaxed**.*

1 I don't believe the story he told us about the robber in the park. – No, it sounded …
2 How about a run along the river? – Let's go, I feel …
3 Some students are watching the show without paying for a ticket, I think that's wrong – I agree, it seems …
4 Hey, have you seen Hanna in her Halloween costume? – No, does she look … in it?
5 That kind of music makes me want to dance. – Same here, it sounds …
6 Do you think we should open a window? – Yes please, it smells … in here.

b **NOW YOU** Look around the classroom and choose two classmates. How do they look? And you? How are you feeling right now?

18

7 That's what friends are for   Basic positions   ▶ 18.3.1b

a We expect a lot from our friends – here are some things good friends might do for you.
Put the words in the right order.

→ always | to me | listen | They
They always listen to me.

1 They | with me | are | angry | never
2 don't | trick | me | ever | They
3 usually | with my opinion | They | agree
4 'Stop: enough is enough!' | sometimes | They | say

5 are | They | ready | for a laugh | always
6 always | They | for me | stand up
7 They | aren't | offline | often
8 me | criticize | They | sometimes

b NOW YOU Are you a good friend? Why – or why not?

8 Newspaper headlines   Basic positions   ▶ 18.3.1c

Here are some headlines from the *Daily News*. Write the first sentence of the
news story, adding the adverbs of manner, place and time in the right order
at the end of the sentence. The verb must be in the past tense.

→ DOG FINDS LOST PAINTING – at the weekend – in a car park
A dog found a lost painting in a car park at the weekend.

1 THE PRESIDENT MEETS THE KING – yesterday – at Buckingham Palace – privately
2 STARBURST CONCERT CANCELLED – last night – unexpectedly – at Wembley
3 GERMANY WINS TOURNAMENT – last Friday – in the Arena in Munich – easily
4 STUDENTS PROTEST AGAINST CUTS – yesterday – at the Brandenburg Gate – loudly
5 LANG LANG PLAYS – last weekend – in the Elbphilharmonie – beautifully
6 500 STOLEN BIKES FOUND – this morning – in a garage in Berlin

9 What a difference a year makes!   Comparison of adverbs   ▶ 18.4

Some students came to our school from another country last year and had a really difficult first term.
After a year, they are now doing much better. Say what has changed using adverbs in the comparative
form.

→ Aikaterina didn't make friends easily. Now she …
*Now she makes friends **more easily**.*

1 She couldn't write fast enough. Now she …
2 Obyda couldn't speak German well. Now he …
3 He didn't copy the words from the board very quickly. Now he …
4 Aysha found it hard to talk very loud in class. Now she …
5 She didn't laugh so much. Now she …
6 Manar had to help at home, so she couldn't work so hard for school. Now she can …
7 She wasn't able to follow lessons well. Now she can …

10 Who works harder? Comparison of adverbs ► 18.4

a Write sentences to compare how classmates Lukasz and Laura do things.

→ *Lukasz works* **harder than** *Laura.*
  Lukasz gets up (just) **as early as** *Laura.*

	Lukasz	Laura
works hard	x x	x
gets up early	x x	x x
dresses smartly	x	x x
laughs a lot	x x x	x x
sings beautifully	x x	x x
goes to bed late	x x	x x x
takes school seriously	x x	x x
talks fast	x	x x

b NOW YOU What about you and one of your friends? Write four sentences to compare how you do things.

→ *Suzie works* **harder than** *me.*

18

✛ 11 I hope to see you soon English verbs instead of German adverbs ► 18.5

These sentences need an English verb to express the same as the German adverb in brackets.

> go on + -ing • happen to • hate • hope • keep + -ing •
> seem to • prefer • ~~used to~~

→ My brother … play the piano. (spielte früher)
  My brother **used to** *play the piano.*

1 The weather doesn't look very good. I … it stays dry.
   (hoffentlich)
2 When I have to travel a long way, I always … going by
   train than by car. (lieber)
3 And I … going by bus. (sehr ungerne)
4 For your homework, please … doing these exercises. (macht weiter)
5 I … be passing the crossing when the cars crashed. (ging zufällig vorbei)
6 I know that your dad has a Porsche, you … reminding me. (erinnerst mich ständig daran)
7 Abby? I can't see her – she … have gone home. (ist wohl nach Hause gegangen)

⊙ **+ 12 Get it right**   Adjectives and adverbs in contrast   ▶ 18

Erklärvideo online:
▶ **Exercise 2**

Find one mistake in each line and correct it. In 3 lines there are no mistakes.

1 The wide known horror story of Frankenstein is really the story of his   → **widely**
2 'monster'. His existence begins when the scientist Dr Frankenstein, who   …
3 is ambitiously to find the secret of life, creates a being out of the body   …
4 parts of dead people. When he adds a spark of electricity, a terrible   …
5 ugly creature is 'born'. He looks really strange and cannot speak proper.   …
6 At first, Frankenstein feels very proudly of his success. But the human   …
7 form is hard born when it or he develops human feelings. He longs for   …
8 human contact and calls his creator 'Father' friendly. But the scientist   …
9 wants absolute nothing to do with the creature that he has put into the   …
10 world and flees from him. The more strongly the monster feels the need   …
11 to love, the more badly is the outcome. The first victims die cruelly at his   …
12 strong hands. Frankenstein begins to chase him farer and farer across   …
13 the world in order to destroy him. The chase ends awful at the North Pole.   …
14 You can read the story as a warning to scientists to be more carefully   …
15 in the future with the inventions that they put into the world.   …

+ 13 The wolf reacted strangely   Adverbs to enhance your style   ▶ 18

18

Using adverbs in your writing helps to make it more lively and informative.

a Read part of this well-known story, which has very few adverbs or adverbial phrases in it. Add at least one to each sentence to improve it. Think carefully about the form and position of your adverbs.

Little Red Riding Hood went to see her grandmother.
She prepared a basket full of food and drink.
She followed the path.
The little girl left the path to collect flowers.
A wolf stopped her.
She told him where she was going.
The wolf went to Grandma's cottage.
He went in and ate the old lady up.
He put on her nightgown and waited.
Little Red Riding Hood arrived.
She was surprised and asked a lot of questions.
The wolf answered her questions.
He swallowed the girl.
The wolf fell asleep and started snoring.
A huntsman came by and heard him …

→ **One spring morning**, Little Red Riding Hood went to see her grandmother in the wood. She **happily** prepared a … **At first**, she …

b Now finish the story. Make your ending as interesting as possible. Remember to use adverbs.

Quick Check

A Complete with the right form of the adverb.

1 happy   – …
2 exact   – …
3 fast   – …
4 friendly – …
5 lucky   – …

6 true   – …
7 stronger – …
8 good   – …
9 fantastic – …
10 bad   – …

B Adjective or adverb? Change the form if necessary.

1 You look (beautiful) in that dress.
2 I saw the shoplifter (quick) slip the perfume into her bag.
3 The latest phone is (extreme) expensive.
4 The whole team did their job very (good).
5 I checked the internet, but my bike store offered me the most (attractive) price.
6 People often feel really (nervous) before a test.
7 Bears can run (incredible) fast.
8 Bats don't (normal) come out during the daytime.

C Put the adverbs in the best position in the sentences.

1 I've travelled through the Channel Tunnel. (never)
2 Please don't forget to wait. (tomorrow night, outside the main entrance)
3 I had remembered to pack my swimming trunks. (luckily)
4 The band had finished playing when all the lights went off. (just)
5 The DJ acted. (in the foyer, strangely, last night)
6 Mike is the first person at the school shop in the break. (always)
7 People mix up *there* and *their*. (sometimes)
8 We've had a lot of good weather. (lately)

D Find and correct the mistakes. There's one in each sentence.

1 The U15 side worked very hardly to win their match.
2 I'll see you after practice at the tram stop, OK?
3 You got the third answer wrongly.
4 Ben worked more hard on the text than Max did.
5 When she went past her teacher, Maxie waved at him really silly.
6 Some bikers wait never for the green light at crossings.
7 I didn't do as worse as I had feared in the test.
8 I was good prepared for my history exam.
9 For your homework, please do these tasks further.
10 Jim is not usually so good organized.

18

19 Nouns

Task	Topic	Example	Englische Grammatik
1	Regular plurals of countable nouns	*Most families take photos on special occasions.*	19.3.2
2	Regular and irregular plurals	*The candidates were young people from different countries.*	19.3.2 19.3.3
3	Nationality words	*The Swiss are great linguists. Many speak fluent French, German and Italian too.*	19.3.5
4	Uncountable nouns	*There isn't much bread left and we don't have any coffee either.*	19.4
5	Countable and uncountable nouns (1)	*The rooms were small: there wasn't room for a lot of furniture.*	19.4.3
6	Other noun types	*Our class wears a uniform. Trousers are forbidden for girls.*	19.5
7	The genitive (1)	*The boys' room is at the top of the house.*	19.6
8	Mixed exercise (1)	*Mrs Evans gave us lots of homework on Monday.*	19.1
9	Gender-related nouns	*A police spokesperson said if a cyclist is texting, they will be fined.*	19.2.2 19.2.3
10	Mixed exercise (2)	*The data was discussed fully with the Americans.*	19.3 19.4 19.5
11	Countable and uncountable nouns (2)	*Her hair was still thick but a few of the hairs had turned grey.*	19.4.3
12	The genitive (2)	*We agreed with one of the girls' suggestions.*	19.6

▶ Quick Check p. 168

1 Plurals   Regular plurals of countable nouns   ▶ 19.3.2

a Fill in the plural forms of these nouns.

beach – ➔ **beaches**   crash – ... (3)   kiss   – ... (6)   pony – ... (9)
body – ... (1)   fly   – ... (4)   mouth – ... (7)   price – ...(10)
car   – ... (2)   key   – ... (5)   knife – ... (8)   toy   – ... (11)

b Use the clues to complete the puzzle with the plural forms of the nouns.

→ Ketchup is made from …
*Ketchup is made from **tomatoes**.*

1 There are some good hiking … in the countryside around Windermere.
2 Steve has four kids – two girls and two …
3 KidsTravel offers holidays for … with three or more children.
4 Two … make a whole.
5 I have been invited to two birthday … this week.
6 This camera takes great …
7 People who steal things are …
8 Many modern houses have flat …

			↓				
1			T				
	2		O				
3			M				
	4		A				
5			T				
6			O				
7			E				
8			S				

2 Yellowstone Park   Regular and irregular plurals   ▸ 19.3.2, 19.3.3

Environmental scientists often have bad news about plants or animals struggling to survive, but sometimes the opposite happens. Choose the correct words to complete this ecological success story.

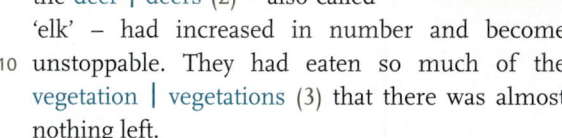

Not many → *people* | peoples know that whole ecosystems can depend on a single species. Yellowstone National Park in the
5 US is a good example. There had been no wolfs | wolves (1) there for over 50 years. Without them, the deer | deers (2) – also called 'elk' – had increased in number and become
10 unstoppable. They had eaten so much of the vegetation | vegetations (3) that there was almost nothing left.
Then, in 1995, wolves were brought back to the park. The return of the predators changed the be-
15 haviour of the elk | the elks behaviour (4). How did this happen? To stay safe, the elk moved in smaller groups. They also stopped going to places where they could be trapped by the wolves, like the deep valleys | vallies (5). Those places started to regener-
20 ate, to have new life | lives (6). Some trees grew five times higher!

The trees helped many other species | specieses (7) to return to Yellowstone Park. Soon there were nine new beaver colonies | 25 colonys (8). The beavers built dams in the rivers, so otters and muskrats, fish | fishes (9), ducks and reptiles could live there again.
There was more. The wolves hunted and killed 30 coyotes too. The numbers of rabbits and mouses | mice (10) then began to grow, which helped feed other animals too. Now there were more foxes | fox (11) and more weasels, and more hunting birds.
But the most interesting thing happened at the 35 river's edges | edges of the rivers (12). Because of the trees, less earth was washed away and the rivers became narrower again. So the return of the wolves changed not only the ecosystem of Yellowstone Park but also its physical geography. 40

19

3 National stereotypes   Nationality words   ▶ 19.3.5

Generalizations about nationalities are not new, but is it time to re-think our prejudices? Complete the text with the correct nationality nouns.

The people of one nation often have funny ideas about the people of another nation. Such ideas are called stereotypes. An example of this might be that the → **French** (people from France) eat frogs and the
5 ... (1) (people from China) eat birds' nests. In the past, people thought that all ... (2) (people from Germany) drank beer and ate sausages and sauerkraut, and that the ... (3) (people from Scotland) drank whisky and ate haggis. And of course a popular ste-
10 reotype is that the ... (4) (people from Britain) can't cook at all. These are rather silly but mostly harmless ideas, often used in jokes. The ... (5) (people from the Netherlands), for example, are rude about the ... (6) (people from Belgium) and the ... (7)
15 (people from England) tell jokes about the ... (8) (people from Ireland).
Isn't it time to forget these old stereotypes and try to understand each other better? Let's not think of ... (9) (the people from Australia) as uncultured

sports lovers, but friendly and honest. The ... (10) 20 (people from Italy) are not chaotic but stylish and passionate. Why talk about how much tequila ... (11) (people from Mexico) drink, when you can focus on their warmth and friendliness? Are the ... (12) (people from Sweden) really boring, or are they 25 sophisticated and modern? And instead of thinking of the ... (13) (people from Switzerland) as cheese-eating yodellers, why not admire their love of peace? And we all know that the ... (14) (people from Poland) are the most hard-working and 30 reliable people in the world, don't we?

Our old ideas are often incorrect, old-fashioned and negative. To live happily together, per- haps we need to under- stand each other better.

⊙ 4 Work experience   Uncountable nouns   ▶ 19.4

Erklärvideo online:
🗎⊙ cornelsen.de/webcodes
+🔊 **Code: repazo**

a Not all of the following nouns are uncountable. Find the uncountable nouns.

> accident • advice • child • equipment • experience • feedback • help • homework • information • job • knowledge • parent • progress • proof • value

b This is Anna's report on her work experience placement. Find and correct her mistakes. There is one mistake per sentence.

→ Anna Langley: A student feedback
Anna Langley: student feedback

1 Here is my report on my work experiences placement at Brent Special School.
2 I had no idea these children needed so much helps.
3 The school had plenty of specialist equipments for playing and learning.
4 I worked with a speech therapist called Emma who had lots of useful advices for me.
5 She even gave me homeworks. She told me to read more about autism and Down syndrome.
6 I was really given more informations than I could remember.
7 I was shocked by the small progresses the children made, but the therapists said that was fine.
8 I think the real proofs of this school's success was in the happy family atmosphere in every classroom.

▶ **5 Bread and butter pudding** Countable and uncountable nouns ▶ 19.4.3

Erklärvideo online:
▶ **Exercise 4**

a Here are the things you need for a pudding which is an old favourite in many British families.
First decide which words are countable and which are uncountable.

> ~~bread~~ • butter • cream • dish • egg • fruit • ~~lemon~~ • milk • slice of bread • raisin • sugar

countable   ➔ *lemon*
uncountable ➔ *bread*

b Complete the recipe with words from your lists.

> If you have any old leftover ➔ **bread**, you don't have to make it into toast or give
> it to the birds. Just follow this simple recipe for a quick and easy family dessert.
>
> Ingredients
> 8 slices of … (1) (leave the crust on)
> 50 g of unsalted … (2) or margarine
> 50 g of dried … (3) (e.g. raisins)
> 275 ml of warm … (4)
> 60 ml of double cream
> 50 g of brown or white … (5)
> the rind of half a … (6) or orange
> 3 eggs

c Choose the correct words to complete the text.

Pre-heat your oven 180°C.

Spread ➔ **a little** | a few of the butter over the bottom of the dish. This will stop the pudding from
sticking to the dish. Butter the bread | breads (1) and cut each slice of bread in half – or into smaller
pieces, if you prefer.
Now arrange four pieces of the bread in the dish and put a few | a little (2) of the raisins on top. Do the
same thing with the rest of the bread and raisins.
Next, mix the milk and the double cream together. You don't need to use much | many (3) cream to make
the pudding richer. Add the sugar and a little | less (4) of the lemon or orange rind. Then mix the eggs into
the milk mixture.
Pour it all over the bread, and bake in the oven for 30–40 minutes. Serve warm with a little | one (5)
more cream or ice cream.

19

6 Translation   Other noun types   ▶ 19.5

a Jonas and his sister Claudia are packing for an exchange visit to the UK. They have some questions and are skyping Tabita, the daughter of their host family in York. Translate the German sentence parts into English.

Jonas → ***All our belongings don't fit*** (Unser Zeug passt nicht alles) into one suitcase. Can we bring two?
Claudia Don't worry. We can always buy something new.
Tabita Just remember: … (Kleidung ist) (1) more expensive in England than in Germany.
Claudia I usually sleep in a T-shirt. Should I bring … (einen Schlafanzug) (2) or a nightdress? And would … (eine schwarze Hose) (3) be better than jeans?
Tabita That's up to you. My parents don't care what you wear. They are more interested in good … (Benehmen) (4).
Claudia Right. We'll do our best. Anything else?
Tabita Well, don't forget to bring … (deine Badehose) (5), Jonas. You love swimming, don't you?
Jonas That's right. Will I need … (eine Sonnenbrille) (6)?
Tabita I don't think so. We usually go to the indoor pool, so there's not a lot of sunbathing.
Claudia Will I need … (eine dicke Strumpfhose) (7)?
Tabita No, you're coming in June. Plus, this is Britain, not the North Pole. Bring … (eine kurze Hose) (8) or a skirt!

b NOW YOU Imagine you're packing for a month's visit to the UK. Make a list of what you would pack.

7 In other words   The genitive   ▶ 19.6

Complete these sentences. Use a possessive form or *of*.

→ This is … (my father, car).
This is **my father's car**.

1 I can't see … (your cousin, face) in the photo.
2 I can tell you … (street, name) where Mr Rogers lives.
3 Those … (children, bikes) are new.
4 … (James, new girlfriend) is from Italy.
5 We often eat fish at … (week, end), on Friday or Saturday.
6 They have changed … (cinema, name). It's called 'The Odeon' now.
7 There was a fire at Henry's house, but he wasn't at home on … (fire, night).
8 … (Pete and Jill, new house) is in France.

8 Get it right   Mixed exercise   ▶ 19.1

Kai asks his exchange student Phil to help him to check his English translation homework. Only two of the sentences are correct. Find and correct Kai's mistakes.

→ Please can you help me with my homeworks? ***homework***

1 My teacher speaks a very good English.
2 We have just had a two weeks holiday from school.
3 I don't like my school uniform because jeans are not allowed.
4 Have you seen the newspaper of yesterday?
5 The news from the Middle East are getting better.
6 My parents say I watch too much soaps on TV.
7 They tell me I'll soon need to wear glasses.
8 I don't want to look like a german Harry Potter!

19

+ 9 The glass ceiling   Gender-related nouns   ▶ 19.2.2, 19.2.3

The glass ceiling is a metaphor used to talk about an invisible barrier stopping people, usually women, from reaching a higher level in a profession. Complete the text with words from the box.

> author • chair • chairman • colleague • flight attendant • ~~friend~~ • gentleman • lady • stewardess •
> they • waiter • waitperson • waitress

Gender equality is nothing new. Women have been fighting for equal pay and equal opportunities for many decades now, and a lot has changed. The Eng-lish language has also changed to match the grow-
5 ing awareness that some words or expressions are simply not OK anymore.
A ➜ *friend* of mine, Linda Gamlin, is the ... (1) of a bestselling book on the subject. In fact, she was originally a ... (2) that I shared an office with years
10 ago: a talented journalist on an in-flight magazine. She was the first to point out that a female member of an airline crew, often called a ... (3), could be given a gender-neutral name like ... (4). This has now become policy for most airlines.
15 Another change is in business and other professional meetings, where the person taking the lead is now hardly ever called the ... (5), regardless of gender.

The politically correct word to use is of course the ... (6) or perhaps the chairperson.
Some people complain that certain changes in 20 language are political correctness gone mad. For British native speakers of English, the word ... (7) for someone who serves you in a restaurant or café sounds rather strange. So in a café in London, for example, you will still hear a woman being called a 25 ... (8) and a man being called a ... (9).
On the other hand, many of us, whatever our gender, would object to the sentence 'Ms Parker, is a ... (10) pilot'. After all, you would never hear anyone say 'Mr Parker is a ... (11) pilot', would you? 30 Whether it's a man or a woman flying your plane, he or she – or should I say ... (12)? – still has to be a qualified pilot!

19

+ 10 The World Happiness Report   Mixed exercise   ▶ 19.3–19.5

What makes people happy? Complete this article from the business section of a British newspaper with the correct singular or plural forms of the verbs and nouns in brackets.

The ➜ *news* (news) from the latest World Happiness Report ➜ *seems* (seem) to be that if you want true happiness, forget about that bigger apartment or those exotic holidays. This year's ... (advice) (1) ...
5 (appear) (2) to be that you should just go and live in Norway instead.
This annual report measures the relative happiness of all the countries of the world. Norway has risen from fourth place in the ranks of the World Happi-
10 ness Report to overtake the previous winner, Den-mark.
Naturally, the ... (politics) (3) of a country also ... (have) (4) an influence on the well-being of its in-habitants. Economic ... (data) (5) ... (be studied) (6)
15 together with social factors in the ... (research) (7) which ... (highlight) (8) several interesting ...

(phenomenon) (9). Of course, the ... (economics) (10) of a country ... (remain) (11) important, but it seems that money isn't everything. Even though the US ... (be) (12) one of the richest counties in the 20 world, the people living there are not as happy as the Norwegians.
The ... (statistics) (13) ... (show) (14) that Norway is joined in the top five by fellow Nordic states Denmark, Iceland, Fin-25 land plus central Eu-rope's Switzerland. And the United States? Only 13th place – so there ... (seem) (15) to be ... 30 (room) (16) for im-provement!

⊙ ✚ **11 The hotel from hell**   Countable and uncountable nouns   ▶ 19.4.3

Erklärvideo online:
▶ Exercise 4

a Have you ever stayed in a five-star hotel? If so, you would expect the very best service. Anthony Cramer was not happy with his hotel. Choose the correct words to complete his letter of complaint to the hotel manager.

Dear Sir or Madam

I am writing to express my dissatisfaction with the service my partner and I received at your hotel last week.

We are ordinary tourists, not business travellers, but we still expect the highest standards from a five-star hotel. ➔ **People** | Peoples like us pay a lot of money for comfortable hotel rooms, but the accommodation | accommodations (1) in your hotel was definitely not five-star quality! The location of the hotel is very poor: we found the immediate surroundings | surrounding (2) disappointing, and we thought the outskirts of your town was | were (3) particularly unattractive.

I am surprised that your hotel ever passed the health and safety requirements. My partner's hairs | hair (4) was burnt when the hairdryer overheated. We were disgusted to find that there were some hair | hairs (5) in the shower. Also, there was never enough shampoo or toilet papers | paper (6), and when we asked for more, we had to wait several hours. Overall, the manner | manners (7) of your employees need to be improved. The staff | staffs (8) clearly should have more and better trainings | training (9) – we wondered if indeed they had had any | one (10) at all?

At mealtimes, there was far too many | much (11) noise coming from the kitchens. At one point we heard some terrible noise | noises (12) which sounded like plates being thrown by an angry chef. However, nothing was done when we reported this at reception.

The worst thing though was when some important paper | papers (13) were stolen from our room. Unfortunately the police was | were (14) never given any of the relevant information | informations (15) despite the fact that the damages | damage (16) to the door of our room was clear evidence of a break-in.

All in all, this was a terrible experience, which I do not want to repeat. I would like you to offer us a refund in full and a written apology for the stress this visit caused me and my partner.

Yours faithfully
Anthony Cramer

b Write the hotel manager's reply and apologize for the problems. Explain what you're going to do to make things better.

19

+ **12 The Kite Runner** The genitive ▶ 19.6

Tariq chose to write about *The Kite Runner* for a school project. Complete his essay with the correct words.

One of my favourite books is *The Kite Runner*, a novel by an Afghani writer called Khaled Husseini. → ***Husseini's bestselling book*** (Husseini | bestselling book) was made first into a film and then a stage
5 play. I have seen both of them.
At … (the beginning | the story) (1), we are in the States with the adult Amir. He is looking back to something that happened to his best friend Hassan 26 years earlier. At that time, Amir's family has …
10 (plenty | money) (2), and Hassan is … (the son | his father | servant) (3). Not only that, but Amir is from a powerful Sunni Muslim background, while Hassan, a Shi'a Muslim, is from an ethnic minority. Despite these differences, … (Amir | father) (4)
15 Baba, encourages … (the boys | unusual friendship) (5).
… (Amir and Hassan | childhood) (6) is full of fun and adventures, but it is during a kite flying competition that Hassan has a traumatic experience. The
20 competition involves … (the string | one boy | kite) (7) cutting the string of another boy's kite. The runner is the person who runs after and brings back the kite that has been cut. Hassan is … (Amir | runner) (8) but, while running for his friend, he is caught by
25 bullies and violently attacked at … (the end | an alley) (9). Amir sees everything but does and says

nothing and then feels so bad that he ends their friendship. He hides some money and a watch under … (Hassan | mattress) (10), making him look like a thief, so Hassan and his father are sent away. 30 Soon Amir and his father also have to leave, because of … (the rise | the Taliban) (11) in Kabul. They escape in … (the back | a truck) (12), taking nothing with them. They move to the States, and it is only years later that the full impact of what Amir did to 35 Hassan hits him. A … (close friend | his father) (13) tells Amir to return to Afghanistan, where he can try to undo the damage he did as a boy.
Any more information will be a spoiler, if you haven't read the book or seen the film. 40
I would just like to add that, in my opinion, … (the stage version | the book) 45 (14) doesn't work very well. The same actor plays the adult and the child Amir, and … (the sight | a middle-aged man) (15) jumping 50 around like a 12-year-old is not very realistic.

Quick Check

A Choose the correct words.

1 Girl's | Girls' football camps are becoming more and more popular.
2 If you want my advice | advices, you'll apologize for what you said.
3 There was a lot of structural damage | damages after the storm.
4 Mum's gone to the dentist's | dentists but she won't be long.
5 I've just torn my new jeans, so now I'll have to mend it | them.
6 There's far too much | many sugar in that pudding.
7 She usually has a toast | piece of toast for breakfast.
8 The boys were tired after their five-mile | five miles run.
9 If you want an | some information on train times, you can look online.
10 Don't blame me, it was my brother's idea | the idea of my brother.
11 My new jeans is | are white. It looks | They look great!
12 The children's | childrens' new football trainer is from France.

B Translate the German sentence parts into English.

1 (Marcos Freundin ist Polin.) She's from Warsaw.
2 Do you have to do (viele Hausaufgaben) tonight?
3 Did you throw out (die Zeitung von Samstag)? Mum's looking for it.
4 I'm told that (Kleidung ist billiger) in the US than in the UK.
5 (Dies ist das Badezimmer von meinen Eltern), so please don't use it.
6 Kenny's parents have given him (wichtige Ratschläge).
7 (Deine Haare sind) much too long.
8 Be careful! (Diese Treppe ist) slippery.
9 I'm afraid (die Nachrichten sind) not very good.
10 (Wo ist meine Brille?) I can't see a thing.

C Find and correct the mistake in each sentence.

1 We need some new furnitures for our new flat.
2 Our teacher always gives us a quick feedback after a test.
3 Have you made any progresses with your homework yet?
4 Myra's pyjamas is too small for her now.
5 The police has just arrived at the scene of the crime.
6 What do you think of my jacket's colour?
7 Do you want a cup tea or would you prefer a coffee?
8 I can't argue with my parent's decision: they're always right.
9 Our school is just a ten-minutes walk from home.
10 When my dog Tess was a puppy, she ate the chair's leg.

20 Articles

Task	Topic	Example	Englische Grammatik
1	Forms and pronunciation of articles	*The hen laid an egg.*	20.1
2	Use of the indefinite article	*He's not an expert but he gives good advice.*	20.2.1 20.2.2 20.2.3
3	Articles with jobs	*She was an actress before she became a politician.*	20.2.3
4	The indefinite article: mixed exercise	*She swims three times a week.*	20.2
5	Use of the definite article	*Religion doesn't really interest me. Do you go to church regularly?*	20.3.2 20.3.3 20.3.6
6	Articles with place names	*Have you ever been up the Eiffel Tower?*	20.3.4
7	Articles with time phrases	*We usually visit our friends in the evening on Monday.*	20.3.5
8	Fixed phrases with or without articles (1)	*She's well qualified on paper – it's a pity she's so chaotic in practice.*	20.2.5 20.3.7
9	Articles with quantities and quantifiers	*All the boys had just half a sandwich each, so it was quite a mean lunch.*	20.2.7 20.3.8
10	Fixed phrases with or without articles (2)	*I read in bed as I couldn't sleep. The bed was too uncomfortable.*	20.3.7
11	Mixed exercise (1)	*A man went into a bar. The bar was full, so the man left.*	20
12	Mixed exercise (2)	*History repeats itself.*	20.3.2
13	Mixed exercise (3)	*Most people in the EU speak more than one language.*	20.3

▶ Quick Check p. 176

1 Pronunciation Forms and pronunciation of articles ▶ 20.1

The way you pronounce articles depends on the word that follows them. Complete the table with words from the box.

accident • apple • ~~book~~ • European • ~~example~~ • hotel • hour • ice cream • image • MP3 player • mistake • ocean • teacher • uncle • uniform • university • visitor • window

a [ə] and the [ðə]	an [ən] and the [ði]
➔ *book*	➔ *example*

2 In other words   Use of the indefinite article   ▸ 20.2.1 – 20.2.3

Rewrite the sentences using the words given, so that the meaning of the second sentence is as similar as possible to the first sentence.

➜ Sara advises her sons regularly. (advice)
   *Sara gives her sons **regular advice**.*

1	Please wait, I will be with you soon. (minute)	Please wait, I will be with you …
2	Keep an eye on Charlie, he can't swim well yet. (swimmer)	Keep an eye on Charlie, he's not …
3	Does Andy Murray come from Ireland? (Irishman)	Is Andy Murray …
4	Our teacher told us what she thought about our presentation. (feedback)	Our teacher gave us …
5	The film was so boring that I fell asleep. (such)	It was … that I fell asleep.
6	He belongs to our local chess club. (member)	He's … of our local chess club.
7	The weather is terrible! (what)	What …
8	I don't need two tickets, thank you. (only one)	I need …, thank you.
9	She told me there was one bus every hour. (an)	She told me there was one bus …
10	The guide informed us incorrectly about the opening times. (information)	The guide gave us … about the opening times.

3 When I grow up...   Articles with jobs   ▸ 20.2.3

a Amy is having a big party on New Year's Eve. Her friends' choice of costume will say something about their childhood dreams and ambitions. Complete what Yuri, Dana and Kai say. Choose to use the correct article or none at all.

Come and celebrate New Year's Eve with us!
The theme this year is
"What did you want to be when you were little?"
There will be a prize for the best costume.
Bring and share party food: 8 till late

Text or email Amy

Kevin
For a while, like most kids, I wanted to be ➜ *a* train driver because my favourite toy was a train set. Then I wanted to be … (1) astronaut, but when I got older, what I wanted most of all was to be … (2) computer scientist. I'm not sure what costume I need for that!

Dana
What did I want to be when I was … (3) kid? When I was about six, most of the girls in my class wanted to be either … (4) ballerina or … (5) actress. In fact, I think most teenagers want to be … (6) celebrity of some sort or other. Me? All I wanted to do was read. So I guess I'll go to Amy's party as a bookworm.

Kai
Most boys want to be … (7) professional footballer or the manager of … (8) English football team in the world, even if they're not … (9) English! Sport was never interesting for me. I've always loved music, and for years my ambition was to be … (10) rock star. So that's my plan for Amy's party!

b NOW YOU What did you want to be when you were little?

20

4 Animal trainers for the movies
The indefinite article - mixed exercise ▶ 20.2

Elisa trains animals for the film industry. Complete the interview with the words *a, an* or *one*. Sometimes no article is necessary.

Interviewer	How did you become ➜ ***an*** animal trainer?
Elisa	I've always loved animals. As … (1) child I was only allowed … (2) dog, but I wanted lots! I got a Saturday job at … (3) beauty salon for dogs but my big chance came when I saw … (4) advert for dogs for the movie '… (5) Hundred and One Dalmatians'. I went along with … (6) of the dogs from the beauty salon and met the Hollywood trainer who was also working on the Harry Potter movies. He introduced me to the right people and they offered me … (7) job. I started training the owls that delivered the mail.
Interviewer	Wow, the owls played such … (8) big role in those movies! So, how many birds have you trained? … (9) hundred, maybe?
Elisa	Oh, I train fifty or sixty animals … (10) year but they're not all birds. During the filming of the Harry Potter series, we probably trained three owls … (11) week. There were a lot of owl scenes! And you have to let … (12) owl rest while another works.
Interviewer	How many times … (13) day do you have to feed owls and what do they eat?
Elisa	When they're working, the owls eat quite … (14) lot: mice, insects, worms and so on. Their food doesn't cost much – just … (15) few euros … (16) kilo.
Interviewer	And how true is the phrase 'wise old owl'? Are owls really clever and quick to learn?
Elisa	Absolutely not! As … rule, (17) they're pretty stupid. The person who first said this was definitely not … (18) owl trainer!

5 Bastoy prison
Use of the definite article ▶ 20.3.2, 20.3.3, 20.3.6

Bastoy island in Norway is an unusual prison. Complete the text by choosing to use or leave out the definite article.

It is normal for criminals to go to ➜ ***prison*** | the prison, but this can mean something completely different in Norway. Bastoy prison island, south of Oslo, gets a lot of criticism | the criticism (1). Many
5 people think life | the life (2) for criminals should not be too comfortable, and Bastoy is very different. Prisoners on this small island live in wooden houses | the wooden houses (3) and not in locked cells. And houses | the houses (4) they live in have
10 keys, which prisoners | the prisoners (5) can keep themselves. Most of them | The most of them (6) hated school | the school (7) when they were younger, but school | the school (8) on Bastoy teaches them useful skills like cooking or woodwork. Prisoners
15 can do farm work or work on ferry | the ferry (9)

that connects the island to the mainland. On Sundays, they can go to church | the church (10) if they wish, because church | the church (11) on Bastoy welcomes everyone. Or they can sunbathe on beach | the beach (12).

For many criminals, history | the history (13) simply repeats itself and they are soon back in prison again. But
25 only 16% of prisoners | the prisoners (14) who were on Bastoy go back to a life of crime. In other prisons across the rest of world | the world (15), the percentage is around 70%.

20

30

20

6 The place name quiz   Articles with place names   ▶ 20.3.4

Complete the sentences with a name from the box, using the definite article if necessary.

> Alps • Atlantic • Belgium • Buckingham Palace • Switzerland • ~~Czech Republic~~ • Himalayas •
> Mediterranean • Netherlands • Red Sea • Times Square • Tower of London • USA

The capital of ➔ **the Czech Republic** is Prague.

1 The highest mountain on earth can be found in …
2 The second largest ocean on the planet is …
3 Over 60% of people in … speak Flemish.
4 … is at the junction of Seventh Avenue and Broadway in New York.
5 California is the most highly populated state in …
6 The stretch of sea between Africa and Asia is called …

7 The King's main London residence is …
8 King Willem-Alexander is the king of …
9 The highest mountain range in Europe is called …
10 British Crown Jewels are kept in …
11 Many people in … speak French and German.
12 Sicily, Majorca and Corfu are among the many islands in …

7 A day in the life of a circus acrobat   Articles with time phrases   ▶ 20.3.5

For a school project, you are interviewing Chloe, a young circus acrobat, about a typical day in her life.

a Complete some questions to ask Chloe. Use *in*, *during*, *on* or *at* with the definite article if necessary.

What time do you get up ➔ **in the** morning?

1 Do you get a day off … Sunday?
2 Are there two shows … weekend?
3 Where do you practise … day?
4 Does the circus tent get very hot … August?
5 What do you talk about … lunch?

6 Do you sleep in a caravan … night?
7 When do you finish … evening?
8 What do you do … winter, when the circus is closed?

b Read what Chloe says about her typical day. Complete the text with an appropriate time phrase from the box.

> ~~in the night~~ • during the week • during the winter • the next morning • in the evening •
> in the morning • at lunch • at the weekend • the night before • by day • in the summer

Working in a circus is fun, and I love it, but it isn't always as glamorous as it seems! I need eight hours sleep, and I'm usually so tired that I rarely wake ➔ *in the night*. I get up at seven or eight … (1), depending on when I went to bed … (2).

I begin my day after a light breakfast with a gymnastics-style warm-up. When it's cold, … (3), this takes longer. … (4), for example in July and August, warming up is much quicker. After my warm-up, I practise the routines for our performance in the circus ring … (5).

After that, we begin our rehearsals. … (6), from Monday to Friday, we have our own ringmaster, but for two days … (7), we might have a guest ringmaster. We discuss any new ideas … (8), which is usually a high protein salad eaten at one o'clock. Acrobats have to watch their weight because any change in your body will make things difficult for your partner. … (9), I just wear old tights and a warm top, but for the show, I look completely different. I wear a sparkling red costume with lots of make-up. The show normally finishes around ten. We all need an hour or so to wind down, but as soon as I get to bed in my caravan, I fall asleep immediately. Then it's up again … (10).

20

8 The job interview Fixed phrases with or without articles ▸ 20.2.5, 20.3.7

Imagine that you're going for a job interview. How can you prepare yourself? What should you expect?
Here are our top tips. Translate the words in brackets to complete the sentences.

Shake hands ➔ **in a friendly way** (auf freundliche Weise),
and make eye contact but not for too long.
Wait until your interviewer asks you to … (Platz nehmen) (1)
before you sit down.
Don't waste any time. You won't have long to … (Eindruck
machen) (2).
You may be a strong candidate … (auf dem Papier) (3),
but you still have to impress them with your personality.
Don't … (etwas dem Zufall überlassen) (4). Do your

homework before the interview and find out all you can about the job.
Show that you have … (Interesse gezeigt) (5) in the firm and what it does.
If a question seems aggressive, answer calmly and … (mit ruhiger Stimme) (6); never get angry.
If you're well prepared, you will … (in der Lage sein) (7) to say why you are the person who should get
this job.
When the interview … (zu Ende geht) (8), thank your interviewer and look confident.

9 What a race! Articles with quantities and quantifiers ▸ 20.2.7, 20.3.8

Carrie has been to an athletics event with her team. She's telling her friend Joel what happened.
Fill in the correct phrase with the help of the words in brackets.

Joel   Hi there! How did your athletics trip to Paris go?
Carrie ➔ **What a week!** (what | week) We had … (such | good time) (1).
Joel   I'm sure you did, you lucky thing! Tell me about it.
Carrie Well, there were two teams, men and women. … (both | teams) (2) came away with medals!
Joel   Really? I thought it was going to be … (rather | difficult challenge) (3)?
Carrie Yeah, but our coach decided we were good enough. It was … (quite | big risk) (4) for him, but it
        paid off. We went by train because flying would have been … (twice | price) (5).
Joel   Did you stay in hotels … (all | time) (6)?
Carrie We did for … (half | time) (7), but that was expensive. Most of us had friends we could stay with.
        I'd contacted a girl I was at school with – it was … (such | surprise) (8) to find that she'd moved
        to France.
Joel   So, tell me about the athletics. What did you win?
Carrie I won the 1000 metres and, honestly, … (what | exciting finish) (9)! I've got a video of it on my
        phone if you want to see it for yourself.
Joel   OK – I've got … (half | hour) (10) to spare!
Carrie Hey, what do you mean? It took me less than ten minutes!

20

10 Man flu – is it real? Fixed phrases with or without articles ▶ 20.3.7

'Man flu' is a name for the stereotypical idea that men complain more when they are ill. Find and correct 10 mistakes in this text

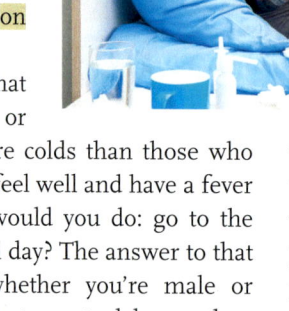

My brother posted this photo yesterday. Poor thing – he has man flu. What, you've never heard of this illness?
5 90 % of men get it! I saw an interesting report about it ~~on the TV~~ ➔ *on TV* yesterday. A recent survey showed that people who go to the work or
10 school by the bus get more colds than those who walk or drive. If you don't feel well and have a fever and a runny nose, what would you do: go to the school or stay in the bed all day? The answer to that depends, it seems, on whether you're male or
15 female. The survey found that men took longer than women to get better after a bad cold. In the practice that means that men go to the bed when they have a cold and stay there for at least three days!

However, maybe man flu is real. The higher level of the hormone testosterone in men 20 means they have a weaker immune system. The study showed that the risk of men getting serious complications is above the average and 25 certainly higher than for women. But does this mean that women are tougher than men or just that they complain less? Many women lose the patience with their partners, at least privately, though they might joke about it in the 30 public in front of their friends. With help of more research, we may learn more one day. Meanwhile, make sure you have plenty of Kleenex ready for the next attack.

11 The silly bank robber Mixed exercise ▶ 20

How smart do you have to be to rob a bank? Most people would say it's always a stupid thing to do, but some bank robbers are more stupid than others! Complete the news article. Use *a, an* or *the.*

➔ *A* man wanted to rob ... (1) main bank in his home town. He ran into ... (2) bank and gave ... (3) note to one of the bank clerks. This poor woman read ... (4) note which said she had to give the man all ... (5) money in their safe. She did what he asked because she thought he
5 might have ... (6) gun. The man took ... (7) money and ran off in ... (8) hurry, leaving ... (9) note with the woman. However, ... (10) police caught him the same day. ... (11) silly man had written ... (12) note on the back of ... (13) envelope. And on ... (14) other side of ... (15) envelope was a name and ... (16) address – his name and address!

+ 12 Dolphin behaviour Mixed exercise ▸ 20.3.2

There are many incredible stories about dolphins and how they communicate and behave with humans. Complete the magazine article. Use *a*, *an*, *one* or *the*. Sometimes no article is necessary.

This week, we are looking at ➔ **the** behaviour of ... (1) dolphins, and especially how they react when someone is in .... (2) danger in ... (3) water. A dolphin uses sonar in ... (4) very special way. Using ...
5 (5) echo system, it can effectively 'see' a human body and all its parts. A dolphin can even hear ... (6) heartbeat of ... (7) unborn baby! Dolphins are ... (8) mammals like us. Could that be ... (9) main reason why they are so willing to help us? According to one
10 of ... (10) world's top dolphin experts, dolphins seem to think and make ... (11) decisions about when they go to help someone. They look at situations and choose who they help and when. This is not just ... (12) theory: there is a lot of ... (13)
15 evidence of dolphins doing this. Harry Cooke, ... (14) wildlife filmmaker, is certainly ... (15) human who has benefited from ... (16) dolphin rescue. In

2017, Henry was filming ... (17) group of dolphins when he noticed ... (18) large shark on ... (19) attack.
20 Three dolphins swam in to protect him. Harry was able to film ... (20) rescue – and that video quickly went viral.

+ 13 English after Brexit Mixed exercise ▸ 20.3

Is the status of the English language changing? Complete this text, using an appropriate article where needed.

Many people in Britain and indeed the world were surprised, if not shocked, when in ➔ **the** referendum of June 2016 ... (1) small majority of people voted to leave ... (2) Europe. What are the conse-
5 quences for ... (3) English language?
English is ... (4) lingua franca in modern Europe. More than ... (5) third of adults already speak English as ... (6) second language, while the figures are only 12% for French and 11% for German. ... (7)
10 majority of secondary school students in ... (8) most European countries now learn English. English is also widely used in ... (9) Asia and ... (10) Commonwealth because of ... (11) colonial history of ... (12) UK.

Any language increases in importance with ... (13)
15 number of people who can speak it. Foreign languages take ... (14) long time to learn, so countries do not quickly change ... (15) ones they speak. In ... (16) European Union, ... (17) most non-native
20 speakers speak English together as the second language of ... (18) choice. But what will happen to English in ... (19) post-Brexit Europe? Will ... (20) status of English decrease in importance? It's too early to tell yet but, as with Brexit, opinions are
25 divided.

Quick Check

A Complete the mini-dialogues with the definite or indefinite article. Sometimes no article is needed.

1 Jim We stayed in … amazing hotel in … small town in … Scotland.
Kate What was … hotel like?
Jim It was … best we'd ever been to.

2 Tracy The plane leaves from … Gatwick. Let's take … taxi to … airport.
Mina What time's … flight?

3 Yuri It's been … horrible day. … sky's really dark already.
Lucy I think there's going to be … storm.
Yuri Let's hope it's not as bad as … storm we had last week.

4 Sam I've got … problem with my tablet.
Eric Call their helpline. They're … experts.
Sam Well, … problem is, … tablet is from … States.

5 Chris I was in … bed last night when I heard … phone ringing somewhere.
Anca Was it your smartphone or … home phone?
Chris Neither. It was on … TV! I'd forgotten to switch it off!

6 Marius I've had … awful headache all day. I think I've got … flu.
Ellie Why don't you go to … doctor's? They're open in … evenings.
Marius Actually, my neighbour's … nurse. I'll ask her advice.

B Choose the correct forms.

1 Ursula wants to go to college | the college in United States | the United States.
2 We spent half a year | a half year in Lisbon. It's such a | so a lovely city.
3 Joe is member | a member of two running clubs: he's amazing athlete | an amazing athlete.
4 What useful | a useful feedback! You must be expert | an expert.
5 Rob is the vegetarian | a vegetarian now, but as child | a child he ate meat.
6 I'll meet you after lunch | the lunch outside Waterloo station | the Waterloo station.
7 They travelled by bus | by the bus. It's half the price | the half price.
8 She has really bad cold | a really bad cold so she's been in bed | in the bed all day.

C Find and correct the mistake in each sentence.

1 I have just read a quite interesting book about dolphins.
2 What do you normally have for the breakfast?
3 My brother goes jogging four times the week, so he's very fit.
4 The most people at the gig were under twenty.
5 When I went to school, everyone wore an uniform.
6 Our travel insurance costs us £130 in the year.
7 He's always dreamt of going into the space as an astronaut.
8 We won't meet again until first week of May.

20

21 Pronouns and determiners

Task	Topic	Example	Englische Grammatik
1	Personal pronouns: subject form and object form	*He gave her a ring, but she gave it back to him.*	21.2
2	Personal pronouns: *it*	*Take your umbrella. – No, I don't need it. It's not raining.*	21.2.3
3	Possessive determiners and possessive pronouns	*She's just a friend of yours, not your sister.*	21.3.2 21.3.6
4	Possessive determiners with parts of the body, clothes etc.	*He's broken his arm.*	21.3.4
5	Possessive determiner + *own*	*He'd love to have a garden of his own.*	21.3.5
6	Personal and possessive pronouns: mixed exercise	*She does things her way, I do them mine.*	21.2 21.3
7	*their/its/of mine:* mixed exercise	*Their cat is no friend of mine. It thinks my yard is its toilet.*	21.2 21.3
8	*you/one/they:* the German 'man'	*What's that dance they do in Brazil?*	21.2.2
9	Reflexive pronouns and *each other*	*The children played by themselves, not with each other.*	21.4
10	Demonstrative determiners and pronouns	*This pan goes on that shelf and these glasses go in those boxes.*	21.5
11	The prop-word *one*	*Which hat do you prefer? – The blue one.*	21.6
12	Mixed exercise (1)	*In my opinion, that problem of yours is one that you could solve by yourself.*	21
13	*each other / one another /* German reflexive verbs	*They complained to one another about the hotel.*	21.4.3 21.4.4
14	Mixed exercise (2)	*We didn't meet the Prime Minister herself.*	21.4.5

▶ Quick Check p. 186

1 Babysitting blues   Personal pronouns: subject and object form   ▶ 21.2

a Sort the pronouns in the box into three groups: pronouns in the **subject form**, pronouns in the **object form** and pronouns that can be both.

> he • her • him • ~~I~~ • it • ~~me~~ • she • they • them • us • we • ~~you~~

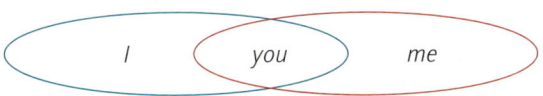

b Judy wanted to see her boyfriend Len tonight, but her mother has other plans. Complete the phone call with an appropriate personal pronoun in its subject or object form.

Len	Hey Judy, where are ➔ **you**?
Judy	Oh hello, Len. … (1) was just going to call … (2). Sorry, I can't come right now.
Len	Why's that? Are … (3) all right?
Judy	No, I'm really fed up. Mum's gone out and left the twins with … (4).
Len	Why didn't your mum take … (5) with … (6)?
Judy	Well … (7) didn't want to. Jemma's fine, full of energy as usual. But Jamie's not well. …'s (8) in bed with a bad cold, and Mum didn't want … (9) to go outside. …'s (10) such a wet day.
Len	But what about … (11)? … (12) had a date, right? Bella and Owen are coming to watch a movie – in fact, … (13) will be here in a minute.
Judy	Sorry, Len. Maybe … (14) three should start watching … (15) without me? I'll join … (16) all as soon as I can. Is that OK?
Len	Well, I suppose so.

c **NOW YOU** Write five sentences about your family. Do you have any brothers and sisters? How old are they? Do you sometimes have to look after them? Use as many pronouns as possible in your answer.

2 Salsa dancing   Personal pronouns: *it*   ▶ 21.2.3

a Dana is writing to her brother Steve from her school trip in Spain. Choose the right pronoun to complete her email.

From:	Dana
Re:	Hi from Spain

Hi from sunny Spain!

Here I am in Cadiz, and so far, this trip is much better than expected – in fact, ➔ he | she | **it** is great! I've already found a new friend – a girl called Anita. He | She | It (1) is from Italy, and her parents have a villa in Rimini. He | She | It (2) sounds amazing – I'm so jealous!
Last night, we had our first salsa lesson. He | She | It (3) was really difficult, but also lots of fun.
In the first session, someone asked Anita to dance. She thought it was another student, but he | she | it (4) was the teacher!
The accommodation isn't too bad this time either. I really like my room. He | She | It (5) is clean and has only four beds. I share him | her | it (6) with three other girls.
There is one thing that worries me. I left my camera in our room, and after lunch he | she | it (7) was gone. The same happened to Anita's sunglasses. It | She | They (8) were on the table next to her bed, but after lunch she couldn't find it | her | them (9).
Must go now – someone's calling my name. He | She | It (10) might be my new best friend Anita!
Hope you're having a good time at college.

Your lovely sister ☺
Dana xxx

21

b This is Steve's reply. Translate the words in brackets to complete his email. Be careful: German 'es' doesn't always translate as 'it' in English.

From: Steve

Re: Hi from Spain

Hi sis,

Nice to hear you're having fun in Spain. I remember when you went on that terrible school camp last year. ➔ **It was** (es war) in the Black Forest, right? And … (es gab) (1) nothing to do, was there? I'm not surprised you … (magst es) (2) much better in Spain, where … (es gibt) (3) parties and dancing lessons.

Maybe next year, we can go on holidays together – I certainly … (hoffe es) (4)! Oh, and you promised to take a lot of photos, so … (vergiss es nicht) (5)!

I'm busy learning for my exams next week, but … (es ist schwer) (6) to concentrate. … (es gibt) (7) so much to learn, and I really need a break. Mum thinks a private tutor would help, but I … (glaube es nicht) (8).

Anyway, enjoy the rest of your holiday. See you soon.
Steve

3 Getting organized   Possessive determiners and possessive pronouns   ▶ 21.3.2, 21.3.6

Do you ever feel the need to get organized and throw out all your old stuff? Jo and Paul have decided it's time to clear out some of their old things. Complete their conversation with words from the box.

her • hers • his • mine • my • of her • of his • of mine • their • theirs • ~~your~~ • your • yours

Jo   I've just read a great article called 'Declutter ➔ **your** life!' – so come on, let's start with the cupboard under the stairs. We might find some things we can sell or recycle.

Paul   We haven't looked in here since Polly and Hari moved into … (1) new flat. A lot of this stuff is … (2).

Jo   Right. This walking stick must be Polly's. I'm sure it's … (3), from when she had … (4) skiing accident.

Paul   Whose camera is this? It's broken anyway, so we can throw it away.

Jo   No, you can't, not if it isn't … (5).

Paul   I think maybe Hari left it here – it's probably … (6) old one. And look, here are some photos … (7), too.

Jo   No, these aren't Hari's. They're … (8) but they're not much good, and I certainly don't want to keep them. Hari is a much better photographer than me, especially his photos of Polly.

Paul   True. He took some great pictures … (9) when she was ski jumping.

Jo   Hey look, here are some of … (10) old video games, from the days when you were still game-crazy! Why don't we give them to that new home for refugees? Paul, are you listening to me?

Paul   Wow, look at this one! This was a big favourite … (11)! I wonder if … (12) old video player's in here somewhere too.

Jo   Paul! We're supposed to be clearing out!

21

4 I hit my head   Possessive determiners with parts of the body, clothes, etc.   ▶ 21.3.4

Match the sentence parts in the table below using the correct possessive determiner.

➔ Hakan cut **his** foot when he stepped on broken glass.

➔	~~Hakan cut~~	her	pocket	while chasing a cat.
1	The dog hurt	our	lives	or you'll lose it.
2	We've changed	their	boots	when I fell downstairs.
3	Many tourists lost	its	arm	about going out tonight.
4	She took off	your	minds	and left them outside.
5	Put that money in	my	~~foot~~	in the terrible tsunami.
6	Last night I broke	~~his~~	paw	~~when he stepped on broken glass.~~

5 Women and fiction   Possessive determiner + own   ▶ 21.3.5

Writer Virginia Woolf spent many years speaking and writing about women's role in literature.

a **Complete the text with words from the box.**

> ~~of One's Own~~ • of her own (x2) • of my own •
> of their own • her own • his own • my own •
> their own (x2) • our own

In 1929, Virginia Woolf wrote an important essay called *A Room* ➔ *of One's Own*. In it, she argued that 'a woman must have money and a room … (1) if she is to write fiction'. Woolf was a wealthy woman, and she and her husband Leonard had … (2) successful company called the Hogarth Press. Leonard published … (3) books and political essays, as well as those of many well-known writers. The couple often stayed with friends, but they had two homes … (4) in fashionable Bloomsbury, London. They also had … (5) house in the country. However, life was not easy and Virginia Woolf sadly took … (6) life in 1941.

Comments

I'm an only child. I can't imagine sharing a room with a brother or sister. My mum's an artist, and when my dad left, she changed the dining room into a studio. Now she has a room … (7) for painting. So now Mum and I both have … (8) space.
Janina, Krakow

I'm a teenage boy who loves rapping and writing poems and songs. I come from a big family, and I don't have a room … (9) – I share with one of my brothers. If I need to spend time on … (10), it's not a problem, though. I just go for long walks and note my ideas on my phone.
Nigel, Bristol

b **NOW YOU** Write a comment like Janina's or Nigel's. How important is it for you to have a room of your own?

6 A lesson in life Personal and possessive pronouns: mixed exercise ▶ 21.2, 21.3

Ruby remembers something that happened to her at school which made her stop and think. Complete the story with the correct pronouns.

At the end of our school year, the class teacher, Mr Taylor, told ➔ **us** that ... (1) were going to take a 'life test'. Some of the other students complained but, personally, ... (2) wasn't worried. Most teachers try to do something different before the holidays be-
5 cause ... (3) know none of ... (4) want to do 'normal' lessons. As I felt quite confident on the day of the test, I worked ... (5) way through all the questions, until the final one which was: 'What's the name of the person who cleans the school building every 10 evening?' I knew this man and I'd seen ... (6) many times, but I'd only really spoken to ... (7) once, and I had no idea what ... (8) name was. I put up ... (9) hand and asked: 'Sir, will ... (10) really matter if I can't answer ... (11) last question?' Mr Taylor smiled 15 and said, 'Definitely.' This taught ... (12) a lesson I won't forget. Nor will I or any of my classmates for-get ... (13) cleaner's name. ... (14) is Harry.

7 Emergency calls *their/its/of mine:* mixed exercise ▶ 21.2, 21.3

By calling 999 in the UK, you can get through to the police, ambulance or fire brigade. But some people call 999 for problems which are not real emergencies. Complete the text with an appropriate pronoun or determiner.

A police spokesman warned that silly 999 telephone calls could have serious consequences. People often forget that other callers' problems may be more important than ➔ **theirs**. ... (1) said: 'All of us in the police force are very busy so ... (2) are asking people to think carefully before making ... (3) 999 call – ... (4) should be for a good reason. Here are some examples of time-wasting calls received this week.'

'I need an ambulance please. Some friends of ... (5) have seen a squirrel in the garden and ... (6) think it's lost one of ... (7) legs.'

'... (8) daughter bought herself a pair of jeans, but they are full of holes! I took ... (9) back but the shop wouldn't give ... (10) my money back. I think the police should know about this.'

'... (11) wife and I are very worried, can you help ... (12)? Can one of ... (13) officers come round to tell ... (14) son to calm down? ... (15) behaviour is becoming very difficult.'

'I need the police please: ... (16) is my daugh-ter's wedding today and ... (17) dress doesn't fit anymore. I need ... (18) to come right now and help ... (19) get into ... (20).'

8 Rio: the marvellous city *you/one/they*: the German 'man' ▶ 21.2.2

Berto has just come back from visiting relatives in Brazil.
He's telling his friend Ann about it. Choose the correct word.

Joel	You've been to Rio, Berto, lucky thing! I think → you | **they** | one speak Portuguese in Brazil, right?
Berto	Well yes, but European Portuguese is a bit different from the Portuguese you | they | one (1) speak in Brazil. There, for example, you | they | one (2) always use the same word for 'you', more like in English, but in Portugal, you | they | one (3) have a formal and an informal word for 'you', like in German.
Ann	Hmm, interesting. My sister Becky is hoping to go to Brazil next year. Do you have any tips for her?
Berto	Sure. And she can check out this website here, look.
Ann	Thank you! I'll tell her. Hey, listen to this from the FAQs: 'Does you | they | one (4) need a visa from the UK?' The answer is: 'UK citizens do not require a visa.' That can't be right, can it?
Berto	Actually, it is correct. You | They | One (5) only need a valid passport and a return ticket! But you | they | one (6) don't let you into the country unless you | they | one (7) have enough money for your stay.
Ann	Fair enough. I know Becky really wants to visit Rio, but on most websites you | they | one (8) say it's quite dangerous. Is that true?
Berto	You | They | One (9) have to be a little careful, just like in most big cities, but they love tourists. You should go too, Ann, it's wonderful.
Ann	Yeah well, maybe I'll get there one day, you | they | one (10) never know!

9 Help yourself Reflexive pronouns and *each other* ▶ 21.4

a Busy parents with big families get very tired and stressed sometimes. Complete the sentences with
the correct pronoun from the box.

> himself • herself • myself • ourselves • themselves • ~~yourself~~ • yourself • yourselves (2x)

Dad	I just read this great article. It says 'you need to have some time to → *yourself* every now and again'. You kids are old enough to look after … (1). I've decided to give … (2) some 'me time' this afternoon. Anna, help … (3) to some sweets to share with the little ones. Be good, all of you, and behave … (4). And take the dogs with you.
Jen	(on the phone) Hi Dad, it's Jen. We were enjoying … (5) in the park. Then the dogs ran off by … (6) and they won't come back. Billy fell and hurt … (7) and Anna's crying. She blames … (8) for everything. What shall we do now?

21

b Describe the pictures. Use a reflexive pronoun or *each other*.

The children are helping
➜ **themselves**.
They are helping
➜ **each other**.

a The teenagers are looking at …
b They are looking at …

a The girls are hurting …
b They have hurt …

a The cats are washing …
b They're washing …

▶ **10 This and that** Demonstrative determiners and pronouns ▶ 21.5

Erklärvideo online:
cornelsen.de/webcodes
Code: donaye

Complete the mini dialogues with *this*, *that*, *these* or *those*.

Maisie Hi is ➜ **that** Innes? … (1) is Maisie. You know … (2) homework we got yesterday?
Innes Do you mean … (3) maths problems we had to do? I gave mine to the teacher … (4) morning.
Maisie No, … (5) language tasks I've got here are for tomorrow, and I'm stuck. Can you help?

Clara I love … (6) jacket you're wearing, Aya.
Aya … (7)? Oh, thanks, it's just something I found in a charity shop.
Clara Is … (8) where you bought the boots you're wearing too?
Aya Excuse me, … (9) boots are brand new and were very expensive!

Sukon Oh dear, I don't think … (10) is the right way. I'm afraid we're lost.
Leo … (11) signs back there weren't very clear. I'll check on my phone.
Sukon Good idea! It's so easy to do … (12) days!

---

11 Afternoon tea The prop-word *one* ▶ 21.6

Two old friends meet in a traditional English tea room. Rewrite the sentences to avoid repetition, using *(the) one* or *(the) ones*.

Amy I'd love a cup of tea. Would you like a cup of tea?
➜ *Would you like* **one**?
Beth I've just had a cup of tea, but OK, I will have another cup of tea, thanks.
Amy Do you want a cake with that? And if so, which cake do you want?
Beth Mmm, I'd love a cake. That cake with the strawberries on top, I think.
Amy I prefer those cakes with cream on. They're delicious.
Beth Yes but I think the cakes with fruit are a bit healthier!

21

+ 12 Modern art   Mixed exercise   ▶ 21

Do you sometimes look at modern art and think 'A five-year-old could have done that'? Three friends are visiting an art gallery. Complete their conversation with appropriate words.

Reka Hey, → *you* guys! What do you think of … (1) painting over there?

Jason Not sure what I think. I mean, anybody could have done that, couldn't … (2)?

Val Well, I know what I think! As you know, I'm teaching … (3) to paint and I reckon … (4) work is better than that!

Reka There's a lot of creativity in a work of modern art, … (5) know.

Jason Creativity or luck? You just need to find someone who believes in you. Look at … (6) painting here, for example. Is that art?

Val Not really. …'s (7) a mess, just a lot of paint splashed onto a canvas. I'm sure if people give … (8) honest opinion, no one really understands what that's meant to be.

Reka I actually like it. I think … (9) function is to make one think, to open … (10) mind. It's powerful and emotive.

Val You sound like an art professor! If you ask … (11), it's just rubbish. In fact, of all the paintings we've seen today, I think it's the worst … (12)!

+ 13 Translation   *each other / one another /* German reflexive verbs   ▶ 21.4.3, 21.4.4

Some frequently used verbs are reflexive in German but not in English. Translate the German sentences into English.

→ Ich denke, Tom sollte sich entschuldigen – das war wirklich unhöflich von ihm.
*I think Tom should **apologize** – that was really rude of him.*

1 Ich wartete am Pool, während meine Freundin sich umzog.
2 Joe und Kelly treffen sich jeden Freitag nach der Arbeit.
3 Sara ist zuhause im Bett – sie fühlt sich heute nicht sehr wohl.
4 Kannst du dir vorstellen, vierzehn Katzen zu haben?
5 Der Fotograf sagte den Schülern, sie sollten sich nicht bewegen.
6 Maite und Rosie freuen sich darauf, einander am Wochenende zu sehen.
7 Bitte komm herein und setz dich.
8 Mama macht sich ständig Sorgen um euch Jungs.
9 Unsere Großmutter erinnert sich sehr genau an ihre Schulzeit.
10 Ich frage mich, ob Katie heute Abend kommt.

21

+ 14 Royal protocol   Mixed exercise   ▶ 21.4.5

How should you behave if you meet somebody royal? There are certain rules and traditions you are expected to know. Choose the correct words.

The British royal family continues to fascinate people from all over the world, not least in Britain → ***itself*** | oneself.
The 'Royals'. You've probably seen them | those (1)
5 on the news but how about actually seeing a king or queen for herself | yourself (2)? As a journalist, the opportunity to meet one of the royal family is an extremely thrilling prospect. But what is the correct etiquette when meeting, for example, the Prince of
10 Wales himself | herself (3)? Does it | one (4) bow or curtsey? Might there | their (5) be any topics of conversation your | you (6) should avoid? And if you meet a princess, what exactly do you call her | herself (7)? Here are some dos and don'ts I wrote to
15 avoid any potential embarrassment in the unlikely event that I should ever meet a royal person oneself | myself (8).
On presentation to a king or queen, the correct form of address is 'Your Majesty', whilst everyone else in
20 the family is just 'Your Royal Highness'. A small curtsey or bend of ones | your (9) knees is required from female visitors, or a short inclination of you're | your (10) head from male visitors. After that, you address the men as 'Sir' and the women as 'Ma'am'
25 – pronounced as in 'jam' and not as in 'arm', so don't make that mistake! We don't want to make fools of us | ourselves (11), do we?

After the introductions, always follow the monarch's lead. Speak only when you're spoken to and do not sit | sit yourself (12) down until they | themselves 30 (13) are seated. The dinner table protocol is very traditional: never start to eat before the king or queen does, of course, and all you ordinary people have to stop eating when themselves | they (14) do, even if you haven't finished dinner itself | your- 35 selves (15). Don't turn | turn yourself (16) round and show your | you're (17) back to a monarch either – that is considered very rude. And the biggest 'no-no' is touching – Michelle Obama her- self | himself (18) famously broke protocol in 40 2009 when she put her arm around Queen Elizabeth II. I wonder if she was amused?

Quick Check

A Complete the sentences with the correct pronoun or determiner.

1 I've known Emma for years, she's a good friend of …
2 These cups are clean, put … in the cupboard, please.
3 We ate … sandwiches sitting on a park bench.
4 That dog in the lake is trying to get … ball.
5 What currency do … use in New Zealand?
6 Take off … shoes, boys, and shut the door.
7 You don't have to shout, I can hear … perfectly well.
8 Did you bring these lovely flowers? – No, it wasn't …

B Complete the sentences using a reflexive pronoun or *each other*.

1 She never takes photos of …, she hates taking selfies.
2 The light switches … off after a minute or so.
3 We hope you all enjoy … this evening.
4 Pat and Brian only think of … . They're so selfish.
5 The two boxers are trying to knock … out, of course.
6 I hurt … while I was running downstairs.
7 Most politicians in Brussels speak to … in English.
8 Her brothers argue a lot but they still respect …

C Complete the mini-dialogues using one of the words from the box where necessary.

> this • that • these • those • (the) one • (the) ones

1 **Alice**   Do you like … jackets here?
   Becky   I don't really like the leather … . … denim … over there are nicer.
   Alice   I just can't find one I like better than … I'm wearing.
2 **Clay**   Here's your shampoo. Did I get the right … ?
   Dorit   Actually, I wanted a large … . Didn't they have any bigger … in the supermarket?
   Clay   Well I only went to the shop on the corner. They only had small … , sorry.
3 **Customer** How much is … dog in the window? … with the sweet face?
   Assistant Sorry, …'s my dog and she's not for sale. Can I interest you in … puppies here?
   Customer A puppy, …'s a good idea! Can I hold … with the blue eyes, please?

D Find and correct a mistake in each of the sentences.

1 Patrica has always wanted an own motorbike.
2 Kevin fell off his skateboard and broke the arm last week.
3 She used to be a very good neighbour of me.
4 Yours is a much better essay than her.
5 We filmed us as part of a school drama project.
6 We agreed that we would see us next week.
7 You don't like red boots? How about these black?
8 I don't feel myself very well today.

21

22 Quantifiers

Task	Topic	Example	Englische Grammatik
1	some, any and no	I'd like some coffee. Have we got any? – Yes, but there's no sugar left. I forgot to buy some.	22.1.1 22.9.1
2	Compounds with some, any and no	Something is wrong here. Does anyone know where Mr Harding is? – Well, there's no one in the staff room.	22.1.2 22.9.2
3	(a) little and (a) few	I need a little help with these boxes. – OK, but I've only got a few minutes.	22.3
4	a lot (of), much and many	There's still a lot of work to do, and we don't have much time.	22.2
5	each, every and any; all	Each of you will be given a task. You may begin writing any time now. Every student must hand in their work at the end of the lesson. I expect all of you to do your best.	22.4.1 22.5
6	both, either, neither, all, none	Both of them can sing, but neither of them can dance. All of the kids are 12 or older, but none are older than 14.	22.5 22.6 22.7 22.8 22.9
7	Mixed compounds	The firefighters looked everywhere, but there was nobody in the building. They couldn't find anyone.	22.1.2 22.4.2 22.9.2
8	Mixed exercise (1)	I had a few minutes before my train left, so I bought something to read at a kiosk.	22
9	both, either, all, neither, none	Laura and Daniel both play the violin. Either of them can help you, but neither of the twins has time today. None of the players protested against the decision. / All of them accepted the decision.	22.5 22.6 22.7 22.8 22.9.1
10	Special uses of some and any	She gave all her money to some so-called expert. I never have any luck at card games. Shirin doesn't like some of her teachers.	22.1.1b 22.4.1b
11	Mixed exercise (2)	The two scientists have both done research on tumour cells.	22

▶ Quick Check p. 193

1 Last-minute planning   *Some, any* and *no*   ▶ 22.1.1, 22.9.1

Erklärvideo online:

cornelsen.de/webcodes
Code: jonuho

Carla and her classmates are selling homemade smoothies at school for a charity project. On the first morning, they meet for a last-minute discussion. Fill in the gaps with *some*, *any* or *no*.

Carla I've brought ➜ ***some*** carrots and grapes with me.
Jack We've got plenty of oranges and bananas too, but we haven't got … (1) apples.
Sue Shall I go and buy … (2)?
Terry Yes, please. And it would be good to get … (3) mangoes and papayas too. But where can you get them?
Özlem You can buy them at … (4) supermarket.
Carla There's … (5) time left for shopping now. But here's … (6) money. You can buy them this afternoon and bring them with you tomorrow.
Rob What about paper cups? Haven't we got … (7)?
Jack Look behind you! There are … (8) right here on the table.
Laurie What if somebody wants to pay with a five-pound note? There's … (9) change in the cash box.
Carla I'll ask Mr Phillips if he's got … (10).

2 The missing mobile   Compounds with *some, any* and *no*   ▶ 22.1.2, 22.9.2

Nick, David and Mehmet are in the classroom, waiting for the lesson to start. Choose the right word.

Nick Has ➜ ***anybody*** | somebody seen my mobile? I can't find it anywhere | somewhere (1).
Mehmet You probably just left it lying anywhere | somewhere (2).
Nick No, I'm sure anyone | someone (3) must have taken it.
David Not anyone | No one (4) here would steal your mobile.
Nick Well, anyone | someone (5) must have. It's anywhere | nowhere (6) in the room
Mehmet Wait a minute. Let me try anything | something (7).
Mehmet takes out his mobile. Anywhere | Somewhere (8) in the room a phone starts ringing.
David I can hear anything | something (9). Hey Nick, isn't that your mobile?
Mehmet Listen, it's in your school bag.
Nick Anybody | Somebody (10) must have hidden it there. I bet it was you two!

3 The end of the book?   (A) *little* and (a) *few*   ▶ 22.3

a Are kids today no longer interested in books and reading? Choose the right word(s) to complete the text below.

According to a new survey, people spend ➜ ***less*** | fewer time reading than ever before. Only a few | a little (1) say that they read at least one hour a day. The group of 16-to-20-year-olds read the fewest | the least (2) of all age groups. They find reading a little | less (3) attractive than watching TV or chatting. This means that fewer | lesser (4) people than ever before are active readers. If this trend continues, in few | a few (5) years
5 the age of the book may come to an end. But few | little (6) people believe that this will really happen.

b NOW YOU Write about your reading habits: Do you spend more or less time reading than you used to? Do you read more or fewer books than your best friend? What kind of books do you like most and what kind least?

4 Our German guest   *A lot (of), much and many*   ▶ 22.2

Hank Krueger from the student newspaper of Culver High School is interviewing Laureen, an exchange student from Germany. Complete the dialogue with words from the box.

> a lot of (2x) • much (2x) • ~~many~~ •
> many (4x) • more (1x) • most (1x)

Hank   Do ➔ **many** people in Germany own their own homes?
Laureen Not as … (1) as in the US. … (2) Germans live in rented apartments than in one-family houses.
Hank   That surprises me. Very … (3) Americans think of home ownership as being, like, a basic right. I mean, almost everybody here owns the place they live in.
Laureen Maybe because houses here don't cost as … (4) as they do in Germany. We've got … (5) housing laws, like how thick the walls have to be and how … (6) energy the house is allowed to consume.
Hank   Wow! Don't … (7) people get angry about that?
Laureen No, not that … (8), I think. … (9) people seem to think it's OK. I mean, it's better for the environment, isn't it?
Hank   You're probably right, but not … (10) Americans would agree with you.

5 Before the test   *Each, every and any; all*   ▶ 22.4.1, 22.5

Students are always nervous before a test. Complete the text with *all, any, each* or *every*. Sometimes more than one answer is correct.

On the morning of their speaking test, ➔ **all** of the students were nervous. When the door of the waiting room opened, the students … (1) entered. … (2) of them looked for the table with their name on
5 it. The teacher asked if … (3) of them felt ready to do the test. She told them that … (4) ten minutes one of them would be called into the exam room. The students nervously watched the door. They knew that … (5) minute now it would open and one of them would be called up. … (6) of them could be 10 next on the list. That was the reason why … (7) of them disliked these speaking tests more than … (8) other kind of exam.

6 The very musical Shrivers

both, either, neither, all, none   ▶ 22.5 – 22.9

a Read the text about the Shriver family. Complete the sentences using the words from the box.

> ~~both~~ • both • either • neither • all (2x) • none

The Shriver family is very musical. Mr Shriver plays ➔ **both** the trumpet and the horn, and Mrs Shriver plays the cello. Mr Shriver is a pharmacist, and his wife teaches at a local school, so … (1) of them is a
5 professional musician. Their twin daughters, Ruth and Sarah, … (2) play the violin, and their older brother Philip plays the flute. … (3) five of them play in the town orchestra.

The 'black sheep' of the family is the younger son Rodney. As a child, he had trumpet and piano les- 10 sons, but he didn't like … (4) of them. Finally his parents gave in and let him take drum lessons. Now he plays in a rock band at his school. … (5) of the other Shrivers share his musical taste, but they … (6) respect his right to make his own decisions. 15

b NOW YOU Who in your family plays a musical instrument? Write three sentences.

➔ **Neither** my mother **nor** my father plays an instrument.

22

7 Ready to leave Mixed compounds ▸ 22.1.2, 22.4.2, 22.9.2

Class 9PH has spent a week at a youth hostel with their teacher, Mr Hill. It's their last day, and they are getting ready to leave. Choose the right word.

Mr Hill Has ➔ anybody | **everybody** finished packing? Have you taken everything | something (1) out of the wardrobes and cupboards?

Cate Sir, I can't find my bag anywhere | nowhere (2).

Mr Hill Have you looked anywhere | everywhere (3)? Bags don't just disappear. It must be anywhere | somewhere (4).

Cate I think it's in my room, but I haven't got the key anymore. I gave it to anyone | someone (5) at the desk ten minutes ago.

Mr Hill Then go to the desk again and ask them to give you the key.

Two minutes later.

Cate Sorry, sir, but there's anybody | nobody (6) at the desk.

Mr Hill Well, there's anything | nothing (7) I can do about it now. Our bus is waiting. Onto the bus, everybody | anybody (8)!

Philip Sir, there's anyone | someone (9) coming down the hall. I think it's the cleaning lady, and she's got anything | something (10) in her hand.

Lara And it looks like Cate's bag. What a surprise!

8 The winners Mixed exercise ▸ 22

Does money make life easier? Find out by completing the text with words from the box below.

> a few • all the (2x) • anything • both • every •
> neither • ~~no~~ • none • some • the two

Fred and Gloria had been married for years. They had ➔ no children and lived a quiet life in a small town. Fred had ... (1) drinks ... (2) weekend at the pub and played the lottery, but he had never won ...
5 (3). Gloria read ... (4) romantic novels she could find at the local library. One day Fred got a letter with ... (5) amazing news: the couple had won half a million pounds. They ... (6) had ideas on how to spend the money: Fred wanted to buy a small car and a
10 holiday house at the coast, whereas Gloria dreamt of moving to London and going on a cruise round the world. ... (7) began arguing over the money; ... (8) of them was willing to give in. In the end, they gave ... (9) money to charity, and the arguments stopped. ... (10) of their friends ever found out what they had 15 done with the money.

✚ 9 Who plays what? *both, either, all, neither, none* ▶ 22.5–22.8, 22.9.1

name	plays
Nicole	tennis, the flute, volleyball, chess, the guitar
Yasmine	badminton, the flute, chess, volleyball
Thomas	tennis, the guitar, football, chess, computer games
Youssef	football, computer games, the guitar

a Make sentences about the teenagers and their activities. Use the phrases *all of them, both of them, neither of them* or *none of them.*

→ Nicole + Thomas: tennis
  Both *of them play tennis.*

1 Nicole + Yasmine: the flute
2 Nicole + Yasmine: football
3 Thomas + Youssef + Nicole: badminton
4 Nicole + Thomas + Yasmine: chess
5 Thomas + Youssef: computer games
6 Youssef + Yasmine + Thomas: the tuba
7 Thomas + Youssef: volleyball
8 Nicole + Thomas + Youssef: the guitar

b Answer the questions.

→ The drama club needs a flute player. Who could they ask: Yasmine or Nicole?
  Either *of them.* | **Either** *Yasmine or Nicole.*

1 A folk band is looking for two guitar players. Who should they ask: Thomas or Youssef?
2 The school band needs more clarinet players. Who should they ask: Yasmine or Nicole?
3 The volleyball coach is looking for a new assistant coach for the girls' junior team. Who could she ask: Nicole or Yasmine?
4 The jazz band needs a saxophone player. Who should they ask: Nicole, Thomas or Youssef?
5 Cheryl is looking for a tennis partner to practise with. Who could she ask: Nicole or Thomas?
6 The school chess club is organizing an open tournament. Who might be interested: Nicole, Yasmine or Thomas?

c NOW YOU Make a table like the one above about you and two your friends. Then write sentences about your activities, the ones you share and the ones you don't share.

22

⊙ ✚ 10 The school talent show *Special uses of some and any* ► 22.1.1b, 22.4.1b

Erklärvideo online:
► Exercise 1

Rob is not a big fan of talent shows. Complete the text using *any, some* or *anybody*.

Our school's annual talent show was almost a complete disaster this year. I wouldn't have gone if my sister hadn't dragged me there. There was hardly ➜ ***any*** advertising for the show because … (1) idiot had torn down all the posters they had put up, so hardly … (2) knew about the event. When we arrived at the school, … (3) twenty people were sitting in the hall waiting for the show to begin. I looked around, but I didn't see … (4) I knew. Well, it could have been a lot worse: most of the kids who performed were actually pretty good. I didn't like … (5) of them, but the rest were OK. When the show was over hardly … (6) applauded. It was pretty embarrassing. The best part came as we were leaving and we met this nice-looking girl from my sister's class. She seemed really happy to see me and said we ought to get together … (7) time. I said I'd be glad and asked her what day. She said … (8) day would be fine with her.

✚ 11 The 3D flop *Mixed exercise* ► 22

Have you ever wondered how 3D movies work? Read the text to find out and translate the German words in brackets into English.

We see objects in three dimensions because we have two eyes. ➜ ***Both*** (beide) eyes focus on the same object, but … (jedes) (1) eye sees the object from a different angle. In the brain, … (die beiden) (2) slightly different images are combined into one three-dimensional image.

3D cinema is based on the same principle. The film camera that is used for making 3D films is really a double camera with two lenses next to each other. … (jede) (3) lens records a separate image. 3D cinemas have double projectors that project … (beide) (4) images onto the same screen. Viewers must wear special glasses that allow … (jedes) (5) eye to see only one of … (die beiden) (6) images.

When Avatar, the first Hollywood blockbuster to be made in 3D, became a smash hit in 2009, … (viele) (7) media experts believed that in … (ein paar) (8) years … (jeder) (9) film would be in 3D. Today, however, … (immer weniger) (10) films are being made in 3D. One reason is the higher cost, … (sowohl) (11) for film studios … (als auch) (12) for film-goers. … (manche) (13) people get headaches or feel sick while watching a 3D film. Film critics say that 3D technology has delivered … (weniger) (14) than it promised: instead of changing the way films are made, it has become simply one more visual trick, a special effect that … (die meisten) (15) viewers quickly tire of and that costs … (mehr) (16) than it is worth.

Quick Check

A Choose the right word from the pair.

1 The Drama Club meets each | every Friday at 4 o'clock.
2 Let's see if you can do the next task without any | some help.
3 Hurry up with the sandwiches – the guests will arrive any | every minute.
4 Does anyone | someone know where Jan is?
5 The maths test was so simple that anybody | everybody could have done it.
6 As we were getting on the bus, the tour guide gave every | each of us a brochure.
7 I've made tea. Would you like any | some?
8 Jackie looked for her notebook, but she couldn't find it anywhere | everywhere.
9 We spent an hour searching the internet, but we only found a few | a little information on our topic.
10 Jason left the both | two girls sitting in the car while he went into the shop.

B Translate the word(s) in brackets.

1 By Friday evening, … (alle) knew that Mandy and Jake had broken up.
2 Germany's biggest folk festival takes place … (jeden) July in Rudolstadt.
3 I phoned Loretta and Chiara, but … (keine) of them knew where Marla was.
4 These LED lamps use … (weniger) energy than conventional lighting.
5 We stopped at a club, but there weren't … (viele) people there, so we left.
6 Steve is one of those people who would do … (alles) to get attention.
7 A few minutes later I saw … (die beiden) tourists go into the information centre.
8 … (Alle Mädchen) I know play hockey.
9 I work … (weniger) in the evening than I used to and get … (weniger) headaches.
10 Ms Carver asked for volunteers, but … (keiner) of the students raised their hands.

C Each sentence contains one mistake. Find and correct it.

1 I know there isn't some margarine in the fridge, so I'll get some later.
2 Nobody of the players knew why Lenny hadn't come to training.
3 Every of the runners is given a number.
4 We get very few rain in this part of the country.
5 Neither Jeremy nor Britta were able to do the task.
6 Are everyone on the bus?
7 There is a train to Leipzig all thirty minutes.
8 Carlo felt lonely because he didn't know somebody at his new school.
9 Let's ask Marie to talk to the headmaster. She could persuade everyone.
10 I asked Tomas and Ben to help me, but none of them had time.
11 All students in my class have new phones.
12 I expect the parcel to arrive every day now.
13 Janos made three suggestions, but I didn't like either of them.
14 Callahan rang the house a couple of times, but noone answered the phone.
15 I'm having trouble with this new software. Could you give me any help?

22

23 Mixed bag

Task	Topic	Example	Englische Grammatik
1	Common mistakes (1)	*We're looking forward ~~to see~~ to seeing you.*	Appendix A
2	Prepositions of place and direction	*The cinema is opposite the bank. Walk along Oak Road and it's on the left next to a café.*	23.2
3	Prepositions of time	*The accident happened in the morning on Friday, at about six.*	23.3
4	Prepositions: fixed phrases	*You might at least say sorry. How about it?*	23.5
5	Connecting sentences	*The flight was cancelled because it had snowed, and so we re-booked.*	24.1
6	Linking with different constructions	*Knowing it was late, she ran home so as not to miss dinner.*	24.1
7	Frequent connectors	*Due to the bad weather, all outside sports such as football and rugby were cancelled.*	24.2
8	Polite ways of talking	*I'd be extremely grateful for some help, if you wouldn't mind.*	25.1.3
9	Short answers and question tags	*She's coming with us, isn't she? I sure hope so!*	25.2.3 25.2.4
10	Informal and formal English	*I am writing to inform you … / Just to let you know …*	25.1
11	Common mistakes (2)	*I ~~know~~ have known Jack since kindergarten.*	Appendix A
12	Structuring argumentative texts	*Firstly, I'm right. Secondly, you're wrong. Therefore, you ought to do what I say.*	24.3.2
13	British and American English	*I haven't gotten used to living in the UK yet.*	25.3

▶ Quick Check p. 203

1 Get it right   Common mistakes   ▶ Appendix A

Find and correct the mistake in each sentence.

➔ The panel discussed <mark>about</mark> the candidates for hours.
The panel discussed the candidates for hours.

1 Tom asked Kathy for help, and she explained him the problem.
2 All what I meant was that you look tired.
3 Mrs Simmons gave her pupils a very good advice.
4 Henry wants that we bring some food to the party.
5 I really enjoyed *The Uncommon Reader* from Alan Bennett.
6 In the park Chloe's dog ran off this morning.
7 What's the opposite from 'sensitive'?
8 We should be doing more to protect the nature.
9 Let's meet us at nine on Friday morning.
10 Mandy's little sister was crying while the film.
11 I'm sure I sent you an email for a week.
12 Why asked you me if you already knew the answer?

2 Where is it? Prepositions of place and direction ▶ 23.2

a Dan and Lisa, a couple from New Zealand, are planning a visit to the UK. Take a look at this hotel brochure and complete the sentences with a preposition from the box.

> behind • by • at • in front of • inside • on • opposite • outside • ~~near~~

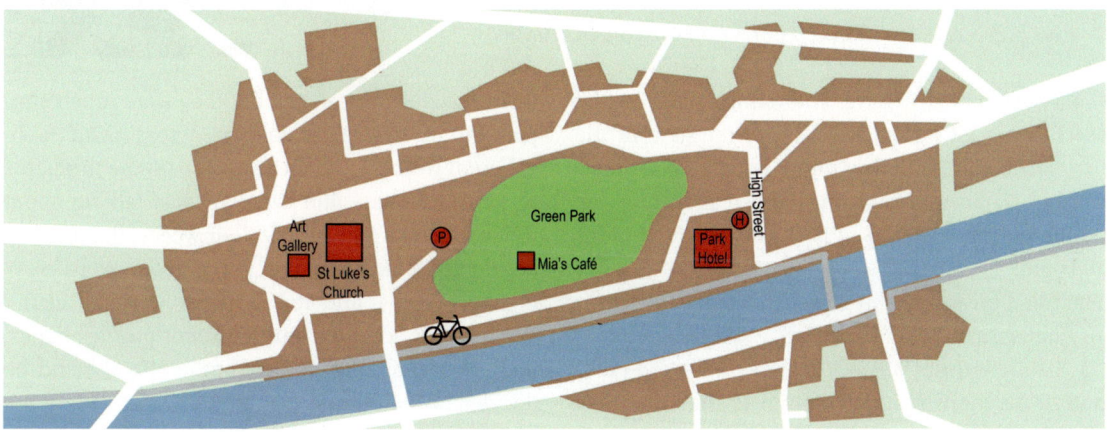

Would you like to spend a few days ➜ *near* London, but far from the noise and stress of the big city? The Park Hotel is the ideal place for your stay. Located in the centre of our beautiful old town, right ... (1) the river, it takes its name from the wonderful park ... (2) the hotel. You can have dinner ... (3) our five-star restaurant and enjoy the view.

There is so much to see and do here that you won't have time to get bored. St Luke's Church ... (4) the corner is well worth a visit. There are a number of fine paintings ... (5) the church, and a really fascinating old graveyard just ... (6) it. And if you're interested in art, there's a gallery ... (7) the church. For those of you who wish to see more of the area, there is a bus stop directly ... (8) the hotel. Come and visit us – you won't regret it!

b Choose the correct prepositions to complete the phrases of directon in Lisa's email to her sister.

| From: | Lisa |
| Re: | Hi sis! |

Hi there

I've just walked ➜ **past** | along someone with a dog like yours, and I thought of you! We're a long way from home but having a good time. We've met some other New Zealanders, who have come from Auckland via | over (1) Los Angeles. They're going in | to (2) Scotland when they leave here, just like us! We all find the hotel a bit noisy, with kids running up and down | in and out (3) the stairs. It's also quite expensive here, and we didn't know when to change our dollars in | into (4) pounds. Dan and I had planned a day trip to London, but we overslept. We ran after | behind (5) the bus to the train station but just missed it. So we hired bikes instead and cycled along | against (6) the river, which was more relaxing. In the evenings, we just have to walk through | across (7) the road for a drink in the park café. And if the weather is good, you can take your drinks out into | onto (8) the terrace.

More news soon.
Love, Lisa

23

3 From word-cross to crossword
Prepositions of time ▸ 23.3

Crossword puzzles are very popular. But who invented them and how have they developed over time? Complete the text with the correct preposition from the box.

> after (x2) • at • ~~for~~ • in (x2) • of • on (x2) • since • until

Crossword puzzles have entertained fans ➜ *for* years, but a lot has changed ... (1) the days of the first word puzzle. Today, many people do a crossword ... (2) Sunday mornings and real enthusiasts
5 do them every evening ... (3) work. So, how did it all begin?
The trend for puzzles in newspapers was started by an Englishman living in the US. ... (4) the winter ... (5) 1914, Arthur Wynne designed a word-cross
10 puzzle for the Christmas edition of the New York World, published ... (6) December 21. ... (7) then, word puzzles had existed, but they were much simpler. But in Wynne's puzzle the 'across' words were different from the 'down' words. ... (8) the time, this was revolutionary and everyone was talking about 15 the word-cross. Then, ... (9) four weeks, the printers accidentally changed the name from word-cross to crossword – and it was never changed again. Wynne experimented with different puzzle shapes, including a circular puzzle, but ... (10) the end he 20 decided on the format that we know today.

4 Careers advice
Prepositions: fixed phrases ▸ 23.5

a Personality tests are designed to match you with a future career, but they don't have all the answers. Ewa has some questions about career tests. Choose the correct phrases in the dialogue.

Ewa Robin, can I ask you something? Are you ➜ in the long run | *in a hurry*?

Robin Not really. In fact | For sure (1), I'm just going home. I usually take the bus, but I don't mind walking with you for a change | for instance (2).

Ewa OK, thanks. I need your advice about careers. My daughter Ellie just can't make up her mind what to do. I thought perhaps you could help – above all | after all (3), you are an expert.

Robin Well, I've been a mentor for a change | for a long time (4). What's Ellie's problem exactly?

Ewa She's been doing lots of careers tests online lately. What do you think of them? In my opinion | In your own words (5), they're pretty useless.

Robin Those tests are just a starting point, but on the one hand | on the other hand (6), they can give your daughter some ideas about possible careers. At last | At least (7) she might be able to cross some careers off her list, and maybe think about others that she hadn't thought of before.

Ewa True. But I do worry. There's so much advice out there, but at the end of the day, she's basically on her own | on duty (8), isn't she?

Robin Not at all | Not at first (9)! She'll have plenty of people to help her. Anyway, whatever she decides to do, everything will be fine in the long run | for a long time (10), as long as she stays true to herself!

b NOW YOU Write your own sentences with three of the phrases you didn't choose in the dialogue.

5 Joining in   Connecting sentences   ▶ 24.1

It's hard to motivate yourself to go outdoors on cold winter days, but you usually feel better if you do. Combine the short sentences into longer ones using the connecting words given in the box.

> although • ~~and~~ • and • because • ~~but~~ • but (2x) • or • so • when • where • which • while • who

→ My friends enjoy cycling. | They love sailing. | They don't do either if it's too windy.
  *My friends enjoy cycling **and** they love sailing **but** they don't do either if it's too windy.*

1 It's winter. | You're not getting much exercise. | That's no reason to be lazy!

   Why not come along with me to the badminton club? | Come along to play indoor tennis.

2 We are all tempted to stay indoors. | It's cold and dark outside.

   I personally go jogging regularly. | I feel terrible if I don't.

   I even went running last week. | It was snowing the whole time.

3 It's cold. | It's windy. | If you have a dog, you have to take it out.

   Toni was walking her dog in a park. | There were other dog walkers in the park.

   She met a guy. | The guy had a dog like hers.

   The dogs played together. | Toni and the guy were talking.

   They agreed to meet again. | This was the start of a beautiful friendship.

6 A frightening incident   Linking with different constructions   ▶ 24.1

a A new crime series on TV starts with a woman who is getting into her car when a man with a knife comes up to her. Rewrite the sentences as one sentence, using the words in brackets.

→ The main character was attacked by a man. The man's face was masked. (whose)
  *The main character was attacked by a man **whose** face was masked.*

1 She wasn't hurt. Her bag was stolen. She was in a state of shock. (but, and)
2 She went to the police station. She wanted to report what had happened. (in order to)
3 She made a statement. She left the police station. (having)
4 She did not want to meet her attacker. She went home a different way. (that's why)
5 She didn't go home immediately. She went to her office first. (instead of)
6 She knew she would be alone. She took the lift to her office. (knowing)
7 She started up her laptop. She wanted to search for a private detective. (in order to)
8 She was scrolling through the list of names. She heard a noise – she clearly wasn't the only one in the office. (while)

b **NOW YOU** Make up your own ending for the story, linking your sentences with different constructions.

23

7 Youth in Iceland   Frequent sentence connectors   ▶ 24.2

Teenage behaviour has been studied in Iceland, resulting in some radical changes. Choose the correct connectors to complete the text.

Twenty years ago, Icelandic teens were among the heaviest-drinking youths in Europe. ➔ Apparently | Finally, it was not enough to just warn teens about drink and drug abuse. Due to | Despite (1) the fact

5 that a lot of money had been spent on special programmes, there were still many problems.

In 1992, 14-16-year-olds in every school in Iceland filled in a form with questions, such as | as well (2) 'How much do you smoke?', 'What do you drink?',

10 'How much time do you spend with your parents?' and so on. This was repeated in 1995 and 1997, and the data was analysed.

As a result of | In spite of (3) this analysis, certain factors became clear. Teens who started drinking,

15 smoking and taking other drugs were often stressed and troubled, whereas | because (4) those who didn't were happier and more successful.

Researchers wanted to find out why. Because of | Apart from (5) sports, organized activities were

clearly important. Moreover | In other words (6), 20 spending time in the family was a key factor. In consequence | In fact (7), teenagers who spent time at home in the evenings were often much happier.

Due to | In spite of (8) this research data, a new national plan called 'Youth in Iceland' was introduced. 25 Laws were changed. On the contrary | For example (9), it became illegal for under-18s to buy tobacco, or to buy alcohol under the age of 20. Children aged between 13 and 16 were forbidden from being outside after 10 pm in winter and midnight in summer. 30 Instead | Namely (10), children spent more time with their parents. The parents were encouraged to ask about school and get to know their children's friends. And the result? Young Icelanders have recently been voted the cleanest-living teens in 35 Europe.

8 Say 'please'!   Polite ways of talking   ▶ 25.1.3

Put the words in the correct order to make more polite versions of the sentences in brackets. Some of them are questions.

➔ please | bags | move | could | you / your | ? (Move your bags.)
Could you please *move your bags?*

1 I'm afraid | seat | that | but | sorry | my | is (That's my seat.)
2 we | would you mind | if | that window | very much | shut | ? (Shut that window.)
3 you | awfully grateful | I'd | could | if | help me | be (Help me.)
4 is | your | just a little | music | for me | loud (Your music's far too loud.)
5 you | it | wouldn't | be better | wore headphones | if | ? (Why don't you wear headphones?)
6 jacket | believe | I | that | mine | is (Hey, that's my jacket.)
7 change seats | if | was wondering | could | I | we (I want your seat.)
8 if | I'll | my own | you don't mind | get | coffee (I don't want you to get my coffee.)

9 Decisions, decisions Short answers and question tags ▶ 25.2.3, 25.2.4

Two students are looking for a flat. Complete the dialogue with the correct short answer or question tag.

Yuri   Did you like the last flat we saw? I'm guessing you didn't like it much, ➜ *did you*?

Zak   It seemed a bit dark, … (1)? Perhaps it was just the red walls. And, of course, if you see a place in the evening, you can't really tell, … (2)? But I was happy with the location.

Yuri   … (3) too. I can imagine living on that street.

Zak   … (4) I. And it's on a good bus route, … (5)?

Yuri   Yes, though the night buses won't run there, … (6)?

Zak   We always could cycle into class, … (7)? Oh, but I forgot to ask if there was somewhere safe to leave bikes.

Yuri   … (8) I. We should really call the owner and ask, … (9)?

Zak   Yes. Tell you what, let's ask if we can view it once more in daylight. We don't have to decide right now, … (10)?

Yuri   Probably not. OK, I'll give her a ring.

✚ 10 Caught out Informal and formal English ▶ 25.1

These phrases are taken from a police interview.
An officer is talking to a young suspect, who uses less formal language than the officer.

a Decide for each phrase whether it's formal or informal English.

> ~~Might I ask why you …?~~ • ~~I dunno!~~ • Should you do that again, … • Me and my mates • But on whose authority …? • Whom did you see …? • I gotta tell you • It's them that did it • Your actions are known to be … • I feel like I'm going crazy • Had we not stopped you, … • We're gonna be in big trouble

formal	informal
➜ *Might I ask why you …?*	➜ *I dunno!*

b Match these phrases with expressions from part a that mean the same.

➜ Why did you …? – *Might I ask why you …?*
➜ I don't know! – *I dunno!*

1 We know your actions are …
2 If we hadn't stopped you, …
3 But who said you could …?
4 I have to tell you
5 My friends and I
6 I feel as if I'm going crazy
7 They did it
8 If you do that again, …
9 Who did you see …?
10 We're going to be in big trouble

23

✚ 11 Practice makes perfect   Common mistakes   ▸ Appendix A

Find and correct the mistakes in each sentence.

➜ I know Jemma since we started school together.
*I **have known** Jemma since we started school.*

1 We suggested to go to the new pizza restaurant.
2 Can someone open the door? I wash my hair at the moment.
3 Did you all your homework last night?
4 She has been standing there since half an hour.
5 I have seen an old friend yesterday evening.
6 He's really looking forward to go on holiday.
7 If I will have time tomorrow, I will call you.
8 We mustn't run, we've got lots of time.
9 Henry left without to say what time he would be back.
10 If you didn't lose your passport, we wouldn't have missed the plane.

✚ 12 Advertising   Structuring argumentative texts   ▸ 24.3.2

a Tanya's class has been asked to write an argumentative essay. She has chosen to write hers about advertising. Choose the correct words to complete the text.

It is almost impossible to avoid advertising which appears everywhere in our lives, ➜ *particularly* | in addition popping up automatically on the internet. Although | But (1) some advertisements can provide
5 genuine product information for customers, many are exploiting a captive audience. As | Moreover (2), so much personal data is now held online that advertisers can target specific people based on their previous actions as consumers. In my opinion, ad-
10 vertising can be seen as actively harmful for several reasons. As | Firstly (3), many advertisements shown nowadays use celebrities or size zero models to promote their products. On the contrary | However (4), not many young women actually look like
15 dolls or models, so | as (5) normal girls are all different shapes and sizes and do not all have perfect skin or the most beautiful hair. Although | Yet (6) they are encouraged to buy clothes, shoes, make up or hair products in order to make themselves look as much like their role models as possible. In conclu- 20
sion | Secondly (7), many products with high budget advertisements are expensive, tempting people to spend more money than they can afford. What's more | But (8), the latest version of everything is promoted. Particularly | Examples of this (9) might 25
be this year's new team kit for football fans or the most up-to-date operating system for computer geeks. However | Consequently (10), people are discouraged from re-using or re-cycling or even buying second-hand. Moreover | In conclusion (11), 30
advertising is powerful, persuasive and pervasive, making us buy things that are not really essential. Genuine and truthful advertisements can be useful, but | therefore (12) as consumers, we should be aware of clever marketing strategies. 35

b Tanya did not structure her essay in paragraphs. Read the text again and divide her text into four paragraphs.

✚ 13 Dialogue   British and American English   ▶ 25. 3

Joel and Hanna are cousins who correspond 'across the pond'. Joel writes to Hanna from his hometown in California, and she replies from Cumbria, in the north of England.

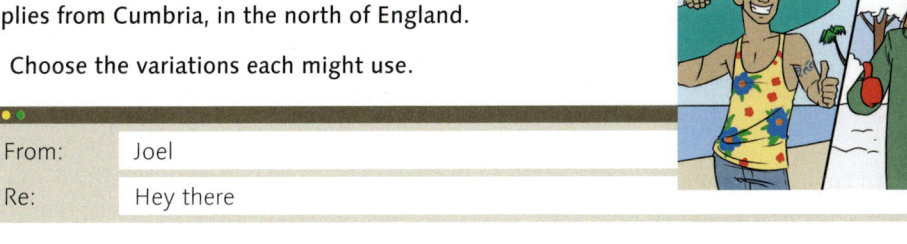

a   Choose the variations each might use.

From:	Joel
Re:	Hey there

Hi Hanna

How's life at college? Did you have your exams yet? And how was this ➜ autumn | **fall** for you? Here it was real | really (1) warm, so I spent a lot of time at the local pool. I'm on the senior swim team | swimming team (2) now, which is much different than last year. Our junior team was good, but junior training was a breeze, and now it sure isn't | certainly isn't (3)! Big news: I now have my driving licence | driver's license (4)! I talked with my mom and she agreed to lend me her car, so I've gotten a lot better. I'm still not great at intersections | crossroads (5) but freeways | motorways (6) are no problem. OK, it's 20 after | past (7) six so I better go get some dinner. I don't write as often as I should, but it'd be awesome to meet with you again – maybe next summer? Maybe we can organize something, OK?

Love to your folks
Joel

From:	Hanna
Re:	Hey there

Hello Joel

Thanks for your mail. I'm at home at the moment. We're on vacation | holiday (8) and I've got plenty of time to write because we've been snowed in from Thursday till | through (9) today! I've never seen so much snow! It's a good job I don't usually like travelling anyplace | anywhere (10) at the weekend. Even the main roads | highways (11) are only 'passable with care'. We've got winter tires | tyres (12) on the family estate car | station wagon (13) but Dad won't let me drive it. I learned to drive in the summer, so I'm not a good winter driver. In fact, I'm not even risking the sidewalks | pavements (14) today. Good to hear you've made it to the senior sports team. As you know, I'm not desperately sporty, but I do play the piano semi-professionally now. My teacher has insisted that I should perform a concerto next term – scary! But you needn't worry about me. Right now, I'm practicing | practising (15) for hours every day – so maybe it's just as well that I can't even get out of the garden | yard (16)!

Love to see you too – shall we make a plan?

Big hugs to all the family
Love, Hanna

23

b Find five more American words and expressions in Joel's email and give their British equivalent. Then do the same thing for Hanna's email. Find five British expressions and give their American counterpart.

Joel's email – American English	British English	Hanna's email – British English	American English
➜ at college	at university	➜ at home	home

c Find the American English equivalents of the words in the clues to complete the puzzle.

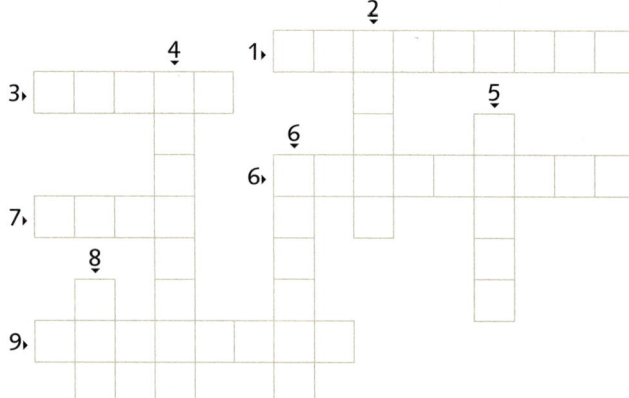

Across

1 holiday
3 handbag
6 pavement
7 queue
9 railway

Down

2 sweets
4 timetable
5 trousers
6 underground
8 petrol

Quick Check

A Complete the sentences with the correct prepositions.

1 I'll meet you … the airport … Monday … nine.
2 Joy comes … car or … her bike when she's not … foot.
3 This dress is … 20 years old, almost 25, in fact, and it's now well … my knees: it's too short!
4 Sorry, I've no cash – can I pay … the drinks … credit card?
5 Ana's staying … us next week, but only … Friday, as she as to work … the weekend.
6 I'm flying … Manchester … Zurich … Sao Paulo.
7 Megan's looking forward … seeing you … the 23rd … April.
8 Tim will arrive … quarter … nine or nine … the latest.
9 We're going … the theatre to see a play … Shakespeare … May.
10 Mariah's married … a guy … Dubai who's one of the richest men … the world.

B Choose the correct words.

1 I don't really know anyone here apart from | instead of you.
2 Henry would very much like to come also | as well.
3 Mr Owen is not in the office and further | furthermore, he will be away all week.
4 Maura's had a difficult life and so | yet she remains positive and cheerful.
5 There are no trains today owing to | following the weather.
6 Linda's on a business trip this month, that is | for example from the 3rd to the 23rd.
7 There was entertainment besides | such as clowns and games for the children.
8 Ted won't be going on holiday because of | in spite of his recent illness.
9 On the one hand | Whereas, you've made a very good point.
10 I saw Hans at the exhibition – I didn't speak to him though | despite.

C Decide if the sentences are formal or informal. Rewrite each sentence to make it more or less formal.

1 Would you mind very much helping me with this?
2 To whom should we send our thanks?
3 I'll be with you asap.
4 Kaitlyn was, like, with you all the time, right?
5 The police believed the man to be in his late forties.
6 I want to see your ticket!
7 Might I suggest that you take an earlier train?
8 Me and my kids, we just had a lovely walk.

D Complete the sentences with question tags or short answers.

1 Molly's dog chases cats. – … (Meine auch.)
2 You don't speak Dutch, … ? (oder?)
3 We didn't watch the news last night. – … (Wir auch nicht.)
4 I really love skiing on fresh snow. – … (Ich auch.)
5 Lotta won't be happy when you tell her, … ? (oder?)
6 I'm your closest relative, … ? (oder?)
7 This car belongs to your neighbour, … ? (oder?)
8 My mother doesn't like jazz. – … (Meine auch nicht.)

23

	Infinitiv	*simple past*	Partizip Perfekt	
A	arise [aɪ]	arose	arisen [ɪ]	entstehen
	awake	awoke	awaken	aufwachen, wecken
B	babysit	babysat	babysat	babysitten
	be	was, were	been	sein
	bear [eə]	bore	borne	(er)tragen
	beat	beat	beaten	schlagen, besiegen
	become	became	become	werden
	begin	began	begun	beginnen, anfangen
	bend	bent	bent	biegen
	bet	bet	bet	wetten
	bind [aɪ]	bound	bound	(ver)binden
	bite	bit	bitten	beißen
	bleed	bled	bled	bluten
	blow	blew	blown	blasen, wehen
	break [eɪ]	broke	broken	(zer)brechen
	breed	bred	bred	züchten
	bring	brought [ɔː]	brought [ɔː]	bringen
	broadcast	broadcast	broadcast	senden (TV usw.)
	build	built	built	bauen
	burn	burnt/ burned	burnt/ burned	(ver)brennen
	burst	burst	burst	platzen
	buy	bought [ɔː]	bought [ɔː]	kaufen
C	cast	cast	cast	werfen
	catch	caught [ɔː]	caught [ɔː]	fangen, erwischen
	choose [uː]	chose [əʊ]	chosen [əʊ]	(aus)wählen
	cling	clung	clung	festhalten
	come	came	come	kommen
	cost [ɒ]	cost	cost	kosten
	creep	crept	crept	kriechen, schleichen
	cut	cut	cut	schneiden

	Infinitiv	*simple past*	Partizip Perfekt	
D	deal [iː]	dealt [e]	dealt [e]	handeln (von)
	dig	dug	dug	graben
	do	did	done [ʌ]	tun, machen
	dream [iː]	dreamt [e]/ dreamed	dreamt [e]/ dreamed	träumen
	drink	drank	drunk	trinken
	drive [aɪ]	drove	driven [ɪ]	(Auto) fahren
	dwell	dwelt/ dwelled	dwelt/ dwelled	(ver)weilen, wohnen
E	eat	ate [eɪ], BE auch: [e]	eaten	essen
F	fall	fell	fallen	(hin)fallen
	feed	fed	fed	füttern
	feel	felt	felt	(sich) fühlen
	fight	fought [ɔː]	fought [ɔː]	(be)kämpfen
	find	found	found	finden
	flee	fled	fled	fliehen, flüchten
	fling	flung	flung	schleudern
	fly	flew	flown	fliegen
	forbid	forbade [æ]	forbidden	verbieten
	forecast	forecast	forecast	vorhersagen
	forget	forgot	forgotten	vergessen
	forgive	forgave	forgiven	vergeben, verzeihen
	freeze	froze	frozen	(ge)frieren, erstarren
G	get	got	BE: got/ AE: gotten	bekommen, (hin)kommen, holen, werden
	give	gave	given	geben, schenken
	go	went	gone [ɒ]	gehen, fahren
	grind [aɪ]	ground	ground	zerkleinern, mahlen
	grow	grew	grown	wachsen

Infinitiv	simple past	Partizip Perfekt	
H hang	hung	hung	(etwas) aufhängen
	hanged	hanged	(jdn.) hängen
have	had	had	haben
hear [ɪə]	heard [ɜː]	heard [ɜː]	hören
hide	hid	hidden	(sich) verstecken
hit	hit	hit	schlagen, treffen
hold	held	held	(fest)halten
hurt	hurt	hurt	verletzen, wehtun
K keep	kept	kept	(be)halten
kneel	knelt/ AE auch: kneeled	knelt/ AE auch: kneeled	knien
know [əʊ]	knew	known	kennen, wissen
L lay	laid	laid	legen
lead	led	led	führen, leiten
lean [iː]	leaned/ BE auch: leant [e]	leaned/ BE auch: leant [e]	(sich) lehnen
leap [iː]	leapt [e]/ leaped	leapt [e]/ leaped	springen, hüpfen
learn	learnt/ learned	learnt/ learned	lernen
leave	left	left	verlassen
lend	lent	lent	(ver)leihen
let	let	let	(zu)lassen
lie [aɪ]	lay [eɪ]	lain [eɪ]	liegen
light	lit/ lighted	lit/ lighted	anzünden
lose [uː]	lost [ɒ]	lost [ɒ]	verlieren
M make	made	made	machen
mean [iː]	meant [e]	meant [e]	bedeuten, meinen
meet	met	met	(sich) treffen
mistake	mistook	mistaken	falsch verstehen

Infinitiv	simple past	Partizip Perfekt	
O overcome	overcame	overcome	überwältigen
overdo	overdid	overdone	übertreiben, zu viel tun
overhear [ɪə]	overheard [ɜː]	overheard [ɜː]	mithören, belauschen
overtake	overtook	overtaken	überholen
P pay	paid	paid	(be)zahlen
put	put	put	stellen, legen, setzen
Q quit	quit/ quitted	quit/ quitted	verlassen, aufhören
R read [iː]	read [e]	read [e]	(vor)lesen
retell	retold	retold	nacherzählen
rid	rid	rid	loswerden, befreien (von)
ride	rode	ridden	reiten, (Rad) fahren
ring	rang	rung	läuten, anrufen
rise [aɪ]	rose	risen [ɪ]	(an)steigen, aufstehen
run	ran	run	laufen, rennen
S say	said [e]	said [e]	sagen
see	saw	seen	sehen
seek	sought [ɔː]	sought [ɔː]	suchen
sell	sold	sold	verkaufen
send	sent	sent	schicken, senden
set	set	set	setzen
sew [əʊ]	sewed [əʊ]	sewn [əʊ]/ sewed	nähen
shake	shook [ʊ]	shaken	schütteln, erschüttern
shed	shed	shed	vergießen, abwerfen
shine	shone BE: [ɒ], AE: [oʊ]	shone BE: [ɒ], AE: [oʊ]	scheinen (Sonne), leuchten
	shined	shined	blank putzen; polieren
shoot	shot	shot	(er)schießen

Infinitiv	simple past	Partizip Perfekt	
show	showed	shown	zeigen
shrink	shrank/ shrunk	shrunk	schrumpfen, einlaufen
shut	shut	shut	schließen, zumachen
sing	sang	sung	singen
sink	sank	sunk	sinken, versenken
sit	sat	sat	sitzen
sleep	slept	slept	schlafen
slide	slid	slid	rutschen
sling	slung	slung	schleudern, werfen
smell	smelt/ smelled	smelt/ smelled	riechen
speak	spoke	spoken	sprechen
spell	spelt/ spelled	spelt/ spelled	buch- stabieren
spend	spent	spent	(Geld) ausgeben, (Zeit) ver- bringen
spill	spilt/ spilled	spilt/ spilled	verschütten
spin	spun	spun	spinnen, schnell drehen
spit	spat	spat	spucken
split	split	split	spalten
spoil	spoilt/ spoiled	spoilt/ spoiled	verderben, verwöhnen
spread [e]	spread [e]	spread [e]	(sich) aus- breiten
spring	sprang	sprung	springen, entspringen
stand	stood	stood	stehen
steal	stole	stolen	stehlen
stick	stuck	stuck	kleben
sting	stung	stung	stechen
stink	stank/ stunk	stunk	stinken
strike	struck	struck	schlagen, treffen
strive [aɪ] (auch: strived	strove	striven [ɪ] strived)	sich bemühen

Infinitiv	simple past	Partizip Perfekt	
swear [eə]	swore	sworn	schwören
sweep	swept	swept	kehren, fegen
swell	swelled	swelled/ swollen	anschwellen
swim	swam	swum	schwimmen
swing	swung	swung	schwingen
T take	took [ʊ]	taken	nehmen
teach	taught [ɔː]	taught [ɔː]	unterrich- ten, lehren
tear [eə]	tore	torn	(zer)reißen
tell	told	told	sagen, erzählen
think	thought [ɔː]	thought [ɔː]	meinen, denken
throw	threw	thrown	werfen
thrust	thrust	thrust	stoßen
tread	trod	trodden/ trod	treten
U understand	understood	understood	verstehen, begreifen
upset	upset	upset	erschüttern, verärgern
W wake	woke	woken	aufwachen, aufwecken
wear [eə]	wore	worn	tragen, anhaben
weave	wove	woven	weben, flechten
	weaved	weaved	sich schlängeln
weep	wept	wept	weinen
wet	wet/ wetted	wet/ wetted	befeuchten
win	won [ʌ]	won [ʌ]	gewinnen
wind	wound [aʊ]	wound [aʊ]	wickeln, aufziehen
withdraw	withdrew	withdrawn	(sich) zu- rückziehen
wring	wrung	wrung	auswringen, verdrehen
write	wrote	written	schreiben

▸ *simple past*: 7.4
▸ Partizip Perfekt: 12.2.2 · 12.3a

Die Zeitformen der Vollverben — The tenses of the full verbs

		Aktiv	Passiv	Aktiv	Passiv
present tense	simple ►6.1	clean/cleans · do/does not clean	am/are/is cleaned	Mr Lee takes Tommy to his drama group every Friday.	Tommy is taken to his drama group every Friday.
	progressive ►6.2	am/are/is cleaning	am/are/is being cleaned	Mr Lee is taking Tommy to his drama group right now.	Tommy is being taken to his drama group right now.
past tense	simple ►7.4 · F	cleaned · did not clean	was/were cleaned	My sister made a cheesecake last night.	This cheesecake was made by my sister.
	progressive ►7.7	was/were cleaning	was/were being cleaned	My sister was making a cake when I came home.	The cake was being made when I came home.
present perfect	simple ►7.1 · F	have/has cleaned	have/has been cleaned	The wind has blown a tree over.	A tree has been blown over by the wind.
	progressive ►7.2	have/has been cleaning		A strong wind has been blowing all day.	
past perfect	simple ►7.9 · F	had cleaned	had been cleaned	I felt proud that I had cooked a meal for ten people.	The meal had been cooked in a wok.
	progressive ►7.10	had been cleaning		When I finally served the meal, I had been cooking for hours.	
will-future	simple ►8.1	will clean	will be cleaned	Julie will record her first song next week.	Julie's first song will be recorded next week.
	progressive ►8.5	will be cleaning		This time next week Julie will be recording her song.	
future perfect	simple ►8.6	will have cleaned	will have been cleaned	By tomorrow, we will have organized all the food and drinks for the party.	Before Amy leaves, a huge farewell party will have been organized for her.
	progressive ►8.6.2 Z	will have been cleaning		By the weekend, we will have been organizing the party for over a week.	
going to-future	►8.2	am/are/is going to clean	am/are/is going to be cleaned	Someone is going to clean the room.	The room is going to be cleaned.

Quellenverzeichnis

S. 11/1: Shutterstock / QQ7; **S. 11/2:** Shutterstock / Mangostar; **S. 12/1 bis 7:** Shutterstock / Rawpixel.com; **S. 12/8:** Shutterstock / Syda Productions; **S. 12/9:** Shutterstock / trubavin; **S. 14/1, 3, 4, 7:** Shutterstock / Photoonlife; **S. 14/2, 6, 8, 9:** Shutterstock / Orca; **S. 14/5:** Shutterstock / Arcady; **S. 14/10:** Shutterstock / Peter Bernik; **S. 20/1:** Shutterstock / Rawpixel.com; **S. 20/2, 3:** Shutterstock / fizkes; **S. 25:** Shutterstock / Dado Photos; **S. 26:** F1online / Imagebroker RM / Juergen Hasenkopf; **S. 27:** Shutterstock / Creativa Images; **S. 28:** Shutterstock / Richard Bowden; **S. 29:** Shutterstock / TraXXXe; **S. 32/1:** Shutterstock / jn.koste; **S. 32/2:** Shutterstock / Lance Bellers; **S. 33:** Shutterstock / Phuong D. Nguyen; **S. 34:** Shutterstock / Kuprevich; **S. 35:** Shutterstock / Jan H Andersen; **S. 36:** Shutterstock / Stokkete; **S. 37:** Shutterstock / Microgen; **S. 39:** Shutterstock / Aquir; **S. 42/1:** Shutterstock / Kennerth Kullman; **S. 42/2:** Shutterstock / James R. Martin; **S. 42/3:** Shutterstock / Georgejmclittle; **S. 42/4:** Shutterstock / Ruth Peterkin; **S. 42/5:** Shutterstock / sirtravelalot; **S. 42/6:** Shutterstock / JM Travel Photography; **S. 42/7:** Shutterstock / dezignor; **S. 42/8:** Shutterstock / Dushlik; **S. 42/9:** Shutterstock / Beloborod; **S. 45:** Shutterstock / Jelena Z; **S. 47:** Shutterstock / Monkey Business Images; **S. 48:** Shutterstock / Alexander Raths; **S. 53:** Shutterstock / Albina Tiplyashina; **S. 54:** Shutterstock / Semiletava Hanna; **S. 58:** Shutterstock / FloridaStock; **S. 61:** Shutterstock / Thomas Barrat; **S. 62:** Shutterstock / Faiz Zaki; **S. 69:** Shutterstock / CKimmortal; **S. 73:** Shutterstock / Muskoka Stock Photos; **S. 76:** Shutterstock / Halfpoint; **S. 80:** Fotolia / Archivist; **S. 81:** Shutterstock / NEstudio; **S. 82:** Shutterstock / sirtravelalot; **S. 83:** Shutterstock / Elena Masiutkina; **S. 86:** Shutterstock / djile; **S. 88:** Shutterstock / Lomaju; **S. 93:** Shutterstock / F8 studio; **S. 94:** Shutterstock / Bobex-73; **S. 95:** Shutterstock / Suzanne Tucker; **S. 96:** Shutterstock / Fabien Monteil; **S. 97/1:** Shutterstock / a_v_d; **S. 97/2:** Shutterstock / Waxen; **S. 97/3:** Shutterstock / Lance Bellers; **S. 100/1:** Shutterstock / stockfour; **S. 100/2:** Shutterstock / Billion Photos; **S. 101:** Shutterstock / goodluz; **S. 102:** Shutterstock / Soloviova Liudmyla; **S. 107:** Shutterstock / Rawpixel.com; **S. 110:** Shutterstock / Matt Gibson; **S. 111:** Shutterstock / Martin M303; **S. 113:** Shutterstock / Iakov Filimonov; **S. 116:** Shutterstock / Lyubov Levitskaya; **S. 119:** Shutterstock / Marian Weyo; **S. 121:** Shutterstock / Lipik Stock Media; **S. 123:** Shutterstock / De Visu; **S. 124:** Shutterstock / Monkey Business Images; **S. 125:** Shutterstock / chuyuss; **S. 128:** Shutterstock / northallertonman; **S. 129:** Shutterstock / Monkey Business Images; **S. 131:** Shutterstock / pathdoc; **S. 134:** Shutterstock / Billion Photos; **S. 135:** Shutterstock / Heike Rau; **S. 140/1:** Shutterstock / Antonio Guillem; **S. 140/2:** Shutterstock / DGLimages; **S. 140/3:** Shutterstock / Alexey Androsov; **S. 140/4:** Shutterstock / Monkey Business Images; **S. 140/5:** Shutterstock / antoniodiaz; **S. 140/6:** Shutterstock / leungchopan; **S. 142/1:** Shutterstock / Sergey Novikov; **S. 142/2:** Interfoto / Hollywood Collection; **S. 143:** Shutterstock / Rawpixel.com; **S. 146/1:** Shutterstock / Max Topchii; **S. 146/2:** Shutterstock / Rido; **S. 149:** Shutterstock / Helen Filatova; **S. 150:** Shutterstock / Patra.K; **S. 153:** Shutterstock / 5 second Studio; **S. 154:** Shutterstock / amstockphoto; **S. 157/1:** Shutterstock / Svetography; **S. 157/2:** Shutterstock / zhu difeng; **S. 161:** Shutterstock / critterbiz; **S. 162:** Shutterstock / M-SUR; **S. 163:** Shutterstock / Africa Studio; **S. 165:** Shutterstock / Samot; **S. 167:** Shutterstock / Don Mammoser; **S. 171/1:** Shutterstock / Matveychuk Anatoliy; **S. 171/2:** Shutterstock / Harvepino; **S. 172:** Shutterstock / kosmos111; **S. 173:** Shutterstock / Photographee.eu; **S. 174:** Shutterstock / Elnur; **S. 175/1:** Shutterstock / Willyam Bradberry; **S. 175/2:** Shutterstock / nito; **S. 178:** Shutterstock / Iakov Filimonov; **S. 179:** Shutterstock / Africa Studio; **S. 180:** bpk / adoc-photos; **S. 182:** Shutterstock / T photography; **S. 183:** Shutterstock / Alison Henley; **S. 184:** Shutterstock / Sweet Art; **S. 185:** Shutterstock / Songquan Deng; **S. 188:** Shutterstock / saschanti17; **S. 191:** Shutterstock / Monkey Business Images; **S. 192:** Shutterstock / photo_oles; **S. 196:** Shutterstock / Levent Konuk; **S. 197/1:** Shutterstock / Jari Hindstroem; **S. 197/2:** Shutterstock / PEPPERSMINT; **S. 197/3:** Shutterstock / Sladic; **S. 199:** Shutterstock / foamfoto;

Illustrationen

Gregor Mecklenburg: Seite 10, 16, 26, 28, 29, 34, 43, 49, 55, 56, 63, 64, 65, 67, 74, 75, 76, 84, 85, 96, 106, 116, 119, 120, 121, 122, 124, 128, 130, 133, 139, 141, 147, 148, 155, 156, 158, 170, 174, 181, 182, 183, 189, 190, 195, 199 und 201.

Englische Grammatik

Übungsbuch
für die Mittel- und Oberstufe

Lösungen

Cornelsen

1 Sentence types and speech intentions

1 Holiday plans

1 Elena has accepted a temporary position at the Oxfam shop in Colchester.
2 Philip is taking part in a trainee programme at an aeronautics firm in Toulouse.
3 Dana is doing a crash course in Italian in Ravenna this summer.
4 Roger is going to help out at his parents' hotel in Bristol in July and August.
5 Oliver has registered for a kitesurfing course in Denmark next month.
6 Jackie has been offered the chance to tour with a youth orchestra in August.
7 Mehmet is doing volunteer work at a summer camp for refugee children.
8 Maleen is visiting her grandparents in Breslau in July.

2 A classroom

a *Suggested answers*
1 There are no windows./There aren't any windows.
2 There is a door.
3 There are a few desks and chairs.
4 There's no teacher in the room.
5 There are no pictures on the walls.
6 There are books on the floor.
b *Individual answers*

3 All wrong!

1 Neil Armstrong wasn't the first man to set foot on Mars. (He was the first man to set foot on the moon.)
2 Koalas don't eat mainly bananas and coconuts. (They eat mainly eucalyptus leaves.)
3 Michael Jackson wasn't shot by a gunman near Central Park. (Michael Jackson died of overmedication. John Lennon was shot near Central Park.)
4 The sun doesn't rise in the west. (It rises in the east.)
5 Mobile phones haven't made communication more difficult. (They have made communication easier.)
6 Bill Gates didn't make a lot of money by manufacturing windows. (He made a lot of money by developing software.)
7 The Golden Gate Bridge doesn't connect San Francisco and Los Angeles. (It connects San Francisco and Marin County.)
8 I won't still be at school in 2045.

4 Information please!

1 Can he speak Welsh too?
2 Does she go to rock concerts too?
3 Do they play football too?
4 Does Jackie have one too?
5 Did he invent the telephone too?
6 Have they sold the old one?
7 Did you see a play too?
8 Has he read the novels too?
9 Do they go on holiday in summer too?
10 Are you going to see a musical too?

5 The London Eye

a 1 How tall is the London Eye?
2 How many passengers fit in one capsule?/How many passengers can one capsule hold?
3 When was it opened to the public?
4 How much did it cost to build?
5 How many visitors are there per year/annually?
6 When is the London Eye open?
b *Individual answers*

6 Schoolyard gossip

1 Who is Mateusz angry at?
2 What are Leyla and Fatma laughing about?
3 Who is Harry waiting for?
4 What is Hanna upset about?
5 Who are Roxanne and Delia talking about?
6 What is Karim thanking Roberta for?
7 Who is Louise staring at?
8 Who is Mr Baxter looking for?

7 A dramatic rehearsal

1 Who caught Danny (when she fainted)?
2 What did Jamal bring her?
3 Who offered to phone for a doctor?
4 What did Yannis feel?
5 Who texted Danny's brother Ron?
6 Who did Ron pick up?
7 Who did the drama teacher phone?

8 An interview with an exchange student

1 What – 2 Which – 3 What is the water temperature like – 4 What kind of – 5 What – 6 Which – 7 what

9 Q&A with Silvia

a 1 No, it hasn't. – 2 Yes, I did. – 3 No, I didn't. – 4 Yes, I have. – 5 No, I won't. – 6 Yes, I can.
b 1 I hope not. – 2 I'm afraid so. – 3 I don't think so. – 4 I hope so. – 5 I'm afraid not. – 6 I guess/suppose so.

10 Walk, don't run

a 1 Don't/Do not park here.
2 Don't/Do not use the lift in case of fire/if there's a fire.
3 Don't/Do not smoke here.
4 Park your car here.
5 Don't/Do not turn left.
6 Don't/Do not take photos here.

7 Watch out for animals.

8 Watch out for falling rocks.

b *Suggested answers*

1 Would you open the door for me, please?

2 Would you mind not smoking here?

3 Could I ask you to change this fifty euro note, please?

4 Would you mind taking a photo of me and my friend?

5 Could you please show me how to use this ticket machine?

6 Could I ask you to help me put my suitcase in the luggage rack?

7 Would you please stop talking? I'm trying to concentrate.

8 Would you mind waiting here until I come back?

11 Secret thoughts

a 1 What smart clothes he's wearing!

2 How handsome he is!

3 What a great sense of humour he has!

4 What a beautiful smile she has!

5 What a pretty face she has!

6 How intelligent she is!

7 What a lucky guy I am!

b *Individual answers*

+ 12 Stressing your opinion

1 Global warming does lead to increased flooding and extreme weather conditions.

2 Every kilometre we drive in our cars does contribute to air pollution.

3 Active volcanoes do emit a huge amount of CO_2 into the atmosphere, but not nearly as much as China's industry.

4 It was Daniel who created our brilliant slogan.

5 It was the junior class that gave us the most support.

6 Publicity is what we need more than anything else.

7 What I liked best was the music.

8 What got on my nerves were the running gags.

9 What made the evening bearable for me was the fantastic lead singer.

10 Hardly ever do you hear of people who dislike travelling.

11 Never before have such large numbers of people been on the move.

12 Only recently have we begun to realize that mass mobility comes at a high price.

+ 13 A lesson in climate politics

Suggested answer

The earth's stratosphere contains a layer of ozone, a form of oxygen. **It is this ozone layer that** absorbs some of the sun's ultraviolet light before it can reach the surface of the earth. Ultraviolet light can cause skin cancer. Beginning in the early **1970**s, scientists observed that the ozone layer was becoming thinner, especially over the Southern Hemisphere. Man-made chemicals called CFCs, used in spray cans and refrigerators, were held responsible. **But it was only in the mid-1980s that experts began to warn** that there could be up to **100,000** additional deaths from skin cancer every year if nothing was done to protect the ozone layer. **It was in 1987 that** the major industrial countries agreed to ban the production and use of CFCs. Since then, the ozone layer has recovered. **What this example shows is** that action taken in time can be effective. Of course, the situation was much simpler than that of global warming. The only cause of the problem was the use of CFCs. **What made it much easier to reach an agreement was** the fact that only a handful of firms produced these chemicals. Furthermore, substitute chemicals that did not harm the atmosphere were already available. Moreover, ordinary people felt personally affected by the threat of skin cancer. By way of contrast, it is difficult to understand the connection between shopping trips in your SUV and flooding in Bangladesh. The link between cause and effect is simply too vague. And – let's be honest – **reducing greenhouse gases does mean** changing every aspect of our lifestyle, not just throwing away the spray cans. But that is no excuse for doing nothing. **Only by drastically reducing our use of fossil fuels can we slow down global warming.**

Quick Check Chapter 1

A 1 Denise and Özlem play tennis every Friday afternoon.

2 There will be a meeting of the student council next Monday

3 John has not been doing very well on his tests recently.

4 We have already discussed this problem many times.

B 1 I won't be at home this Christmas.

2 Marco didn't do his homework yesterday.

3 Leonie and Jenna didn't want to join the Photo Club.

4 Eating junk food isn't/is not good for you.

C 1 Who designed the poster?

2 Why did the girls leave the concert early?

3 When will the band meet for a rehearsal?

4 What does Kieran do at the local gym?

5 How did the class go to Salisbury?

6 How many friends has Tina invited to her party?

7 Who did Henrike meet at Kate's party?

8 Who did Sarah give the letter to?

D 1 Which – 2 What – 3 what – 4 How is your brother feeling – 5 What – 6 is

E 1 did – 2 do – 3 It was – 4 what – 5 had ... been

2 The simple sentence and its elements

1 Who does what? – a game

a 1 Flight attendants serve the passengers food and drink.
2 Pharmacists sell their customers medicine.
3 English teachers teach their students English.
4 Tour guides show tourists interesting sights.
5 Hotel receptionists give hotel guests the room keys.
6 Lawyers offer their clients legal advice.

b 1 Flight attendants serve food and drink to the passengers.
2 Pharmacists sell medicine to their customers.
3 English teachers teach English to their students.
4 Tour guides show interesting sights to tourists.
5 Hotel receptionists give the room keys to hotel guests.
6 Lawyers offer legal advice to their clients.

c 1 They serve them to the passengers.
2 They sell it to their customers.
3 They teach it to their students.
4 They show them to tourists.
5 They give them to hotel guests.
6 They offer it to their clients.

2 Please help me!

a 1 But then I said something wrong to her, and since then she refuses to even look at me.
2 The biggest mistake of my life was when I introduced my best friend to her. / The biggest mistake of my life was when I introduced her to my best friend.
3 Nadia had mentioned to me her wish to go back to her homeland a couple of times.
4 Nevertheless, I was shocked when she announced her decision to the class.
5 You should report the incident to the police.
6 A good teacher should be able to point out to you the weak points in your writing. / A good teacher should be able to point out the weak points in your writing to you.
7 Could you describe your family situation to me in more detail?

b *Individual answers*

3 A trip to Tunisia

1 over – 2 off – 3 back – 4 in – 5 around – 6 down – 7 over – 8 out – 9 up – 10 back

4 In the library

1 This novel is so exciting, I just can't put it down.
2 I'm not a horror fan. A while ago I picked up a copy of a Stephen King novel, but after the first few pages I put it back on the shelf.

3 Excuse me, is this photocopier out of order? – No, just press the button to turn it on.
4 I keep forgetting my user number. – Maybe you should write it down.
5 If you enjoy reading, you should join the Reading Club. – The Reading Club? Sounds cool. I'll have to check it out.

5 I thought you were my best friend!

1 for – 2 at – 3 to – 4 through – 5 of – 6 in – 7 at – 8 about

6 Sorry, what did you say?

a 1 What/Who do you worry about?
2 What/Who are you thinking of?
3 What/Who did you hear about?
4 Who did you speak to?
5 Who/What did he tell you about?
6 What did you ask him for?
7 What did he promise to help you with?

b *Individual answers*

7 Tomorrow Utopia

a 1 There will be peace in all countries of the world by 2050.
2 You will not find human drivers on public roads anymore.
3 Researchers will have discovered a cure for AIDS in a few years.
4 In the near future all housework will be done by robots.
5 People will often live to 100 years or even older.
6 Everywhere in the world people will have access to clean water.

b *Individual answers*

8 Christine's debut

1 sounded exciting – 2 get nervous – 3 stay calm – 4 felt sick – 5 seemed strange – 6 looked very friendly – 7 was a great success

+ 9 America's first black president

a 1 In 2008, Barack Obama was elected President of the United States.
2 At the time, black activists considered Obama's victory the beginning of a new chapter in race relations.
3 Today, many people find the expectations placed on Obama unrealistic.
4 Nevertheless, Obama is considered an outstanding figure in US political history.
5 For one thing, he made affordable health care a reality for all Americans.
6 The Affordable Care Act of 2010 was nicknamed 'ObamaCare' by the media in honour of its creator.

b *Individual answers*

+ 10 A difficult time in life

Adolescence is a difficult time in the lives of children and their parents. Quarrels **erupt** over seemingly trivial issues. Parents refuse to see why they should **tolerate** their son's or daughter's eccentric, unpredictable behaviour. Formerly docile teens suddenly start **contradicting** their elders at every turn. Attempts at **discussing** differences of opinion typically end in shouting matches. All too often, parents just **despair** and wait for the storm to **subside**. They might be more understanding if they were to **recall** their own adolescence. Many of the conflicts their children are **experiencing** are similar to the problems they had as teenagers.

Adolescence is primarily a behavioural trial period: teens are **exploring** new behaviours as they search for their own identity. If parents kept this in mind, they might regard their children's sudden changes of mood more calmly.

Quick Check Chapter 2

A 1 plays computer games in his free time – 2 explain to me – 3 when he showed it to me – 4 made her a leader – 5 put them back on the shelves – 6 What are you guys laughing at? – 7 why don't you try it on – 8 looked angry – 9 students will get most – 10 is considered one of the greatest

B 1 Mr Flanagan showed his class a film about life on the Aran Islands. / Mr Flanagan showed a film about life on the Aran Islands to his class.
   2 Hakan met Karim at a café in the city centre yesterday afternoon. / Yesterday afternoon Hakan met Karim at a café in the city centre.
   3 I mentioned to her that I was leaving for the States at the weekend.
   4 Ms Gomez made her children dinner before she left the house. / Ms Gomez made dinner for her children before she left the house.
   5 'That's a lovely necklace you're wearing.' – 'Thanks. My aunt bought it for me.'
   6 I never buy fresh fish at the supermarket.
   7 The parcel service delivered the books to the shop on Friday.
   8 Filiz was elected chairperson at the first meeting of the year.

C 1 Then you can turn it off.
   2 Why don't you take them off?
   3 Well, you could tidy it up.
   4 Why don't you send them back?
   5 Then you can just leave it out.
   6 No, please put it back on my desk.

D 1 Who have you bought it for? / Who did you buy it for?
   2 Who did you give it to?

3 Who have you heard it from? / Who did you hear it from?
4 What are you waiting for? / What do you have to wait for?
5 What did she thank you for?
6 What did you get so angry about?

3 Full verbs

1 Spelling matters

a

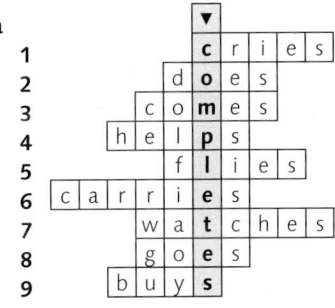

b 1 controlling – 2 dying – 3 hoping – 4 offering – 5 planning – 6 playing – 7 sitting – 8 smoking – 9 stopping – 10 swimming – 11 working

2 Pinocchio often lies

1 is trying – 2 grows – 3 begins – 4 is planning – 5 cries out – 6 gives – 7 teaches – 8 runs – 9 gets – 10 starts – 11 has – 12 knows

3 Pronunciation matters

-d: lived – played – seemed – tried
-t: helped – laughed – picked – shopped – washed – wished
-id: hated – needed – painted – waited – wanted

4 He came, he saw, he overcame his fear

a

1 become – 2 began – 3 chosen – 4 ate – 5 gone – 6 grew – 7 hidden – 8 hit – 9 made – 10 saw – 11 shot – 12 spoke – 13 won – 14 written

b 1 made – 2 began – 3 grew up – 4 went –
5 hit – 6 shot – 7 hid – 8 saw – 9 spoke –
10 wrote – 11 was – 12 became

5 She's known him since kindergarten

a

		Tense	Time
Bev	Sorry Anja, I can't talk now, I**'m** just **going** out.	present	present
Anja	To Elmer's? I heard he **is having** a party tonight.	present	future
Bev	Oh, I didn't realize you **knew** him.	past	present
Anja	Yeah, I**'ve known** Elmer for years.	pres perfect	present
Bev	When **did** you last **see** him?	past	past
Anja	I **haven't seen** him for ages.	pres perfect	present
Bev	Well, if you **met** him in the street, …	past	future
	… you **wouldn't recognize** him.	past	future
Anja	Really? Anyway, **are** you busy tomorrow?	present	future
Bev	Yes, I**'m working** all day, I'm afraid.	present	future
Anja	If you **had** five minutes now …	past	present
Bev	Listen, I**'ll ring** you back in a minute, OK?	future	future

b 1 Ich bin gerade dabei zu gehen.
2 Ich kenne Elmer schon seit Jahren.
3 Wann hast du ihn zuletzt gesehen?
4 Wenn du ihn auf der Straße treffen würdest, würdest du ihn nicht wiedererkennen.
5 Hast du morgen schon etwas vor?
6 Wenn du jetzt fünf Minuten Zeit hättest, …

6 Who usually cooks? Who's cooking now?

a 1 often cooks – 2 doesn't eat – 3 is he preparing – 4 happens – 5 make – 6 tastes – 7 makes – 8 is boiling over – 9 Does he often make – 10 does – 11 needs – 12 usually clears up
b *Individual answers*

7 What do you know?

1 doesn't matter – 2 do you mean – 3 own –
4 don't understand – 5 are bringing out –
6 believe – 7 costs – 8 are selling – 9 smells –
10 'm not buying – 11 seems – 12 love –
13 **prefer** – 14 enjoy – 15 's working –
16 sounds – 17 's studying – 18 talks about –
19 think – 20 tells

8 I could smell smoke

a 1 heard – 2 saw – 3 saw – 4 noticed –
5 seemed – 6 felt – 7 thought – 8 seemed –
9 smelled – 10 seemed – 11 saw – 12 felt
b *Individual answers*

+ 9 It's the thought that counts

1 're thinking – 2 do … think – 3 thinks –
4 depends – 5 is depending – 6 depends –
7 measures – 8 measure – 9 is measuring –
10 expect – 11 'm expecting – 12 expect – 13 've been meaning 14 means – 15 means – 16 does … hold – 17 don't hold – 18 is holding

+ 10 What's been happening?

1 is living – 2 lived – 3 had been doing – 4 had been living – 5 sought – 6 had crossed – 7 hid – 8 didn't manage – 9 fell – 10 destroyed – 11 changed – 12 didn't go – 13 didn't have – 14 did she feel – 15 will have been living – 16 will have learned – 17 have decided – 18 am – 19 am – 20 need

Quick Check Chapter 3

A 1 offering *[no doubling of consonants]*
2 carried *[-y changed to –ie]*
3 showed *[simple past, not past participle]*
4 done *[form of 'to do', not 'to be']*
5 smoking *[-e ending in the infinitive]*
6 stopped *[doubling of consonants]*
7 stood *[form of 'to stand', not 'to stay']*
8 felt *[form of 'to feel', not 'to fall']*
D 1 preferred – 2 left – 3 opening – 4 happened – 5 Tying – 6 lied – 7 coming – 8 read
C 1 does it belong – 2 don't believe – 3 wants – 4 is imagining – 5 do you mean – 6 is thinking – 7 are enjoying – 8 don't suppose
D 1 I live in Berlin. I've lived here / I've been living here for ten years. Before that I lived in Frankfurt.
2 Tim and I are playing / are going to play tennis tomorrow. We always play tennis on Wednesdays. We've been playing together since 2016.
3 We're just eating dinner. We usually eat at eight o'clock. My mother doesn't eat meat – she is a vegetarian.

4 The verbs *be, have* and *do*

1 Are you tired?
a 1 F, A – 2 F, A – 3 A, A – 4 A, A, F – 5 A, A, F – 6 A, A, F

b 1 having – 2 does – 3 is – 4 being – 5 have – 6 don't have / do not have – 7 have – 8 don't do – 9 to do – 10 (to) have

c *Individual answers*

2 Is Venice sinking?
1 are connected – 2 is used – 3 is known – 4 is estimated – 5 is kissing – 6 is rising – 7 is happening – 8 will be covered

3 There's a lot to see
1 there is / there's – 2 there are – 3 there are – 4 there will be – 5 There is / There's – 6 There are – 7 there were – 8 there was – 9 there were – 10 there was – 11 there were – 12 Is there

b *Individual answers*

4 He doesn't have any brothers or sisters
a 1 had – 2 didn't have – 3 don't have – 4 won't have – 5 having – 6 doesn't have – 7 has – 8 have – 9 has – 10 had

b 1 Did China have a single-home policy in the 1970s? – No, it didn't. It had a single-child policy. 2 Did Cheng's grandparents have more than one child? – No, they didn't. They only had one child. 3 Will Cheng have any brothers or sisters in the future? – No, he won't. He will always be an only child. 4 Does Cheng have private guitar lessons? – No, he doesn't. He has piano lessons. 5 Does his life only have good sides? – No, it doesn't. It has negative sides, too. 6 Do kids like Cheng have a lot of free time? – No, they don't. Their days are very busy.

c *Individual answers*

5 Having a good time?
a 1 Do they normally have a cooked lunch? – No, they don't. They have just a sandwich. 2 Did John have a good bike ride yesterday? – No, he didn't. He had a long walk. 3 Will Clare have a glass of cola later? / Is Clare going to have a glass of cola later? – No, she won't / isn't. She'll have a glass of juice. / She's going to have a glass of juice. 4 Are they having an argument at the moment? – No, they aren't. They're having a friendly conversation. 5 Do they usually have a coffee in the evening? – No, they don't. They have a cup of tea.

b 1 are having a short holiday – 2 to have a break – 3 are having a really bad time – 4 had an upset stomach – 5 have a game of tennis – 6 had a fight – 7 had an accident – 8 were having a ride – 9 is having an operation – 10 will have a nervous breakdown

c *Individual answers*

6 I haven't seen you for ages
1 Have you had – 2 have been – 3 has been – 4 Have you ordered – 5 have – 6 haven't stopped – 7 has happened – 8 hadn't heard – 9 had split up – 10 will have been

7 Do it yourself
a **do:** a test – the dishes – the housework – the ironing – the shopping – very well – your hair- your homework
make: a cake – a cup of tea – a mess – a mistake – lunch – the beds

b 1 do the ironing – 2 makes a mess – 3 does the shopping – 4 made a cake – 5 made lunch – 6 do the dishes – 7 make a cup of tea – 8 doing housework

c *Individual answers*

8 Don't believe everything you read
a 1 don't always tell – 2 Don't share – 3 Do think – 4 Don't rush – 5 Does … offer – 6 don't need – 7 does … match – 8 Don't send – 9 don't forget – 10 doesn't seem

b 1 didn't think – 2 didn't do – 3 didn't look – 4 don't do – 5 don't feel – 6 doesn't matter

c *Individual answers*

+ 9 Being a lifeguard
a 1 What does it mean to be a Duty Officer?
2 How long have you been doing this job?
3 How did you train for it?
4 Does your mind wander?
5 Do you often have to stop kids messing about?
6 How do you do that?
7 Have you got used to doing shifts yet?
8 What do you like least about your work?
9 What qualities does a lifeguard need to be good at the job?
10 What do you do in your leisure time?
11 And what do you think you will be doing in ten years' time?
12 Have people become more health conscious in recent years?
13 Why is swimming such a good way to keep fit?
14 I hate the chlorine in swimming pools, don't you?

b *Suggested answers*
Do as a full verb: Could you tell us what you <u>do</u>? / that all the staff are <u>doing</u> what they're supposed to

be <u>doing</u>/have <u>done</u> all sorts of things in between/
You have to <u>do</u> a life-saving award/I've been <u>doing</u>
staff training at regular intervals.

Be as a full verb: I<u>'m</u> a lifeguard and a Duty
Officer./Yeah, when it<u>'s</u> quiet./which <u>is</u> the
National Pool Lifeguard Award./There<u>'s</u> lots of time
for thinking/It<u>'s</u> nice water.

Have as a full verb: We <u>have</u> with us this morning/
I don't <u>have</u> a problem with being strict./I don't
seem to <u>have</u> a lot of leisure time/Buxton pool
doesn't <u>have</u> as much chlorine/made me feel like
<u>having</u> a swim!

Do as an auxiliary verb: <u>Doesn't</u> sound very
interesting, <u>does</u> it?/I <u>don't</u> have a problem with
being strict./they <u>don't</u> tend to argue/I <u>don't</u> think
I look like a pushover/Yes, I <u>do</u>

Be as an auxiliary verb: making sure everything<u>'s</u>
running smoothly/I've <u>been</u> travelling/you<u>'re</u>
basically just standing on the side/More and more
older people <u>are</u> coming to us/You<u>'re</u> watched all
the time

Have as an auxiliary verb: <u>have</u> done all sorts of
things in between/if you<u>'ve</u> told them straight/Yes,
I <u>have</u> really./I'll <u>have</u> completed all my staff
training/Talking to you <u>has</u> almost made me feel
like having a swim

+ 10 So you want to be a spy?

a 1 being – 2 were started – 3 have changed – 4 do
you need – 5 was – 6 there are – 7 do – 8 don't
put

b 1 No, she didn't. A colleague of hers said she'd be
good at surveillance.
2 No, she wasn't. She was joking when she said that.
3 No, they weren't. They were originally recruited
from the army.
4 Yes, it has. A lot has changed since then.
5 No, it didn't. It lasted three hours.
6 No, she wasn't. She was selected because she
stayed calm.
7 No, you don't. You don't have to be like 007 to
become a spy.
8 No, they aren't. Intelligence agents are forbidden
to share secrets with anyone.
9 Yes, it does. It matters because you might
become a target for blackmail.
10 No, you shouldn't. Don't put anything on social
media.

Quick Check Chapter 4

A 1 is, will be – 2 Being, be, is – 3 Don't be, isn't/'s
not – 4 weren't, were – 5 won't be – 6 wasn't,
would be – 7 aren't, am – 8 'm not, being

B 1 have, don't have – 2 were having, had – 3 used
to have – 4 had had – 5 Have you had – 6 hasn't
had

C 1 done – 2 made – 3 making – 4 make –
5 doing – 6 do

D 1 There are three – 2 weren't very nice – 3 Did
the girls do – 4 Your brother has – 5 Don't be so
silly – 6 He made a few – 7 What is Paul doing? –
6 Do you do much sport?

5 Modal verbs

1 Can you or can't you?

a 1 can, can't – 2 can't, can – 3 can't, can – 4 can,
can't – 5 can't, can – 6 can't, can – 7 can,
can't – 8 can, can't

b *Individual answers*

2 Making your dreams come true

a 1 are able to – 2 wasn't able to – 3 was able
to – 4 'll be able to – 5 'll be able to – 6 weren't
able to – 7 be able to – 8 are able to – 9 aren't
able to – 10 won't be able to

b 1 *[no change]* – 2 couldn't – 3 *[no change]* –
4 couldn't – 5 *[no change]*

3 You mustn't leave your bike here

1 You're allowed to fill up your water bottles.
2 You mustn't eat here.
3 You mustn't use your mobiles.
4 You mustn't go into this room.
5 You're allowed to take a book to read.
6 You mustn't ride your bikes.

4 Rules, rules, rules

a 1 We were allowed to help ourselves to drinks from
the fridge.
2 We weren't allowed to leave glass bottles lying
around.
3 We weren't allowed to make fires anywhere in
the grounds.
4 We were allowed to use their barbecue area.
5 We were allowed to take sports equipment from
the cupboard.
6 We weren't allowed to climb on the table-tennis
tables.

b They will be allowed to/won't be allowed to +
individual answers

5 A new school

1 needn't – 2 needn't – 3 needn't – 4 needn't –
5 must – 6 mustn't – 7 mustn't – 8 mustn't

6 London for beginners
a 1 have to – 2 must/have to – 3 must – 4 don't have to – 5 must – 6 must – 7 have to – 8 have to

b *Individual answers*

7 Do it yourself
1 'll have to – 2 'll have to – 3 have to – 4 don't have to/won't have to – 5 had to – 6 have to – 7 doesn't have to – 8 didn't have to – 9 don't have to – 10 'll have to

8 Don't worry
a 1 Her parents should/ought to arrange extra lessons.
2 She should/ought to join a group of students when they go outside in the break.
3 She shouldn't/oughtn't to wait to be asked.
4 She ought to/should talk to the teacher and tell her about it.
5 She should/ought to ask a classmate to lend her the notes.
6 She shouldn't/oughtn't to be afraid of making mistakes.

b *Individual answers*

c 1 You're supposed to stand in the queue for lunch.
2 You're not supposed to talk during registration.
3 You're supposed to join at least on after-school club or activity.
4 You're supposed to do homework at home, not at school.
5 You're not supposed to eat or drink during lessons.
6 You're not supposed to come to school in flip-flops.

9 Could you help me?
1 Will you wake me at 7.30, please?
2 Can I use the microwave, please?
3 Could you possibly collect me from the station at 10 pm, please?
4 Can I open the window?
5 Couldn't I stay out a bit later?
6 Could you please prepare a packed lunch for me for tomorrow?

10 Where is everyone?
1 would – 2 must – 3 may – 4 might – 5 might – 6 must – 7 will – 8 could

11 A weekend in Berlin
1 may – 2 have to – 3 don't have to – 4 have to – 5 can – 6 couldn't – 7 had to – 8 didn't have to – 9 ought to – 10 might – 11 must – 12 can – 13 mustn't – 14 needn't

+ 12 To eat or not to eat?
1 We'd better wait/should wait/ought to wait for the others.
2 They should hurry up/ought to hurry up a bit.
3 They're supposed to be the best in town.
4 They really should have/ought to have a delivery service.
5 Remember, we're (supposed) to be at the cinema by eight.
6 Then we'd better leave/should leave/ought to leave in five minutes
7 Those who are hungry should just grab an apple or a banana.
8 Okay, the others ought to be/should be along any moment now.

+ 13 Work experience
a 1 *are to* is stricter – 2 *are never to* is stricter – 3 *must* is stricter – 4 *are supposed to* is stricter – 5 *have to* is stricter – 6 *ought to* is stricter

b *Suggested answers*
1 Right. On day one you <u>must</u> arrive in good time and present yourself to your supervisor. In fact, you <u>should</u> leave home at least ten minutes earlier than usual in case anything happens on the way.
2 You <u>shouldn't</u> dress too casually, especially on your first day. And from then on, you <u>must never</u> leave the grounds of the firm during working hours without informing your supervisor first.
3 You are getting a great opportunity for work experience and <u>ought to</u> make good use of it. But if you are ever worried about anything, you <u>have to</u> phone me at school straight away, remember that.
4 For instance, if you find yourself photocopying and making coffee all day, you <u>don't have to</u> do those jobs; you <u>ought to</u> be learning about careers and the workplace there.
5 You <u>are to</u> hand in your written report one week after your return to school, so you<u>'d better not</u> leave it too late to start.
6 At the end of your time, you <u>should</u> have learned a lot about the workplace – and you <u>may</u> want to present your experience to the rest of the class.

+ 14 It could have been worse
1 should have looked – 2 could have been killed – 3 must have noticed – 4 could have used – 5 might have slowed down – 6 should have been avoided – 7 Couldn't they have thought – 8 would have saved

+ 15 Shall we go now?

1 Would you help yourselves to tea and biscuits from the buffet?
2 Shall we all introduce ourselves, to begin with?
3 Could you all mark your home country with a flag on this map?
4 May I present a short film about our school?
5 Would you wait here while I fetch the head teacher to speak to you?
6 Will you join us when we go to the town hall to meet the Mayor?

+ 16 Would you say that again?

1 needn't wait / don't have to wait – 2 was to return / had to return – 3 couldn't swim / wasn't able to swim – 4 needn't come / don't have to come – 5 should have asked / ought to have asked – 6 is to do / has to do / must do – 7 is supposed to be – 8 wasn't allowed to use – 9 has to share / must share – 10 must get vaccinated / should get vaccinated / ought to get vaccinated – 11 should have arrived / ought to have arrived – 12 are not to cross / mustn't cross – 13 won't be able to see – 14 must be – 15 Can't you make

Quick Check Chapter 5

A 1 Sorry, I won't be able to help you tomorrow.
2 She had to go to the dentist yesterday.
3 Students weren't allowed to take knives to school when I was on exchange in the US.
4 Mum had to collect me from soccer practice last Tuesday.
5 They didn't have to do any homework last week.
6 They can go / are allowed to go home early today.
B 1 Yesterday I was able to talk to my tutor.
2 You needn't / don't have to go swimming with us, but you are very welcome to join us.
3 Can you speak Italian?
4 You needn't do it if you don't want to.
5 The sign says you aren't allowed to drink the water from the tap.
6 Aren't you supposed to put bottles and cans into your suitcase?
7 Tim doesn't have to work this weekend.
8 Our new flat is much nicer than the old one. We should have moved years ago.
C 1 mustn't / aren't allowed to – 2 are to / must – 3 had to, were able to – 4 needn't – 5 Shall – 6 had better / should / ought to – 7 won't be allowed 8 might / may
D 1 ought to – 2 won't be allowed to – 3 mustn't – 4 Did you have to – 5 had better not – 6 Would – 7 oughtn't to have – 8 was able to

6 Present tenses

1 'He, she, it …'

-s: enjoys – feels – hears – knows – leaves – likes – needs – owns – says – sleeps – speaks – takes – thinks – wakes up – wears – works
-es: goes – misses – teaches – watches
-ies: flies – hurries – studies – tries – worries

2 The day starts early

1 leave – 2 wakes up – 3 goes – 4 has – 5 tries – 6 hears – 7 needs – 8 wear – 9 knows – 10 worries – 11 comes – 12 feels – 13 sleep – 14 enjoys – 15 watches

3 About Joe

1 Does the new job interest him? – Well, it offers a lot of opportunities but it doesn't pay very well.
2 Does Joe miss his home town? – Of course, he misses his girlfriend but he skypes with her most evenings.
3 Do Joe and his girlfriend meet every weekend? – No, they don't see each other more than twice a month.
4 Does Joe have many hobbies? – He doesn't have much free time but he tries to go jogging after work.
5 Does his girlfriend do a lot of sport? – Yes, she does more sport than Joe because she doesn't work such long hours.
6 Do they want to move to Edinburgh? – No, they like the city but they don't want to live there.

4 What do they usually do?

a 1 He never plays tennis in the winter.
2 He doesn't often cycle to school.
3 He is sometimes late for class.
4 He and his mates often discuss sport.
5 He doesn't always eat healthy food.
6 He always goes to the gym at the weekend.
b 1 Mike and Basia always play tennis together on Fridays.
2 Basia sometimes cycles to school but Mike never cycles – he's too lazy.
3 Mike is always late, but Basia is never late for school.
4 They often discuss sport.
5 Mike sometimes eats healthy food, but Basia doesn't.
6 Mike never goes to the gym. Basia usually goes to the gym at the weekend.
c *Individual answers*

5 Great minds think alike

a 1 i – 2 e – 3 f – 4 g – 5 a – 6 c – 7 h – 8 b – 9 d
b *Suggested answers*
 1 Man bekommt, was man bezahlt. / Qualität hat ihren Preis.
 2 Alles, was du brauchst, ist Liebe.
 3 Aller guten Dinge sind drei.
 4 Stille Wasser gründen tief.
 5 Übung macht den Meister.
 6 Geld wächst nicht auf Bäumen.
 7 Was man sät, das wird man ernten. / Wie man in den Wald hineinruft, so schallt es heraus.
 8 Jeder macht mal Fehler.
 9 Paare, die zusammen Spaß haben, bleiben auch zusammen. / Gemeinsame Hobbies verbinden.

6 I'm working this summer

 1 Jules is picking strawberries at Hall Farm for four weeks.
 2 Petra is helping out in the corner shop until September.
 3 Toni is selling ice creams in the park for a month.
 4 Helena is working as a lifeguard at the swimming pool for a while.
 5 Bertie and his brother are stacking shelves at the supermarket for six weeks.
 6 Tasha is looking after dogs at the local kennels until she goes on holiday.

7 I'm still waiting

 1 Are … coming – 2 'm sitting – 3 are … doing – 4 'm trainspotting – 5 'm … joking – 6 'm waiting – 7 are running – 8 'm joining – 9 isn't stopping – 10 's happening – 11 's looking for – 12 aren't having

8 Usually … but not today

 1 She usually relaxes in her bedroom but today she's lying on the sofa.
 2 She usually has lessons at school but today she's studying alone.
 3 She usually plays in a band but today she's listening to iTunes.
 4 She usually meets friends in town but today she's chatting online.
 5 She usually helps in the garden but today she's watching her dad.

9 A survey

 1 'm not doing – 2 do you shop – 3 buy – 4 get – 5 do you go – 6 're buying – 7 stays – 8 Do you find – 9 hope – 10 don't think

10 What a mess!

 1 knows – 2 loves – 3 doesn't want – 4 needs – 5 suggests – 6 doesn't need – 7 feels – 8 promises – 9 doesn't agree – 10 owns

+ 11 Choose and explain

a 1 'm sitting – 2 always get – 3 're staying – 4 're having – 5 's beginning – 6 's improving – 7 knows – 8 loves – 9 isn't worrying – 10 always get up – 11 jump – 12 does – 13 'm planning – 14 often run – 15 's swimming – 16 generally explore – 17 want – 18 are you doing – 19 hope – 20 's waiting
b 1 C – 2 A – 3 D – 4 C/D – 5 E – 6 E – 7 B – 8 B – 9 C – 10 A – 11 A – 12 A – 13 E – 14 A – 15 C – 16 A – 17 B – 18 D – 19 B – 20 C

+ 12 The world is getting hotter

 1 Are … taking – 2 are increasing – 3 is melting – 4 (is) freezing – 5 is affecting – 6 are multiplying – 7 are spreading – 8 are dying – 9 is becoming – 10 is causing – 11 are suffering from – 12 are not getting – 13 are getting – 14 are occurring – 15 are not doing

+ 13 Reader's review

a A thickens, becomes, live, increases
 B finds, envies, visits, frightens
 D lives, gets
 E continues, has, stops
 G witnesses, sees
 H fantasizes, enjoys
 I doesn't remember, retains, don't believe, warn
b 1 C – 2 E – 3 D – 4 B – 5 A – 6 H – 7 G – 8 I – 9 F
c *Individual answers*

Quick Check Chapter 6

A 1 We usually help each other when we work as a team. / Usually, we help each other when we work as a team.
 2 She's always excellent at time management.
 3 Do you sometimes regret taking on too many projects? / Do you regret taking on too many projects sometimes?
 4 They don't always spend enough time checking their answers.
 5 The dog normally sleeps at my feet under my desk. / Normally the dog sleeps at my feet under my desk.
 6 Paula never goes to the dentist if she can avoid it.
 7 My car hardly ever starts first time on cold mornings.
 8 We're rarely the last to arrive at parties.
 9 He doesn't usually get so anxious about meeting new people. / Usually, he doesn't get so anxious about meeting new people.
 10 They frequently argue about who's going to do the washing up.

B 1 is babysitting – **2** come – **3** Do you think –
4 forget – **5** don't make – **6** 's snowing – **7** 's
becoming – **8** don't often print – **9** is going
up – **10** does it cost

C 1 stars – **2** always cries – **3** doesn't play – **4** I
think – **5** don't usually eat – **6** is working – **7** 're
running – **8** Does he know – **9** I don't believe –
10 doesn't make

D 1 Jules doesn't have a new car.
  2 I don't see the point in going outside in this
    weather.
  3 She doesn't remember her accident. She doesn't
    know what happened
  4 Please don't leave your trainers out in the
    corridor.
  5 We're not planning / We aren't planning to visit
    you today.
  6 Jennie's new jeans don't go well with her top.

7 Past and perfect tenses

1 A checklist

a regular: locked – packed – texted – wrapped
  irregular: done – driven – fed – forgotten –
  given – hidden – taken – told – written

b I've locked the cupboard.
  I haven't hidden my diary yet.
  We've fed the cat.
  We haven't wrapped Grandma's present.
  We've texted Dad.
  Mum has bought the train tickets. / She's bought the
  train tickets.
  Mum hasn't given the key to our neighbour. / She
  hasn't given the key to our neighbour.
  Mum has told Grandma when we're arriving. / She's
  told Grandma when we're arriving.

2 Have you ever tried frogs' legs?

a yesterday, last week, three days ago

b 1 Have you ever been to England?
  2 Have you ever been to hospital?
  3 Have you ever broken your mobile phone?
  4 Have you ever flown first class?
  5 Have you ever lost your keys?
  6 Have you ever won a prize?
  7 Have you ever ridden a horse in your life?
  8 Have you ever spent the night in a five-star hotel?
  9 Have you ever seen a bad accident?
  10 Have you ever cooked dinner for ten people?

c *Individual answers*

3 Nothing much has changed in my life

a 1 Every morning since 1990 I've woken up in this
    cage.

  2 I've eaten about 15,000 lettuces in the last
    40 years.
  3 I've always wanted to go on holiday to Africa.
  4 My human helpers have always been kind to me.
  5 I've never had to go to the vet.
  6 But I haven't had any adventures either.
  7 I've often asked myself if I will live to 100.

b *Suggested answers*
  How many lettuces has Gilbert eaten in the last 40
  years?
  Has Gilbert ever had to go to the vet?
  Has he had any great adventures?

4 Consequences

  1 c – **2** f – **3** g – **4** e – **5** b – **6** h – **7** d – **8** i – **9** a

5 What have they been doing?

  1 She's been sleeping.
  2 They've been shopping.
  3 It's been swimming.
  4 They've been playing football.
  5 He's been skiing.
  6 She's been climbing.

6 I've been playing for 11 years

a for a week – since last month – for ages – since I
  left you – for centuries – for many days – since
  we last talked – since Christmas – for a long time

b 1 They've been playing for four hours.
  2 I've been writing my blog since January.
  3 She's been taking riding lessons for six months.
  4 My brother has been saving for his bike since
    Christmas.
  5 They've been working on the pitch for seven
    months.
  6 I've been having dancing classes since last year.
  7 They've been learning Spanish for three years.
  8 We've been running since eight o'clock.

7 Keep trying

  1 has been helping / 's been helping – has helped /
    's helped
  2 have been seeing / 've been seeing – have just
    seen / 've just seen
  3 have been learning / 've been learning – have
    learned / 've learned
  4 have been writing / 've been writing – have
    written / 've written
  5 have been trying – hasn't tried
  6 have been saving – haven't saved

8 A history quiz

  1 When did the Berlin Wall fall? – c
  2 The New York terrorist attacks were carried out
    on September 11 th .... – c

3 How many years did the First World War last? – a

4 Who wrote *Romeo and Juliet*? – b

5 The famous song *Yesterday* was first sung by … – c

6 Which political leader did not win the Nobel Peace Prize? – b

7 On which country was the first atomic bomb dropped? – a

8 The first *Star Wars* movie was made in the year … – b

9 About Jo

a simple past: in 2014 – When? – at the weekend – yesterday – last night – on Tuesday – at 8:30 – ago
present perfect: just – never – ever – not … yet – so far – since – always

b 1 got married – 2 moved house – 3 have lived – 4 haven't had – 5 retrained – 6 has always worked – 7 came, died – 8 haven't seen

c *Individual answers*

10 Everyone has an alibi

a 1 were enjoying – 2 was staying – 3 was lying – 4 weren't working – 5 was visiting – 6 was making
The first Kramer twin stole the Crown jewels.

b *Individual answers*

11 The moon was shining

1 were singing – were sounding out – stepped – caught – froze

2 was smashing – were being thrown – heard – felt

3 was moving – was shaking – was going on – broke – whispered

4 were coming – were being pushed back – were not even fighting/weren't even fighting – were stopped – stood – covered

12 Extraordinary talents

a 1 had … written – 2 had been chosen for – 3 had … designed – 4 had used – 5 had been signed – 6 had … won – 7 had spoken

b *Individual answers*

13 Not my lucky day

1 met, had seen – 2 had saved up, wasn't – 3 couldn't, had been thrown out – 4 had … found out, took -5 didn't seem to be, had sold out – 6 told, had got

14 The boy who cried wolf

a 1 had been putting up – 2 had been repairing – 3 had been selling – 4 had been feeding – 5 had been digging up – 6 had been playing

b 1 realized – 2 had been lying – 3 went – 4 had been hiding – 5 knew – 6 had been waiting – 7 jumped out – 8 attacked – 9 enjoyed

15 Things used to be different

a 1 They used to smoke there.

2 A lot of/Many students used to go to single-sex schools.

3 There used to be many/lots of corner shops around.

4 You used to have to wear swimming caps in pools.

5 You didn't use to be allowed to vote at 18.

6 Women used to have to ask their husbands when they took a job.

7 They didn't use to have smartphones and the internet.

8 Most male teachers used to wear ties to school.

b *Individual answers*

16 Sports and me

1 used to play – 2 broke – 3 had to stop – 4 have been going riding – 5 went – 6 used to take – 7 have never done – 8 Have you ever asked – 9 were playing – 10 saw – 11 promised – 12 used to play – 13 has that been stopped – 14 have been asking – 15 said – 16 has never done – 17 talked – 18 have practised/have been practising

+ 17 A job interview

1 How long have you been living/have you lived in Bavaria?

2 We moved here eight years ago.

3 I have lived/have been living in Munich for five years.

4 I have been playing/have played tennis since my 10th birthday.

5 I passed my Abitur last year.

6 You're writing for the newspaper. When did you start doing that?

7 I haven't decided yet which subject I want to study.

8 Have you ever lived abroad for more than three months?

+ 18 The story of a rescue

1 was walking – 2 had got in – 3 drove – 4 was approaching – 5 stopped – 6 was heading – 7 saw – 8 were flashing – 9 were coming – 10 had already reached – 11 ran – 12 looked – 13 was speeding – 14 took – 15 said – 16 didn't know – 17 was happening – 18 started – 19 whistled/was whistling – 20 passed – 21 had only just made – 22 had just happened – 23 was waiting – 24 waved/was waving – 25 had recorded

+ 19 Tricky tenses

a 1 Yes – 2 Gina – 3 Yes – 4 Yes – 5 Yes – 6 No – 7 No – 8 Yes – 9 No

b 1 When I came in, everyone was sitting there and talking, but when the Queen entered, everybody stood up.

2 My friend has just gone to New York, but I've never been there.

3 How long has your car been in the garage? You took it there last week, right?

4 Kelly has had a headache all morning. Yesterday she didn't feel well either.

5 How many albums did John Lennon record, and how many has Adele recorded so far?

6 Jo finally had her hair cut last week. She has never had it cut so short before.

+ 20 Rachel's year abroad

a 1 flew – 2 was confronted – 3 made – 4 did – 5 didn't have – 6 was – 7 had taken – 8 had met – 9 had had – 10 had stood up – 11 was living – 12 was trying – 13 had changed – 14 had lived – 15 had been lost – 16 had got – 17 wondered / was wondering – 18 had always been – 19 had had – 20 was / had been – 21 have missed – 22 have become – 23 have decided – 24 have learned / learned

b *Individual answers*

Quick Check Chapter 7

A 1 since – 2 ago – 3 for – 4 since – 5 yet – 6 for – 7 yet – 8 ago

B 1 We've been living / We've lived in this part of town for eight years.

2 Sam looks a bit green in the face – that's the third ice cream she's eaten today.

3 I didn't see him yesterday.

4 I've had this watch since my fourteenth birthday.

5 I've only just arrived. When did the party start?

6 We haven't read a play by Shakespeare yet.

7 How long have you known your dance partner?

8 He took the flight the day the holidays started.

C 1 used to go – 2 was turning – 3 had taken – 4 hasn't collected – 5 has been preparing – 6 didn't want – 7 had been expecting – 8 have gained

D 1 have learned – 2 was putting – 3 I've been preparing – 4 didn't use to – 5 didn't you tell – 6 have followed / 've followed – 7 had already started – 8 didn't give – 9 ten years ago – 10 didn't hear

8 Expressing future time

1 Wait, I'll help you!

1 b – 2 f – 3 a – 4 g – 5 d – 6 h – 7 e – 8 c

2 An exchange trip

a 1 I don't suppose (that) I'll talk much at the beginning.

2 I don't expect I'll get enough to eat.

3 I hope I'll have a room of my own.

4 I think there'll be a school bus.

5 I'll probably meet other German students.

6 I'm sure I'll be able to do a lot of sports there.

7 I guess the teachers will be stricter there.

8 I definitely won't have much free time.

9 I don't expect I'll skype with my parents every day.

10 I wonder if I'll get homesick.

b *Individual answers*

3 Plans for the future

a 1 Anna and Ayse are going to go on a work and travel tour.

2 Leon is going to become an au pair somewhere.

3 Jonas is going to do nothing for a couple of months.

4 Finn, Yuri and Emma are going to cycle across the Alps.

5 Nasrin is going to apply for a job at the local supermarket.

6 Karim is going to do a hotel management training course.

7 Hanna and Darius are going to spend the summer in Auckland.

8 Lily is going to apply for a placement at a film production company.

b *Individual answers*

4 What's going to happen?

a 1 The woman is going to miss the bus.

2 The girl in lane four is going to win.

3 The seagull is going to steal his fish and chips.

4 The students are going to do a test.

5 The player is going to score a goal.

6 The girl is going to lose her phone.

7 The girl is going to light a rocket.

8 The drone is going to land in the river.

b *Individual answers*

5 A shopping trip

1 's going to rain – 2 'm going to buy – 3 will be – 4 'm going to be – 5 Are we going to check out – 6 will be – 7 are going to buy – 8 'll pay – 9 'll have – 10 won't be

6 Are you coming with us?
1 Pietro   I'm making pizza for you at the weekend.
2 Pietro   I'm skyping with my parents after dinner.
3 Mrs Brown   I'm having coffee with Jo on Tuesday afternoon.
4 The dog   Is anyone taking me for my walk today?
5 Kelly   My friend Suzie is helping me revise Maths tonight.
6 Mr Brown   Steve is coming over for dinner next Friday.
7 Kelly   Charlie and I are meeting on Thursday after school.

7 Summertime
1 'll be sightseeing – 2 will you be doing – 3 'll be sitting – 4 will be rock climbing – 5 'll be working – 6 will be cycling

8 We leave at 8.51
1 meet – 2 leaves – 3 arrives – 4 don't have – 5 starts – 6 finishes – 7 doesn't leave – 8 will have – 9 will pay – 10 return/will return – 11 miss/will miss – 12 will we get

9 Next year ...
1 We're going to the mountains
2 Are you coming
3 I'll switch on
4 will you be living
5 I'm not going to light
6 I won't get through
7 What are you going to change
8 I bet I won't keep
9 we don't fill
10 we'll be

+ 10 Maths problems
a 1 He'll have saved enough in ten months' time.
2 No, he won't have arrived. He'll arrive an hour later.
3 Our oil reserves will have run out by about 2060.
4 The tortoise will have left the lawn (twenty seconds earlier).
b Individual answers

+ 11 The optimist
a 1 My grandad would like to retire this year.
2 Our family is certain to move/to be moving to a bigger house before summer.
3 My sister hopes to marry in September.
4 Our cat is about to have kittens.
5 I expect to pass my school leaving exam at the end of term.
6 The girl I fancy is sure to fall madly in love with me.
7 But my football team is unlikely to stay in the league at the end of the season.
b Individual answers

+ 12 Challenges ahead – but progress too
1 will be facing – 2 won't just be sitting – 3 will become – 4 will have advanced – 5 won't just do/won't just be doing – 6 will also read/will also be reading – 7 will make – 8 will stabilize – 9 won't spill – 10 will be able to transplant – 11 won't want – 12 grow up – 13 will be able to provide – 14 will all be living – 15 will have been perfected – 16 will drop/will have dropped – 17 will have been developed – 18 will be able to – 19 are likely to – 20 are you going to do/will you be doing/will you do

Quick Check Chapter 8
A 1 are you coming – 2 won't be able – 3 'll drive – 4 're meeting – 5 'll help – 6 're going – 7 'm not going – 8 won't open again
B 1 about to – 2 'm going to take – 3 will be waiting – 4 will you have left – 5 has – 6 's not going to – 7 don't – 8 're spending
C 1 I'll help you – 2 it's going to snow – 3 we'll be out – 4 is going to become a vet – 5 you're going to crash – 6 are spending – 7 We will call you – 8 We are spending
D 1 because I won't have done my homework yet. – 2 I'm going to scream! – 3 it's at 7 pm. – 4 'll help you – 5 are you going to book/order? – 6 she'll be looking after her grandchildren.

9 The passive

1 How your time is spent
a 1 A – 2 P – 3 P – 4 A -5 P – 6 P -7 P – 8 A
b Individual answers

2 How often is it done?
a 1 How often are the beds made? – They are made every day.
2 How often are the bins emptied? – They are emptied every day.
3 How often are the baths and toilets cleaned? – They are cleaned every day.
4 How often is the television checked? – It's checked every day.
5 How often are the towels changed? – They are changed every day.
6 How often is the mini-bar refilled? – It's refilled every day.
b 1 Are the windows cleaned every day? – No, they aren't cleaned every day.
2 Are the mirrors polished every day? – No, they aren't polished every day.
3 Is the grass in the garden cut every day? – No, it isn't cut every day.

4 Is the fire alarm tested every day? – No, it isn't tested every day.

5 Is the restaurant menu updated every day? – No, it isn't updated every day.

6 Is the dining room redecorated every day? – No, it isn't redecorated every day.

c *Individual answers*

3 A quick quiz

1 When was the World Cup played in Germany? It was played in Germany in 2006.

2 Where was the world's first underground railway built? It was built in London.

3 Where were the first modern Olympics held? They were held in Athens.

4 Who was the Eurovision Song Contest won by in 2012? It was won by Lena.

5 What was the first animated Disney movie called? It was called Snow White and the Seven Dwarfs.

6 When was Germany officially reunited? It was officially reunited in 1990.

7 Who was the first antibiotic discovered by? It was discovered by Alexander Fleming.

8 Who was Google invented by? It was invented by Sergey Brin and Larry Page.

4 Town hit by earthquake

a 1 Someone has rescued a missing walker from a Swiss mountain.
MISSING WALKER RESCUED

2 Kids have found ten little dogs in a rubbish bin in Corby.
TEN LITTLE DOGS FOUND IN CORBY RUBBISH BIN

3 A gold medallist has opened a new swimming pool.
SWIMMING POOL OPENED BY GOLD MEDAL-LIST

4 The police have arrested the bank robbers.
BANK ROBBERS ARRESTED

5 A German film has won an Oscar.
OSCAR WON BY GERMAN FILM

6 A hurricane has destroyed thousands of homes.
THOUSANDS OF HOMES DESTROYED BY HURRICANE

b 1 Two girls have been injured by a crocodile.

2 A new German chancellor has been elected.

3 Holiday cottages have been burnt down in Cornwall.

4 A/The chief of police has been arrested for shoplifting.

5 A new shopping centre has been opened in Manchester.

6 A top model has been voted the worst dressed celebrity.

5 The window had been broken

a 1 had been shot – 2 hadn't been killed – 3 had already been taken – 4 had been broken – 5 had been searched – 6 had been emptied – 7 had been stolen – 8 had not been found – 9 had been used – 10 had been left

b 1 Had the burglar been seen by anyone before he entered the house?

2 Had he been attacked by the dog before he shot it?

3 Had the burglar been informed by someone that there was jewellery in the house?

4 Had anyone been seen watching the house in the days before the break-in?

5 Had this house been broken into before?

6 Had the same fingerprints been found in other break-ins in this area?

6 What will be done when?

1 will be reserved – 2 will be expected – 3 will be worn – 3 will the final reservation be made – 5 will be done – 6 will be offered – 7 will be ordered – 8 will be booked – 9 won't be finished – 10 will be completed – 11 won't be announced – 12 will the teachers be invited

7 It must be done

1 All the equipment in the gym can be used, but only at your own risk.

2 ID cards must be shown at reception.

3 No food or drink (except water) may be brought in.

4 Towels and water bottles should be picked up and litter (should be) put in the litter bin.

5 Each piece of equipment must be cleaned for the next user.

6 Only clothing suitable for working out should be brought.

7 No boots, street shoes or sandals must be worn.

8 No photographs may be taken in the gym or the changing rooms.

8 Where were your jeans made?

a 1 is known – 2 are made – 3 was called – 4 has been used – 5 was sold – 6 was opened – 7 have been destroyed – 8 are produced – 9 has been reduced – 10 has been introduced

b 1 Gold wasn't sold in Levi's first New York store. Things like cotton material were sold.

2 His San Francisco store wasn't opened in 1851. It was opened in 1853.

3 Cheap jeans aren't destroyed in India and China. They are produced/made there.

4 A lot of oil isn't used in the making of jeans. A lot of water is used.

5 The lives of the factory workers won't be saved by the 'Worker Well-being' program. They will be improved.

c *Individual answers*

9 Who stole the Mona Lisa?

1 The *Mona Lisa* was stolen by an Italian called Vincenzo Perugia from the Louvre in Paris. / The *Mona Lisa* was stolen from the Louvre in Paris by an Italian called Vincenzo Perugia.

2 Edvard Munch's famous painting *The Scream* was taken from a Norwegian museum in 2004.

3 Munch's stolen painting was found by detectives in 2006, but it had been treated badly (by the thieves).

4 Vincent van Gogh's *Poppy Flowers* was stolen from a museum in Cairo in 1978.

5 Ten years later, Van Gogh's stolen painting was discovered in Kuwait (by police), but in 2010, the museum was broken into again.

6 Two men were arrested, but the painting hasn't been seen since.

7 Picasso's *Le pigeon aux petits pois* was stolen in Paris but it was thrown into a rubbish bin when the art thief got scared.

8 The bin was emptied by Parisian rubbish collectors. The rubbish was taken away and the painting was probably destroyed.

10 Vandals or victims?

1 Schools had been broken into.

2 The repairs will have to be paid for.

3 The police say that the vandals should be talked to.

4 We know that bullied kids are always being laughed at.

5 In troubled homes, kids were always being shouted at.

6 Social workers suggested that these kids haven't been brought up properly.

7 From a very young age some of the children had been looked after by unqualified babysitters.

8 Special family situations should be considered in these cases.

11 The stuff that dreams are made of

1 Since the days of Sigmund Freud, many books have been written about that topic.

2 Dreams are often illogical, but they are accepted as normal.

3 And no matter if a dream is clear or confusing, most of our dreams are forgotten.

4 Three teenagers were asked this question.

5 I often dream that I am laughed at because of my clothes.

6 I often dream that I'm running a marathon and my shoes have been taken just before the start.

7 I was followed everywhere by a monster with a long tail.

8 In the end, we talked about it and when our problem had been solved, the dreams stopped.

12 Were you given a form to fill in?

a 1 Then I was given a card with my name on it.

2 I was shown around the school.

3 After that, I was taken to the teachers' room.

4 I was offered a cup of coffee.

5 I haven't been introduced to any of the children yet.

6 I wasn't asked if I had any brothers or sisters.

7 I was invited to watch a lesson.

8 I'm going to be told more tomorrow.

b 1 Were you given a card with your name on it? – No, I wasn't given a card. I was given an ID badge.

2 Were you shown around the school? – No, I wasn't shown around the school. I was shown around one classroom.

3 Were you taken to the teachers' room? – No, I wasn't taken to the teachers' room. I was taken to the canteen.

4 Were you offered a cup of coffee? – No, I wasn't offered a cup of coffee. I was offered a light lunch.

5 Have you been introduced to any of the children yet? – No, I haven't been introduced to any of the children yet. I've been introduced to all the dinner ladies.

6 Were you asked if you had any brothers or sisters? – No, I wasn't asked if I had any brothers or sisters. I was asked a lot of questions about my parents.

7 Were you invited to watch a lesson? – No, I wasn't invited to watch a lesson. I was invited to teach a lesson.

8 Are you going to be told more tomorrow? – No, I'm not going to be told more tomorrow. I'm going to be told more next week.

+ 13 Super talented?

a 1 Having been told how much the tickets cost, she changed her mind.

2 Having been sent an advert for free tickets to the talent show, she applied for some.

3 Two tickets having been awarded (by the TV sponsor), she invited a friend.

4 Her friend having been invited, she waited for his answer.

5 His answer having been received, she arranged where to meet him.

6 Arrangements having been made to meet outside the TV studio, they stood in a long queue.

b *1* e – *2* f – *3* a – *4* c – *5* g – *6* h – *7* d – *8* b

+ 14 Bees need to be protected

a 1 must not be ignored – 2 is worth remembering – 3 have to be pollinated – 4 must be protected – 5 must have been affected – 6 dislike being moved – 7 is to be feared – 8 to be given – 9 being attacked – 10 to be passed

b *Individual answers*

+ 15 It is thought that

a 1 has been proven to be – 2 is believed to be – 3 is known to have been – 4 are thought to have been – 5 is believed to have been – 6 could have been – 7 are said to be – 8 seems to have been

b were used – are called – were brought – have been found – have been discovered

+ 16 They're known to be rich

1 Billionaires' Quay is known to be home to the world's super yachts.
2 The Cote d'Azur is said to be the playground of the rich and famous.
3 It is thought that yacht owners here are among the wealthiest people in the world.
4 This year Antibes is expected to be much quieter than usual.
5 Taxes on fuel are known to have risen from 15% to 55%.
6 It is thought that this rise will cost the boat owners up to 20,000 euros a week.
7 It is expected that such an increase will upset many super yacht owners.
8 Some billionaires are reported to have complained to the French president.

Quick Check Chapter 9

A 1 was used – 2 is understood – 3 has been repaired – 4 will be sold out – 5 had already been made – 6 Have … been written
B 1 could be found – 2 should be shut – 3 must be returned – 4 may be taken – 5 should have been finished – 6 cannot be tolerated
C 1 These days a lot of food shopping is done on Sundays.
2 We were told to help ourselves to tea or coffee.
3 My coat has been taken by accident. This is not mine!
4 *Lord of the Rings* was written by J.R.R. Tolkien.
5 In 2016 the Tour de France was started in Yorkshire.
6 Tom was asked for all his contact details by the bank manager.
D 1 It is believed – 2 caused by ice – 3 must not be worn – 4 written by – will be talked about for many years – 6 thought to have been built
E 1 were shown – 2 has been advised – 3 was recommended – 4 were told – 5 was advised – 6 is expected

10 The infinitive

1 A gap year in Canada

a 1 She plans to/is planning to go to Canada for a year.
2 She hopes to/is hoping to find a family that will take her on as an au pair.
3 If that doesn't work out, she'll try to find a part-time job.
4 Her English teacher has offered to help her with the application.
5 She needs to earn enough money to get by on her own.
6 She expects to become really good at English during her year in Canada.
7 If she manages to find a job in Quebec, she can practise her French too.
8 She has decided to do translation work when she comes back to Europe.

b *Individual answers*

2 After the test

a 1 Jared says the speaker was difficult to understand.
2 Tom thinks he is sure to get a good mark.
3 Lisa is unhappy because the last two tasks were impossible to do.
4 Larry is afraid to see his test score.
5 Carl believes that it is pointless to worry about your score.
6 The teacher tells the class that it is important to learn from your mistakes.

b *Individual answers*

3 Before the class trip

1 He reminded them to bring their ID cards with them.
2 He advised them to exchange their money at a local bank.
3 He allowed them to explore London in groups of three or more in their free time.
4 He warned them not to go anywhere on their own.
5 He encouraged them to use their English.
6 He asked them to thank their parents for their support.

4 Susan's Halloween party

1 Ron and Peter were the last guests to arrive.
2 Jackie was the last guest to leave.
3 Mehmet was the first guest to leave.
4 Felicia was the only guest to come by bus.
5 Ron and Peter were the only guests to come by car.
6 Jackie was the only guest to wear a ghost costume.
7 Mehmet was the only guest to wear a vampire costume.

5 That's the way to do it

a with infinitive: ability – attempt – courage – decision – need – plan – reason – right – strength – time – will – willingness – wish
with *of* + gerund: advantage – danger – dislike – dream – idea – hope – risk – thought – possibility
with either: chance – opportunity – way

b 1 We want to give you the opportunity to show / of showing us your talent.
2 Is there any possibility of booking an earlier flight?
3 Everyone has the right to form their own opinions.
4 The class made a final attempt to persuade the teacher to put off the test.
5 As a vet, Carmen is now living her dream of working with animals.
6 We'll continue the search as long as there is still hope of finding survivors.
7 I was surprised at Ted's willingness to support our campaign.

6 A problem for you to solve

1 It's too late for us to start over again.
2 That box is too heavy for you to carry.
3 Here's a list of mistakes for you to correct.
4 She gave me a worksheet for you to do in class.
5 Shakespeare's English was difficult for the students to understand.
6 That's no reason for you to get (so) angry.

7 Miriam's questions

Suggested answers
1 Miriam isn't sure who to talk to if she has a problem.
2 She wants to find out what to do if she loses her room key.
3 She doesn't know where to get an adapter for her laptop.
4 She wants to find out how to meet other new students.
5 She isn't sure which travel pass for public transport to buy.
6 She doesn't know how to find a cheap second-hand bike.

8 Giving (and taking) advice

a *Suggested answers*
1 Why not phone him?
2 I'd rather/sooner put it in writing.
3 Why not write him a letter?
4 I'd rather/sooner text him.
5 You'd better not have that conversation on the phone.
6 I'd rather/sooner not see him ever again.

b *Suggested answers*
1 I'd rather/sooner sleep a little longer.
2 Why not try wearing contact lenses?
3 I'd rather/sooner spend a quiet evening at home.
4 You'd better see a doctor about that.
5 I'd rather/sooner go for a pizza.

9 A day in the life

1 saw/noticed – 2 watched/saw – 3 heard – 4 saw/noticed – 5 noticed/saw – 6 watched – 7 watched/saw – 8 saw/noticed – 9 listened to / heard

10 Lucky Steve

1 lets – 2 make – 3 let – 4 let – 5 make – 6 lets – 7 makes

11 Help wanted!

1 to – 2 to – 3 ø – 4 to – 5 to – 6 ø – 7 ø – 8 to – 9 ø – 10 ø

12 How (not) to take a test

1 He told them not to copy from their neighbour.
2 He told them not to write more than one answer to each question.
3 He told them not to forget to write their name at the top of the page.
4 He didn't tell them to copy from their neighbour.
5 He didn't tell them to write more than one answer to each question.
6 He didn't tell them to forget to write their name at the top of the page.

+ 13 Time to clean up

1 He wanted to go scuba diving. But his dream of exploring an underwater paradise came to an abrupt end when he found himself surrounded by plastic trash.
2 That was when he felt the need to do something about this problem.
3 He made the decision to collect photos of beaches ruined by plastic pollution.
4 He saw the chance to reach / of reaching large numbers of people via the internet.
5 When he returned home, he started a website called DrasticPlastic.net to give people the possibility of posting photos showing the effects of plastic pollution.
6 Niels is also grateful to research institutes for their willingness to let him use their photos of plastic found in marine animals.
7 To date, more than 40,000 people have taken the time to post photos from all over the world.
8 Niels thinks this is a good way to call / of calling attention to a worldwide problem.

14 The fairy bell

Suggested answers

1 to settle the argument – **2** to fetch the old iron pot – **3** tells him to turn off the lights – **4** tells the farmers to come – **5** for everyone to take his turn – **6** asks the owner to turn the lights on – **7** orders the farmers to show him their hands – **8** to have white hands – **9** afraid to touch the pot

+ 15 Shakespeare's theatre

1 be performed – **2** to have been working – **3** to be connected – **4** to have already been – **5** to have been built – **6** to have ended

Quick Check Chapter 10

A **1** Don't forget to phone Grandpa this afternoon.
   2 The head teacher refuses to discuss the matter.
   3 The ranger warned us not to make a campfire.
   4 Our coach expects us to win the match on Saturday.
   5 My parents invited our Australian cousins to visit us this summer.
   6 Aleksandra's dad taught her to speak Russian.
   7 We helped Cara (to) move into a new flat last weekend.
   8 Jake's girlfriend persuaded him to sign up for a dancing course.

B **1** I am/was sorry to hear about your accident.
   2 Leroy is glad to be back home in Atlanta.
   3 You are old enough to make your own decisions.
   4 My parents think I'm too young to stay out all night.
   5 The last two tasks were too difficult for Vitali to solve.
   6 It wasn't easy for me to say goodbye to my friends.
   7 Farah's parents think it's important for her to get good marks.
   8 Will it be possible for us to make a day trip to Greenwich?

C **1** My mum asked me to look after my little brother.
   2 Our teacher reminded us to bring our ID cards on Monday.
   3 How could you forget to close the windows before leaving the house?
   4 I still haven't worked out how to change my settings on this site.
   5 Rakhida promised to help us with the posters for the concert.
   6 The band members agreed to meet an hour earlier for the sound check.
   7 The angry hotel guest demanded to speak to the manager.
   8 We decided to take the train instead of driving.
   9 Hillary Clinton was the first woman to run for president.
   10 Larissa hopes to win a prize in the competition.

D **1** I can't afford to go away this summer.
   2 If you don't mind, I'd rather wait for the bus.
   3 My parents don't want me to study medicine.
   4 The teacher made the students leave their mobiles outside the room.
   5 We're driving to the coast this weekend. Would you like to come with us?
   6 You ought to have told me earlier about your problem.
   7 I expect you to help me with the project.
   8 This song always makes me feel sad.

11 The gerund

1 Talking about hobbies

   1 Playing computer games has become extremely popular.
   2 Making a video is much easier than it used to be.
   3 Performing in a musical is great if you enjoy singing and dancing.
   4 Writing poems is an unusual hobby.
   5 *Collecting stamps is a bit old-fashioned.*
   6 Lying on the couch isn't really a hobby at all.
   7 Dancing in a group is a good way of staying fit.
   8 Doing volunteer work shows that you are someone who cares.
   9 Joining a debating club is a good way to practise speaking skills.

2 A dream career?

   1 Luis is considering accepting the offer.
   2 Luis says he would enjoy having the chance to concentrate on his sports skills.
   3 He says he wouldn't mind practising a lot every day. / He says he wouldn't mind having to practise a lot every day.
   4 But he would miss seeing his friends every day. / But he would miss being able to see his friends every day.
   5 And he would have to give up going to all-night parties.
   6 Luis can't help wondering if it really is the right decision.
   7 He admits feeling unsure about leaving home.
   8 But then he imagines playing in a major-league team some day.

3 What belongs where?

a verb + gerund: practise, finish, dislike, keep, mention
verb + infinitive: hope, decide, seem, offer, plan, expect, promise, want
verb + gerund or infinitive: start, hate, continue, prefer, begin

b *Suggested answers*

I love living abroad – my family and I are all very happy here in Germany.
My best friend doesn't like / hates doing home-work – so he's normal!
I enjoy reading novels, especially on holiday.
My friend Toby wants to be rich and famous – me too!
I prefer doing sport with my friends than alone.
My friends and I all expect to pass our exams – well, we hope to pass them!
My friend Jenny plans to babysit for her neighbour to earn some extra pocket money.

4 A bank robbery

1 walking – 2 waiting -3 to talk – 4 noticing –
5 to say – 6 to get – 7 to write down

5 Talking about feelings

1 We were very disappointed about not making it to the final.
2 Jared is proud of winning first prize for his short story.
3 Catriona's really sad about not coming to my party.
4 I wasn't interested in going to the cinema (with Marco).
5 I'm really sorry about/for hurting your feelings.
6 Sandra is very nervous about taking her driving test tomorrow.
7 Tarik is really angry about leaving his mobile in the café.
8 We were glad about not having to rewrite our essays.

6 Liz and Jeremy

1 Jeremy earns extra pocket money by doing garden work for the neighbours. / By doing garden work for the neighbours, Jeremy earns extra pocket money.
2 Before meeting her friends in the afternoon, Liz finishes her homework.
3 Jeremy sometimes leaves the house without doing / having done his homework.
4 Jeremy wants to do a gap year after finishing school.
5 Liz wants to study drama instead of doing a gap year.
6 Liz and Jeremy get on well, in spite of being very different.

7 Travel-India.com

1 What's the best way of finding a good hostel?
2 What is the main reason for not travelling alone?
3 What about the risk of eating the wrong food?
4 How great is the danger of getting robbed?

5 What are the advantages and disadvantages of travelling by train?
6 Is there any chance of seeing the 'real' India?
7 What about the possibilities of finding help in an emergency?

8 A difficult task

1 I'm busy doing the next task.
2 There's no point asking him.
3 I had a hard time understanding 5 a.
4 It's no use sitting here if I can't solve the tasks.
5 How about asking Mr King for a couple of tips?
6 It's not worth asking him.

9 Josh's dream

1 Josh often dreams of making it big in the music scene.
2 He sometimes thinks about leaving school and touring with his band.
3 His parents think he should concentrate on getting better marks at school.
4 Josh seldom worries about failing his exams.
5 He's sure he will succeed in passing all his courses.
6 He's looking forward to finishing school and spending more time on his music.

+ 10 The hotel theft

1 He warned the staff against withholding information.
2 He thanked the barman for giving him a useful tip.
3 The hotel manager criticized the chambermaid for leaving the door of one of the rooms open.
4 The chambermaid blamed the bellboy for not locking the door.
5 Carnaby suspected the chambermaid of not telling the complete truth.
6 In the end Carnaby accused the chambermaid of stealing / of having stolen the jewellery.
7 The hotel manager congratulated Carnaby on solving / on having solved the crime so quickly.

+ 11 What teens hate most

a *Suggested answers (the opening words are inter-changeable)*

1 They hate being treated unfairly.
2 They can't stand being talked down to.
3 They dislike being stared at.
4 They object to not being taken seriously.
5 They hate being pushed around by authority figures.
6 They complain about being expected to conform.
7 They dislike being given advice by older people.
8 They are fed up with being constantly told what to do by their parents.

b *Individual answers*

Quick Check Chapter 11

A 1 going – 2 writing/to write – 3 to be – 4 doing – 5 to watch – 6 to phone – 7 painting – 8 playing – 9 smoking – 10 walking

B 1 forward to seeing – 2 idea of leaving school and joining the navy – 3 trouble (in) installing – 4 possibility of seeing – 5 useful for making – 6 get used to living – 7 succeeded in persuading – 8 afraid of breaking

C 1 Please close all windows before leaving the building.
2 I can't believe Sharon would just move away without saying goodbye.
3 You can improve your English by learning five new words a day/every day.
4 I can remember meeting you for the first time.
5 Are any of you interested in visiting the museum?
6 The sun is shining — let's walk instead of going by bus/taking the bus.

D 1 Priscilla is so publicity-hungry – I think she actually enjoys being chased by paparazzi.
2 The head teacher congratulated the students on winning the prize.
3 I would like to thank you for being/for having been so patient with me.
4 Daniel dislikes being treated like a child (by his parents).
5 Paul apologized for being late.
6 Nobody likes the feeling of being laughed at.

12 Participles

1 What's what?

a 1 beschädigt – 2 deprimierend – 3 verängstigt/erschrocken – 4 frustrierend – 5 entspannend – 6 schockiert – 7 überraschend – 8 besorgt

b 1 a broken leg – 2 a fallen tree – 3 a helping hand – 4 a talking bird – 5 a buried treasure – 6 a sleeping cat – 7 a fried egg

2 A fascinating city

a 1 interested – 2 thrilled – 3 confusing – 4 surprised – 5 boring – 6 amazing – 7 moving – 8 tired

b *Individual answers*

3 Who's who?

a 1 Mirella is the girl talking to Jamal.
2 Claire is the girl using the notebook.
3 The girl sitting next to Claire is Kathy.
4 Thanh is the guy sitting on Claire's left.
5 The girl holding a coffee cup is Shana.
6 And the guy taking the photo is me, of course!

b 1 Cars steered by computers – no longer science fiction
2 The food served in our cafeteria is awful
3 Photos posted online never really go away
4 Stuff bought on the internet isn't always cheaper
5 Some films made for TV are better than Hollywood
6 Why children born into poor families stay poor

4 My dog Toby

1 When I open the door, he doesn't come running up to me, because he knows I don't like it.
2 Instead, he remains sitting on his bed until I call him.
3 Then I get his lead and we go walking in the park.
4 At first he just stood there looking at me with a confused expression on his face.
5 Then he went running after a cat.
6 In the end, I had to go looking for him.

5 Hanging out

a 1 looking – 2 chatting – 3 talking – 4 telling – 5 sitting – 6 smiling – 7 touching

b *Individual answers*

6 Down by the lake

1 saying – 2 standing – 3 confused – 4 walking off – 5 sitting – 6 talking – 7 hiding/hidden – 8 climbing – 9 rushing – 10 hugging

7 What happened when?

1 While visiting her aunt in Teheran, Sarina learned to speak a little Persian.
2 Seeing a man with a gun, Mrs Higgins phoned 999.
3 Finding a cat at her door, Rani took it inside and gave it some milk.
4 While training for the competition, Sam injured his leg.
5 While walking to school, Karel found a handbag full of money.
6 Hearing a loud crash, the kids all ran to the window.

8 Changes

1 I bet she (has) had her hair dyed.
2 The city council had it torn down a couple of years ago.
3 My parents had it painted last month, so I had to clean it out.
4 Yes, the town had a new one built last year.
5 He wasn't happy with it, so he contacted a professional speech writer and had parts of it rewritten.
6 Yeah, they did, but after the accident they had it repainted a different colour.

9 A well-written story

1 Tight-fitting – 2 freshly prepared – 3 carefully constructed – 4 time-saving – 5 well-organized – 6 much-repeated

10 At the department store

1 take – 2 put – 3 make/making – 4 carrying – 5 go – 6 close – 7 talking – 8 open – 9 hanging – 10 grinning

+ 11 Don't keep me waiting

a 1 b – 2 b – 3 a – 4 a – 5 b – 6 b – 7 a – 8 b
b Individual answers

+ 12 It's a small world

a 1 (While) Having tea in a sidewalk café, I saw my ex-girlfriend walk by.
2 Going into a bookshop to buy a map, I was surprised to find a former classmate of mine at the cash desk.
3 (While) Cycling through the Yorkshire Dales, I had to stop to repair my bike.
4 Looking into my toolkit, I discovered that a tool was missing – the one I needed.
5 (While) Sitting next to my bike and wondering what to do, I heard a car stop just behind me.
6 Having repaired my bike, he drove off, and I continued my tour.
7 Having finally reached Cowgill, I felt very hungry, so I went into the first café I found.
8 Looking up to give the waitress my order, I saw that it was my cousin Jeanne.
b Individual answers

+ 13 The Golden Gate Bridge

1 (Being) Surrounded by water on three sides, for many years the city of San Francisco was cut off from the rest of the Bay area.
2 Looking for an alternative to ferry traffic, the Board of Supervisors asked the city engineer to examine the possibility of building a bridge across the Golden Gate Strait.
3 The Department of War was against the project, fearing that any kind of bridge would hinder navigation in the Bay.
4 (Being) Determined to get their bridge, the Supervisors hired engineer Joseph Strauss to oversee the project.
5 Having already designed and built several large bridges, Strauss was confident that he could make the project succeed.
6 Strauss insisted on high safety standards, spending $130,000 on a huge safety net.
7 The bridge was painted bright orange, making it easier to see in the fog.

8 The Golden Gate Bridge, used by over 120,000 people daily, is one of America's most famous landmarks. / Used by over 120,000 people daily, the Golden Gate Bridge is one of America's most famous landmarks.

+ 14 Does the Web really connect us?

Suggested answer

Social scientists talk about bonding and bridging as the two main forms of social connection. Bonding means the connection between people belonging to the same group; bridging refers to creating ties between members of different groups.

When the internet was still young, many thought it would become the ultimate bridging tool, uniting people around the world in one global village. Now we know that the opposite is true. People use the internet very selectively, reading only opinions that support their views and forming communities with others of a similar background and political perspective. Instead of making people broader-minded, the internet tends to strengthen the views we already have, making us less tolerant toward those who disagree.

Of course, the internet has also brought benefits, for example for members of social minorities, e.g. gay, lesbian and transgender individuals, who are now able to link up with others facing similar challenges.

Another group that has benefitted from the bonding talent of the internet consists of people suffering from rare diseases. Whereas in the past it was almost impossible for these individuals to find advice and support, today there are dozens of online self-help groups, making it possible for people who will never meet in person to swap information on therapies and medication.

Quick Check Chapter 12

A 1 thrilled – 2 disappointed – 3 interesting – 4 repainted – 5 annoyed – 6 confusing – 7 amused – 8 looking

B 1 People living in glass houses shouldn't throw stones.
2 The money found in the bag had been stolen the day before.
3 Four of the people killed in the crash were tourists from Australia.
4 Passengers flying on to New York are asked to go to Gate 7.
5 The buildings damaged by the earthquake had to be torn down.
6 The girl sitting next to Philip is my sister.

C 1 English-speaking – 2 freshly painted – 3 fast-talking – 4 meat-eating – 5 well-written – 6 hard-working

D 1 The paintings stolen from the museum were never found.

2 Leon's brother went to Mali as part of a peace-keeping mission.

3 Photos edited on a computer sometimes look unnatural.

4 Nina was really excited when she heard about the concert.

5 My laptop keeps crashing. – Why don't you have it repaired?

6 All of the issues mentioned here will be dealt with in the next chapter.

7 There are a lot of fast-moving action scenes in his latest film.

8 Kensington has many houses built in the 18th century.

9 Cycling through Brandenburg, I saw a wolf.

10 Generally speaking, IT specialists have well-paid jobs.

13 Main clauses and subordinate clauses

1 Teens and phones

a 1 [MC] – 2 [SC] – 3 [SC] – 4 [MC] – 5 [MC] – 6 [SC] – 7 [MC] – 8 [MC]

b *Suggested answers*
As a recent study of communication habits discovered, many teens don't like talking on the phone. (2)
They mostly use messaging services because they prefer texting to talking. (3)
When asked about their reasons, teens say that it's faster to type a text message than to talk to someone. (6)

2 No excuses!

a 1 and – 2 but – 3 so – 4 or – 5 but – 6 so

b *Suggested answers*
1 wouldn't be back before 8 – 2 it was broken – 3 go hungry – 4 I had to clean it up – 5 I was already late – 6 I couldn't come to the rehearsal

3 Sport and you

a 1 Some people are allergic to sport because they think it's really hard work.

2 When you do sport every day, it gets much easier.

3 Sport can even help you to think clearly. I often get my best ideas while I'm jogging.

4 Sport is good for your health as long as you stay within your limits.

5 Even though you may feel tired at first, you'll feel more energy with every workout.

6 You can choose any sport you like unless you have a health problem.

7 Go to your doctor for a checkup before you begin doing a really tough sport.

b *Individual answers*

4 Emily's first trip to Germany

1 because – 2 until – 3 As soon as – 4 where – 5 While – 6 as – 7 After – 8 as soon as

5 Caught in the act

1 c – 2 f – 3 a – 4 h – 5 d – 6 e

+ 6 Lilly and Lucy

a 1 C – 2 F – 3 D – 4 A – 5 A – 6 E – 7 A – 8 C – 9 H – 10 G

b *Individual answers*

+ 7 Elizabethan London

Suggested answers

1 While Elizabeth I was queen, …

2 As there were frequent plagues, …

3 If a fire broke out, …

4 Before the Metropolitan Police was created in 1829, …

5 Although city life was dangerous, …

6 When the Elizabethan Age ended, …

Quick Check Chapter 13

A 1 because – 2 whenever – 3 since – 4 but – 5 unless – 6 or – 7 yet – 8 so

B 1 or – 2 if – 3 when – 4 so that – 5 unless – 6 so – 7 Every time – 8 While

C 1 as – 2 Every time – 3 Wherever – 4 whereas – 5 Although – 6 as long as

D 1 When the doorbell rang – 2 until I come back – 3 Every time I hear – 4 If you don't like – 5 While Samantha was waiting – 6 Julio told me that [*no comma*] – 7 looking as if – 8 stepped back so that she could

14 Conditional sentences

1 Traveling to Celle
1 If − 2 When − 3 if − 4 if − 5 When − 6 If −
7 when − 8 when

2 If A, then B
1 c: *If the temperature falls below 0° C, water freezes.*
2 d: If the battery is weak, the yellow light starts to blink.
3 g: If you right-click the icon, the context menu opens.
4 f: If you choose the 'portrait' option, the camera focusses on the face.
5 b: If the ice is less than 15 cm thick, skating isn't allowed.
6 a: If there isn't enough rain, the young plants die.
7 e: If the winter is mild, some birds don't fly south.

3 Before the exam
a 1 If his alarm doesn't ring, he won't wake up early.
2 If he doesn't wake up early, he'll miss/he will miss the early bus.
3 If he misses the early bus, he'll have to take/he will have to take the later bus.
4 If he takes the later bus, he'll feel/he will feel nervous when he arrives at school.
5 If he feels nervous, he won't get a good mark.
6 If he doesn't get a good mark, he won't pass.
b *Individual answers*

4 Good advice
a 1 c: *If you aren't part of the solution, you are part of the problem.*
2 f: If you want to hear good advice, listen to your heart.
3 d: Don't walk if you can fly.
4 b: If you don't do what you love, you'll never love what you do.
5 e: You'll never win if you're not willing to lose.
6 a: If you try, you may fail.
7 g: If you don't try, you've already failed.
b *Individual answers*

5 Studying abroad
1 If I was accepted by a US college, I would get a room in a students' hostel.
2 I would never feel lonely if I lived in a students' hostel.
3 It wouldn't be so expensive if I got a scholarship.
4 If I needed more money, I could/would look for a part-time job.
5 If you studied in the US, we wouldn't be able to visit you often.
6 There would be no one to look after you if you were ill.

7 You would/might feel lonely if you left all your friends behind.
8 If we didn't have three other children, we could think about letting you study abroad.

6 Boring holidays
a *Suggested answers*
1 If we had a car, I could go to the disco in Bradford.
2 If my girlfriend was here, I would have somebody to hang out with.
3 If one of my friends had a party, I would/might get an invitation.
4 If my PC worked, I could play computer games.
5 If I had enough money, I would/could get it repaired.
6 If there was a shop in our village, maybe I could get a part-time job.
b *Individual answers*

7 Maybe
1 If I buy a lottery ticket, maybe I will win the jackpot.
2 If I bought a lottery ticket, I probably wouldn't win anything.
3 If I enter the race, I will come in first.
4 If I entered the race, I would come in last.
5 If I get an 'A' on the exam, my parents will be happy.
6 If I got an 'A' on the exam, my mum would be shocked.

8 Things could have been different
1 If Shirin had gone to the audition, she would/could/might have got a part in the musical.
2 If Frank hadn't overslept, he wouldn't have arrived late for his job interview.
3 If Pauline hadn't forgotten her umbrella, she wouldn't have got (so) wet on the way to school.
4 If Carlo hadn't spent all his money on a new mobile, he could have gone to the concert.
5 If the Bakers' car hadn't broken down, they could have gone on holiday.
6 If Spike hadn't barked, the man wouldn't have run off/might have broken into the house.

9 Chances
1 If I studied creative writing I could/might write a bestselling novel.
2 If I became an astronaut I could/might fly to Mars.
3 If I had a brilliant idea, I would/could found a startup.
4 If I did research, I could/might win a Nobel Prize.
5 If I had gone to dancing school, I could have developed my talent.

6 If I had become a dancer, I could/would/might have travelled around the world.

7 If I had travelled around the world, I would have met interesting people.

8 If I had met interesting people, I would/might not have married your grandfather.

10 If you'd worked harder ...

1 you had – 2 you would – 3 you had – 4 you had – 5 you would – 6 You would

11 What really happened?

1 Yes, he did. – 2 No, he can't. – 3 No, she isn't. – 4 Yes, she does. – 5 No, he isn't. – 6 Yes, he did. – 7 No, she doesn't. – 8 No, she can't. – 9 Yes, he did. – 10 No, he isn't.

12 Uncle Horace

1 If I had invested in Microsoft back then, I would be a multimillionaire today.

2 If I had more money, I would start my own consulting firm./If I had had more money, I would/could/might have started my own consulting firm.

3 If I hadn't broken my leg in 1972, I would have run in the Olympics.

4 If I had gone into politics when I was younger, I could/might be President today.

5 I could/might have become a Hollywood star if I had concentrated on my acting talent while I was in college.

6 If I weren't always so busy, I would write my autobiography./If I hadn't always been so busy, I would have written my autobiography.

7 If you kids take my advice, you will become just as successful as I am./If you kids took my advice, you would/could/might become just as successful as I am.

+ 13 Flatsitting

1 as long as – 2 providing – 3 unless – 4 in case – 5 as long as – 6 unless

+ 14 What if ...?

a *Individual answers*

b *Individual answers*

Quick Check Chapter 14

A 1 if – 2 When – 3 When – 4 if – 5 If – 6 When – 7 when – 8 when

B 1 will miss – 2 don't do – 3 starts – 4 will take – 5 don't have – 6 aren't – 7 doesn't want – 8 will be

C 1 didn't have – 2 wanted – 3 hadn't been – 4 would have lent – 5 were – 6 could/would have driven – 7 wouldn't have to – 8 would have had

D 1 If Karol had worked harder, he would have got better marks.

2 If you can't do the tasks alone, ask Francine for help.

3 If Tarik didn't have to help his parents, he could come to the party.

4 If our train had arrived on time, we wouldn't have missed the beginning of the concert.

5 I'm expecting a visitor — send her into my office when she arrives.

6 If I was/were a filmmaker, I would make a film about the food industry.

7 If I hadn't failed my maths exam, I'd be at university now.

8 We'll be late for the show if we don't catch the next bus.

9 Let me know if there is anything I can do for you.

10 If Piotr hadn't broken his leg, he could have played for our team.

15 Indirect speech (Reported speech)

1 What's that, dear?

1 He says he and I/we came in his new car.

2 He says he has never been to this village before.

3 He wants to know if you have been living in this house for long.

4 He says his parents had a holiday home not far from here.

5 He says his mum and dad don't live together anymore.

6 He says that he and I/we will be getting married soon.

7 He says he hopes you can come to the wedding.

8 He says that I will definitely send you an invitation.

2 A wet weekend

1 said – 2 told – 3 said – 4 tells – 5 told – 6 said – 7 told – 8 said

3 The perfect family?

1 He said (that) they ordered pizzas on Wednesday after football training, and Friday was fish and chips night.

2 Lillian said (that) they all had breakfast at different times, and they all got home at different times too, so it was hard to eat together.

3 Mandy said (that) her mum left the house first and had a coffee at work.

4 Jed said (that) they didn't have breakfast together but his parents wanted them to have their evening meal together.

5 Yuri said (that) they were all perfectly healthy so he was not complaining.

6 Lillian said (that) they had Sunday lunch with her grandparents.

7 Mandy said (that) on weekdays, they didn't have time for breakfast in their house.

8 Jed said (that) his dad was a better cook than his mum, so he made dinner for them every night.

4 Alibi

1 Finn said (that) they had met at half past five, but Susie said they had met at six.

2 Susie said (that) they had had a quick snack in a sandwich bar on East Street, but Finn said they had eaten at the new curry place.

3 Finn said (that) Susie had always been interested in Spanish films, but Susie said that Finn had wanted to see an old Spanish film.

4 Susie said (that) they had bought tickets at the box office, but Finn said they had booked tickets online.

5 Finn said (that) they had walked to the Show-room, but Susie said they had taken a bus there.

6 Susie said (that) they had had time for a drink, but Finn said they hadn't had a drink.

7 Finn said (that) he hadn't even had time to go to the toilet, but Susie said he had gone to the toilet.

8 Susie said (that) she had hated the film, but Finn said they had both enjoyed it.

5 So little time

1 Joel also said he would love to hike to Machu Picchu if he could.

2 He admitted that he really should learn Spanish before he went.

3 Len said he would probably tour Eastern Europe by train.

4 He added that he wouldn't go to Warsaw because he had been there before.

5 Ollie told us he might stay with his aunt and uncle in Sydney.

6 He explained that he couldn't go to Australia without visiting Uluru.

7 Patsy thought she might not go far because she'd like to see more of the British Isles.

8 She decided that she would definitely visit the Shetland Islands.

6 Questions, questions

1 How long have you lived in the village?
2 Have you left school?
3 What courses have you studied?
4 Do you have a clean driving licence?
5 Can you stay calm in an emergency?
6 How far do you walk every day?

7 How many pets do you have?
8 What kind of dogs do you prefer?

7 They wanted to know

1 what the password for the internet connection was – 2 how they could get onto the balcony – 3 where you kept the key – 4 if they could use the garden – 5 why the freezer had been switched off – 6 how to use the microwave – 7 if they should write a review on the internet – 8 if they could get some of their money back

8 Party planners

1 asked the children to invite – 2 promised not to be here – 3 warned us not to start – 4 advised me not to let – 5 offered to help me – 6 told Pam to make – 7 suggested having dinner – 8 told me not to forget

9 Be kind to yourself

a don't drink too much tea or coffee – try some natural health products for stress or panic attacks – Try eating less sugar – Have a healthy diet of fresh fruit and vegetables. – taking more exercise, like a regular walk in the park or a swim – spend less time in front of the computer screen – manage your time better – say 'no' or 'I need more time' – I could show you some relaxation tech-niques like breathing or simple yoga exercises

b 1 She warned me not to drink too much tea or coffee.
2 She advised me to try natural health products.
3 She asked me if I ate properly.
4 She suggested eating/that I eat less sugar.
5 She recommended that I should have a healthy diet.
6 She suggested taking/that I take more exercise.
7 She advised me to spend less time in front of the computer screen.
8 She proposed that we (should) talk about managing my time better.
9 She advised me to say no.
10 She offered to show me some relaxation tech-niques.

c Individual answers

10 My hero

a 1 had always been – 2 would say – 3 was – 4 might be – 5 thought – 6 was – 7 didn't matter – 8 was going – 9 managed – 10 had taught – 11 would … be – 12 had played – 13 felt – 14 had been – 15 had been thinking – 16 could – 17 had felt – 18 had made

b Individual answers

11 Change of plan

1 She said she was going to the doctor's the following day.
2 Then she said she wasn't feeling very well at that moment/then. She thought she might have caught a cold.
3 So I said she really should try to rest all that week.
4 Mikey said he was too busy that day.
5 Mikey said he had tried to call me several times the previous week/the week before.
6 I said I had had some terrible news the day before.
7 Then I told him our favourite café had closed down two days earlier.
8 Mikey said that was OK because we could all meet there at his place.

+ 12 Stay safe

1 is recommended that – 2 told – 3 you to prepare- 4 advised – 5 advise you to – 6 are warned not to eat

+ 13 Wish you weren't here

1 A leading travel agent said 'A number of anti-tourist protests have taken place in some of Europe's most popular holiday destinations.'
2 Spanish activists complained that tourism was killing neighbourhoods.
3 A spokesperson said 'Today's model of tourism displaces families and harms the environment.'
4 Various tour operators said 'Spain is rather full. We have had an all-time high in tourist numbers to Spain this year.'
5 A Venetian restaurateur told us 'These huge ships have become symbols of the impact of mass tourism.'
6 He said that each ship might bring 3000 visitors, who all arrived at the same time. Their old city could not take so many people.
7 He said 'This will harm the foundations of the city, which are already very fragile.'
8 A member of the UN said that this was a very serious problem that needed to be discussed in a very serious way.

+ 14 Guerrilla gardening

Suggested answer

I asked a fashion designer from Los Angeles what guerrilla gardening was exactly. He said that guerrilla gardening was when the people who lived in cities made their city greener in secret. He explained that they did this by planting flowers at night, growing a garden and seed bombing. He argued that seed bombing wasn't aggressive at all. He told me that when he found an empty piece of land, he threw down handfuls of seed in 'earth bombs'. He said

that most cities were short of green places. He advised me to look around me and I would see lots of places that could be transformed. He disagreed with the term activist, and said that all sorts of people were interested in improving life in the city. He informed me that in LA, you couldn't get fresh fruit without driving to a store. He explained that he had dug up the grass outside his house and (had) planted sunflowers and banana trees. He told me that his plan for the future was to plant edible gardens everywhere.

The woman I spoke to agreed that guerrilla gardening was technically illegal. She said you had to make sure first that the land was vacant. She also advised to make the space better. She went on to say that the most important rule was not to let anyone catch you doing it. She then showed me a gadget she had designed for digging holes. She thanked me when I said I thought it was clever and said she was proud of that one. Her second gadget could shoot out flower seeds into wasteland. In her opinion, children would be able to enjoy the flowers and butterflies. She warned me that sometimes they came up against authorities and that they had to fight them. She told me about a woman who had fought back and had won, so the garden had remained.

Quick Check Chapter 15

A 1 Bella said she really didn't like hot milk.
2 Neil asked Paula if she wanted to come with him.
3 Jude told me to answer the phone for him.
4 Karim thought it might snow there.
5 Lilly asked Bill to help her/if he could help her with her homework.
6 Laura wanted to know what time the last bus was.
7 Ina told Josh she would call him the next day.
8 Ryan agreed (that) that lemon cake was delicious.
9 Owen wondered if he would need a coat.
10 Faye told us (that) she had seen that film when it first had come out.

B 1 didn't want – 2 had always done – 3 meant – 4 hadn't enjoyed – 5 were – 6 had had – 7 would prefer – 8 going – 9 would cost – 10 had asked

C 1 Bella   'I prefer vegetarian food.'
2 Neil   'I'm going to the beach.'
3 Jude   'Was the call for me?'
4 Karim   'Can I borrow a warm sweater?'
5 Bill   'I'll meet you at the station tomorrow.'
6 Laura   'Has it been raining?'
7 Ina   'I know how much the tickets cost.'
8 Ryan   'Help yourself to a drink, Jane.'
9 Owen   '(Be careful!) Don't touch the hot plates.'
10 Faye   'Are you going by yourself?'

D **1** told us not to forget – **2** told us to take – **3** when the show ends – **4** Belinda told me – **5** tell me the time – **6** what I was studying – **7** wants me to help her – **8** if I usually went

16 Relative clauses

1 The bag snatcher

Suggested answers

1 These are the men who/that were playing chess.
2 This is the girl who/that was checking her mails.
3 This is the woman who/that was sitting on a bench.
4 This is the handbag that/which was stolen.
5 This is the young man who/that passed on his bike.
6 This is the plane that/which flew over the park.
7 This is the man who/that stole the handbag.
8 This is the cap that/which the bag snatcher lost.

2 Which one?

1 The book I lent (to) you last week.
2 It's a nonprofit organization Matt Damon founded in 2009.
3 The one I ate before I came here.
4 It's the bike I bought second hand a couple of years ago.
5 The film we watched last weekend.
6 The one I painted for the competition.

3 That boy I told you about

1 Lucas is the guy/boy (who/that) Ken is waiting for.
2 Spots is the dog (that) Harry is running after.
3 Roger is the guy/boy (who/that) Camilla is shouting at.
4 Lucy is the girl (who/that) José is flirting with.
5 Laszlo is the guy/boy (who/that) Tarek is laughing at.

4 Parents and their jobs

1 She's the one whose mother is a ballet dancer.
2 She's the girl whose father is a diplomat.
3 Brian's the guy whose mother writes fantasy novels.
4 He's the one whose father is a bodyguard
5 She's the girl whose parents are opera singers
6 She's the one whose father works as a stuntman.

5 Cleaning up

1 Who's – **2** who's – **3** Whose – **4** whose – **5** who's – **6** whose

6 The birth of a vampire

a *1* d: Bram Stoker, who became famous as the author of Dracula, was born in Dublin in 1847.

2 c: He was still a student at Trinity College when he became the theatre critic for the Dublin Evening Mail, which at that time was the leading Irish newspaper.
3 b: Through his work as a theatre critic he became friends with Henry Irving, who was one of the best-known actors of his time.
4 a: Stoker later became the manager of the Lyceum Theatre in London, which belonged to Irving.
5 f: Stoker had begun writing fiction early in life and he wrote many novels, but his biggest success was *Dracula*, which was published in 1897.
6 g: Before he began writing, Stoker spent many years studying the folklore of Transsylvania, which he never visited in person.
7 e: Stoker's charismatic vampire Count Dracula, whose bite makes vampires of his victims, has inspired authors, playwrights and filmmakers from F. W. Murnau to Stephenie Meyer.

b *Individual answers*

7 Sports Day at Hatherford

1 During the 400-metre race Brian Kennedy fell and hurt his leg, which meant that he had to spend the rest of the day on the bench.
2 The volleyball team of Form 10 BH won all their matches, which made them very proud.
3 Bertie Lewis won the 5000-metre run, which didn't exactly come as a surprise.
4 At lunch break, some of the teachers showed their sports talent, which gave everyone something to laugh at.
5 Linda Moretti broke the school record for girls' long jump, which made her friends cheer wildly.
6 Kelly Mulligan cleared 170 cm on the high jump, which no one had ever done before.

8 From starlet to superstar

1 From 2010 to 2013, Grande played a character in the popular TV series *Victorious*, which brought her national attention.
2 In 2013 she released her first studio album, which was called *Yours Truly*.
3 Her second album, *My Everything*, which made Grande famous, was a huge success.
4 In 2017, Grande, whose third album, *Dangerous Woman*, was released in 2016, went on a world concert tour.
5 At the end of her concert in Manchester Arena on May 22, a bomb exploded, killing 23 people who/that were leaving the concert hall.

6 Grande organized a benefit concert for the victims, which took place in Manchester on June 4.

+ 9 The water crisis

1 yes – 2 yes – 3 yes – 4 no – 5 no – 6 yes – 7 no – 8 yes – 9 yes – 10 yes

+ 10 Crowdfunding

1 The American Committee of the Statue of Liberty, which was responsible for raising money to build the pedestal, had great difficulty finding enough supporters.

2 Joseph Pulitzer used his newspaper *The New York World* to start a fundraising campaign, with which he solved the problem.

3 He received money from more than 160,000 people, most of whom donated less than a dollar.

4 Modern crowdfunding began with the rise of the internet, which makes it easier to reach large numbers of people in a short time.

5 Rock musicians who/that needed money for a tour or a new album were among the first to discover the possibility of raising money by getting many people to donate relatively small sums.

6 Often there are special prizes for those who/that donate larger amounts, for example an autographed CD or a backstage invitation.

7 Since then, crowdfunding has become a billion-dollar business that/which is often used by start-ups to raise capital for new projects.

8/9 Websites such as Kickstarter and Indiegogo connect people who/that have new ideas with others who/that are willing to support them.

10 To date, more than 10 million people worldwide have donated to online campaigns, which shows that crowdfunding in one form or another is here to stay.

+ 11 First impressions

a 1 A friend of mine had given me the phone number of the youth hostel in Mannheim, where I planned to stay.

2 The train I was travelling on had a breakdown, so I arrived two hours late.

3 I phoned the youth hostel, but the man I talked to told me they were full up.

4 I left the station and looked around for streets where there might be a cheap hotel.

5 But all the hotels I went to had no free rooms.

6 The reason why all hotels were booked out was the trade fair in Mannheim.

7 Not knowing what else to do, I went to a nearby park and looked for a quiet bench, where I spent my first night in Germany.

8 But the person I shared my first German breakfast with has turned out to be a really good friend.

b 1 The position for which you have applied has also been advertised internally.

2 The assessment centre to which suitable applicants will be invited will take place on 13 March.

3 The contract must be signed and returned within two weeks from the date on which it was received.

4 As soon as the contract is signed, we will have a meeting, at which we will discuss the next steps.

5 The project is similar to others on which I have worked before.

6 Would it be possible for me to receive a list of the other people with whom I will be working on this project?

Quick Check Chapter 16

A 1 who/that – 2 who/that – 3 whose – 4 which – 5 which – 6 who/that – 7 whose – 8 which – 9 which – 10 which – 11 whose – 12 who

B 1 no – 2 yes – 3 yes – 4 no – 5 yes – 6 no – 7 yes – 8 yes – 9 yes – 10 no – 11 no – 12 yes

C 1 Sri Lanka, which is in the Indian Ocean, used to be called Ceylon.

2 Jeanette remembered to bring her pocket calculator to the maths lesson, which surprised everyone.

3 Passengers who are travelling on to the US [*no comma*] should go to Gate 10.

4 Only students whose marks are B- or higher can take part in the programme.

5 Hey — isn't this the flash drive (that) you were looking for?

6 Don't believe everything (that) Melissa tells you.

7 Winning that prize was the best thing that could have happened to you.

8 My girlfriend Sandra, whose family comes from Poland, [*comma*] speaks four languages.

9 We need the names of all the customers to whom this letter was sent/this letter was sent to.

10 Kathleen? That's the girl who's sitting next to Robert.

17 The adjective

1 Taller, younger

a bad, worse – far, further/farther – fast, faster – fit, fitter – good, better – *heavy, heavier* – light, lighter – old, older – poor, poorer – rich, richer – short, shorter – *tall, taller* – young, younger

b Alex is shorter, older, heavier and worse at maths. He's better at English, faster over 100 m, his school journey is longer and he is (a bit) richer.

2 Everyone has an opinion

a 1 most fantastic – 2 more difficult – 3 most famous – 4 most useful – 5 fastest – 6 more bored – 7 the most beautiful – 8 slower

b *Individual answers*

3 As easy as pie

a 1 as pretty as a picture
2 as hungry as a wolf
3 as quick as a flash
4 as busy as a bee
5 as tough as old boots
6 as dry as dust
7 as hot as fire

b 1 as dry as dust
2 as hot as fire
3 as quick as a flash
4 as tough as old boots
5 as busy as a bee
6 as poor as a church mouse

4 Comparisons quiz

a 1 London is bigger than Berlin.
2 Saturn is further than Mars.
3 Mont Blanc is higher than the Zugspitze.
4 A diamond is more expensive than a ruby.
5 A lion is faster than an elephant.
6 Shakespeare is more difficult to read than Rowling.
7 Football is more popular than cricket.

b 1 Berlin is not as big as London.
2 Mars is not as far as Saturn.
3 The Zugspitze is not as high as Mont Blanc.
4 A ruby is not as expensive as/less expensive than a diamond.
5 An elephant is not as fast as a lion.
6 Rowling is not as difficult as/less difficult than Shakespeare.
7 Cricket is not as popular as/less popular than football.

c *Individual answers*

5 Teacher talk

1 nearest – 2 further – 3 last – 4 next – 5 latest

6 Which one's for me?

1 The round one is for Sherrin.
2 The square one is for Alex.
3 The huge one is for Moritz.
4 The two long ones are for Leon.
5 The black one is for Lisa.
6 The two tiny ones are for Kinda.

7 Cheaper, but not the cheapest

a 1 The Twilight Dream is the fastest. The Homie is slower/not as fast. The Rambler is the slowest.
2 The Twilight Dream is the most expensive. The Rambler is not as expensive/cheaper, and the Homie is the least expensive/cheapest.
3 The Twilight Dream is the longest, the Rambler is shorter and the Homie is the shortest.

b *Individual answers*

+ 8 The best thing about school

a 1 The most difficult thing about languages
2 The nice thing about school sport/PE
3 – that's the great thing about it
4 on the most interesting part
5 The most important thing
6 The funny thing
7 to do (some) good
8 the unexpected

b *Individual answers*

+ 9 The rich and the poor

a Gebt/Überlasst/Bringt mir eure Müden, eure Armen, …

b 1 [no prop word] – 2 [no prop word] – 3 men and women/people – 4 [no prop word] – 5 [no prop word] – 6 [no prop word] – 7 people – 8 people/men and women/citizens – 9 [no prop word] – 10 [no prop word] – 11 [no prop word] – 12 [no prop word]/people/men and women – 13 people/men and women – 14 [no prop word]/people/men and women

Quick Check Chapter 17

A 1 small – … – smallest
2 … – nicer – nicest
3 tidy – tidier – …
4 … – easier – easiest
5 bad – … – worst
6 … – more difficult – most difficult
7 boring – … – most boring
8 … – more important – most important

B 1 more expensive than – 2 as interesting as – 3 tea is better – 4 higher than last year's – 5 the latest forecast – 6 the nearest to my home – 7 Only the fittest people – 8 the most unpopular item – 9 much better than – 10 easier than

C 1 a green one – 2 The most exciting thing about travelling – 3 the poor – 4 the big ones – 5 nothing worse than – 6 the most environmentally friendly – 7 as long as – 8 pretty as a picture – 9 only – 10 The older, the more forgetful
D 1 easier – 2 bigger – 3 more expensive – 4 worse – 5 more exciting – 6 heavier

18 The adverb

1 I can usually do this easily

a slow – normal – angry – easy – terrible – full – quick – true – basic – good
b slow, slowly – normal, normally – angry, angrily – easy, easily – terrible, terribly – full, fully – quick, quickly – true, truly – basic, basically – good, well
c 1 easily – 2 angry – 3 well – 4 normal – 5 good – 6 truly

2 We loved Katzi dearly

a 1 kind – 2 quickly – 3 easily – 4 happy – 5 usually – 6 normally – 7 beautiful – 8 quietly – 9 safe – 10 good – 11 carefully – 12 finally – 13 close – 14 sad – 15 well
b 1 The kind people – 2 we called them quickly – 3 We chose her easily – 4 a happy member – 5 She usually stayed out – 6 (she) normally returned – 7 four beautiful kittens – 8 (Katzi) quietly carried them off – 9 a safe place – 10 a good mum – 11 (she) looked after them carefully – 12 we finally moved – 13 some close friends – 14 We were very sad – 15 (our friends would) look after Katzi well

3 Jakob's knee problems

a adjective: quick – friendly – cheerful – helpful
adjective & adverb: daily – early – fast – far
adverb: fantastically – badly – exactly – shyly
b 1 daily – 2 quickly – 3 far – 4 fast – 5 in a friendly way – 6 politely – 7 cheerfully – 8 well
c 'Well' can be an adjective when it's used in the sense of 'fit' or 'healthy'.

4 It's hardly a problem

1 free, freely – 2 fairly, fair – 3 close, closely – 4 lately, late – 5 mostly, most – 6 near, nearly

5 What is really important to you?

a 1 terribly – 2 hardly – 3 absolutely – 4 totally – 5 incredibly – 6 an absolutely
b Individual answers

6 I feel fine

a 1 suspicious – 2 fit – 3 unfair – 4 scary – 5 cool – 6 stuffy
b Individual answers

7 That's what friends are for

a 1 They are never angry with me.
2 They don't ever trick me.
3 They usually agree with my opinion.
4 They sometimes say, 'Stop: enough is enough!'
5 They are always ready for a laugh.
6 They always stand up for me.
7 They aren't often offline.
8 They sometimes criticize me.
b Individual answers

8 Newspaper headlines

1 The President met the King privately in Buckingham Palace yesterday.
2 The Starburst concert was cancelled unexpectedly at Wembley last night. / The Starburst concert at Wembley was cancelled unexpectedly last night.
3 Germany won the tournament easily in the Arena in Munich last Friday.
4 Students protested loudly against the cuts at the Brandenburg Gate yesterday.
5 Lang Lang played beautifully in the Elbphilharmonie last weekend.
6 Five hundred stolen bikes were found in a garage in Berlin this morning.

9 What a difference a year makes!

1 Now she can write faster.
2 Now he can speak German better.
3 Now he can copy the words more quickly / quicker.
4 Now she can talk more loudly / louder.
5 Now she laughs more.
6 Now she can work harder for school.
7 Now she can follow lessons better.

10 Who works harder?

a Laura dresses more smartly than Lukasz.
Lukasz laughs more than Laura.
Lukasz sings (just) as beautifully as Laura.
Laura goes to bed later than Lukasz.
Lukasz takes school (just) as seriously as Laura.
Laura talks faster than Lukasz.
b Individual answers

+ 11 I hope to see you soon

1 hope – 2 prefer – 3 hate – 4 go on – 5 happened to – 6 keep – 7 seems to

+ 12 Get it right

1 widely – 2 [no mistake] – 3 ambitious – 4 terribly – 5 properly – 6 proud – 7 hardly – 8 in a friendly way/manner – 9 absolutely – 10 [no mistake] – 11 worse – 12 further and further – 13 awfully – 14 careful – 15 [no mistake]

+ 13 The wolf reacted strangely

a *Suggested answer*

One spring morning, Little Red Riding Hood went to see her grandmother in the wood.
She happily prepared a basket full of food and drink.
At first, she followed the path.
Later, the little girl unwisely left the path to collect flowers.
Suddenly, a wolf stopped her.
Naively, she told him where she was going.
The wolf immediately went to Grandma's cottage.
He went straight in and ate the old lady up in one bite.
Quickly, he put on her nightgown and waited patiently in bed.
Not long after, Little Red Riding Hood arrived on the scene.
She was understandably surprised and nervously asked a lot of questions.
The wolf answered her questions in Grandma's voice.
But then at the first chance, he swallowed the girl hungrily.
Finally, the wolf fell asleep and started snoring loudly.
At that moment, a huntsman came by and heard him.

b *Suggested answer*

The man immediately realized what had happened. He carefully cut open the wolf's stomach. Within a minute, both Grandma and her granddaughter jumped out unharmed. The wolf escaped with a great leap out of the window. After all their adventures, the three people happily shared the food and drink.

Quick Check Chapter 18

A 1 happily – 2 exactly – 3 fast – 4 in a friendly way – 5 luckily – 6 truly – 7 more strongly – 8 well – 9 fantastically – 10 badly

B 1 beautiful – 2 quickly – 3 extremely – 4 well – 5 attractive – 6 nervous – 7 incredibly – 8 normally

C 1 I've never travelled through the Channel Tunnel.
2 Please don't forget to wait outside the main entrance tomorrow night.
3 Luckily, I had remembered to pack my swimming trunks.
4 The band had just finished playing when all the lights went off.
5 The DJ acted strangely in the foyer last night.
6 Mike is always the first person at the school shop in the break.

7 People sometimes mix up *there* and *their*.
8 We've had a lot of good weather lately.

D 1 worked very hard – 2 see you at the tram stop after practice – 3 got the third answer wrong – 4 worked harder – 5 waved at him in a really silly way – 6 Some bikers never wait – 7 do as badly as I had – 8 well prepared for – 9 please go on doing these tasks – 10 so well organized

19 Nouns

1 Plurals

a 1 bodies – 2 cars – 3 crashes – 4 flies – 5 keys – 6 kisses – 7 mouths – 8 knives – 9 ponies – 10 prices – 11 toys

b 1 paths – 2 boys – 3 families – 4 halves – 5 parties – 6 photos – 7 thieves – 8 roofs

2 Yellowstone Park

1 wolves – 2 deer – 3 vegetation – 4 the behaviour of the elk – 5 valleys – 6 life – 7 species – 8 colonies – 9 fish – 10 mice – 11 foxes – 12 edges of the rivers

3 National stereotypes

1 Chinese – 2 Germans – 3 Scottish – 4 British – 5 Dutch – 6 Belgians – 7 English – 8 Irish – 9 Australians – 10 Italians – 11 Mexicans – 12 Swedish – 13 Swiss – 14 Polish

4 Work experience

a advice – equipment – experience – feedback – help – homework – information – knowledge – progress – proof

b 1 my work experience placement – 2 needed so much help – 3 specialist equipment – 4 lots of useful advice – 5 gave me homework – 6 more information – 7 the small progress – 8 proof of this school's success

5 Bread and butter pudding

a countable: dish – egg – *lemon* – slice of bread – raisin
uncountable: *bread* – butter – cream – fruit – milk – sugar

b 1 bread – 2 butter – 3 fruit – 4 milk – 5 sugar – 6 lemon

c 1 bread – 2 a few – 3 much – 4 a little – 5 a little

6 Translation

a 1 Clothes are more expensive in England than in Germany.
2 Should I bring pyjamas or a nightdress?
3 And would black trousers be better than jeans?
4 They are more interested in good manners.

5 Well, don't forget to bring your swimming trunks, Jonas.
6 Will I need sunglasses?
7 Will I need thick tights?
8 Bring shorts or a skirt!

b *Individual answers*

7 In other words
1 I can't see your cousin's face in the photo.
2 I can tell you the name of the street where Mr Rogers lives.
3 Those children's bikes are new.
4 James' new girlfriend is from Italy.
5 We often eat fish at the end of the week, on Friday or Saturday.
6 They have changed the name of the cinema. It's called 'The Odeon' now.
7 There was a fire at Henry's house but he wasn't at home on the night of the fire.
8 Pete and Jill's new house is in France.

8 Get it right
1 speaks very good English – 2 a two week holiday – 3 *[no mistake]* – 4 yesterday's newspaper – 5 is getting better – 6 too many soaps – 7 *[no mistake]* – 8 a German Harry Potter

+ 9 The glass ceiling
1 author – 2 colleague – 3 stewardess – 4 flight attendant – 5 chairman – 6 chair – 7 waitperson – 8 waitress – 9 waiter – 10 lady – 11 gentleman – 12 they

+ 10 The World Happiness Report
1 advice – 2 appears – 3 politics – 4 has – 5 data – 6 is studied – 7 research – 8 highlights/has highlighted – 9 phenomena – 10 economics – 11 remains – 12 is – 13 statistics – 14 show – 15 seems – 16 room

+ 11 The hotel from hell
1 accommodation – 2 surroundings – 3 were – 4 hair – 5 hairs – 6 paper – 7 manners – 8 staff – 9 training – 10 any – 11 much – 12 noises – 13 papers – 14 were – 15 information – 16 damage

+ 12 The Kite Runner
1 the beginning of the story – 2 plenty of money – 3 the son of his father's servant – 4 Amir's father – 5 the boys' unusual friendship – 6 Amir and Hassan's childhood – 7 the string of one boy's kite – 8 Amir's runner – 9 at the end of an alley – 10 Hassan's mattress – 11 the rise of the Taliban – 12 the back of a truck – 13 close friend of his father's – 14 the stage version of the book – 15 the sight of a middle-aged man

Quick Check Chapter 19
A 1 Girls' – 2 advice – 3 damage – 4 dentist's – 5 them – 6 much – 7 piece of toast – 8 five-mile – 9 some – 10 my brother's idea – 11 are, They look – 12 children's

B 1 Marco's girlfriend is Polish. – 2 much homework – 3 Saturday's paper – 4 clothes are cheaper – 5 This is my parents' bathroom – 6 some important advice – 7 Your hair is – 8 These stairs are – 9 the news is – 10 Where are my glasses?

C 1 We need some new furniture for our new flat.
2 Our teacher always gives us quick feedback after a test.
3 Have you made any progress with your homework yet?
4 Myra's pyjamas are too small for her now.
5 The police have just arrived at the scene of the crime.
6 What do you think of the colour of my jacket?
7 Do you want a cup of tea or would you prefer a coffee?
8 I can't argue with my parents' decision: they're always right.
9 Our school is just a ten-minute walk from home.
10 When my dog Tess was a puppy, she ate the leg of the chair.

20 Articles

1 Pronunciation
a [ə] or the [ðə]: *book* – European – hotel – mistake – teacher – uniform – university – visitor – window
an [ən] or the [ði]: *example* – accident – apple – hour – ice cream – image – MP3 player – ocean – uncle

2 In other words
1 Please wait, I will be with you in a minute.
2 Keep an eye on Charlie, he's not a good swimmer yet.
3 Is Andy Murray an Irishman?
4 Our teacher gave us feedback after our presentation.
5 It was such a boring film that I fell asleep.
6 He's a member of our local chess club.
7 What terrible weather!
8 I need only one ticket, thank you.
9 She told me there was one bus an hour.
10 The guide gave us incorrect information about the opening times.

3 When I grow up…

a 1 an – 2 a – 3 a – 4 a – 5 an – 6 a – 7 a –
8 an – 9 *[no article]* – 10 a

b *Individual answers*

4 Animal trainers for the movies

1 a – 2 one – 3 a – 4 an – 5 A – 6 one – 7 a –
8 a – 9 A – 10 a – 11 a – 12 one – 13 a –
14 a – 15 a – 16 a – 17 a – 18 an

5 Bastoy prison

1 criticism – 2 life – 3 wooden houses – 4 the
houses – 5 the prisoners – 6 Most of them –
7 school – 8 the school – 9 the ferry –
10 church – 11 the church – 12 the beach –
13 history – 14 the prisoners – 15 the world

6 The place name quiz

1 the Himalayas – 2 the Atlantic – 3 Belgium –
4 Times Square – 5 the USA – 6 the Red Sea –
7 Buckingham Palace – 8 the Netherlands – 9 the
Alps – 10 the Tower of London – 11 Switzerland –
12 the Mediterranean

7 A day in the life of a circus acrobat

a 1 on – 2 at the – 3 in the / during the / by – 4 in –
5 at/during – 6 at – 7 in the – 8 in / in the

b 1 in the morning – 2 the night before – 3 during
the winter – 4 In the summer – 5 in the evening –
6 During the week – 7 at the weekend – 8 at
lunch – 9 By day – 10 the next morning

8 The job interview

1 take a seat – 2 make an impression – 3 on
paper – 4 leave anything to chance – 5 taken an
interest – 6 in a quiet voice – 7 be in a position –
8 comes to an end

9 What a race!

1 such a good time – 2 Both (the) teams –
3 rather a difficult challenge – 4 quite a big
risk – 5 twice the price – 6 all the time – 7 half
the time – 8 such a surprise – 9 what an exciting
finish –10 half an hour

10 Man flu – is it real?

people who go to work or school – by bus – go to
school – stay in bed – In practice – men go to
bed – above average – women lose patience – in
public – With the help of

11 The silly bank robber

1 the – 2 the – 3 a – 4 the – 5 the – 6 a –
7 the – 8 a – 9 the – 10 the – 11 The –
12 the – 13 an – 14 the – 15 the – 16 an

+ 12 Dolphin behavior

1 *[no article]* – 2 *[no article]* – 3 the – 4 a –
5 an – 6 the – 7 an – 8 *[no article]* – 9 the –
10 the –11 *[no article]* – 12 *[no article]* – 13 *[no
article]* – 14 a – 15 one – 16 a – 17 a – 18 a –
19 the – 20 the

+ 13 English after Brexit

1 a – 2 *[no article]* – 3 the – 4 the – 5 a – 6 a –
7 The – 8 *[no article]* – 9 *[no article]* – 10 the –
11 the – 12 the – 13 the – 14 a – 15 the –
16 the – 17 *[no article]* – 18 *[no article]* – 19 *[no
article]* – 20 the

Quick Check Chapter 20

A 1 an – a – *[no article]* – the – the
2 *[no article]* – a – the – the
3 a – The – a – the
4 a – the – the – the – the
5 *[no article]* – a – the – the / *[no article]*
6 an – the – the – the – a

B 1 college – the United States
2 half a year – such a
3 a member – an amazing athlete
4 useful – an expert
5 a vegetarian – a child
6 lunch – Waterloo station.
7 by bus – half the price
8 a really bad cold – in bed

C 1 quite an interesting book – 2 for breakfast –
3 four times a week – 4 Most people – 5 a
uniform – 6 £130 a year – 7 going into space –
8 the first week of May

21 Pronouns and determiners

1 Babysitting blues

a subject: he – *I* – she – they – we
object: her – him – *me* – them – us
both: it – *you*

b 1 I – 2 you – 3 you – 4 me – 5 them – 6 her –
7 she – 8 He – 9 him – 10 It – 11 us – 12 We –
13 they – 14 you – 15 it – 16 you

c *Individual answers*

2 Salsa dancing

a 1 She – 2 It – 3 It – 4 it – 5 It – 6 it – 7 it –
8 They – 9 them – 10 It

b 1 there was – 2 like it – 3 there are – 4 hope
so – 5 don't forget – 6 it's hard – 7 There
is – 8 don't think so

3 Getting organized
1 their – 2 theirs – 3 hers – 4 her – 5 yours –
6 his – 7 of his – 8 mine – 9 of her – 10 your –
11 of mine – 12 my

4 I hit my head
1 The dog hurt its paw while chasing a cat.
2 We've changed our minds about going out tonight.
3 Many tourists lost their lives in the terrible tsunami.
4 She took off her boots and left them outside.
5 Put that money in your pocket or you'll lose it.
6 Last night I broke my arm when I fell downstairs.

5 Women and fiction
a 1 of her own – 2 their own – 3 his own – 4 of
their own – 5 their own – 6 her own – 7 of her
own – 8 our own – 9 of my own – 10 my own
b Individual answers

6 A lesson in life
1 we – 2 I – 3 they – 4 us – 5 my – 6 him –
7 him – 8 his – 9 my – 10 it – 11 your –
12 me – 13 our – 14 It

7 Emergency calls
1 He – 2 we – 3 their – 4 it – 5 mine – 6 they –
7 its – 8 My – 9 them – 10 me – 11 My –
12 us – 13 your – 14 our – 15 His – 16 It –
17 her – 18 you – 19 her – 20 it

8 Rio: the marvellous city
1 they – 2 they – 3 they – 4 one – 5 You –
6 they – 7 you – 8 they – 9 You – 10 you

9 Me time
a 1 yourselves – 2 myself – 3 yourself – 4 yourselves – 5 ourselves – 6 themselves –
7 himself – 8 herself
b 1 a The teenagers are looking at themselves.
1 b They are looking at each other.
2 a The girls are hurting each other.
2 b They have hurt themselves.
3 a The cats are washing themselves.
3 b They're washing each other.

10 This and that
1 This – 2 that – 3 those – 4 this – 5 these –
6 that – 7 This – 8 that – 9 these – 10 this –
11 Those – 12 these

11 Afternoon tea
Beth   I've just had one but OK, I will have another
one, thanks.
Amy   Do you want a cake with that? And if so,
which one do you want?
Beth   Mmm, I'd love one. That one with the
strawberries on top, I think.

Amy   I prefer those ones with cream on. They're
delicious.
Beth   Yes but I think the ones with fruit are a bit
healthier!

+ 12 Modern art
1 that – 2 they – 3 myself – 4 my (own) –
5 you – 6 this – 7 It – 8 their – 9 its –
10 one's – 11 me – 12 one

+ 13 Translation
1 I waited by the pool while my friend was changing.
2 Joe and Kelly usually meet after work on Fridays.
3 Sara's at home in bed – she's not feeling very
well today.
4 Can you imagine having fourteen cats?
5 The photographer told the students not to move.
6 Maite and Rosie are looking forward to seeing
one another at the weekend.
7 Please come in and sit down.
8 Mum worries about you boys all the time.
9 Our grandmother remembers her school days
very clearly.
10 I wonder if Katie will come tonight.

+ 14 Royal protocol
1 them – 2 yourself – 3 himself – 4 one –
5 there – 6 you – 7 her – 8 myself – 9 your –
10 your – 11 ourselves – 12 sit – 13 they –
14 they – 15 yourselves – 16 turn – 17 your –
18 herself

Quick Check Chapter 21
A 1 mine – 2 them – 3 our – 4 its – 5 they –
6 your – 7 you – 8 me
B 1 herself – 2 itself – 3 yourselves – 4 themselves – 5 each other – 6 myself – 7 each
other – 8 each other
C 1 these, ones, The … ones, the one
2 one, one, ones, ones
3 that, The one, that, these, that, the one
D 1 her own motorbike – 2 broke his arm – 3 neighbour of mine – 4 than hers – 5 We filmed
ourselves – 6 see each other – 7 these black
ones – 8 don't feel very well

22 Quantifiers

1 Last-minute planning
1 any – 2 some – 3 some – 4 any – 5 no –
6 some - 7 any – 8 some – 9 no – 10 any/some

2 The missing mobile
1 anywhere – 2 somewhere – 3 someone – 4 No one – 5 someone – 6 nowhere – 7 something – 8 Somewhere – 9 something – 10 Somebody

3 The end of the book?
a 1 a few – 2 (the) least – 3 less – 4 fewer – 5 a few – 6 few
b *Individual answers*

4 Our German guest
1 many – 2 More – 3 many – 4 much – 5 a lot of – 6 much – 7 a lot of – 8 many – 9 Most – 10 many

5 Before the test
1 all – 2 Each – 3 all – 4 every – 5 any – 6 Any – 7 all – 8 any/every

6 The very musical Shrivers
a 1 neither – 2 both – 3 All – 4 either – 5 None – 6 all
b *Individual answers*

7 Ready to leave
1 everything – 2 anywhere – 3 everywhere – 4 somewhere – 5 someone – 6 nobody – 7 nothing – 8 everybody – 9 someone – 10 something

8 The winners
1 a few – 2 every – 3 anything – 4 all the – 5 some – 6 both – 7 The two – 8 neither – 9 all the – 10 None

9 Who plays what?
a 1 Both of them play the flute.
2 Neither of them plays football.
3 None of them play badminton.
4 All of them play chess.
5 Both of them play computer games.
6 None of them play the tuba.
7 Neither of them plays volleyball.
8 All of them play the guitar.
b 1 Both of them. / Both Thomas and Youssef.
2 Neither of them. / Neither Yasmine nor Nicole.
3 Either of them. / Either Nicole or Yasmine.
4 None of them.
5 Either of them. / Either Nicole or Thomas.
6 All of them.
c *Individual answers*

10 The school talent show
1 some – 2 anybody – 3 some – 4 anybody – 5 some – 6 anybody – 7 some – 8 any

11 The 3D flop
1 each – 2 the two – 3 Each – 4 both – 5 each – 6 the two – 7 many – 8 a few – 9 every – 10 fewer and fewer – 11 both – 12 and – 13 Some – 14 less – 15 most – 16 more

Quick Check Chapter 22
A 1 every – 2 any – 3 any – 4 anyone – 5 anybody – 6 each – 7 some – 8 anywhere – 9 a little – 10 two
B 1 everybody/everyone – 2 every – 3 neither – 4 less – 5 many – 6 anything – 7 the two – 8 All (of) the girls – 9 less, fewer – 10 none
C 1 there isn't any margarine – 2 None of the players – 3 Each of the runners – 4 very little rain – 5 was able to – 6 Is everyone – 7 every thirty minutes – 8 he didn't know anybody – 9 persuade anyone – 10 neither of them – 11 All (of) the students – 12 any day now – 13 any of them – 14 no one answered – 15 give me some help

23 Mixed bag

1 Get it right
1 she explained the problem to him – 2 All I meant – 3 some very good advice – 4 wants us to bring some food – 5 *The Uncommon Reader* by Alan Bennett – 6 Chloe's dog ran off in the park this morning. – 7 the opposite of – 8 protect nature – 9 Let's meet – 10 during the film – 11 a week ago – 12 Why did you ask me

2 Where is it?
a 1 by – 2 opposite – 3 at – 4 on – 5 inside – 6 outside – 7 behind – 8 in front of
b 1 via – 2 to – 3 up and down – 4 into – 5 after – 6 along – 7 across – 8 onto

3 From word-cross to crossword
1 since – 2 on – 3 after – 4 In – 5 of – 6 on – 7 Until – 8 At – 9 after – 10 in

4 Careers advice
a 1 In fact – 2 for a change – 3 after all – 4 for a long time – 5 In my opinion – 6 on the other hand – 7 At least – 8 on her own – 9 Not at all – 10 in the long run
b *Individual answers*

5 Joining in

1 It's winter, so you're not getting much exercise but that's no reason to be lazy! Why not come along with me to the badminton club or to play indoor tennis.

2 We are all tempted to stay indoors when it's cold and dark outside. I personally go jogging regularly because I feel terrible if I don't. I even went running last week although it was snowing the whole time.

3 It's cold and windy, but if you have a dog, you have to take it out. Toni was walking her dog in a park where there were other dog walkers. She met a guy who had a dog like hers. The dogs played together while Toni and the guy were talking. They agreed to meet again which was the start of a beautiful friendship.

6 A frightening incident

a 1 She wasn't hurt but her bag was stolen and she was in a state of shock.

2 She went to the police station in order to report what had happened.

3 Having made a statement, she left the police station.

4 She did not want to meet her attacker. That's why she went home a different way.

5 Instead of going home immediately, she went to her office first.

6 Knowing she would be alone, she took the lift to her office.

7 She started up her laptop in order to search for a private detective.

8 While she was scrolling through the list of names, she heard a noise – she clearly wasn't the only one in the office.

b *Individual answers*

7 Youth in Iceland

1 Despite – 2 such as – 3 As a result of – 4 whereas – 5 Apart from – 6 Moreover – 7 In fact – 8 Due to – 9 For example – 10 Instead

8 Say 'please'!

1 Sorry but I'm afraid that is my seat.

2 Would you mind very much if we shut that window?

3 I'd be awfully grateful if you could help me.

4 Your music is just a little loud for me.

5 Wouldn't it be better if you wore headphones?

6 That jacket is mine, I believe. / I believe that jacket is mine.

7 I was wondering if we could change seats?

8 I'll get my own coffee, if you don't mind. / If you don't mind, I'll get my own coffee.

9 Decisions, decisions

1 didn't it – 2 can you – 3 Me – 4 So can – 5 isn't it – 6 will they – 7 couldn't we – 8 Neither/Nor did – 9 shouldn't we – 10 do we

+ 10 Caught out

a formal: *Might I ask why you … ?* – But on whose authority … ? – Whom did you see … ? – Your actions are known to be … – Should you do that again, … – Had we not stopped you, …
informal: *I dunno!* – I gotta tell you – Me and my mates – It's them that did it – I feel like I'm going crazy – We're gonna be in big trouble

b 1 Your actions are known to be … – 2 Had we not stopped you, … – 3 But on whose authority … ? – 4 I gotta tell you – 5 Me and my mates – 6 I feel like I'm going crazy – 7 It's them that did it – 8 Should you do that again, … – 9 Whom did you see … ? – 10 We're gonna be in big trouble

+ 11 Practice makes perfect

1 suggested going – 2 I'm washing my hair – 3 Did you do all your homework – 4 for half an hour – 5 I saw an old friend – 6 looking forward to going – 7 If I have time – 8 We don't have to run – 9 left without saying – 10 If you hadn't lost

+ 12 Advertising

a 1 Although – 2 Moreover – 3 Firstly – 4 However – 5 as – 6 Yet – 7 Secondly – 8 What's more – 9 Examples of this – 10 Consequently – 11 In conclusion – 12 but

b Paragraph 1: It is almost impossible (l. 1) […] for several reasons (l. 11)
Paragraph 2: Firstly, many advertisements (l. 11) […] as possible (l. 20).
Paragraph 3: Secondly, many products (l. 21) […] buying second-hand (l. 30).
Paragraph 4: In conclusion, advertising (l. 30) […] clever marketing strategies (l. 35).

+ 13 Dialogue

a 1 real – 2 swim team – 3 sure isn't – 4 driver's license – 5 intersections – 6 freeways – 7 after – 8 holiday – 9 till – 10 anywhere – 11 main roads – 12 tyres – 13 estate car – 14 pavements – 15 practising – 16 garden

b Joel's email: at college / at university – did you have your exams yet / have you had your exams yet – much different than / very different from – team was good / team were good – I now have / I've now got – talked with / talked to – I've gotten / I've got – go get / go and get – meet with / meet (up with)
Hanna's email: at home / home – I've never seen / I never saw – a good job / a good thing – travelling /

traveling – at the weekend / on the weekend –
insisted that I should perform / insisted that I
perform – you needn't worry / you don't need to
worry

c

					2▼					
	4▼	1► v	a	c	a	t	i	o	n	
p u r s e				a			5▼			
c		6▼		n			p			
h	6► s	i	d	e	w	a	l	k		
l i n e	u		y			n				
8▼	d		b			t				
g	u		w			s				
r a i l r o a d										
s	e		y							

Quick Check Chapter 23

A 1 at, on, at – 2 by, on, on – 3 over, above – 4 for,
by – 5 with, until, at – 6 from, via, to – 7 to, on,
of – 8 at, to, at – 9 to, by, in – 10 to, from, in

B 1 apart from – 2 as well – 3 furthermore –
4 yet – 5 owing to – 6 that is – 7 such as –
8 because of – 9 On the one hand – 10 though

C 1 formal: Please help me with this.
2 formal: Who should we thank?
3 informal: I'll join you as soon as possible.
4 informal: Kaitlyn was with you all the time,
wasn't she?
5 formal: The police believed the man was in his
late forties.
6 informal: Please can you show me your ticket?
7 formal: You should take an earlier train.
8 informal: My children and I have just had a lovely
walk.

D 1 So does mine. / Mine does too. – 2 do you –
3 Neither did we. / We didn't either. – 4 So do I. / I
do too. / Me too. – 5 will she – 6 aren't I –
7 doesn't it – 8 Neither does mine. / Mine doesn't
either.